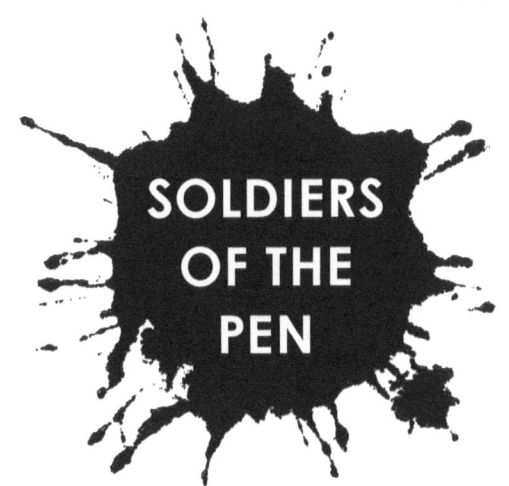
SOLDIERS OF THE PEN

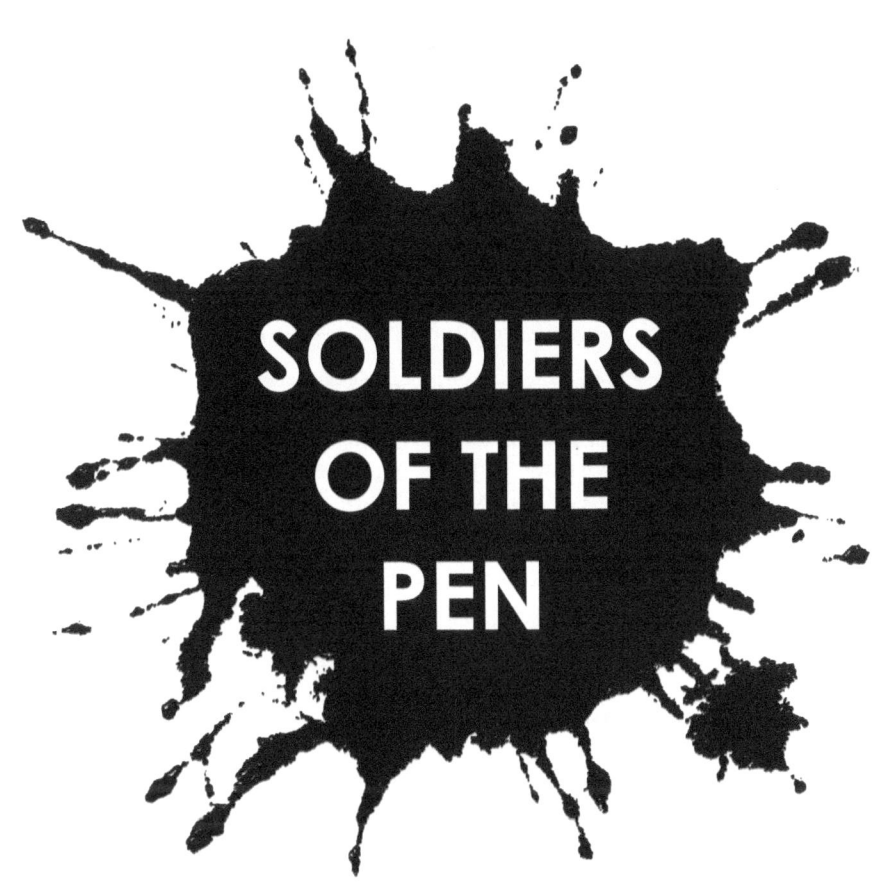

SOLDIERS OF THE PEN

The Writers' War Board
in World War II

Thomas Howell

UNIVERSITY OF MASSACHUSETTS PRESS
Amherst and Boston

Copyright © 2019 by University of Massachusetts Press
All rights reserved
Printed in the United States of America

ISBN 978-1-62534-387-1 (paper); 386-4 (hardcover)

Design by Jen Jackowitz
Set in Adobe Garamond Pro
Cover design and illustration by Thomas Eykemans

Library of Congress Cataloging-in-Publication Data
Names: Howell, Thomas, 1944– author.
Title: Soldiers of the pen : the Writers' War Board in World War II / Thomas Howell.
Other titles: WWB in WWII | Writers' War Board in World War II
Description: Amherst, MA : University of Massachusetts Press, [2019] |
Includes bibliographical references and index. |
Identifiers: LCCN 2018019163 (print) | LCCN 2018025788 (ebook) | ISBN 9781613766347 (e-book) | ISBN 9781613766354 (e-book) | ISBN 9781625343871 (pbk.) | ISBN 9781625343864 (hardcover)
Subjects: LCSH: Writers' War Board. | World War, 1939–1945—Propaganda. | Propaganda, American — History — 20th century. | Authors, American — 20th century — Societies, etc. | World War, 1939–1945 — United States — Mass media and the war. | World War, 1939–1945 — United States—Literature and the war. | World War, 1939–1945 — United States—Motion pictures and the war.
Classification: LCC D810.P7 (ebook) | LCC D810.P7 U375 2019 (print) | DDC 940.54/88673 — dc23
LC record available at https://lccn.loc.gov/2018019163

British Library Cataloguing-in-Publication Data
A catalog record for this book is available from the British Library.

Lyrics of "Dear Friend," "We're on Our Way," and selected verses of "Ol' Man Author" by Oscar Hammerstein II are published by agreement with Hammerstein Properties LLC.

Excerpt from *They Burned the Books*, a radio play by Stephen Vincent Benet. Copyright © 1942 by Stephen Vincent Benet. Renewed 1970 by Thomas C. Benet, Rachel Benet Lewis, Stephenie Benet Mahin. Used by permission of Brandt and Hochman Literary Agents, Inc. All rights reserved.

Excerpts of two poems by Edna St. Vincent Millay. "The Murder of Lidice" from *Life* (October 17, 1942). Copyright 1942, © 1969 by Edna St. Vincent Millay and Norma Millay Ellis. "Poem and Prayer for an Invading Army," originally broadcast on June 6, 1944, by the National Broadcasting Company and read by Ronald Colman. Copyright 1944, © 1971 by Edna St. Vincent Millay and Norma Millay Ellis. Reprinted with permission from The Permissions Company, Inc., on behalf of Holly Peppe, Literary Executor, Edna St. Vincent Millay Society, www.millay.org.

First stanza and three additional lines of "Don't Let's Be Beastly to the Germans," a song by Noel Coward. Copyright © 1943 by Noel Coward from *The Complete Lyrics of Noel Coward*, ed. Barry Day, 1998, Methuen Drama, an imprint of Bloomsbury Publishing Plc.

FOR OUR DAUGHTERS

Kate and Jenny,
the brightest stars in our universe

CONTENTS

Preface ix

Introduction 1

Chapter 1
The History and Function of the Writers' War Board 15

Chapter 2
Propaganda for the Military 54

Chapter 3
Home Front Propaganda 87

Chapter 4
Propaganda on America's Allies and Enemies 131

Chapter 5
The Controversial Hate Campaign 169

Chapter 6
Shaping the Peace 208

Chapter 7
Reflections on the Writers' War Board 239

Notes 255

Index 307

PREFACE

I ORIGINALLY BECAME INTERESTED in the use of propaganda in wartime America when I encountered the World War I activities of George Creel and his Committee on Public Information (CPI). While the CPI pioneered many techniques, it took liberties with the truth and ultimately gave government propaganda a bad name. Fearing similar excesses, Congress shackled its World War II successor, the Office of War Information (OWI), with strict guidelines and constant scrutiny. When I discovered the Writers' War Board (WWB), a shadowy propaganda organization partly subsidized by the OWI, I became intrigued. Further examination of over one hundred WWB files in the Library of Congress indicated the depth and complexity of its story. Although this volunteer group of twenty well-known New York writers collaborated with the OWI, it did not fall under congressional jurisdiction. With little supervision, WWB members were free to handle a host of activities that the government's official propaganda agency could not or would not undertake. The board's dominating chairman, mystery writer Rex Stout, further piqued my interest since I had read several of his books. When my early efforts to locate published references to the group came up almost empty, I knew I had found an untouched field of study, and I was hooked.

One of my greatest challenges in researching the WWB has been identifying the pieces of propaganda written at its behest. I was astonished to find that this small group successfully recruited thousands of authors around the United States to help with its work. They would prepare and submit pieces to local and national publishers after the board notified them of upcoming topics to develop. However, these materials ordinarily made no reference to the WWB, which preferred to remain behind the scenes. One of the primary reasons that this organization has not been fully investigated is the fact that its role was not routinely acknowledged during the war. I had to track down its propaganda output by carefully perusing its correspondence, newsletters, weekly minutes, and annual reports. My study makes clear the significance of the WWB as a unique, private propaganda organization that received funding from the government to sway American attitudes.

I could not have completed this study without the cooperation of many others. Professor Burl Noggle first called my attention to the WWB files, and three individuals provided early inspiration and support—my colleague Dr. Mary D. Bowman, Linda Fite, and especially my mother, Hazel Hall Howell. Both of my daughters, Kate and Jenny Howell, offered constant encouragement and help. I am most grateful for the assistance of Jeff Flannery and the excellent staff at the Manuscript Division of the Library of Congress, as well as the librarians at William Jewell College and Boston College. Several readers, including Professor Allan Winkler, examined my manuscript. I appreciate their positive feedback and crucial suggestions for improvement. Special thanks go to Brian Halley, my editor at the University of Massachusetts Press, whose patience, guidance, and encouragement from start to finish were essential. Above all others stands Donna Jo Walker Howell, my wife, personal editor, research associate, and equal partner in all things. She put her heart and soul into the later stages of this project and gave me the impetus to complete it.

INTRODUCTION

THE WRITERS' WAR Board (WWB) was a small but influential American organization that helped federal agencies and the military generate propaganda in World War II with partial funding from the government. It also assisted several private organizations with their war-related efforts and mounted its own campaigns. Its propaganda so pervaded the home front that it helped to mold the nation's wartime culture. Chaired by mystery writer Rex Stout, the group of twenty men and women included Book of the Month Club editor and popular radio show host Clifton Fadiman, bestselling novelist Paul Gallico, Broadway lyricist Oscar Hammerstein II, and radio commentator William Shirer. These experienced authors in the New York City area were primarily political liberals from both parties who supported the policies of President Franklin D. Roosevelt.

Although they could generate ideas and use their clout to complete projects with speed and finesse, they alone could not have produced and quickly disseminated all of the organization's propaganda. Fortunately, these talented few were able to enlist the help of more than four thousand of their colleagues around the United States. The group's main goals were uniting the public in the war effort and advocating measures to prevent a third global conflict. To address these concerns, WWB members not only followed the administration's agenda but also denounced racism and demanded harsh peace terms for Germany. Some of their proposals were considered radical at the time. They called for the establishment of a centralized world government that wielded authority over every nation and had the power to deter internecine conflicts, and they encouraged

Americans to hate the entire population of Germany, ordinary citizens as well as Nazis.

The WWB was established in December 1941 at the instigation of the Treasury Department to help sell defense bonds. By the time of its first meeting, America had entered the war, and the board decided to expand its scope to help other departments and bureaus. From 1942 to 1945 its members volunteered their services without compensation, and they and their cadre of writers produced subtle and blatant propaganda in virtually every format—speeches, magazine and newspaper articles, editorials, plays, radio programs, songs, poems, short stories, films, books, pamphlets, posters, cartoons, and comic books. The group's power derived from its ability to generate and disperse promptly high-quality materials that met specific needs. Within its first six months of operation, federal officials recognized its value and began to support it financially. The WWB became a quasi-government organization that was a formidable propaganda mill. Journalist and author Lewis Gannett considered the group "incredibly active," and WWB chairman Rex Stout estimated that the manuscripts it instigated weighed over three tons.[1]

To insure a continuous supply of propaganda materials, the WWB notified authors and media personnel about projects in advance so that they could prepare materials and publicize each campaign. Whenever it could, the board acted as a clearinghouse, matching writers with jobs that they were best qualified to handle. While the WWB did not have the budget to compensate these authors, it was able to direct them to agencies and organizations that would pay for their services. Board members and staff kept up a voluminous correspondence with writers around the country and with each of the groups that the board assisted. Of necessity the WWB also cultivated good relationships with publishers, radio network executives, heads of newspaper syndicates, and others in the communications industry that could distribute its propaganda nationwide in a timely fashion. The board established its headquarters in New York City to make the best use of these contacts. The metropolis was then the center of book and magazine publishing as well as art, theater, music, and dance. The city had ten daily newspapers including the preeminent *New York Times* and was home to the world's largest news organization, the Associated Press. Government agencies in Washington were within easy reach by train. At a time when radio was the most pervasive media, New York boasted the corporate offices of all four networks—Mutual, CBS, NBC Red, and NBC Blue, the last of which became ABC in October 1943. Since the majority of national programs were broadcast live, the city had daily contact with citizens across the United States. It offered the board several ways to keep in touch not only with media outlets in urban areas but also with small town newspapers, clubs, churches, radio stations, and other sources of community information.

PROPAGANDA IN THE UNITED STATES BEFORE WORLD WAR II

Many board members had become acquainted with one another through their participation in interventionist organizations established after war broke out in Europe in the fall of 1939. They received training in producing and using political propaganda as they urged the U.S. government to become involved in the conflict and tried to stir up public support for intervention. However, these groups were divided about the level of America's involvement. The aggressive Fight for Freedom Committee and similar organizations believed that military action was necessary while groups like the Committee to Defend America by Aiding the Allies wanted the United States to provide other kinds of assistance without deploying its troops. Both interventionist camps opposed those who demanded that the government remain neutral and take no action. Among these isolationists were fascists, pacifists, members of special interest groups such as the National League of Mothers of America, and religious ultra-conservatives like Father Charles Coughlin, who headed the anti-Semitic Christian Front. In September 1940 these and many other isolationist organizations banded together in an umbrella group called the America First Committee (AFC). Several influential newspapers supported the AFC's viewpoint including Colonel Robert McCormick's *Chicago Tribune* and William Randolph Hearst's *San Francisco Examiner*.[2]

The board's methods of producing and distributing propaganda may be compared to those of three American organizations that operated between 1916 and 1918: two private groups—the Vigilantes and the National Board for Historical Service (NBHS)—and one government agency, the Committee on Public Information (CPI). Before the United

States entered the conflict, a handful of writers founded the Vigilantes in December 1916: Hermann Hagedorn, Porter Emerson Browne, Charles Hanson Towne, and Julian Street. Their idea was to produce patriotic poems and other works as a way of encouraging the government to prepare for the conflict. The Vigilantes eventually grew to include over four hundred authors, journalists, artists, and publicists like Booth Tarkington, Hamlin Garland, Emerson Hough, Theodore Roosevelt, and Ida M. Tarbell.[3]

After Congress declared war against Germany in April 1917, the group took on additional jobs, working for free with several government agencies including the CPI. The Vigilantes promoted Liberty Loans, the conservation of food and fuel, and the War Savings Campaign. At the time Browne called propaganda "the deadliest known weapon" in the enemy's arsenal, and he accused the Germans of using it maliciously in "encouraging treason; aiding and abetting sedition; cultivating depression; [and] fanning the fires of . . . disunion, disorganization, anarchy, and disaster." He insisted, "It can be defeated only by a weapon adapted to do combat with it, . . . the written and the spoken word." The Vigilantes used their talents to expose the cunning of the Germans and denounce prejudice in America. When German propaganda distributed in Russia presented the United States in an unfavorable light, CPI officials enlisted the group's help in counteracting the negative publicity. The Vigilantes also assisted private organizations including the Red Cross, the YMCA, the Chamber of Commerce, and the Boy Scouts.[4] In a similar fashion in World War II, the WWB worked with the Office of War Information (OWI) and helped federal agencies and private groups with some of the same types of campaigns.

A second group of writers that assisted the government in World War I was the National Board for Historical Service. Its founding was instigated by John Franklin Jameson, who had helped to organize the American Historical Association. The NBHS ran an editorial service for the CPI and became so closely allied with official policy that it acted as "an unofficial arm of the government."[5] These historians produced a variety of propaganda materials including magazine and newspaper articles and pamphlets. They contacted other members of their profession throughout the country and periodically supplied them with written materials to guide them in making their own contributions to the war.⁶ Historian Harold A. Wolff once proposed to the WWB that it organize a committee similar to the NBHS, but the authors rejected his idea, arguing that their work was not historical in nature. If any material needed a stamp of authenticity, the writers could easily obtain it from one or more well-known historians like Allan Nevins, who served the board in an advisory capacity.⁷ Although the NBHS aimed most of its output at the readers of scholarly journals and learned magazines and rarely succeeded in placing the erudite works of its members in widely distributed newspapers or popular magazines, it may be considered a forerunner of the WWB, which developed a similar editorial service at the OWI's request. As the NBHS had done previously, the board maintained contact with authors throughout the nation who were responsible for producing propaganda materials, but the WWB wanted these items to be geared to the general public rather than the educated elite.

On April 13, 1917, one week after America entered the war, President Woodrow Wilson created the Committee on Public Information. Members of the WWB were most heavily influenced by this group, which developed new techniques of persuasion and set the benchmark for all subsequent efforts in the field. The original purpose of the CPI was to handle news from the government, but its chairman, journalist George Creel, also concentrated on encouraging American support for the war even when fighting on the battlefield remained at a stalemate for months at a time. Meeting only once with his fellow committee members—the secretaries of state, war, and the navy—Creel took complete charge of the organization, which has been called "America's first 'propaganda ministry.'"⁸ Given carte blanche by Congress, he used both ethical and spurious means to shape public opinion, censoring unfavorable material and producing some 75 million pieces of propaganda from posters to pamphlets. He enlisted 75,000 volunteers to give short speeches about the war effort and placed war-related material in films and books as well as magazines, newspapers, and cartoons.⁹

The CPI chairman said that his aim was to create a "passionate belief in the justice of America's cause that [would] meld the people of the United States into one white hot mass instinct with fraternity, devotion, courage, and deathless determination."¹⁰ Unfortunately his overly zealous efforts caused the CPI to make extravagant promises, use overheated rhetoric, and deliberately falsify information on more than one occasion. It soon earned a reputation as the "Committee on Public Misinformation." Despite its early admonition to volunteer speakers to avoid "hymns of hate," the CPI ultimately put out intentionally fabricated works such as a booklet on the bogus *German-Bolshevik Conspiracy* and "That Monstrous Thing Called Kultur," an advertisement that falsely pictured German soldiers crucifying captured civilians.[11] Creel, of course, denied using questionable methods and denounced his attackers. He disingenuously claimed, "Our effort was educational and informative throughout, for we had such confidence in our case as to feel that no other argument was needed than the simple straightforward presentation of facts."[12] Learning of the CPI's deceptive tactics after the war, Americans felt hoodwinked and became skeptical about propaganda in general and government-sanctioned propaganda in particular. But they could not stop its proliferation in other fields, especially business.

In the 1930s Joseph Goebbels, Adolf Hitler's minister of propaganda, brilliantly used the tactics of the CPI to manipulate public attitudes in Germany.[13] Anxiety about the effectiveness of his propaganda machine and dismay over the false reports promulgated by the CPI caused Americans to blanch at the idea of establishing another government-sponsored propaganda organization.[14] President Franklin Roosevelt consistently rejected requests to create such an agency in 1940 and 1941, but six months after Japan propelled the United States into World War II, he finally established the Office of War Information. To allay the public's legitimate fears concerning misinformation and manipulation, Congress immediately placed restrictions on the new agency. Conservative Republicans and southern Democrats had another reason to oppose the OWI: they considered it to be a subversive tool that the Roosevelt administration used to promote its liberal agenda. Throughout the war they closely controlled it and even tried to wipe it out altogether at one point.[15] Ironically, their stringent regulations and persistent monitoring created a need for a private group like the WWB that could generate government propaganda without congressional interference.

Members of the board were proud of the help they gave to the war effort, and they never flinched from identifying the WWB as a propaganda organization. In 1928 Edward Bernays, a former CPI employee who became the "father of public relations," praised those who shape public opinion. He argued that they hold ultimate power: "The conscious and intelligent manipulation of the organized habits and opinions of the masses is an important element in democratic society. Those who manipulate this unseen mechanism of society constitute an invisible government which is the true ruling power of our country."[16] Considering the members of the WWB to be part of a theoretical invisible government stretches the point, but Bernays's comment underscores the fact that the WWB exerted a significant influence even though its work often went unacknowledged. It was especially effective in promoting the government's agenda, mobilizing the public in support of the war effort, and espousing liberal causes. The hostile Hearst press once referred to the organization as "one of the greatest propaganda machines in history," undoubtedly a disparaging exaggeration. However, the group regarded the epithet as a compliment instead of a slur.[17] The description may have been more accurate than anyone could foresee at the time.

EARLY GOVERNMENT FUNDING

Since the Writers' War Board was established five months before Roosevelt set up the Office of War Information, the New York group initially came under the jurisdiction of the Section of Volunteer Talents in the Office of Civilian Defense (OCD), an agency within the Office of Emergency Management (OEM). At first board members paid for materials and stenographic help out of their own pockets and depended heavily on volunteers to handle routine secretarial tasks. When expenses rose to $150 per member (about $2,300 in 2018 currency), the group asked the government for funding since it was working with several federal agencies. In January 1942 Rex Stout, WWB chairman, approached the OCD but was sent packing. However, when he tried again the following month, he was able to arrange a March 5 meeting with I. J. Meade, regional manager of the Division of Central Administrative Services of the OEM. Meade allowed the WWB to acquire an office and stenographer, justifying those ongoing expenditures under the OCD's mandate to "promot[e] . . . activities designed to sustain the national morale and to create opportunities for constructive civilian participation in the Defense Program."[18]

In April Stout began to look for an executive secretary to coordinate projects and supervise volunteers. Within a month the government agreed to hire Frederica L. Barach as a civil service employee of the Office of Facts and Figures (OFF), another branch of the OEM.[19] The OFF's Production Division took over the responsibility of handling the board. Headed by Henry Pringle, 1932 Pulitzer Prize winner for his biography of Theodore Roosevelt, the division consisted of a small staff of researchers and writers who prepared materials on war-related topics for government publication. Pringle made arrangements for the WWB to fill all requests for outside writers that came to his office.[20] Despite Barach's efficient work and partial funding from both the OCD and OFF, in late spring 1942 the board was forced to turn down virtually all assignments from private sources and some from government agencies too. When pleas for assistance came in, the group typically replied, "We are so swamped with requests from various government departments that it is physically impossible for us to take on any more assignments until and unless our staff and office space are considerably expanded."[21]

Another government group, the Arts Council of the OCD, rescued the board by providing the increased funding it needed. The council's driving force was actor Melvyn Douglas, a consultant whose job was to maintain contact with organizations that could supply writers, artists, musicians, and actors to fill wartime requests from government agencies. If one of them needed a muralist, for example, the Arts Council would contact the Chicago Museum of Art or the Museum of Modern Art in New York. Once Douglas heard about the WWB, he was eager to enlist its help. In April he met with thirty New York writers and became convinced that greater funding for the board would be of mutual benefit. He worked out a deal with its members, who agreed to use OCD money only in ways acceptable to that agency. In May the WWB established a policy that requests from government departments would be cleared with Douglas. If he did not approve an assignment, the board would decline it. On a few occasions the group overlooked this policy in order to start a project that was urgent or one they felt was certain to receive routine approval. Even in these cases, however, Douglas had the final say.²² This arrangement between the OCD Arts Council and the WWB did not last long, but it helped to establish the board's regular government subsidy.

RELATIONSHIP WITH THE OWI

Once the Office of War Information was established, it assumed many of the duties of the OCD and the OFF such as providing financial support for the WWB. The OWI's domestic, overseas, and administrative branches shared the cost.²³ Overall responsibility for the group rested with OWI director Elmer Davis, who had been a popular radio commentator. Having served as a member of the WWB for a short time, he understood its capabilities. Davis shared his general supervisory functions with Robert Sherwood, who headed the agency's Overseas Division. As a Pulitzer Prize–winning dramatist, Sherwood already knew several board members.²⁴ Various offices within the Domestic Branch handled day-to-day contact with the group. At first the job was given to Chester Kerr, head of the Book Bureau; however, Dorothy Ducas of the Bureau of Publications and Graphics carried on most of the correspondence with the group early on. When author Oscar Schisgall became head of the new Book and Magazine Bureau, he took the job of maintaining a convivial relationship with the board, which kept him informed with periodic written reports on its activities. Throughout the war the OWI continued to request the WWB's help with difficult projects and activities that congressional opponents of the agency might question.

Twenty-five years after the war, former OWI deputy director Leo Rosten applauded the achievements of the board and acknowledged that it undertook an "immense variety of tasks" and was "extremely useful" to Washington agencies.²⁵ Chief among those agencies was the Office of War Information, which endured several early upheavals. Before the end of its first year of operation, OWI assistant director Gardner Cowles changed the leadership of the Domestic Branch. OWI head Elmer Davis, a Democrat, had hired Cowles, a moderate Republican, to deflect criticism of the agency from congressional conservatives. Since Cowles was a newspaper publisher who had links to business and advertising, he recruited executives from those two industries to work with him. Writers and artists at the OWI feared that their new bosses would use advertising techniques to play up the propaganda value of the war material they produced, thus compromising its factual content. In April 1943 the disgruntled employees resigned en masse, leaving a tremendous gap.[26]

Congress made two other moves against the OWI that year. First, it forced the agency to take drastic action by reducing the budget of the Domestic Branch. Its Bureau of Publications and Graphics ceased to operate even though it had printed a huge volume of materials for a variety of government departments. According to one historian, after that time the OWI became "a coordinating agency" that did not have the ability to do much on its own.[27] The second blow came near the end of 1943. Conservatives that had frequently criticized the agency because of its close ties to the Roosevelt administration attempted to abolish it. That maneuver failing, they decided to press for a full reorganization of the Domestic Branch. The shuffle brought many changes that included combining the book and magazine divisions under Schisgall.[28] The board took no position on these upheavals, but it recognized the problems they created. When the OWI writers resigned, WWB members stepped in to help, and when the publications office closed, they used their contacts to direct government bureaus to the people and services they needed. More importantly, the board continued to carry on and expand some of the liberal initiatives that Congress forced the OWI to drop.[29]

Schisgall did not dictate any hard-and-fast rules to the WWB or try to intervene in its everyday affairs. He specifically outlined the board's relationship to the government in an exchange of letters with Stout in 1944:

> My own feelings on the matter . . . are these: The Writers' War Board ought to continue as a volunteer agency which is completely independent of O.W.I. I know this is the way you are now operating; if I repeat the obvious, it's simply because I feel it's the right way to go on from this point. . . . Whatever the O.W.I. pays to maintain liaison with the Writers' War Board is money paid to recognition of the services the Board can and does give to the war program; but such payments are not to be construed as indicating that the O.W.I. controls the actions and the decisions of the Writers' War Board; nor, on the other hand, that the O.W.I. is in any way responsible for such actions.[30]

Stout concurred with Schisgall, noting that his explanation "states clearly and properly the status of the Writers' War Board and its relation to the Office of War Information."³¹ Although the connection between the group and the Roosevelt administration was undeniably close, Stout always contended that "there was no government control of the board's activities. None whatever," and the OWI's Rosten agreed that the problem "simply did not exist."³² Nevertheless, WWB members occasionally worried about becoming subordinate to the government agency.³³ Board employee Selma Hirsh sympathized with them and said that she wished to keep the organization from being "infected with the government bug—a deadly virus."³⁴ Contacted in 1969, board member Clifton Fadiman grudgingly admitted, "We were for the most part, I suppose, an arm of the government."³⁵ None of the WWB members would have made such an acknowledgment during the war, but Fadiman's comment seems justified in light of the group's subsidy and its frequent assignments for government departments.

SIGNIFICANCE OF THE WRITERS' WAR BOARD

This study emphasizes three assertions about the Writers' War Board. First and foremost, the organization was an aggressive and unfettered purveyor of government propaganda. Because of its quasi-governmental status, the WWB could claim the advantages of being a government agency and a private organization at one and the same time. Since it was on the federal payroll, government groups frequently sought its assistance. In addition to having an entrée into each department of the cabinet, the board had access to a host of individuals, companies, local officials, and other resources that considered it imperative to comply with government requests related to the war effort. Equally important, the board took full advantage of the government's franking privilege, which allowed it to distribute its publications at federal expense without paying postage. The group's status as a private organization also proved to be beneficial. It insured that the board did not operate under the same restrictions as the OWI. Furthermore, the WWB had the freedom to accept or reject assignments from federal agencies, to launch campaigns on its own, and to take requests from organizations outside the government without worrying about the approval of or interference from overseers. Aware of the board's unique position, the Roosevelt administration periodically contacted the group about making an argument or taking a stand that it wished to have publicized but dared not handle itself because of political expediency. In these cases the board outwardly appeared to oppose the government's position even though it was acting on behalf of the administration. Roosevelt liked the idea of using private organizations to promote the government's agenda. When some officials suggested that the administration become involved in a divisive, prewar congressional debate, the president replied, "Couldn't it be done with voluntary organizations and people?"[36]

Board members strongly believed in the views they espoused and were aggressive in pursuing their campaigns, even those that proved to be unpopular or drew controversy. They exploited their influence on occasion by publicly supporting a position before the government announced its official policy in hopes of prodding the administration into taking a particular view, moving faster, or pushing the envelope. Board members produced well-written propaganda materials for every type of publication from posters to comic books to intellectual treatises in order to appeal to all segments of the population. They were unconcerned about building their reputations, making a profit, or getting publicity. Although they were independent thinkers, they worked together harmoniously to achieve their sincere, often idealistic desire to help win the war and secure a lasting peace. Their devotion to these goals, their talents, and their concern for liberal causes made this volunteer group a formidable organization.

A second assertion of this study is that the board was a vital force in the domestic culture of wartime America. Early in the war the WWB became an integral part of a government effort to persuade Americans to set aside differences, find common ground, and unite behind the war. Board members were smart about their appeals, drawing the attention of Americans by writing and distributing articles and letters to the editor that were signed by famous people and by adding a touch of humor when they could. The writers urged the public to abide by government regulations including price controls and rationing and to save their money rather than go on spending sprees, which might cause inflation by creating a scarcity of goods. These New York–based authors promoted good relations with America's allies by distributing information on each nation, and they asked for contributions to relieve the suffering of people in war-torn countries. In regards to the German enemy, however, they wanted to stamp out all feelings of sympathy. They fomented hatred for the entire population of the country and argued against the widespread notion that "good Germans" existed. They emphasized the nation's brutality by organizing commemorations of Nazi book burning and the razing of a Czech village, and they insisted on harsh peace terms for Germany to prevent it from starting another global war. Administration officials approved of this anti-German effort and privately encouraged it. In a plethora of campaigns WWB members made speeches on the war, organized rallies to sell bonds, promoted books that supported their arguments, distributed dramatic scripts for local performances, and helped to set up special celebrations such as Infantry Day and I Am an American Day. The board's ubiquitous propaganda touched virtually every American home.

The third assertion central to this study is that the board played an influential role in promoting liberal democracy, especially after Congress reorganized the OWI and curtailed its activities in that cause. Fighting isolationists, the WWB supported internationalism and pushed the government to take a leading role on the world stage. It produced a pledge for peace that encouraged Americans to promise allegiance not only to their own country but also to a future world organization that would have the power to stop aggression and enforce peace. While board members could not achieve this goal, their vision of people working together for the common good persists today as nations and industries have become increasingly global in outlook. The WWB also made inroads in helping to change traditional attitudes through its campaigns to enlist females in the military. Its arguments outlining what they could contribute to victory by taking an active role helped to give a number of women the confidence to seek opportunities outside of home and family. Although the board's propaganda did not overturn ingrained societal attitudes on this issue, it prompted people to rethink their assumptions. WWB members far and away considered their most successful liberal effort to be their campaign against prejudice, a subject that few individuals and organizations were willing to tackle directly. The group not only brought the problem of intolerance to the attention of the general public but also specifically targeted media personnel who often used stereotypes in their depictions of people of different racial and ethnic backgrounds. The board's clever presentation of the issue at a mock theatrical show convinced many decision-makers of the need for improvement and caused an immediate change for the better.

While the members of the Writers' War Board were volunteers, their level of commitment to the government and its war work was so strong that they often seemed to be civilian soldiers wielding their pens to defeat the enemy and create a better world. Their two goals of uniting the country behind the war effort and establishing lasting peace were idealistic, but the group never wavered in its commitment to both. Some of the stands it took proved unpopular, but each served a purpose. The board produced pro-Soviet propaganda not because it supported communism but because the United States needed to work with its Russian ally on the battlefield and at the peace table. Its effort to arouse hatred of all the citizens of Germany was not motivated by conscious racial bias but by repeated acts of German aggression, which triggered two global wars in the first half of the twentieth century. WWB members felt that Germany had to be completely defeated in order to prevent further conflicts. So these authors marched off to make war in their own way, flags flying, full speed ahead.

CHAPTER 1

THE HISTORY AND FUNCTION OF THE WRITERS' WAR BOARD

THE HISTORY OF the Writers' War Board does not start with its first meeting in January 1942 nor with its chairman, Rex Stout, the man who single-handedly shaped the organization. It begins in 1941 with the Treasury Department and one of its new employees. After Germany provoked war in Europe by invading Poland on September 1, 1939, Americans became increasingly concerned about a possible attack. Both interventionists and isolationists saw the wisdom of bolstering the country's defenses. In order to finance the initiative, the Treasury Department created Series E savings bonds for defense. On April 30, 1941, Franklin Roosevelt called on citizens to form "one great partnership" by investing in their nation as he himself publicly purchased the first new bond from Treasury Secretary Henry Morgenthau Jr.[1] Department officials knew that they would have to publicize the bonds continually to keep money flowing into the government's coffers from millions of small savers who could not afford to buy several bonds at a time. On November 1 Morgenthau's office hired thirty-nine-year-old Julian Street Jr., former journalist and radio executive, to develop an "education program designed to create awareness of the world situation and build up a confidence in government, stimulate production, explain tax needs, and sell government bonds."[2]

Street had begun his career as a reporter for the Paris edition of the *New York Herald Tribune* and had subsequently worked for eleven years at the NBC radio network where he eventually headed the magazine publicity department. In 1939 he took a public relations job as secretary of the Museum of Modern Art before moving to the Treasury Department.[3] During his first five weeks in his new position, Street spent "a good 80 per cent" of his time promoting bond sales. Soon he became aware that

"Secretary Morgenthau wanted someone to mobilize writers behind the Treasury's Defense Savings Program."[4] He was in a unique position to handle the job because of his work with writers and artists and because of his familial ties. He was well aware of the contributions that professional authors could make to the government's fundraising campaigns since his father had been a founding member of the Vigilantes. As the son of novelist and Princeton professor Julian Street, young "Pete" had come into contact with prominent men and women of letters from an early age. Those connections continued after his 1925 marriage to the daughter of prominent New York banker and financier Frank A. Vanderlip.[5]

Within his first month at the Treasury, Julian Street Jr. went to see Luise Sillcox, executive secretary of the Authors' League of America. That visit set in motion a series of events that eventually led to the formation of the Writers' War Board. Street himself came to feel that instigating the founding of the organization was one of his most important early achievements as a government consultant. Once America formally declared war in December, his primary task shifted into "mobilizing for the War Finance Campaign the talents of the writers and artists of America as a great national resource on which to draw in wartime." In order to maintain his connections to both groups, he set up a second office in New York. For two and a half years Street divided his time between the political capital and the cultural capital of the country, spending three days in each office.[6]

Unfortunately, the origins of the WWB are somewhat nebulous because he and Stout gave differing versions of the group's establishment. Street included his account in an unpublished report to Treasury official Peter Odegard entitled "High Lights of My Work with Writers and Artists for the Treasury Department: November 1, 1941 to January 31, 1946." Street focused on his visit with Sillcox; Stout made no mention of her. Instead, the WWB chairman contended that Street had talked with playwright and stage actor Howard Lindsay, president of the Authors' League.[7] Perhaps Street did both although he does not say so. The differences in the two accounts are puzzling but not totally contradictory, and the two can be woven together to make a fairly coherent report of the inception of the organization.[8]

Street said that he contacted Sillcox in November before the United States entered the war, but he gave no date. He requested that the Authors' League consider forming a small committee to help the Treasury

Department promote the sale of defense savings bonds by undertaking a variety of writing assignments. Sillcox told him frankly that the group had refused propaganda requests during World War I, but she admitted that some writers, including Lindsay, had begun to discuss ways they might help the government in light of the profound success of the Nazi propaganda machine. She promised Street that his request would be considered at the next board meeting. The following week Sillcox notified him that Stout "had been appointed by the League to form a Treasury Writers' Committee."[9]

Stout may never have known of the existence of the ninety-one-page document Street submitted to the Treasury in November 1946, but Street obviously had heard the chairman's account of the founding of the Writers' War Board. Although he never seems to have contested Stout's story publicly, Street wrote to Odegard, "How would you like to know a little of the God's truth about how the Writer's War Board got started? This is one version of it. As [syndicated columnist] Drew Pearson would say 'now it can be revealed.'" Unlike Street, Stout never mentioned any action by the league's board of directors. In a 1968 interview, the WWB chairman, who served as president of the Authors' League for more than ten years during the 1950s and 1960s, stated that the organization's charter prohibited members from engaging in projects not exclusively connected with the writing profession. In his account Stout focused on Lindsay's role in setting up the committee. Regardless of whether Lindsay found out about the government request from the league office or from Street, the playwright was sympathetic to the Treasury's request. He believed that a number of writers would be willing to offer their services to the government, and he asked his longtime collaborator Russel Crouse to create a special committee. Although Crouse was willing to help, he did not want to head the group, and he recommended the outspoken interventionist Stout. Lindsay wasted no time in contacting the novelist, but Stout was cautious. He insisted that he be allowed to select the committee members himself and stipulated that the group be autonomous, with no official connection to the Authors' League or any other organization. As a way of insuring the committee's independence, Stout suggested that members have sole responsibility for obtaining financial backing for the group. Lindsay assented to these conditions, and Stout immediately began to draw up a list of possible recruits.[10]

Street was disheartened on learning about the new committee: "I was disappointed that [the Authors' League] had not consulted me as to what sort of chairman I thought I would work with best and what sort of committee would be most useful to the Treasury needs." He worried that he might encounter the same kind of problems that Ferdinand Kuhn, his friend and Treasury colleague, had experienced when he had worked with a volunteer group of writers previously. They had overstepped their authority by claiming to speak for the department and by trying to control public relations. Street emphasized to Sillcox and Stout that "the Treasury would have to work closely with the committee and guide its policies." Unaware of the full scope of Street's apprehensions, Stout telegrammed invitations to a dozen or so notable authors, most of them Pulitzer Prize winners. He told Street that he thought two or three might accept and that he planned to fill the rest of the committee with writers from different fields. Street remembers that Stout sent the telegrams on December 6. Because the Japanese bombed Pearl Harbor the following day, the chairman received a better response than he had anticipated, and he set the first committee meeting for Tuesday, January 6, 1942, in New York City. Stout gives the date of the WWB's founding as December 9 without specifying a reason. Perhaps by that date he had received a sufficient number of replies from the writers he contacted to form his committee. He convened the one and only meeting of the Treasury Writers' Committee with five other authors in attendance: Crouse, Clifton Fadiman, Oscar Hammerstein II, Pearl Buck, and John P. Marquand. Street also came, but he was not invited into the meeting room until the writers had conferred for half an hour.[11] The group initially organized as the Writers' War Committee but retained that name for only a few months. In late April it became the Writers' War Board.[12]

THE SIX ORIGINAL MEMBERS OF THE BOARD

From beginning to end the board's irascible chairman dominated every aspect of its work. Having just turned fifty-five on December 1, Rex Todhunter Stout was the second oldest board member, but his years neither slowed his actions nor mellowed his opinions. He was one of the board's most interesting members and easily the most controversial.

Even though his formal education ended with a high school diploma, Stout made two fortunes by his ingenuity and drive. Born of Quaker parents, he grew up in Kansas and later served in the navy as a warrant officer on President Theodore Roosevelt's yacht. After a variety of jobs Stout turned to writing for magazines and began contributing to both humanitarian and radical causes. He even gave money to found the left-wing periodical *The Masses* and served for a brief period on its executive board, but he resigned within a year because of its association with communism. Nevertheless, this brief involvement led to charges later in his life that he was either a communist or a communist sympathizer. In 1916 Stout turned to business. He developed an idea his brother Bob had for a banking system that allowed students to save money through a program at their schools. The two operated the Educational Thrift Service on a nationwide basis for ten years and became wealthy men.[13]

Even then, Stout retained his interest in liberal causes and the literary world, serving as the first president of Vanguard Press, which was founded in 1926 to publish affordable left-wing books. At the age of forty he retired comfortably and produced four novels, but they had limited sales. When the Depression depleted his savings in 1933, he made his writing pay by creating the wildly popular fictional detective Nero Wolfe. A wealthy gourmand and eccentric who was devoted to his orchids, Wolfe rarely left his New York brownstone but solved each case after ruminating about the facts collected by his assistant. Over the next forty years Stout published more than seventy short stories and novels featuring the corpulent sleuth. By the time the WWB was founded, the author had a worldwide reputation. In 2000 he was one of five nominated as "Best Mystery Writer of the 20th Century." A steady stream of works brought Stout a second fortune and enough free time for his favorite causes.[14]

The bestselling writer seems to have taken little interest in world affairs until the 1938 Munich Conference at which British prime minister Neville Chamberlain tried to keep the peace by allowing Germany to take over the Sudetenland, a section of Czechoslovakia. Stout reported that the British capitulation to the Nazis gave him his "first belly-ache" and caused him to "star[t] making speeches, debating [the isolationists], going on the radio to answer them, doing all [he] could to wake people up to the danger."[15] Believing that Hitler's aggressive tactics were a threat not only to Europe but also to the rest of the world, Stout campaigned ardently for American intervention, cheerfully describing himself as a "warmonger." He supported organizations such as the Century Group, the Committee to Defend America by Aiding the Allies, and the Associated Leagues for an Immediate Declaration of War. As early as November 1940 he argued that the United States should be engaged in the fight.[16] Since the Committee to Defend America was unwilling to go that far, Stout became involved in the Fight for Freedom Committee, which vigorously promoted armed intervention. During the first year of the group's existence, the author was one of its most popular speakers, appearing at its pro-war rallies, debating isolationists on the radio, and otherwise encouraging interventionist sentiment.[17]

In October 1941 Stout helped to found Freedom House and became one of the prominent leaders of the organization, which continues to promote democratic principles around the globe.[18] He also joined the Council for Democracy, a group organized as a service and liaison agency for the interventionist organizations, and he served as master of ceremonies for its 1941 radio broadcast *Speaking of Liberty*.[19] The following year Stout became president of the antifascist organization Friends of Democracy, a position he retained throughout the war. The group specialized in sensational denunciations of American isolationists and right-wing extremists. One of its pamphlets labeled the America First Committee "a Nazi front" and accused it of being "a transmission belt by means of which the apostles of Nazism are spreading their antidemocratic ideas into millions of American homes."[20]

Stout himself never shied from public controversy and attracted heckling and other challenges at some of his public appearances. His barbed commentary and aggressive attacks won the lasting enmity of the isolationists. He repeatedly denounced their most prominent spokesman, Charles Lindbergh, and called the aviation hero a "quitter" when Lindbergh resigned his commission in the Army Air Corps after Roosevelt publicly criticized him. Stout even suggested in a radio broadcast that Lindbergh would become the collaborationist president of the United States if Hitler succeeded in his conquests.[21] In 1942 Stout published a book entitled *The Illustrious Dunderheads*, a collection of quotations from American isolationists.[22] His onslaughts brought replies in kind. Congressman Hamilton

Fish III of New York, a Nazi sympathizer who was one of Stout's favorite targets, called the novelist a "Communist and more dangerous to America than Earl Browder [general secretary of the Communist Party of the United States from 1934 to 1945]."[23] A writer for the isolationist *Chicago Tribune* detected a "fanatical gleam" in Stout's eye and declared him to be a member of several communist front organizations.[24]

Beginning in August 1942 and continuing through early October 1943, Stout regularly made a fifteen-minute broadcast called *Our Secret Weapon* each Friday evening over the CBS radio network. With the assistance of Freedom House, he read about fifteen statements put out by the Axis news services and then exposed them as falsehoods. The program attracted a sufficiently large audience to be commercially sponsored during its last year.[25] Stout's wartime activities also involved two other organizations. In 1943 he assumed the presidency of the Authors' Guild of America, a group associated with the Authors' League, and the following year he began to head a new organization that he had helped to found, the Society for the Prevention of World War III (SPWW3). It argued for a stringent peace settlement that would forestall Germany's economic recovery and keep the nation from starting a third conflict. After the Marshall Plan and other postwar programs thwarted that goal, the group advocated a strong global government that could keep the peace. The SPWW3 continued to operate until 1972.[26]

Throughout the years that the WWB existed, Stout was indefatigable, working six or seven days a week, even during the holidays.[27] Because he did not want to waste time on the long journey back and forth to his country mansion just north of New York City, he moved his wife and two daughters to a downtown apartment.[28] Eventually he found it necessary to take three extended absences from the WWB: one after a bout of pneumonia in December 1943, six weeks during the summer of 1944 when he had to write another Nero Wolfe novel to bolster his finances, and two months in early 1945 when he went to Europe on a trip sponsored by the U.S. Army Air Forces.[29] Stout was the only one to devote himself to the board's work so completely; other members usually made an effort to keep up a semblance of their normal schedules. Although he was the kind of man who used strong language and provoked it in others, under his direction the Writers' War Board achieved its goals with some occasional disagreements but no lasting animosities or personal attacks. Several members contacted individually twenty-three years after the end of the war unanimously agreed on the effectiveness of his leadership. The words of executive secretary Frederica Barach are typical: Stout was "an extraordinary executive and dedicated day to day, . . . a superb executive."[30] Despite the fact that all decisions were made by majority vote, Stout's opinions pervaded, and his dynamic personality was the force behind most of the board's actions. In the words of one board member, "If there ever was one, Rex was the autocrat of the breakfast table."[31] With those he respected, Stout would always listen to objections, and occasionally he could be persuaded to withdraw his opinion or revise it. Although he alienated some people by his strong advocacy of certain ideas, he convinced many others to assist the board with his tactful persuasiveness, exercised either in person or in his writing, which could be quite charming and endearing as well as humorous.

The most valuable and influential member of the WWB aside from Stout was Clifton Fadiman. During the chairman's brief absences, the group usually chose "Kip" as acting head. Fadiman admired Stout and acknowledged his influence: "He was for many years my guru. To him, more than anyone else, I owe whatever basic understanding I have of World War II. He understood the Germans long before most of us did."[32] Something of a phenom, Fadiman had spent ten years at the Simon and Schuster publishing firm in the early 1930s, rising to the position of editor in chief before taking the prestigious job of book editor at the *New Yorker* at the age of twenty-nine. By the time he joined the WWB in 1942, he was on the editorial boards of the *Encyclopedia Britannica* and the Book of the Month Club. His fame reached its zenith between 1938 and 1951 when he hosted *Information Please*, a popular and well-respected radio program. The heart of the show, Fadiman purveyed culture to the masses every week. Americans admired his versatile intellect, ingenuity, sense of humor, penchant for repartee, prodigious memory, and encyclopedic knowledge.[33] For the WWB Fadiman took on a variety of jobs despite his busy schedule. Since he was a guaranteed drawing card, the organization regularly called on him to make appearances and host events as well as write propaganda. The group tapped his talents so often that Fadiman complained to Stout about the workload: "If there isn't enough talent in the War Board to spread the jobs around, the hell with the War Board."[34] Fadiman took a two-month "vacation" from the WWB at the end of 1944 and resigned twice. He was persuaded to return each time and continued to do more than his fair share until the organization shut its doors.[35]

A second member that Stout considered especially important was Oscar Hammerstein II. Both Fadiman and Hammerstein were with the board from its organization to its dissolution. Although trained as a lawyer, Hammerstein rose to fame and fortune working with leading composers on a string of popular musicals including the prewar hit *Show Boat*, which featured his song "Ol' Man River." By the time World War II began, he was one of the highest paid authors in the world. In 1942 his career entered its most productive phase when he and Richard Rodgers began collaborating. Their works included the Broadway blockbusters *Oklahoma* (1943), *South Pacific* (1949), *The King and I* (1951), and the iconic *Sound of Music* (1959).[36] One of Hammerstein's colleagues described him as a "gentle, quiet man, . . . a great doer rather than a great talker." For that reason the names of other board members appear in the records more frequently and more prominently than Hammerstein's.[37] However, he chaired the Music War Committee of both the WWB and the American Theater Wing, an organization best known today for presenting the Tony Awards. He fielded all requests for World War II songs that the board received and contributed a number himself. His best was "The Last Time I Saw Paris," which he wrote in 1940 after German troops took control of the French capital. While none of the war songs he wrote on behalf of the WWB were so inspired, each addressed a need. An example is "Dear Friend," which he and Rodgers composed in 1944 for the Fifth War Loan Drive. It encouraged Americans to support the cause of "living free" by donating money for their sons in the armed forces:

Dear friend,
Dear friend, this is a touch.
We won't go into explanations,
But when boys need help so much,
They always call on their relations, dear friend.
Traveling on foreign shores,
Is expensive as can be.

It isn't our fault or yours
It's the high cost of living free, dear friend.
To know that we can count on you
Is all we need to know.
Just say that you'll see us through,
And we'll finish up the show, dear friend.
We still need aeroplanes and guns,
So dig down in your jeans
And please oblige your loving sons,
Your Army, your Navy, your Marines—
Dear friend.[38]

Another member present at the board's initial meeting was Russel "Buck" Crouse, the first person Authors' League president Howard Lindsay recruited to serve on the WWB. The two men had worked together since 1934, and their twenty-eight-year collaboration continues to be described as the American theater's most successful. They produced *Arsenic and Old Lace* (1941) and adapted two autobiographical books into successful plays that were later made into movies: *Life with Father* (1939), which ran on Broadway for over seven years—still the record for a nonmusical—and *The Sound of Music* (1959), from which the screenplay was adapted.[39] Crouse molded the board by insisting that Stout head the group. For the organization Crouse wrote plays and regularly contributed a column to the British army magazine *Parade*.

The final two who attended the WWB's initial meeting were the illustrious novelists Pearl S. Buck and John P. Marquand. Each had won a Pulitzer Prize in the 1930s, and Buck had received the 1938 Nobel Prize in literature.[40] Although the two made a few public appearances for the board, neither was devoted to the organization, rarely attending its meetings or participating in its campaigns because of their prior commitments. Also, both lived outside the New York area. Such was their stature, however, that the board continued to display their names on its letterhead even after Buck resigned in July 1943 because she objected to the group's stand on some issues.[41] Nevertheless, she and Marquand continued to help the WWB from time to time.

Eventually twenty-nine writers sat on the war board including Stout, but no more than twenty served at one time. While the group remained remarkably stable for the most part, Buck was not the only one who resigned. Five left in 1942 including Elmer Davis, who became head of the OWI. Others making an early exit were Sam B. Eubanks, executive vice president of the American Newspaper Guild; journalist George Britt; author Henry Fisk Carlton; and screenwriter Sidney Buchman. None of their names figure prominently in the minutes. Two additional members, journalists Robert Bellaire and Henry Pringle, had no real opportunity to contribute to the board because they joined the group in 1945 just as it began curtailing its activities in anticipation of the end of the war. Both drama critic Hobe Morrison and Jean Poletti, a politically active clubwoman who had worked in advertising, became part of the board in 1944. Although they made significant contributions to the group, each served for just over one year. (Poletti's husband was former New York lieutenant governor Charles Poletti.) Most of the board's work was carried out by fifteen men and women. In addition to Rex Stout, Clifton Fadiman, Oscar Hammerstein, and Russel Crouse, this core group included Carl Carmer, Paul Gallico, Jack Goodman, Alan Green, Rita Halle Kleeman, Christopher LaFarge, Robert J. Landry, Margaret Leech, Katharine Seymour, William Shirer, and Luise Sillcox. Robert T. Colwell periodically had to leave the group because of his wartime service with the Office of War Information-Overseas and the Psychological Warfare Department of the Third Army. Less active members of the board were Franklin P. Adams and Samuel Grafton.[42]

WRITERS WHO ASSISTED THE WWB

Street had originally envisioned a small committee that would work exclusively with the Treasury, but the board did not confine itself to one department, and requests for assistance began to pour in from several government agencies. WWB members wrote all the propaganda early on, but they soon recognized the need for additional help, especially since Buck and Marquand were unavailable for regular duty. To enlist a large contingent of colleagues to handle the workload, the WWB turned to

Luise M. Sillcox, the person Street had contacted at the Authors' League. As secretary-treasurer of that organization and its subordinate groups, the Dramatists' Guild and the Authors' Guild, she maintained contact with writers around the country, and those men and women considered her their advocate. Even though she was not an author, she had tackled their common problems from copyright infringement to income tax issues, had fought to establish basic royalty fees for both amateur and professional works, and had administered a benevolence fund for sick or indigent writers.[43] After her tenure of almost fifty years, author John Hersey characterized Sillcox as "the memory, the spur, the conscience, the will, and the cheerful heart" of the Authors' League.[44] Recognizing her commitment to writers and her invaluable information, Stout asked Sillcox to join the board in early 1942 because the WWB needed to expand its reservoir of talented contributors. The files of the Authors' League and its two affiliates provided the names of thousands of journalists, radio scriptwriters, commentators, playwrights, poets, and authors of fiction and nonfiction, a number of whom lived in the immediate vicinity of New York and could be contacted quickly.[45]

In late March and early April 1942, the board sent a comprehensive questionnaire to approximately three thousand members of these professional organizations and to any others who had contacted the board about volunteering their services. The WWB aimed to register all of them whether they had international reputations or were known only in their local areas. To select appropriate writers for specific assignments, the board collected information regarding their fields of expertise, foreign language abilities, preferred types of writing, previously published works, and publishers. About 2,200 writers answered the first survey, and the Authors' League eventually took over the job of classifying their responses. After eliminating crackpots and total amateurs, the WWB encouraged the rest to help with the war effort. It continued to recruit authors throughout the war and managed to register some five thousand by 1944. Most helpful was a short list that the board developed of conscientious authors who could be counted on to meet a quick deadline and produce suitable, polished materials that required little editing.[46]

The WWB's efforts to tap other sources of talent were not as successful. At the suggestion of board member Rita Kleeman, the group contacted foreign writers living in the United States to help with its campaigns. Kleeman, who had made her name with a 1935 biography of Franklin Roosevelt's mother, *Gracious Lady: The Life of Sara Delano Roosevelt*, was important to the WWB because of her prominent role in several influential groups including the National Council of Women, the National Federation of Business and Professional Women's Clubs, and the Pan-American Women's Association.[47] She had contact with many of the authors in exile through the international writers' organization PEN. The board established a Foreign Writers' Committee in late 1942 and named as chair Manuel Komroff, who had lived overseas and was personally acquainted with a number of European authors. The WWB hoped that these writers could serve as "propaganda instruments," addressing American audiences in English about circumstances in the writers' native countries and making appeals to their compatriots living in the United States in their mother tongue. The committee began to conduct interviews and send out questionnaires to find foreign writers willing to cooperate on such projects. Symposia were held, and several articles by foreign writers appeared in various publications, but the committee never achieved the results the board envisioned for two reasons, one practical and one philosophical. Despite their reputations in their homelands, most of the foreigners had trouble connecting with American publishing houses, which had become more selective because of the wartime paper shortage. Furthermore, these authors had developed their own political opinions and were not always willing to present the WWB's point of view. After such problems surfaced, the board decided that its efforts should be directed elsewhere, and the committee ceased to be active in less than a year.[48]

The WWB also hoped to coordinate its efforts with those of other writers' organizations that could help promote board campaigns. At the end of 1942 the board made overtures to the Canadian Writers' War Committee, established in October. Stout met with the group on November 9 and spoke at a public meeting in Toronto the following day. However, his trip convinced him that the Canadians could not be of much help. The two organizations exchanged some materials, but they did not work together on any projects.[49] Looking for more insight into regional perspectives and additional opportunities to develop local contacts, the WWB tried to establish connections with groups in two U.S. regions. It had little difficulty in securing the cooperation of Chicago radio scriptwriters headed by Ruth Wallister. She and her colleagues aided the board in publicizing several of its projects in the Midwest and throughout the country.[50] However, the Hollywood Writers' Mobilization (HWM) on the West Coast was not very helpful.

In the summer of 1942 Melvyn Douglas of the Office of Civilian Defense had promoted contact between the two groups. Once both organizations had participated in a few joint activities of minor importance, the prospect for their continued collaboration seemed good. Although the HWM was never as active as the board, it had engaged in some similar projects: enlisting writers for documentary films, preparing plays for use in army camps, and producing a radio series.[51] HWM chairman Robert Rossen arranged to visit the WWB, and the two organizations planned to cosponsor a writers' conference in October 1943. However, the board backed out of the arrangement, believing that some of the ideas of the Hollywood group would not be productive. Rightly or wrongly, WWB members felt that the HWM viewed them as unwelcome outsiders and resented their efforts in California. Furthermore, they discovered that Rossen's group had occasionally tried to bypass their organization even while the HWM was considering working with the New Yorkers. Compounding the problem was the fact that the two groups did not see eye to eye on several issues including the terms of peace.[52] The Hollywood writers were more conservative and had little interest in promoting the board's liberal ideas. Consequently, the two went their separate ways, operating independently of each other for the rest of the war.

At first the WWB had difficulty keeping all of its registered writers informed about ideas for compositions on timely war-related topics. In 1943 it gave the challenging task to the Assignments Committee, headed jointly by Sillcox and volunteer Martha McCleery. The group's main purpose was to generate propaganda on the grassroots level by drawing on the talents of authors living throughout the United States. To that end the committee created a mailing list of competent writers and sent them periodic messages in the hope that they would write or stimulate a special editorial, a local radio show, a discussion group, or, at the very least, a letter to the editor of their local newspaper. In this way the board could promote regional interest in a topic of national concern. For example, it asked authors residing in agricultural states to urge farmers to increase production, and it encouraged those from heavily wooded states to remind readers of their patriotic duty to prevent forest fires.[53] The number of letters the WWB received from local authors indicates the organization's success in involving them in the war effort. At the board meeting on May 19, 1943, the Assignments Committee was able to report that local writers had provided "active, even astonishing cooperation along many lines."[54]

Once the sporadic messages of the Assignments Committee proved successful in generating local propaganda, the WWB decided to produce a newsletter each month about its present and future activities. In some ways it was similar to the bimonthly *Magazine War Guide* put out by the Office of War Information. The board was in charge of distributing that publication along with occasional issues of its supplement to magazine editors and writers on the WWB's mailing list. Both carried suggestions for background stories, plot ideas, articles, and editorials on themes the government planned to publicize in three months' time. Sometimes the *Supplement* dealt with a single topic or targeted specific kinds of periodicals like "Action Magazines," "Confession Magazines," and "Love and Western Love Magazines."[55] In October 1944 the OWI estimated that the 2,000 guides distributed up to that time had stimulated a total of 7,500 magazine articles.[56]

The board began to send its *Writers' War Board Report* to 2,500 authors on April 15, 1943. Readership eventually reached 3,500 to 4,000 writers who had sufficient ability or local prominence to stimulate some action on its suggestions.[57] WWB members wrote most of the articles, and volunteer Jane Grant compiled and edited each issue. Although unimpressive in appearance, the single typewritten sheet printed on both sides normally dealt with four to six WWB projects. A few articles merely presented information, but most enlisted support. For example, the newsletter of September 1, 1943, publicized (1) an effort by the Office of Price Administration to encourage housewives to abide by the rationing system, (2) a projected series of short sketches on typical Americans for the OWI to distribute overseas, (3) a report on WWB recruitment projects for the Women's Army Corps, (4) an announcement about a radio program to launch new war songs each week, and (5) the board's own campaign for racial tolerance. Each issue indicated the topics on which written materials were currently needed or would soon be required. If the authors immediately pursued one or more of the suggested subjects, they knew they could find a market for their work, whatever form it took—article, script, novel, speech, editorial, letter, and so on. In early 1945 Grant gave up her job as editor, complaining that the board neither allowed her to attend its meetings nor gave her access to board minutes that could have helped her prepare each issue.[58]

Despite her resignation, Grant is an excellent example of the kind of help the WWB was able to attract. This daughter of a Missouri farmer became a *New York Times* reporter. During the 1920s she cofounded the *New Yorker* magazine and made her mark as a strong advocate of women's rights by helping to found the Lucy Stone League. Another extremely capable volunteer was Nina Bourne, a young employee at Simon and Schuster who worked under the tutelage of board member Jack Goodman. She went on to spend seven decades in the publishing industry, becoming an icon credited with the success of several modern classics including Joseph Heller's *Catch-22*. At her death at age ninety-three, renowned editor Robert Gottlieb praised her as "*the* genius of book-publishing ads."[59] The board enlisted seventy-one other volunteers to serve on the Advisory Council that it created in April 1942. Among these illustrious writers were novelist John Steinbeck; poets Langston Hughes and Stephen Vincent Benet; dramatists Eugene O'Neill, Thornton Wilder, and George S. Kaufman; and commentator Edward R. Murrow.[60] Not simply a rubber stamp, the council played a vital role in guiding the WWB and helping shape its positions. When the board tackled highly debatable issues, it thoughtfully considered the viewpoints of the group. Advisory Council members also served on WWB committees and took writing assignments and speaking engagements, sometimes on very short notice.

OTHER WWB PUBLICATIONS

The WWB developed three publications in addition to the *Writers' War Board Report*. Mailed at the government's expense, these specialized newsletters went to writers, cartoonists, journalists, radio broadcasters, and others who could disseminate the board's propaganda and mold public opinion. Even though these publications were short, mimeographed bulletins of no more than six pages, they proved to be so effective that the board routinely used them to bolster almost all of its campaigns. Each mailing bore the name and address of the board and included some version of this instruction: "All this material is yours to use, cut, excerpt. It is cost-free; credit-free; copyright-free." Sometimes an issue reassured recipients that "everything is cleared for your use" or specified "no credit to Writers' War Board necessary."[61]

The Brief Items Committee established in 1942 produced two of these publications. The group's original function was to create and circulate to media outlets war-related slogans, catch phrases, wisecracks, radio plugs, newspaper fillers, poetry, and short articles to promote the sale of war bonds and other Treasury Department initiatives. Because it needed a steady supply of material, the board canvassed its registered writers to identify those with advertising experience. Around two hundred agreed to assist the committee in producing ideas throughout the war.[62] In 1943 advertising executive Julian Brodie took charge of the committee, and on June 15 it began to publish *Brief House Organ Items from the Writers' War Board*. This monthly publication went to major corporations that printed a regular bulletin or other type of "house organ." Collectively these bulletins reached more than 30 million employees. *Brief House Organ Items* was originally sent to 500 companies but that number swelled to 2,600 firms before circulation ceased in June 1945.[63]

Even though many house organs had previously carried some war-related propaganda, the WWB felt that it was ineffective because it was often stilted, blatant, and blandly anonymous. Committee members punched up the material they sent out by attaching it to the name of a well-known writer or entertainer. The prominence of this individual would encourage editors to print the piece so that its propaganda message, which had been finessed and personalized, would have more of an impact. The first *Brief House Organ Items* issue contained an article on war bonds under the byline of striptease performer Gypsy Rose Lee as well as one by Rex Stout on the postwar world.[64] The WWB or its affiliated writers would produce most of the articles and sometimes obtain permission to use the name of a well-known individual in the byline. At one time or another this publication carried articles supposedly by Academy Award–winning actor Fredric March on world organization, FBI director J. Edgar Hoover on the security of war information, singer Bing Crosby on maintaining the war effort, and many others. Even the names of popular fictional characters on the radio were used: Fibber McGee promoted war bonds, and ventriloquist's dummy Charlie McCarthy assisted in explaining income tax withholding. Occasionally a piece by a nonmember appeared, but such items were usually reprinted from other sources.[65] In addition to four or five short articles of a few hundred words each, every edition contained one or two poems, a few inspirational fillers of one or two sentences, and, invariably, a cartoon that featured Joe Palooka or some of Joe's associates. Drawn by Ham Fisher, it always plugged a current campaign.[66] The board considered the response to this service excellent even though it had no consistent statistical data to show the number of times the house organs "picked up" WWB pieces. Periodic checks revealed that the percentage of corporate publications using one or more items rose from an early average of 22 percent to 30 percent. Even if this medium continued to reach only one-third of the employees of large companies, it circulated WWB propaganda to at least 9 million readers each month.[67]

Less than a year after *Brief House Organ Items* appeared, the committee began to issue a second publication for another crucial audience, American soldiers. The first issue of *Brief Army Camp Items from the Writers' War Board* went to editors at military posts in March 1944. Between 1,100 and 1,150 of them received a monthly copy of pieces that they could modify and include in the publications distributed to the soldiers stationed at each base. The *Brief Items* publications for both house organs and army camps contained some of the same material, but they also included articles tailored to the targeted groups. For example, each bulletin encouraged Americans to buy war bonds, but civilian employees received that message more often than those in the military. On the other hand, the WWB urged soldiers to fight for the unconditional surrender of the Axis nations while it asked those at home to support that effort. Even the cartoon characters differed: Joe Palooka was a war worker in *House Organs* but a private first class in the *Army Camp* issues.[68]

Another WWB publication was the short-lived *Bulletin to Cartoonists* that began on May 3, 1944, and continued once a month from August until soon after Germany surrendered the following May. Aimed at a limited audience of artists whose works regularly appeared in newspapers and magazines throughout the country, it had the fewest recipients. Like the *Report*, it carried written descriptions of campaign ideas, but these were geared to visual presentation. The first issue emphasized nationwide problems through articles such as "We Are Not Keeping Military Secrets" and "Can We Glamourize Economy?" and it offered suggestions about ways to depict those subjects through drawings. During the time it was produced, the *Bulletin* won an enthusiastic response from the 270 or so comic magazine editors, comic strip artists, and editorial cartoonists who received it.[69]

EDITORIALS, ARTICLES, PLAYS, AND SPEECHES

In addition to its newsletters, the board regularly distributed editorials, newspaper articles, and plays free of charge. The group's all-important editorial service originated in May 1943 with a request from Sutherland Denlinger, a representative of the OWI's Domestic News Bureau. He complained that war-related news released by the government was not reaching the public, citing the fact that it received almost no mention in the nation's editorial columns even though it was printed on official letterhead. He approached the WWB about helping to disseminate this information because the board had an excellent reputation for getting material into local publications and because it was composed of prominent individuals who attracted attention. The group agreed to prepare and distribute one set of editorials each month using facts supplied by the OWI. However, the board made one stipulation: its members insisted on their right to include some information on their private campaigns. The OWI agreed.[70] The first set of editorials went to about seven hundred newspapers that August. Rather quickly the number of recipients increased until more than 1,600 American newspapers received the mailings. Even though most of them had circulations of less than 100,000, the board was able to cover every area of the United States without duplication. Robert L. Duffus, an experienced journalist, handled the operation. Into his hands fell the task not only of editing the articles but also of doing much of the writing initially. WWB members and writers on the board's list also contributed to this service, which continued through July 1945 with Duffus as head until December 1944.[71] Editors appreciated the freedom to modify the pieces as they saw fit and liked the fact that they did not have to contend with legal issues concerning attribution and payment.

From four to eight war-related editorials were in each set although five were most often included. Typically, at least two of them dealt with the board's own projects, but the pattern varied. Three of the editorials for August 1943 were written at the request of the OWI. One explained fuel oil rationing, another urged the public not to travel, and a third defended the government's anti-inflation measures. The board also provided an editorial about the need for racial tolerance, one of its private initiatives. Four editorials for April 1944 supported OWI campaigns to eliminate venereal disease, suppress the black market in gasoline, popularize the infantry, and improve soldier morale by encouraging cheery letters from home. Two others concerned the WWB campaigns for racial equality and for a harsh peace settlement.[72]

The WWB considered its editorial service to be a great success. To keep track of the frequency of its use and the specific papers that carried the editorials, the OWI was supposed to hire a newspaper clipping service to locate and collect the articles. However, the plan proved to be impractical. The editorials were often difficult to identify since they were unsigned, modified in a variety of ways, and printed under different titles. However, in its files the board kept letters from government agencies and newspaper editors about this service, and they indicate that both groups appreciated the board's monthly offerings. A Wisconsin editor admitted, "Of literally pounds of franked releases received by us daily, yours is the only one we really look forward to, and the one which is the most utilizable."[73] Only a few dissented. One editor from Texas characterized the WWB as "a busy bunch with as many ideas as a dog has fleas, and scarcely a day passes when the nation's editorial desks fail to receive a fistful of articles—giving three rousing cheers and a tiger for some aspect of the war effort, or hissing down someone or some idea board members decide is detrimental to same."[74] Because the tone of the vast majority of the letters was positive, Barach observed in 1944, "The reception to the editorials continues to be enthusiastic, and more and more government agencies in Washington keep putting pressure on us to use [these pieces] to support their causes."[75]

Not so successful was the effort of the Syndicate Committee led by WWB member Carl Carmer. It provided articles to the Associated Press, the International News Service, Gannett News Service, and several other newspaper syndicates. The group maintained an especially close relationship with the Newspaper Enterprise Association (commonly referred to as the NEA), which served six hundred newspapers that had a combined readership of 12 million. One of the WWB articles it distributed was little more than a rewrite of a War Department recruiting release; however, because Paul Gallico's name appeared in its byline, several papers carried it. Although the committee submitted a number of much stronger pieces to the syndicates, only a few appeared. Furthermore, wary editors would not consider using any WWB material on controversial issues that might turn readers away. Realizing that they could not count on these news services to disseminate their propaganda, frustrated board members dissolved the Syndicate Committee in 1943. Even so, the WWB did not entirely abandon the effort because the syndicates provided a guaranteed nationwide audience through the newspapers they served. During 1944 the group submitted to the NEA a series on war themes using the same ploy that had worked with the Gallico article: each editorial was purportedly written by one of more than fifty public figures including senators, ministers, scholars, and widely known authors.[76] Many of these were reprinted across the country.

Finally, the WWB began a script service in July 1942 to disseminate propaganda and answer the public demand for patriotic material that surfaced as soon as America entered the war. Erik Barnouw, then a teacher of journalism at Columbia University, headed the committee responsible for acquiring and distributing the scripts. When Barnouw resigned to join the script department at NBC, the chairmanship went briefly to Louella Hoskins, professor of journalism at New York University. Later the job came back to Barnouw before it was finally placed in the hands of WWB member Robert Landry in 1944. Regardless of the changes in its chair, the committee continued to function smoothly. With the cooperation of the Association for Education by Radio, the committee obtained a mailing list of more than 250 stations. It expanded the list to include a variety of local community groups and commercial radio stations, requiring the latter to air productions of the material on a strictly noncommercial basis. Mailings ultimately went to more than 835 recipients, and other groups could obtain copies on request. The committee made all of the monthly scripts continuously available by compiling a comprehensive catalog.[77]

Both original scripts, some of them written at the group's behest, and scripts previously broadcast on the radio were in the board's collection. The committee saw that they were easy to stage, required only a small cast, and could be adapted for younger actors and audiences. Most of the leading radio writers of the day contributed at least one play to the WWB without charge. The first script that the group distributed was *They Burned the Books* by Stephen Vincent Benet. Originally prepared for an early board project, it had already aired nationwide. Subsequent scripts ran the gamut of WWB concerns: food shortages, the performance of the Russian Army, the treatment of returning war veterans, world organization, and the problem of anti-Semitism. The "hate Germany" theme was used most frequently while racial tolerance was second in emphasis. If a campaign were particularly urgent, two or three plays on topics related to it might be included in a single mailing. Board members clearly valued this service, praising it and continuing to help with it throughout the war.[78]

Preparing speeches about the war became another integral part of the board's duties. Almost immediately after its organization, the WWB received pleas for addresses on various subjects from both government agencies and private organizations like the Veterans of Foreign Wars. During its first year the board established the Speech Writers Committee and gave the job of handling all requests to volunteers Nina Bourne and Elinor Green of Simon and Schuster. Under the chairmanship of WWB member Alan Green, who took over in 1943, the committee began to furnish a few speakers in the vicinity of New York and along the East Coast. Board members Christopher LaFarge, Rex Stout, Clifton Fadiman, and Paul Gallico as well as Advisory Council member John Gunther and other well-known personalities like radio commentator Raymond Gram Swing agreed to present war-related subjects to American troops and organizations closely connected to the military. The committee also arranged for speakers to present the WWB's point of view in radio debates, many of which were broadcast nationally. In 1943 alone the group sent representatives to fifteen of these programs.[79]

Green likewise pushed to increase the number of "war talks" that the WWB put out. Anticipating the needs of each new campaign, committee members made suggestions for speeches without waiting for a specific request. They wanted to have on hand addresses of varying lengths that covered relevant issues and could be used to launch a campaign or focus on its salient points. Recognizing that the speeches it generated could spread its propaganda message throughout the country, the committee printed a circular listing each one and briefly explaining its content. Soon it produced a catalog of twenty-seven titles similar to the one compiled by the War Scripts of the Month Committee. After the board mailed it to radio stations and civic, educational, and church organizations, requests for specific speeches increased. By February 1944 Stout estimated that the WWB had sent out approximately nine thousand war talks and that seven or eight thousand had actually been delivered. That summer the board heavily publicized the service to stimulate even more use. As a result the demand for copies rose to almost eight hundred requests monthly.[80]

Board members and associate writers anonymously authored the speeches, which had to meet rigid standards of clarity, effectiveness, and doctrine. Only one of every four submitted was accepted by the committee. Each had to be written in a simple, straightforward style so that it could be delivered effectively by almost anyone. Among the thirty-seven or so speeches in the complete catalog were two companion pieces, "Can We Trust Our Allies at the Peace Table?" and "Not Just Allies—Friends." Some, like "Our Enemy—Madame Butterfly" and "Horror Is Their Pleasure," denounced the Axis nations. Others, including "How Writers Can Help Win the War" and "A Challenge to Every Woman," concerned the home front, and several dealt with the postwar period, among them "Our Chances of Avoiding World War III" and "A Bad Half Hour for the Average Man." All were revised periodically to keep them up to date so that they could be used throughout the war. Many speakers delivered them verbatim even though they bluntly declared the board's viewpoint on controversial issues, which was sometimes antithetical to public consensus. Stout marveled, "It is surprising how much you can get in a speech that is contrary to the opinion of the group hearing it and still have the speech accepted."[81] For that reason he and the board's other authors did not hesitate to insert the liberal views of the WWB and the Roosevelt administration into their speeches, believing that they might sway some audience members and not offend others.

BOOK AND MOVIE PROMOTIONS

Throughout its existence, the WWB used books and movies to help mold public opinion and reinforce the viewpoints of its members. These promotions became an integral part of most of the group's campaigns.[82] When the board generated propaganda on the evil nature of the German enemy, it advertised several works including *The War against God*, edited by WWB member Carl Carmer. He presented statements from Axis leaders and prominent citizens declaring that their countries were at war with Christianity. Religious leaders from Allied nations then weighed in, refuting the comments and identifying their cause with Christ.[83] Board members developed a number of activities to promote the books they recommended, most of them newly published works of nonfiction, and occasionally they came up with special ideas for particularly significant volumes. Even without the board's input, these books would have been reviewed, but the board was in a unique position to exploit their propaganda value. With contacts in the fields of literature and entertainment, WWB members could boost sales by quickly drumming up suitable comments from well-known individuals. As was its habit, the board usually did the writing and then secured permission to use a famous name. Actor Humphrey Bogart once wrote the group, "Fortunately for me and my peace of mind and conscience, I think the way you fellows think—so as soon as the book gets here, I'll send you my weighty and considered endorsement which you'll have to write."[84]

The board's radio contacts helped the WWB arrange author interviews and on-air forums that focused on each work. The group also used its own publications to tout books and call them to the attention of radio commentators, journalists, and writers across the country who could give them favorable mention. One of the WWB's more intriguing approaches was to create a controversy by arranging for one reviewer to praise a work and a second to attack it. The two would gain further attention by critiquing each other's comments. At one point the board asked its staff to formulate a list of the different types of book promotions it had used. The resulting report covered two typewritten, single-spaced pages.[85] While WWB members claimed to oppose censorship on principle, they brushed aside that position on occasion. They had no problem working to prevent the publication of books that did not present the slant they liked. Stout nimbly skirted the issue of censorship by arguing that freedom of expression did not include the right to publish.[86] If works they opposed were already in circulation, board members tried to discourage sales with bad book reviews and other ploys. Frankly conceding the hypocrisy involved, Fadiman argued that the importance of the goal justified the board's exception to liberal principles and admitted that the group tried to "avoid in any way any appearance of attempting censorship or coercion."[87]

Beyond promoting books, the group publicized recently released movies that delivered a board-approved message. Members initially hoped to influence screenwriters and directors from the inception of their ideas to the completion of their films, but the New Yorkers lacked contacts in the California-based film industry. In the fall of 1942 they sent WWB member Robert Colwell to Hollywood to see what could be done to develop their clout. With the help of some West Coast acquaintances of board members, he arranged a meeting with scriptwriters and others that proved to be discouraging. He reported, "We are not likely to have much success 3000 miles away influencing war films."[88] More than a year later, Clifton Fadiman wrote his brother William, a movie executive, to ask if the board might obtain "first story treatment" for proposed movies dealing with the war. This privilege would have given board members access to scripts before filming began, a time when they could suggest revisions. However, Fadiman's request seems to have been ignored.[89]

The group resorted to rating movies in its *Writers' War Board Report*. Each production could earn one to five "bombs" or one to five "duds" depending on its portrayal of the war. The 1943 film *For Whom the Bell*

Tolls received one dud because "the propaganda value of Hemingway's novel has been largely eliminated while several negative aspects have been italicized." Another movie released that year, *Watch on the Rhine*, garnered four bombs for "exposing fascism as an urgent personal matter for everyone."[90] At least some industry insiders took notice. In 1945 producer David O. Selznick indignantly complained about the board's "vicious attack" when it gave a rating of two duds to his 1944 movie *Since You Went Away,* starring Claudette Colbert and Joseph Cotton. Despite the fact that the film concerned the American home front, the WWB reviewer faulted it for being "devoid of any mention of the fundamental issues of the war."[91] That year movie executive Martin Starr reported to Barach that producer Cecil DeMille had become "the laughing stock of the trade" after the WWB gave a "damning review" of three duds to his 1944 movie about a naval war hero, *The Story of Dr. Wassell*, which starred Gary Cooper. He added that DeMille would "practically die rather than offend the War Board."[92]

Despite the reactions of Selznick and DeMille, the board was frustrated that its appeals were largely unheeded. Perhaps the organization made no headway because the film industry had already developed a strong relationship with the OWI. That agency exerted extensive influence over moviemakers, especially in regard to the production of war-related films. If the OWI did not approve of a particular movie, it would contact the Office of Censorship and block its distribution overseas. Because the industry was driven by profit and publicity, no one involved in it considered producing a film that the government would ban immediately. After much grumbling from movie executives, the OWI used the threat of censorship to obtain cooperation in producing films that promoted democracy, antifascism, and support for all of America's allies including Russia and China. The board had hoped to go further, prodding filmmakers into addressing liberal concerns such as the issue of racial prejudice and the portrayal of African Americans. On that particular point the OWI consistently "buckle[d]" without making any effort to control racial stereotyping or to encourage Hollywood to portray more African Americans including black soldiers. No producers or writers wanted additional guidelines proposed by the WWB or any other group, and the board reluctantly gave up its attempts to push for more substantive changes in American movies such as the depiction of fully realized minority characters.[93]

HANDLING REQUESTS THROUGH WWB COMMITTEES

What made the WWB unique was the level of talent of its members combined with their commitment to promote the war, lasting peace, and the government's liberal agenda. Had they not been so focused, this group of opinionated individuals might well have had difficulty working together. Their weekly meetings were scheduled every Wednesday afternoon from two to six o'clock although they sometimes continued for eight or nine hours. These gatherings were not held at the WWB office but at the Authors' League office at 6 East 39th Street. At this neutral venue, members felt that their activities as a private organization could be considered openly.[94] During these sessions members discussed all matters including the deluge of requests, ongoing projects, problems that required special attention, and general policy guidelines such as procedures for the office staff. Sometimes representatives of a government agency or private organization would attend to plead their case. Many also sought advice about the kind of campaign they should develop or the publicity they should use for greatest effect. Although the board discouraged such time-consuming visits, they were a common occurrence.

To determine which projects to accept, the WWB used two tests. Alan Green characterized the first as a "yardstick marked with two scales": Could the WWB help to win the war or secure a durable peace by taking on the project? Both the test and Green's metaphor echoed the president's words. In his fireside chat broadcast two days after Pearl Harbor, Roosevelt used the term "yardstick" and assured Americans, "We are going to win the war and we are going to win the peace that follows."[95] If either part of the first question could be answered in the affirmative, the board would consider the second test: Was the project viable? Members examined each request to determine whether they had the resources to complete it within a reasonable timeframe given their other campaigns. If a proposal satisfied both criteria, they usually accepted it unless their workload prevented them from taking on additional assignments. As soon as they approved a request, WWB members frequently began to come up with ideas immediately. After a deluge of suggestions on everything from publicity angles to helpful contacts, between thirty and fifty realistic possibilities for each project usually emerged. Brainstorming regularly took up much of the meeting time, and some on the board came to believe that they were among the early users of the technique.[96]

Once board members accepted an assignment, they would send it to a standing committee or create a special committee to deal with it. Their action depended on whether they thought the request could be dispatched quickly or required time and additional effort. Standing committees like the War Script of the Month Committee and the Speech Writers Committee had recurring duties while the "campaign committees" were usually short-lived groups that disbanded as soon as the projects they addressed came to an end. One example is a committee of only two members that the WWB set up after staffers at the OWI pointed out that the first stanza of the national anthem ends in a question: "O say, does that star-spangled banner yet wave / O'er the land of the free and the home of the brave?" They believed the little-known fourth stanza might work better during the war because it makes a positive statement about the country's ability to achieve victory:

O thus be it ever when freemen shall stand
Between their lov'd home and the war's desolation!
Blest with vict'ry and peace, may the heav'n rescued land
Praise the power that hath made and preserv'd us a nation!
Then conquer we must, when our cause it is just,
And this be our motto—"In God is our trust,"
And the star-spangled banner in triumph shall wave
O'er the land of the free and the home of the brave.[97]

Committee members Robert Landry and Margaret Leech, both of whom sat on the board, produced several ideas and succeeded in introducing Americans to the stanza by persuading Kate Smith, the most popular vocalist on radio, to sing it on her show week after week. When the board received reports that her example was being followed widely, it dissolved the committee and moved on to more substantive projects.[98] The WWB's real spadework was done in these two types of committees, a few of which had as many as eighteen members, depending on the difficulty of the tasks to be handled. Generally at least one person from the board or its Advisory Council was included.[99] Nearly eighty committees operated at one time or another, four of them established jointly with other organizations.

Among the standing committees were "issues committees" that involved campaigns the board itself instigated on topics such as racial tolerance, lasting peace, and international cooperation. Because these matters were dear to the hearts of WWB members, they did not relegate them to a single campaign but incorporated them into numerous projects. The writers established only a few of these committees because they regularly handled such concerns together as one body. Another type of standing committee maintained contact with various branches of the media and secured their cooperation on WWB projects. These included the Newspaper Syndicate Committee and the Radio Committee. The latter was particularly active since television, still in its infancy, was relatively unknown at the time. Another media committee was the Comics Committee. It included cartoonists C. C. Beck, writer and illustrator of Captain Marvel, and George E. Marcoux, creator of the Supersnipe comic book series that was extremely popular at the time.[100] The WWB found that comic books provided an especially effective outlet for propaganda because they reached a large male audience including soldiers and teenaged boys soon to be drafted.[101] Some young men read almost nothing else, and sales tripled between 1940 and 1945.[102] Because these illustrated works were exempt from scrap-paper recycling, they were often kept and reread or passed on to others. Referring to the board's deliberate use of comic books and comic strips, Barach wrote in 1943, "We believe that many subjects can be handled by [the comics] without interfering with their entertainment value while making use of their power."[103]

"Pulp" magazines were also widely read. Each was a collection of fiction on a single subject that appealed primarily to male readers: adventure tales, westerns, science fiction, detective and mystery stories, or depictions of war. Titles included *Men in Combat, Thrilling Western, Man's Life,* and *Ellery Queen's Mystery Magazine*.[104] Under the leadership of Frederick C. Painton, who wrote popular fiction and served as a frontline war correspondent for *Reader's Digest*, the Pulp Writers' Committee maintained contact with the Office of War Information and with authors working in the genre.[105] The board was even able to persuade some well-known mainstream authors to write propaganda pieces for these publications, which had a combined circulation of 15 million. Rex Stout cajoled Faith Baldwin, wildly popular writer of romances and novels about women, into contributing by telling her that she "had the knack" to handle these readers. Reluctantly consenting, she wryly suggested that her tombstone carry the inscription, "Here lies the hack / Who had the knack." Stout rejoined in kind: "If it makes you gulp to write for a pulp, at least there is the advantage of being introduced to about ten million bozos and bozoesses who never spent two bucks for a book and probably never will. You meet a lot of nice people that way."[106] Again and again Stout and others on the board used their personal charm, wit, and gift for persuasion to recruit a remarkably high level of talent for board projects.

Sometimes standing committees were dissolved because their purpose could not be achieved. Such was the case with the Committee on Cooperation with the Churches. Always looking for additional avenues of support, the board considered the extensive religious community in the United States, which reached a vast audience each week. It came up with the idea of providing sermon topics and outlines as well as other materials demonstrating the rightness of the Allied cause and the morally wrong actions of the Germans and the Japanese. Committee members made contacts, being careful to avoid religious groups that espoused pacifism or isolationism. But they soon ran into more serious problems. The differences among religions and the multiple Christian denominations made it difficult to produce one set of general materials that would appeal to all believers. Additionally, the board had hoped to receive help with the project from the publishers of religious books, but they showed no interest.[107] Recognizing the insurmountable difficulties, the WWB abandoned its plans and shut down the committee.

The board counted on its members not only to contribute to the work of its committees but also to keep it apprised of trends in the media, developments on the battlefront, and concerns at home. It expected them to write propaganda, offer useful suggestions, and make contacts for each campaign. For advice about preparing propaganda for radio broadcast, the WWB turned to four of its members in the industry: Katharine Seymour,

Hobe Morrison, Robert Landry, and William Shirer. Freelancer Katharine Seymour, who chaired the Radio Committee from 1942 to 1944, was widely respected as one of the first radio scriptwriters. Working for the fledgling NBC network during the late 1920s, she had gained experience handling almost every kind of script. In 1931 she and John Tilden Waite Martin produced and later revised *Practical Radio Writing: The Technique of Writing for Broadcasting Simply and Thoroughly Explained*, a textbook still useful in the twenty-first century. When serious illness compelled Seymour to leave the WWB, Stout recruited Hobe Morrison.[108] During his short tenure with the board in 1944 and 1945, Morrison worked in the radio department of the Young and Rubicam advertising agency where he had access to information about upcoming programs. Except for that job, Morrison spent most of his career from 1937 into the 1970s at *Variety*, the trade paper of the entertainment business.[109]

A second *Variety* veteran was WWB member Robert J. Landry. His reputation rested on the controversial commentaries he had produced as the paper's radio editor, but for most of the war he served as director of program writing at the CBS network. After the conflict, he also returned to *Variety*, where he spent thirty years as managing editor.[110] Another CBS employee, William Shirer, was a news reporter and commentator that had become a fixture in the 1930s with his frequent reports from Europe. He moved to Berlin after Germany invaded Poland and was the chief American voice from the German capital until he left in December 1940, fearing arrest by the Gestapo. His 1941 account of that experience, *Berlin Diary*, became a bestseller, and crowds flocked to his appearances during his periodic returns to the United States. In 1960 he published his masterwork, *The Rise and Fall of the Third Reich*, which remains a classic on the era.[111] Whenever he was in New York, Shirer contributed to the WWB, and the organization agreed with many of his views about Hitler and the menace that the Germans posed.

The WWB asked Seymour and the other members of the Radio Committee to weigh in when it considered mounting its own radio program. The aim of *Across the Board* was to deliver exactly what the organization wanted to convey without having to compromise or negotiate with networks, producers, or sponsors. Board members created a pilot script to indicate how the program would combine lighthearted banter with factual information about current campaigns. Although NBC was willing to fit the proposed program into its schedule, Seymour and others were skeptical. She expressed her reservations to Stout: "We're trying to win the war and win the peace and also provide entertainment and get a respectable Crossley [audience rating] all in one half-hour program and I'm afraid the total effect on listeners will be confusion."[112] Largely on her recommendation, the group dropped the idea.

WWB members Paul Gallico, Christopher LaFarge, and Carl Carmer observed military engagements firsthand and provided their colleagues background information on the war. In 1944 Gallico became European editor and war correspondent for *Cosmopolitan*. Although he had made his name as one of the most widely known and well-paid sportswriters in America, he left newspaper journalism in 1936 and moved to England to pursue freelance work. He earned a worldwide reputation by writing a bestselling novella based on his popular 1940 short story "The Snow Goose."[113] Another of the board's most consistent and effective propagandists was Christopher LaFarge, best known for his novels in verse including *Each to the Other* (1939). His experiences in 1943 as a war correspondent for *Harper's Magazine* inspired *East by Southwest*, his book of short stories set against the fighting in the South Pacific.[114] Also that year Carl Carmer traveled on naval missions to gather information about submarines and the everyday life of their crews for the WWB. Before the war he had worked as assistant editor of *Vanity Fair* and *Theatre Arts Monthly* and had served as a director of the American Civil Liberties Union. This "well-bred sophisticate" collected folk songs and wrote books about the culture and history of Alabama and his native New York. Particularly noteworthy was his 1934 nonfiction bestseller, *Stars Fell on Alabama*.[115]

For advice on public relations matters, the board frequently looked to three WWB members whose careers were rooted in the advertising industry. From 1929 to 1946 Robert T. "Bob" Colwell worked with the largest ad agency in America, J. Walter Thompson. He became a vice president of the company and later served as its "top creative adviser." After the war he helped establish the highly successful firm of Sullivan, Colwell, and Bayles.[116] When he was in New York, Colwell contributed to WWB projects whenever he could. Both of the other admen were among the group's most active members. Alan Baer Green was only twenty when he established an advertising agency with Julian Brodie. It flourished after Green created a dramatic type of book advertising for Viking Press. The youngest member of the board was Canadian Jack Goodman, who became a naturalized American citizen in 1939. Although he had started his career at the Green-Brodie agency, he moved to Simon and Schuster in 1935 and remained there for twenty-two years. Throughout the war he served as its advertising manager and editor in chief. Eventually he rose to become a vice president and a member of its board of directors. According to one source Goodman "was adored by almost everyone in the company," and a *New York Times* writer described him as "legendary" more than fifty years after his unexpected death in 1957 at the age of forty-eight.[117] Well before the war these board members had developed second careers as successful authors and had seen one of their works made into a movie. Colwell wrote stories, magazine articles, plays, and scripts for popular radio programs. Green produced stories and books with other writers including Brodie and Goodman. Goodman also collaborated with publisher Albert Rice Leventhal. Green's solo effort, *What a Body!* won the 1950 Edgar Allan Poe Award for best first mystery novel.[118]

Most of the board members worked arduously on their committee assignments. A good example is Margaret Leech, who won two Pulitzer Prizes for her histories, one in 1942 for *Reveille in Washington, 1860–1865*, and one in 1960 for *In the Days of McKinley*.[119] Throughout the war she chaired a committee charged with producing magazine articles each month that were designed to encourage good relations between the United States and Great Britain. Only two members, both journalists, followed in the footsteps of Buck and Marquand, rarely attending meetings or participating in WWB activities. Franklin Pierce Adams or "F.P.A." was a well-known humorist and the oldest board member at sixty-one. His witty column, "The Conning Tower," was carried in one New York newspaper or another from 1911 until September 1941 with a brief lapse during World War I. He was also a popular panelist on *Information Please*, the radio program that Clifton Fadiman hosted.[120] Adams's efforts for the WWB included a bit of committee work, a handful of appearances, a few pieces of propaganda, and some doggerel, his stock-in-trade. The board saw even less of *New York Post* editor Samuel Grafton, a passionate crusader often considered the most liberal American columnist of his day. Despite his lack of attention to WWB affairs, the outspoken, provocative, and sometimes abrasive writer periodically used his attention-getting style to promote WWB causes in editorials and speeches as well as in his syndicated column, "I'd Rather Be Right."[121]

COLLABORATION WITH PRIVATE ORGANIZATIONS

Rarely did the WWB handle large campaigns entirely by itself. Aside from help from the government agency or private organization that had requested assistance and from its store of writers, the board often worked in conjunction with several private groups including the American Theater Wing, the Council on Books in Wartime, and two organizations that Stout headed, the Friends of Democracy and the Society for the Prevention of World War III. One other nonprofit sometimes contributed to the campaigns that the WWB had agreed to assist, but the two did not usually work together for several reasons. The War Advertising Council was originally designed to create advertisements for the war effort. Now known as the Ad Council, it continues to produce public service announcements and other forms of advertising for the public good on topics such as pollution and health.[122] The council and the board were similar in several respects. Both began to operate in early 1942, both had close ties to the OWI, and both produced propaganda to sell bonds, recruit soldiers, and the like.

In other ways, however, the two groups were very different. While the WWB liked to work behind the scenes without calling attention to itself, the council trumpeted its every action and claimed sole responsibility for any triumphs. Touting its accomplishments was one way that it could facilitate the growth and development of business during the war and lay the groundwork to take advantage of postwar economic opportunities. The two organizations also differed in their approach to Roosevelt and his administration. The board supported the liberal policies of his government and did not criticize the president publicly. Even so, the group sometimes tried to influence administration officials by declaring its position on an issue before the government took a stand. The council, however, did nothing more than pay lip service to Roosevelt since its members were mostly conservatives who opposed New Deal liberalism.[123] Critics have leveled two charges against the War Advertising Council. The first is that its members presented a "dangerously distorted picture of the Second World War" in their business-supported ads.[124] Such a barrage of them blanketed the country that advertising "dominate[d] domestic war propaganda"[125] The second accusation is that they controlled the OWI. The businessmen on the council had strong connections to Republicans in Congress who supported the move to place advertising executives in charge of the OWI's Domestic Branch. Critics later claimed that the takeover was so complete that it marked the death of government information. A 2012 study of advertising during the war confirms the extent of the takeover and the resulting shift from emphasizing information to promoting advertising.[126]

As the board's workload increased during its first year of operation, Stout continued to press government officials for additional space and clerical assistance. On August 28, 1942, the WWB finally moved into more adequate quarters in the Chanin Building at 122 East 42nd Street. Stout estimated that about 85 percent of the group's efforts went toward government projects.[127] To deal with them efficiently, the board eventually opened a satellite site in Washington, DC, late that year, and they picked Selma G. Hirsh to run it with the aid of a single clerical employee. Hirsh had had experience writing radio scripts for the Smithsonian before she began working for the Office of Civilian Defense, where she came to the attention of WWB members. As part of her duties she received and evaluated government requests before sending them to New York for board approval. If they were granted, she determined the work that needed to be done and the talent it required. Her position frequently took her to New York to consult with board members, writers, and others. Before arranging the delivery of the finished work to the appropriate government agency, she reviewed it to confirm that it met the specifications of the job and conformed to government policy statements.[128]

The work of Frederica Barach, whose official title for government purposes was liaison officer of the OWI, was inextricably tied to the success of the Writers' War Board. Educated at Vassar, she had served as a book editor and taught creative writing at Sarah Lawrence College. She juggled her work with her busy home life as mother of two young boys and wife of Dr. Alvan L. Barach, a famous New York pulmonologist who pioneered several breakthroughs in the field. At the New York office, "Freddy" handled the board's day-to-day activities, supervised its staff, dealt with visitors, and kept up with its correspondence. She maintained contact with a vast body of writers and made more job assignments to them than anyone else although most of her letters were of a routine nature. Her frequent memos to individual board members included reminders about contacts they were to make; assignments they had agreed to work on; acknowledgments to write; and appointments, meetings, upcoming events, and approaching deadlines. WWB members constantly testified to her superb abilities, competence, and pleasant demeanor. Street described her as "glorious," and, in a passing reference to Shakespeare's Sonnet 18, commented that everybody compared her to a summer's day.[129]

Barach not only collected all of the requests and regularly presented them to the board but also spent part of her time on projects that the board conducted on its own or on behalf of a nongovernmental organization. For these campaigns she was compensated, if at all, with funds not tied to the OWI subsidy. One of her most difficult responsibilities was keeping the board's governmental and private projects strictly segregated.[130] The six women who worked under Barach at one time or another, among them Ellen Tannenbaum and Voltarine Feingold, performed secretarial functions and occasionally provided research assistance to writers involved in WWB campaigns. Only one employee, Stout's personal secretary, was not paid by the OWI but by the chairman himself. Ten to fifteen regular volunteers supplemented the work of the full-time staff members, and numerous others came to lend assistance on one or more occasions. Many of them helped Barach with the board's private campaigns, which she alone could not handle in addition to her other duties. In times of critical need, the board hired extra help, but the staff was usually able to carry out most of the group's functions.[131]

FINANCIAL OPERATIONS OF THE WWB

The OWI subsidy, never very large, increased each year and allowed the Writers' War Board to keep both of its offices open. A financial statement for 1942 indicated expenditures of $2,777.40, but the government contributed only $2,237.27, leaving a deficit of more than $500.[132] The salaries of WWB employees came from separate funds. OWI administrative officer Selma Hirsh received the highest pay, $3,800 per year.[133] As a clearinghouse that connected authors to employers, the board did not have a significant payroll. Even though its expenses were minimal, the OWI subsidy alone could not cover them all. When members found that the board needed money, they often chipped in themselves or asked their agents, publishers, or friends for help.[134] Some writers who received work through WWB channels voluntarily gave the New York group a portion of the money they received, but no major inflow of funds came from such gifts, which were entirely at the discretion of each author. A few individuals outside the board also made contributions, most of them less than twenty-five dollars each.

Unfortunately the board's annual reports contain no statements about the organization's budget after 1942, and no financial summaries are located in either the Writers' War Board files in the Library of Congress or the Rex Stout Papers at Boston College. The only extant records pertaining to the board's finances come from proposed budgets the OWI submitted to Congress for approval in 1944 and 1945. The amount that the OWI anticipated for the operation of the board in 1944 totaled $28,352 including employee salaries, but it estimated that overtime pay and other items would drive the amount to $37,628.78.[135] What percentage of the board's 1944 income this figure represents is a matter of conjecture. Stout undoubtedly kept a close eye on funding since his wife, Pola, was Finance Committee chair. He asserted many years after the war that the government subsidy usually met only one-fourth of the board's requirements, but that percentage is difficult to substantiate.[136] When Congress pressed the OWI to justify the WWB's subsidy in 1944, Schisgall gave a glowing account of the organization's work:

> For the money we spen[d] in maintaining liaison with the Writers' War Board, we have the services of almost 5000 writers; we reach thousands of newspapers, more than 600 radio stations; and have a vast army of writers ready to cooperate in the Government's war work. I can think of no other way in which the talents and the efforts of so many writers can be organized for the Government's benefit. The money laid out to maintain liaison with this organization is repaid a hundred fold in the work the Writers' War Board produces.[137]

In 1945 the OWI planned to spend $31,210 on the board, but it probably used only half that amount because its subsidy stopped in June after the war in Europe ended. None of these figures include one of the most important government contributions to the board: the franking privilege. Most of the group's mass mailings required no payment to the postal service. When the OWI stopped the board's subsidy in 1945, Stout estimated that the organization would need $35,000 to continue operating.[138]

Even though there appear to be no financial records concerning the board's 1943 budget, some information is available about private contributions that year. Donor John D. Rockefeller Jr. gave the WWB $1,500, and Marshall Field added $2,000 to its coffers. In addition, an unidentified WWB member contributed about $4,200.[139] Such sums were anomalous, a one-time boon. Indeed, a 1943 form letter the WWB sent to almost one hundred people requesting financial assistance drew virtually no response.[140] More typical were the donations received from January 1 to October 1 the following year, which totaled $11,500 from fifty-nine individuals.[141] For specific projects that strained the budget, Stout was often able to obtain funding from Isidore Lipschultz, a wealthy associate of his in Freedom House and the Society for the Prevention of World War III. Lipschultz was a Belgian diamond merchant who had moved to the United States in 1938 after leading anti-German activities in his native country. He occasionally supported the board and several other antifascist organizations from behind the scenes.[142]

In an interview board member Alan Green stated that the WWB was a collection of some of the most talented people in the country, and his comment seems well justified.[143] While several of them had written some political propaganda for the cause of interventionism, others were entirely new to the genre. However, they were fast learners. Their craft had taught them how to catch the attention of readers, touch their hearts, make them laugh, or cause them to squirm. The writers realized at the outset that their propaganda needed to reach every age group if they were going to promote unity at home. But they could not have produced the amount of work they did without the help of the media and writers from every area of the nation. Time and time again the WWB called on its members to use their connections not only to their professional colleagues but also to people of influence, wealth, and power including actors, artists, politicians, broadcasters, publishers, and magnates of banking, business, and industry. It was the job of the board to exploit these contacts for WWB campaigns, to drive the committees to keep up their output, and, always, to contribute propaganda pieces including speeches, editorials, and magazine articles. They spent long hours working without pay although they were usually compensated for their travels on behalf of the organization.

The convergence of three elements—America's involvement in the war, the volunteer group of well-established writers in New York, and congressional interference in the affairs of the government's official propaganda agency—created a unique propaganda organization that could work from within the government or outside it. Because of its early accomplishments the WWB came to the attention of Joseph Goebbels. On November 22, 1942, a Berlin radio broadcast sarcastically denigrated the group: "A new propaganda organization has been set up in Washington recently, consisting of some thirty-five hundred American writers, headed by Rex Stout, well-known detective story and pulp magazine writer. . . . Now we have the explanation why so many of the war stories released in Washington have so strong a flavor of Chicago gangsterism." Stout was not perturbed. Characterizing himself as a "man of goodwill," he replied in kind: "I wish [Goebbels] the best. I hope he is boiled in the very *best* oil—none of that ersatz stuff."[144]

CHAPTER 2

PROPAGANDA FOR THE MILITARY

THE BOARD USUALLY responded more quickly to requests from the military than from any other source no matter what the assignment might be. One example is a small project the group undertook in March 1943 to help procure canines for the armed forces. Even for this minor effort to publicize Dogs for Defense and inform citizens that they could lend their dogs for duty as well as donate them, the group pursued several ideas. Aside from running an informational squib in the *Writers' War Board Report*, it set up radio interviews and prepared a promotional jacket for a Book of the Month Club selection on dogs in combat. At the instigation of the board, Faith Baldwin wrote the article "Taffy at War," and the WWB arranged for its publication in *Cosmopolitan*. She called attention to the program, commenting that it "contributes to defense and to attack. It is part of our armed services."[1] The Assignments Committee also went to work, contacting the writers on the WWB's list about producing news stories, editorials, and speeches on the subject in their local areas. However, it cautioned them not to use pictures of tearful children bidding farewell to their beloved pets.[2] While the board did a good job with this brief campaign, it spent far more time on several major projects for the armed services. Some were related to the recruitment and orientation of soldiers and sailors while others were matters of morale, healthcare, and the treatment of veterans.

RECRUITMENT

Recruitment was among the earliest of the board's efforts, and it occasioned some of the group's greatest successes and most disappointing failures. In March 1942 the WWB received an urgent request from the War Department to mount an all-out campaign to expand the Army Air Forces. Military leaders expected no difficulty in recruiting 150,000 pilots, whose job was well-known and relatively glamorous, but they anticipated a problem in securing an equal number of navigators, bombardiers, and tail gunners as well as over a million ground crew members to keep the planes flying. The board, itself just becoming organized, appointed a committee composed of Clifton Fadiman and John Marquand. With some assistance from Russel Crouse, they conceived an approach that proved quite successful. When contacting the group's cadre of writers, the two circulated a list of suggestions about ways to publicize the air force jobs that rarely received media attention. They asked the authors to incorporate one or more of these "slants" in their magazine articles, editorials, poems, novels, and other compositions.

One of their suggestions advised stressing that recruits did not need a college degree. Another emphasized the importance of noncombat fliers in the Air Transport Service.[3] Each slant targeted a specific problem or need:

- Popularize the bombardier and the navigator as against the pilot.
- Popularize the work of the tail gunner as against the bombardier and the navigator; try to remove the false impression that the tail gunner's job, which is a hazardous one, is necessarily a shortcut to suicide. . . .
- It takes 12 or 15 men on the ground to get a plane up in the air. Hundreds of thousands of ground-crew mechanics must be trained. They are just as valuable as the fliers themselves and they should receive as much attention.[4]

The slants also cautioned that accidents might occur during training and stressed that the military was not looking for daredevils but responsible fliers who could save themselves and their valuable equipment if need be. Surprisingly, the list invited writers to create a humorous aerial gunner or other character that could become a popular figure representing the Army Air Forces. Although such a figure never emerged, the board's efforts yielded much favorable publicity. In fact, creating slants worked so well that the WWB used the technique in several campaigns.[5]

In the hope of stimulating even more newspaper and magazine articles, the board came up with another successful idea that it repeated for other recruitment projects: trips for media personnel to observe members of a particular branch of the service in action. In April it sent Dorothy Thompson, the "First Lady of American Journalism," to spend two days at Langley Field in Virginia.[6] Subsequently she offered continuing support for the air force in her column "On the Record." Later the WWB asked feature writer Katharine Brush to visit three airfields, and she produced a variety of pieces picked up by the syndicates.[7] On July 16 the board arranged for thirteen writers of fiction to go to Washington for official briefings and exhibitions of flight crews and ground crews at work. At least three stories on the air force resulted from this trip, one in a weekly magazine aimed at high school students, another for members of a nationwide lodge, and a third targeting female readers of romance magazines.[8] Because the WWB did not want women to think that air force jobs were hazardous lest they should inhibit their husbands, relatives, and boyfriends from signing up for such positions, the organization instigated an article in a women's magazine claiming that the casualty rate among fliers was not abnormally high. It also placed an article on the special problems of aviators' wives in the *New Yorker* and suggested subjects on the air force to bestselling author and war correspondent W. L. White. He turned them into two books and a series of articles that continued well after the original campaign ended.[9]

Throughout 1942 a number of articles and works of fiction appeared in "slick" magazines that had large circulations. *Look* pointed out that ground crews "must match the men in the air in resourcefulness, in know-how, in courage," and the *Saturday Evening Post* emphasized the desperate need to fill those important positions. Veterans of past wars learned about the vastly increased uses of aviation in war and the necessity of securing more money and men for the Army Air Forces. An article in *Country Gentleman* apprised farmers of the military uses of gliders and called for additional pilots to man them. Other pieces written under WWB auspices included a story about the Air Ferrying Command and one about naval antisubmarine fliers. The group also assisted in writing an article on the heroics of the air force during Japan's invasion of the Philippine Islands.[10]

Under their guidance the dangerous jobs of bombardier and tail gunner were turned into glamorous positions. The *Saturday Evening Post* published one of the most successful stories the board ever delivered in terms of propaganda effect, "Bombardier" by Paul Gallico. An admiring pilot describes its determined hero: "He's got hunting blood. He signed up for bombardier from way back. He's no washed-out pilot or flop navigator. Ever since he's come into the Air Force, he's done nothing else but eat, sleep, live, and dream bombing. He just wants to bomb." Gallico downplayed the danger of the position and touted the job as "the most wonderful job in the war," "the top card in the deck," and "one of the things that sets you apart."[11] Stout also contributed to the cause, mentioning a bombardier in his Nero Wolfe novella *Not Quite Dead Enough*, which was published in abridged form in *American Magazine* that December. The magazine had already carried an article on a tail gunner who bragged that his work was "the most thrilling job in this man's war." He elaborated, "I'm twenty-five and I know that most of the fellows my age think the pilots have the best job. I don't think so now that I'm an aerial gunner. I see how important my job is. An aerial gunner is on his own. If he shoots too long and burns up his guns, if he exhausts his ammo, then he's endangering his comrades and his plane. He's got to have horse sense, and like to shoot rather than eat." Newspaper syndicates also bought articles on the subject including "The Gunner's the Man" by WWB member Franklin Adams.[12] The popularity of the position may well have persuaded Joseph McCarthy to call himself "Tail Gunner Joe" as he rode his questionable war record to political success in 1946.

A photographic survey of fliers in *Look* prominently featured ground crews, bombardiers, and gunners while passing lightly over the pilots. Other newspaper and magazine stories appeared that had no specific propaganda message but made favorable reference to the Army Air Forces. An excellent example from 1944 is Faith Baldwin's serial romance "Change of Heart" in *Collier's*.[13] By the end of this WWB campaign, most magazines had established their own contacts with the public relations section of the War Department, which readily supplied as much aviation material as they could reasonably publish. Rounding out the field of coverage was a cheaply priced book for boys that the board had encouraged a publisher to print, *How Every Boy Can Prepare for Aviation Service* by Keith Ayling.[14] The group also arranged for posters and asked two thousand writers to produce air force slogans and mottoes. Finally it stimulated the writing of two songs for the campaign, "The Bombardier Song" (words by Lorenz Hart and music by Richard Rodgers) and "I Wanna Marry a Bombardier" (words by Mack David and music by Leonard Whitcup).

The latter, which made the Hit Parade list, emphasized the romantic talents that a man with the physical condition, self-confidence, and steady nerves of a bombardier would undoubtedly possess.[15]

In addition to the songs, board members counted 523 articles, 24 syndicated columns, 12 stories, 3 broadcasts, 1 novel, and a handbook for which they were directly responsible. All were distributed or broadcast nationwide, and almost all reflected at least some of the slants that the WWB listed. In addition, there were uncounted slogans, short pieces, or indirect mentions of the air force in other works. Such statistics are a rarity since the board did not keep careful records of its output in subsequent campaigns. This effort, however, attracted so many recruits for the jobs of bombardier and gunner that the air force asked the board to stop publicizing them. Its task completed, the WWB combined its committees on the air force and the army.[16] From start to finish the campaign was a classic example of what the group could accomplish. It heightened the respect that other organizations and government agencies had for the board and brought in other assignments.

More than a year later the board made an additional effort for the Army Air Forces after the advertising agency working on cadet recruitment requested the WWB's assistance in obtaining magazine coverage. Gallico headed the project, and mailings went to the writers and editors of pulp and slick magazines in November 1943. The December *Writers' War Board Report* explained the initiative:

> The restless, impatient seventeen year old boy, still one year away from draft age and the big fight, may now . . . enlist in the Air Corps Enlisted Reserve and take the physical and mental examinations which, when he reaches the ripe old age of eighteen, will qualify him without further tests to begin his training for his wings.
>
> A blue and silver Air Corps lapel button will be awarded to successful candidates. This button, worn by the civilian boy, advertises to all the world and especially to the girls of his acquaintance that he has been accepted by the Air Force.[17]

Results were soon apparent. *Liberty Magazine* published a fictional account of a young man's eager entry into the air cadets. A serial in the *Saturday Evening Post* used the air cadet program as part of its background.

Mechanix Illustrated also referred to it, and *Rotarian* included a picture story on the cadets. Milton Caniff drew a sequence on the young recruits for his nationally syndicated comic strip *Terry and the Pirates*. The pulp magazines were especially cooperative. *Ranch Romances*, *True Detective*, *Master Detective*, and *Air Ace* immediately carried materials on the cadets. Other stories and articles were under development when the advertising agency asked the board to halt its efforts because more than enough young men had enlisted.[18]

In its first year of operation the WWB also worked on recruitment for the merchant marine, a naval auxiliary. It played a critical role in providing oil and other supplies to American troops overseas. At the request of Mark O'Dea, director of the Bureau of Public Relations for the Maritime Commission, the board designated Margaret Leech to head a special committee to publicize this service, which was essential if not glamorous. At its suggestion Advisory Council member Edna Ferber wrote "Lifeboat," a story that traced a merchant ship from its construction to its delivery of vital cargo across the Atlantic. It also persuaded former merchant seaman Robert Carse, an experienced author of pulp fiction, to travel on a merchant ship and record his observations. Carse got far more than he anticipated when he signed on as an officer on the S.S. *Steelworker*. It was part of the PQ16 convoy to Murmansk, Russia, in May 1942, one of the most dangerous of all merchant marine runs. Carse lost all of his careful notes when his ship was sunk, but he survived to tell the harrowing tale in "We Fought Through to Murmansk," a serial that the WWB arranged to put in the *Saturday Evening Post*. The group also promoted Carse's book on the subject, *There Go the Ships,* a classic of its kind still in print.[19]

Another merchant seaman, S. Edward Roos, told his story in *American Magazine*. With the help of a ghostwriter that the board contacted, he praised the "thousands of heroes without uniform, crews of the tanker fleet," and acknowledged their contribution: "Without the oil they carry, battleships won't cruise, airplanes won't fly, tanks won't charge."[20] Rita Kleeman published a story in *This Week* about the heroic actions of deceased merchant seaman Lawrence H. Gianella. Partly because of her efforts, in 1943 he was posthumously awarded the Merchant Marine Distinguished Service Medal and a ship was named in his honor, both at that time and again in 1985.[21] The WWB subsequently considered forming a Merchant Seaman Relief Committee, but it gave up the idea when the government organized an official group to address the problem. Once it concluded that O'Dea was doing a thorough job of publicizing the service, Leech's committee dissolved.[22]

By 1944 the number of merchant marine recruits had dropped again even though voyages across the Atlantic were a good deal safer because convoys received much better protection. Serious risks remained and were an obvious deterrent, as was the drudgery of the work. Board members tried to help the group a second time but were unable to make the job appealing. They could not duplicate their earlier success, especially in attracting experienced seamen who could step into vacant positions without much additional training. Robert Carse agreed to write both a piece for the Newspaper Enterprise Association (NEA) syndicate and a script for a movie short entitled *Men for Merchant Marine*.[23] The board's *Report, Bulletin to Cartoonists,* and editorial service cranked out material, and the organization sent special mailings to radio commentators. Kleeman placed a brief story about a merchant marine captain in the *Saturday Evening Post*, and the board secured a few references in obscure pulp magazines and the publications of fraternal orders, but little of real benefit resulted from these efforts. Taking a different approach, the WWB contacted sportswriters and newspaper editors about including recruiting materials in their sports pages, which had a large male readership. Although Gallico was the logical choice to head the initiative because of his past experience in sports journalism, he was overseas at the time. Franklin Adams took the job instead, having briefly served as a sportswriter early in his career. The campaign produced a few items including one mention in Al Laney's column "Views of Sport" in the *New York Herald-Tribune*, but the subject never received widespread coverage. For once the board came up short of ideas. Since members had nothing else to contribute, they dropped the project, but O'Dea's office continued to request their assistance.[24]

WOMEN IN THE MILITARY

The newly formed women's branches of the service also looked to the WWB for help with recruitment. When the Women's Army Auxiliary Corps (WAAC) was established in May 1942, more than fifty thousand women signed up, and the U.S. Army envisioned as many as 1.5 million females in uniform. Initial appeals had played on the patriotism of the nation's women and centered on the slogan "Release a Man for Combat." When the army made a special effort to expand the corps to 150,000 less than a year later, those approaches no longer worked. Since females had not been allowed to enlist in previous wars, women had no models to follow, and many were reluctant to volunteer. Several feared army life and training while others were apathetic. Some believed that single women who signed up for duty would put men off. Americans were generally uninformed and had no understanding of the jobs that the WAAC did. Almost everyone had heard the disparaging remarks of those who did not like the idea of women in the military.[25] Decision-makers in the army exacerbated these problems. They lacked experience in recruiting women, training them, and insuring that their expectations and needs were met.[26]

In March 1943 the WAAC addressed these issues by launching a recruiting campaign that was the most thorough in the history of the army.[27] The advertising agency Young and Rubicam had principal charge of the project. Both the army and the agency asked the WWB to contribute ideas and place stories and articles in magazines and on the radio since board members were familiar with the outlets, the process, and the writers. Following its proven tactic for gaining publicity, the group also scheduled a tour of the five major WAAC training centers. Ten writers, editors, and radio personalities plus fashion photographer Toni Frissell agreed to make the trip from April 16–18, 1943. They found good conditions, enthusiastic interviewees, inspiring stories, and attractive servicewomen. On April 17, the board broadcast a fifteen-minute nationwide radio show about the tour. Crouse hosted *Salute to the WAACS,* and Jack Goodman supplied the casual but carefully worded script. Participants included Advisory Council member Katharine Brush and journalist Alice Hughes.[28]

The board made certain that information on the WAAC continued to be carried over the airwaves. Hughes prepared two full broadcasts about the WWB trip on her radio program, *A Woman's Views,* and returned to the subject of women in uniform periodically.[29] An episode of the soap opera *This Life Is Mine* saw the heroine join the WAAC and work her way through a variety of useful tasks and heart-wrenching romances. The serial *Green Valley, U.S.A.* devoted a week to the WAAC in June. Scripts of the show *Blondie* made frequent references to the corps and incorporated the board's suggested slants.[30] The New York writers even managed to arrange a second network program for the campaign. After some feverish searching through American history, WWB members and WAAC officials decided that Molly Pitcher was a suitable American heroine whose image, if polished a bit, could be used as a symbol for servicewomen. The legendary colonist had supposedly put down her water pitcher to take her husband's place in combat, firing a cannon after he was wounded in the Revolutionary War.[31]

No small consideration was the convenient fact that Molly's heroism had occurred on June 28, 1778. Since the 165th anniversary of her bold action was fast approaching, Irwin Nathanson wrote a script dramatizing her heroics and driving home the point that "the Army honors WAACS, the Army respects WAACS, and—by the shades of Molly Pitcher—it needs WAACS."[32] A duly inspired member of the corps then told her story, and speeches followed by such notables as General James Bowers and Academy Award–winning actor Spencer Tracy. The program was broadcast on NBC at 6:45 p.m. on Saturday, June 26, 1943. The governor of New Jersey signed a WWB-prepared statement proclaiming Molly Pitcher Day, and in cooperation with the magazine *Harper's Bazaar*, the board conducted a nationwide contest for department store window displays on the Molly Pitcher theme.[33]

The overall strategy for the WAAC campaign was to deemphasize patriotism and focus on familiarizing the public with the work of the corps and the good side of military life.[34] Under Fadiman's leadership the WAAC Committee compiled and distributed a list of slants about ways that writers might handle the subject. The board urged them to emphasize the "smart-looking" uniforms, the "fine relationship" between men and women in the armed services, the need for female recruits, the advantages their military experience might bring them after the war, and, most importantly, the better-than-average chance of finding a husband. The WWB specified that pretty women should be pictured to dispel the notion that WAACs were unattractive. It saw that a servicewoman was selected "Miss Subways" for July. With that recognition came free publicity via a picture poster of the honoree in uniform displayed prominently in all New York subways that month. When the corps prepared its new recruiting brochure, a Frissell photograph of four cheerful WAACs appeared on the cover.[35]

Through the efforts of the WWB, various women's magazines did their part. *McCall's* periodically carried information on women in the service in its "Washington Newsletter" section. It also printed several of Frissell's photographs featuring members of the corps shown at inspection, in a beauty shop, on a boat with a handsome soldier, and engaged in activities like swimming and playing table tennis. Hildegarde Fillmore's accompanying article included practically all of the WWB slants:

> When you meet these WAAC officers you are touched by the fact that they combine the competence of top-drawer business executives with the skill and sympathy of ultra-modern college deans. . . . A WAAC told me that a girl often gets to know the soldier she is replacing. And the boys tell us they aren't sorry to leave a desk job for active duty. . . . Does her job spoil a girl's natural individuality? Well, watch the crowded stag line at one of their dances, or look at the bulletin board crammed with invitations to nearby functions, and you have your answer.

Fillmore goes on to mention that the women in uniform are delighted with the opportunity for job training and feel "set apart" because they can "relieve a man for combat duty."[36]

Harper's Bazaar devoted most of its July issue to women in uniform, and *Vogue* and *Ladies Home Journal* also carried features.[37] In July *Cosmopolitan* ran "The Lieutenant Meets the WAAC," a story it bought through the auspices of the board. On July 11, *This Week* saw its popular fictional character Arizona Spratt join the WAAC, buoyed by properly ennobling sentiments: "I didn't want any of those pink pants war jobs, which I'd get on account of being a Spratt. A lot of good men haven't been too good to go in where they could share some of the tough going of the boys that are fighting for us, . . . so I just went out and enlisted in the WAACS."[38] In August *American Magazine* used a photogenic servicewoman as its cover girl, and *This Week* did the same on August 8. The pulp magazines played every angle of the romantic possibilities. "The Women's Army" by Carter Sprague was one example that appeared in the August issue of *Thrilling Love*.[39] By then the WAAC had become an official branch of the service known as the Women's Army Corps (WAC) with concomitant rank and pay.

Newspaper publicity was another vital part of the campaign. The board sent copies of *McCall's* "Washington Newsletter" to several hundred papers in the hope that editors across the country would use its material on women in the military. Brush wrote columns for the Bell newspaper syndicate while Hughes composed several for King Features. Beginning in September the board's editorial service furnished pieces on the corps for local newspapers, and for some time thereafter the group occasionally placed articles in newspapers or instigated a mention by regular columnists to keep the WAC in the public eye.[40] To refute concerns by parents and religious leaders that military service endangered the moral character of women and undercut church attendance, the board contacted denominational publications and arranged for church dignitaries and religious news writers to visit WAC training centers and photograph servicewomen engaged in activities such as attending chapel.[41]

In 1953 the government published a history of the corps by former officer Mattie E. Treadwell, who served as assistant to Colonel Oveta Culp Hobby, WAC commander. *The United States Army in World War II; Special Studies: The Women's Army Corps* mentions only two WWB activities—the creation and placement of several magazine articles by prominent authors and the writers' tour of training facilities. Although board records indicate that the group accomplished much more, their efforts did not pay off. Members were disappointed when recruiting fell well short of revised goals that WAC officials had reduced. Treadwell pulled no punches: "When the drive was finished and the score counted it was revealed as a miserable—almost an incredible—failure."[42] The board may have encouraged some citizens to begin modifying their views about servicewomen, but it could not spur change rapidly enough. Even so, Colonel Hobby was impressed by the group's ingenuity and ability. She wrote Fadiman, "I feel that nothing that has been done for the WAC has had the impact of the work which the Writers' War Board has accomplished."[43] While board members continued to support the drives for women recruits, preparing pamphlets for an Air WAC campaign and persuading poet-historian Carl Sandburg to write a script for a movie short, their attitude was one of increasing resignation. Finally in June 1944, after they had worked on recruitment extensively and continuously with "discouragingly little effect," the writers suggested to WAC officials that the only way to fill their quotas might be through national conscription. The board actually considered a campaign to promote this idea but quickly concluded that it had no chance.[44]

Even though the WWB had become discouraged about its efforts on behalf of the WAC, it could not refuse to develop a campaign for the WAVES (Women Accepted for Volunteer Emergency Service) of the U.S. Naval Reserve. Established on July 30, 1942, the naval equivalent of the WAC contacted the board in early September 1943. This campaign was basically a repeat of the WAC endeavor although WWB members were able to generate a few new approaches. The WAVES Committee chaired by Kleeman kicked it off by arranging for staff members of the leading women's magazines to observe the training of female recruits at the U.S. Naval Station in Jacksonville, Florida. The September 14–17 trip generated an outburst of publicity with articles in *Vogue*, *Mademoiselle*, *Harper's Bazaar*, *True Confessions*, *Woman's Press*, and *This Week*. All leaned heavily on photographs to demonstrate the personal attractiveness of the WAVES, the excitement of their lives, and the excellent conditions under which they worked. The texts strongly emphasized their interesting and important jobs, their good character and morale, and their opportunities for romance.[45] The board followed these articles with an appeal to alumni publications asking them to feature graduates of their institutions who had entered the women's services. Over forty sent evidence of cooperation.[46]

Frustrated by the disappointing response from women, Kleeman tried a new tactic—taunting. She wrote a rather testy piece that ran in a few WWB publications in January 1944 and subsequently appeared in some newspapers. Ostensibly written by a "mere male [who] wonders what is the trouble," the editorial carried the title "What's the Matter Girls?" and implied that the dearth of female recruits indicated a lack of proper spirit among them.[47] The committee generated additional articles by scheduling another trip for writers to the Naval Recruiting

School at Hunter College in New York and obtained a WWB radio script on the WAVES by Robert Colwell. It was first performed by the acting team of WWB Advisory Council member Howard Lindsay and his wife, Dorothy Stickney. As before, the board also tried to involve the religious press to dispel rumors that WAVES were immoral. However, the coverage in various outlets was not as complete as it had been for the WAC campaign. Skeptical about attracting women who had refused their previous appeals, board members did not press the media for more publicity since most outlets felt that they had already done all they could to promote women in the service. Because the recruitment goals for the WAVES were more realistic—and much lower—than those of the WAC, the shortfall was not as serious, but the board was acutely aware that it had failed once again.[48]

In a blatant and perhaps desperate attempt to convince the public that female service in the armed forces would be an advantage rather than an obstacle to resuming normal life after the war, the board made two final efforts. One was an article it distributed on the training of women recruits entitled "WACS and WAVES Make Wonderful Housekeepers." It claimed that "the Army and Navy may not know it but they are running the best school in the country for *brides*."[49] Another was a piece for *Glamour* in which Stout took Kleeman's taunting one step further. Trying to rile the 10 million American women eligible for military duty into taking action, he accused them of being "slackers" who did "not care that much about winning the war." He called the reasons they gave for not joining the women's services "flimsy alibis."[50] As Stout intended, his hostile comments drew controversy, tweaked some consciences, and provoked articles in reply, but they did not inspire any substantive change in the number of recruits for either of the women's services. The New York writers found that their most intense efforts could not quickly or easily dislodge the personal fears many women had about becoming one of the first females to enlist in the U.S. military, especially when those fears were combined with parental obstructionism and traditional societal attitudes about a woman's place.

Despite these obstacles the WWB did not flinch when it was contacted about working on a limited campaign for the U.S. Cadet Nurse Corps in 1944 because the need was critical. Most of this effort was confined to the New York area with local radio interviews, newspaper reports, and speeches, but the WWB sought some national publicity as well. An article ran in *Parents' Magazine,* and cadet recruitment was covered in the network radio shows *Broadway Matinee* and *When a Girl Marries.* The OWI reported widespread use of the board's editorial "From Jitterbug to Angel." Through the cooperation of the Music War Committee of the American Theatre Wing, the team of composer Irving Graham and lyricist Bob Sour came up with the ballad "A Woman's Place," which delivered the straightforward message, "A woman's place is where she's needed and she's needed in the Cadet Nurse Corps."[51] In July 1945 the board put out a final call for WAVES in the medical field, citing the current number of wounded sailors and the battles against Japan that loomed ahead. However, it did not follow this appeal with specific projects since it was winding down its operation and had already lost its OWI subsidy.[52]

ORIENTATION

In addition to its work on recruitment, the WWB helped with the orientation of soldiers. In 1942 and 1943 it created and distributed materials including a series of pamphlets on various countries to give soldiers being stationed overseas the practical information and background history they needed. The board took a further step by enlisting speakers to discuss the language and culture of these areas. Authors who had resided abroad like Janet Flanner (France), Hendrick Van Loon (Holland), and Francis Hackett (Denmark) agreed to give presentations.[53] Beginning in the spring of 1944 the WWB stepped up these activities as the army began to realize the need for educating soldiers on several war-related subjects such as the history of the conflict, the nature of the enemy, and postwar plans. The WWB established a committee under Alan Green to help orientation officers around the country keep the troops informed. It instigated pamphlets such as *Know Your Enemy* and *Cartels: The Menace of Worldwide Monopoly,* which explained the international economic power of the Germans. The organization put them into kits that also contained information about the land and people of each allied nation, some of it supplied by the individual countries themselves. In keeping with its liberal agenda, the WWB added items on racial tolerance and international cooperation in the postwar world along with a carefully prepared bibliography of works that supported the board's views on a peace settlement.[54]

The WWB also provided a number of articles to *Army Talk*, a fact sheet for orientation officers. Examples are "What Victory in Europe Means to the Home Front" by economist John Kenneth Galbraith, "Is International Organization Practical?" by educator Arthur Upham Pope, and "What Part Can Religion Play in the Fight for Democracy?" by clergyman Henry Atkinson.[55] Since the army found that the average soldier responded better to such material when a civilian expert in the field presented it, the WWB held meetings in April and May 1944 to enlist well-qualified speakers and to discuss the subjects they wished to develop. Among them were "Post-War Problems in the Balkans," "American Fascism," "The United States Is a Pattern for a United World," and "Nazism Is Merely One Expression of the German Spirit." Green told one prospective speaker to make "any talk which will give the boys a better understanding of the war's background and purposes."[56] Although the board made occasional suggestions to speakers, it did not attempt to control their talks; however, the speakers were clearly a select group. Only those whose views were approved by the war board were invited to participate.

Most who agreed to speak gave regularly scheduled addresses at bases and hospitals in the New York area. Beginning in May the board sent one or two individuals per month on two-week nationwide tours of the Air Transport Command, which had posts in several states including Texas, California, Montana, Michigan, and Kansas. In late summer 1944 the twenty-six East Coast bases of the First Air Force were added to the agenda. This unit provided so many speaking opportunities that the board's Orientation Committee divided it into eight areas in order to avoid overworking any presenter. By December the WWB was using fifty speakers per month, and their addresses were delivered in places that could accommodate audiences of several thousand soldiers. Within a month the board started declining any further assignments, but that move seems to have been unnecessary. The number of these orientation sessions soon began to drop because of concerns about their content.[57] At several locations speakers supplied by the board stirred up controversy when they discussed issues dear to the group's heart like racial prejudice, American fascism, postwar relations with Russia, and hatred of all

Germans. Reports from the speakers convinced the WWB that the opposition came from conservative base command officers who did not care for the board's liberal agenda. Some of them apparently held isolationist sentiments or repudiated the idea of racial equality. Without giving any specific reason the army either abbreviated many of the programs or canceled them altogether. By May 1945 it had dropped the entire First Air Force circuit. Whether ideological differences existed or not, the approaching end of the war in Europe was undoubtedly the military's primary reason for terminating most of the orientation activities.[58]

MORALE

Once recruits had enlisted, received training, and completed orientation, the vast majority of them headed overseas. In new and unfamiliar surroundings they often faced a combination of fear, homesickness, loneliness, boredom, hardship, depression, and frustration. To help them cope, the military tried to provide entertainment and recreational activities that would keep the soldiers occupied during their off-duty hours. It also set up a radio network that broadcast some popular programs and informed them about events on the home front. Sympathetic to the needs of the troops, the Writers' War Board and other organizations worked to boost soldier morale. In 1942 the board supplied twenty-eight dramatic scripts for the program *Command Performance*, which was broadcast to American troops overseas.[59] One WWB initiative the following year was a program on the Armed Forces Radio Network called *Yarns for Yanks*. It featured Hollywood stars reading short stories for the men and women in uniform. Board members selected appropriate fictional works based on a single criterion: "If you were stuck in a fog-bound isolated camp in Alaska, even without chewing gum, what kind of story would you like to listen to on the radio?"[60] Other WWB activities ranged from supplying jokes and skits to advocating better treatment for the wounded to promoting civilian understanding of the various jobs within the military.

During the three and a half years of America's involvement in the war, the WWB sponsored contests to recognize writing talent in the army and navy. Winners received war bond prizes, some contributed by civilian dramatists.[61] The board's most consistent service to soldiers throughout the war began early in 1942 when Colonel Marvin Young of the Special Services Division of the War Department approached its members about providing scripts, songs, gags, and the like for use by the troops in staging camp shows. The board formed a committee under the able chairmanship of Dorothy Rodgers, wife of composer Richard Rodgers. The Committee on Scripts for Soldier and Sailor Shows was one of the board's oldest, and Stout felt it was "most active and useful."[62] It provided free materials for the troops to use in putting on their own shows for entertainment. The committee sent out from thirty to fifty items per month in the beginning and greatly increased that number over time. The material came from three main sources: previously used sketches, monologues, and other short pieces from revues and vaudeville acts; dramatic sequences and slightly altered comedy scripts from radio shows like those of Jack Benny, Fred Allen, Charlie McCarthy, and Fibber McGee and Molly; and original short plays that the WWB solicited.[63]

Throughout the war those on the board as well as committee members like dramatist George S. Kaufman coaxed work from their colleagues and contributed their own writings to insure a constant supply of appropriate plays and sketches. A number of leading dramatists including Russel Crouse, Clifford Odets, and Robert Benchley contributed one or more scripts free of charge, and the committee was able to obtain all of the material at no cost to the government. In total it supplied some three thousand plays and other presentations, several hundred of which were entirely new. These were published for the exclusive use of the armed services in folios distributed to American troops around the world. The board's files contain evidence of the widespread use of the scripts and of repeated expressions of gratitude from all concerned for the committee's unwavering service.[64]

The WWB also facilitated the work of two private organizations that regularly helped soldiers, the well-established American Red Cross and the new USO (United Service Organizations), founded in 1941 at the urging of President Franklin Roosevelt. Representatives of the latter approached board members in 1942 and asked them to publicize the purpose and function of the USO and to provide materials for its camp shows for the troops. The group established two committees, but the one designed to help with the camp shows ceased to operate within a year because the USO changed course.⁶⁵ Instead of mounting its own productions using WWB scripts, the organization decided to sponsor a series of large professional shows produced by the American Theater Wing with well-known Hollywood entertainers like comedian Bob Hope. Except for a brief burst of activity in the summer of 1945, the board was not involved in USO productions after early 1943.⁶⁶

In contrast, the group's efforts to help the American Red Cross continued throughout the war. Again WWB members set up two committees. One provided publicity for the frequent Red Cross blood drives, periodically generating fresh advertising ideas to keep donors coming back. The second committee assisted with the annual Red Cross fundraising campaign. In 1943 the WWB recruited writers and speakers, plugged the drive in its publications, and oversaw the creation and distribution of promotional materials to more than nine hundred radio stations. The following year the board placed articles highlighting the wartime work of the Red Cross in several national magazines including *Good Housekeeping*, *McCall's*, and *Country Gentleman*. For the 1945 effort, the board furnished the Red Cross campaign with twenty-four radio spot announcements, a radio drama, and six articles by authors like Paul Gallico and John Gunther.⁶⁷ The group's help to both the USO and the Red Cross ultimately benefited American soldiers, one of the main goals of the WWB.

Inexplicably board members shied away from two of the war's early race-related controversies even though they strongly supported racial equality in other instances. In August 1942 the WWB declined to criticize segregation in the armed forces, asking only that the army provide better food for black soldiers on troop trains.⁶⁸ Perhaps they felt that calling attention to the problem would give African Americans good reason not to enlist, but their reasoning is a matter of conjecture. Furthermore, they decided not to become involved in the debate over segregating blood. Prior to Pearl Harbor the Red Cross, which controlled the American blood supply, had excluded blacks as donors. On January 21, 1942, it reversed that policy but segregated the blood so that whites did not receive it. This humiliating practice infuriated African Americans, who raised as much protest over it as over any other blatant act of discrimination during the war.⁶⁹

After several people urged board members to join the protest, the WWB polled its Advisory Council. Overwhelmingly that group disapproved of the Red Cross policy and urged the board to take action. However, council member Howard Lindsay strongly objected. He pointed out that many Americans had been taught to believe the fallacy that black blood presented a danger to whites, and he took a stand on behalf of the troops: "I cannot ask any person, however ignorant, prejudiced, or superstitious, to incur wounds in battle in my defense . . . and be subjected to a blood transfusion which horrifies and revolts him." He added that making the matter public would be a disservice to many of the soldiers, whose morale would be shaken if the Red Cross changed its policy. His argument convinced Stout, who replied, "For myself, I have never seen a case better put than you put that one; and I agree with you."[70] The board did not pursue the issue, the policy remained in place, and the situation continued to be an insult to African Americans until 1950, when the Red Cross stopped segregating blood. The argument that a change in the Red Cross policy would have drawn strong opposition from either soldiers or civilians has recently been challenged. Whether or not Lindsay's point had any validity, his comments caused the board to miss an opportunity to promote tolerance by rejecting a false assumption based on race.[71] The group's decision not to denounce segregation among the troops and in the blood supply was antithetical to the liberal views of its members and to their goal of unifying the nation. Two years later the organization made up for this inexcusable lapse by launching a vigorous campaign against racial prejudice.

PUBLICIZING MILITARY JOBS

Major Frank Mason of the Bureau of Public Relations in the War Department visited the board on July 8, 1942, to ask about using all media outlets to inform the public about certain military matters. He specified several subjects to focus on such as cooperation between the army and navy, but some of them were technical in nature and required writers with expertise in making complicated information comprehensible to average readers. WWB members immediately established an Army Committee under the chairmanship of radio commentator and military analyst George Fielding Eliot, an Advisory Council member. It produced dozens of articles and stories for both popular publications and specialized periodicals such as *Firepower*, the ordnance magazine.[72] The committee also worked on Mason's suggestion to publicize specific jobs in the military in order to emphasize the contributions of ordinary soldiers who received little or no attention. This effort drew widespread public attention and proved to be a tremendous morale booster because many of the troops felt that the routine jobs they did were neither understood nor appreciated.[73]

The campaign started small as the Army Committee attempted to polish the image of one of the more unpopular branches of the service, the military police (MPs). It urged radio commentators to give MPs favorable mention, and it publicized the group in newspaper editorials and columns. The board also arranged a factual article in the *Saturday Evening Post* that stressed the importance of MPs and pointed out that their qualifications, their attitudes toward soldiers, and their methods of handling problems had vastly improved. The New York group contacted Matt Taylor, whose fictional accounts of policeman hero Dan McGarry regularly appeared in the Sunday newspaper supplement *This Week*. He agreed to transfer McGarry to the military police to help with the campaign. Through his stories Americans learned that being an MP was a "big-time job," and that "every job everywhere is important, in the army."[74]

The WWB project expanded in May 1943 when the Army Service Forces (ASF) requested the board's help in drawing attention to its work, which was relatively unknown despite the fact that it involved about one-third of the army's personnel. Its duties included handling construction projects (Corps of Engineers), supplying food and fuel for the troops (Quartermaster Corps), and operating battlefield communications (Signal Corps). Its Transportation Corps, Medical Corps, Ordnance Department, and Chemical Warfare Service carried out a variety of other tasks. According to one article, "When the invasion of Europe is opened, the ASF will have the colossal task of supplying every item the invasion needs from tanks to safety pins."[75] The OWI assembled most of the materials and ideas for the publicity drive, and the board used its contacts with experienced writers and media outlets to instigate more than fifty magazine articles, essays, and the like. One was a photographic study by Margaret Bourke-White highlighting several ASF jobs.[76]

The WWB scored one of its greatest successes in 1944 for the Army Ground Forces. Early in February military personnel approached the board about a morale problem. They felt that the public was not aware of the essential part that foot soldiers played in winning the war. Infantry representatives admitted that their men depended on the help of all branches of the military, but they argued that this assistance had little meaning unless the ground forces succeeded in capturing territory. WWB members agreed and began to conceive ideas for an all-out publicity campaign centered on the celebration of an "Infantry Day."[77] They established a committee under the leadership of correspondent James Putnam to make the arrangements. It selected June 15, 1944, for the event, the anniversary of George Washington's appointment as commander in chief of the Continental Army and, arguably, the anniversary of the founding of the American infantry. The War Department liked the idea, and General Lesley James McNair, commander of the infantry, signed appeals to newspapers to help with the campaign. Clifton Fadiman contacted radio scriptwriters, George Fielding Eliot pulled in his fellow commentators, and Paul Gallico asked writers of fiction for help. The initiative snowballed until it included well over one hundred projects in the three months that it lasted.[78]

In a fact-based article in *Argosy*, Eliot acknowledged the accouterments of modern warfare but reserved his highest praise for the infantry: "We are entranced by the complexity, the fury and the ingenuity of machine war; but victory still goes, at the last, to the side whose infantry can move forward and take and hold ground. That is the pride and glory of the foot soldier—the mud-slogging doughboy who knows that, whatever happens, upon his weary shoulders rests the final responsibility for victory."[79] Columnist Frank Sullivan lamented the fact that the reports of war correspondents from the front lines often ignored the tough job of the ground soldier: "The doughboy? Ah, he is down in the nice clean sewer picking nits out of his shirt and leading a pretty unglamourous life which never moves a correspondent to raptures."[80] Among other columnists and broadcasters who called attention to infantrymen were Eleanor Roosevelt, Earl Godwin, Adelaide Hawley, Imogene Wolcott, Ernie Pyle, and Edgar

Ansel Mowrer. The main characters in the comic strips *Superman* and *Joe Palooka* joined the effort. The prestigious *New York Times* was inspired to make an editorial comment that the war board applauded: "We know that with all our steel for combat, our planes, tanks, self-propelled guns and other engines of war, it is the flesh and blood infantry that will have to clinch the victory that we and our allies seek."[81]

Newspaper maps marked the advance of the Army Ground Forces with a black line that became synonymous with the infantry. The WWB played up the description. As Eliot put it in a piece that ran in one of the board's publications, "The little black line on the map, that's the payoff. That's where the infantry is. That's the yardstick of victory or defeat."[82] Sheldon Stark celebrated the moniker in a poem published in *Look* magazine. He referred to the infantrymen as "the thin black line" and praised them for being "out in front of the other corps / The rest of the army behind them."[83] As part of its campaign the board produced two editorials, "Hats Off to the Infantry" and "How Far Can You Walk?" Several hundred newspapers carried one or both of them. The WWB provided the newspaper syndicates with additional material on the subject, and all of them distributed it in one form or another.[84]

Radio shows of all the national broadcasting networks paid tribute to infantrymen and so did the Broadway team of Rodgers and Hammerstein. They produced one of the few songs written for the war effort to make a real impact. Hammerstein first sang "We're on Our Way" at a WWB meeting to enthusiastic applause. Its repeated words (step by step, foot by foot, yard by yard, mile by mile) mimic the rhythm of walking. Performed on the air and later recorded on Decca Records by the choral group Fred Waring and his Pennsylvanians, the song looks toward ultimate victory:

There's a good time comin' when we all get home,
But you can't get home by givin' in!
So take all you're takin' and give all you got.
There's a good time comin' when we win!
Step by step
(Wadin' through the water),
Foot by foot

(Climbin' up the beach),
Yard by yard
(Sloggin' through the mud),
Mile by mile
(Chokin' in the dust),
The infantry's movin' up.
The infantry's movin' in.
The infantry's movin' on and on and on!
Yea, brother! Verily, yea!
Hallelujah! We're on our way![85]

The campaign climaxed with Infantry Day, which brought national publicity and parades in training camps, army posts, and cities around the country. In New York infantrymen marched in a Fifth Avenue parade that drew over 700,000 spectators, and Mayor Fiorello La Guardia held a ceremony honoring eight heroes in the Army Ground Forces. During the Fifth and Sixth War Loan Drives (June 12–July 8 and November 2–December 16, 1944), the infantry continued to receive special attention.[86] The army reported that the improvement in morale among the foot soldiers was so marked that it considered the campaign an immediate success. General McNair, who was not usually generous with his praise, acknowledged the WWB's role:

> I am writing this letter now because of the apparent success of the Infantry Day idea, which I am informed, was originated by your committee. There appears to be no doubt that much was accomplished as a result of this idea toward bringing the Infantry nearer to its proper place in the people's mind.
>
> In my opinion each member of your committee deserves a large share of the credit for an achievement which means much to this most important branch of the armed services.[87]

The infantry campaign succeeded so well that articles continued to appear on the subject even after it ended. A story in the March 1945 issue of *American Magazine* by WWB member Christopher LaFarge pictured foot soldiers as average Americans with heroic qualities, "a million little

GI's from Hat Creeks in all of the forty-eight states, all of them decorating the Infantry." But he indicated that their grueling job was still not properly acknowledged by many on the home front. Private Krasek, the central character, explained: "One guy went home, and he's back here now. He says it's all the air force or the submarines. Or the paratroopers. He says, you say you're in the Infantry when someone asks, and they say, 'Oh?' like if you said you was in the business of hauling manure."[88]

The publicity campaign for the ground forces had one negative side effect: it made members of the Army Medical Corps feel unappreciated. Many Americans did not recognize that the medical corps had responsibility for tending the wounded on the battlefield and mistakenly gave the Red Cross credit for the dangerous job. As long as the Army Ground Forces with which the medics worked were also forgotten, the morale of both groups remained about the same. However, when the WWB's campaign brought a "sensational change" in the public attitude toward the infantry, the medics began to feel isolated.[89] Board members agreed to work on the problem and put LaFarge in charge. He saw that appropriate pieces were hastily written and inserted in several WWB publications. In November 1944 the *Bulletin to Cartoonists* put the problem to the nation's artists: "One of the most dangerous and courageous jobs in any branch of the Army has been that of the Army Medical Department. Confused with the Red Cross it is only the medics, the enlisted men, and officers who tend the wounded on the field of battle. The work they have done has been given very little publicity, and in some instances their morale has suffered. Can we give these men some of the recognition they deserve?"[90] The board's editorials, its monthly *Report*, and its materials for the NEA syndicate devoted space to the medics. Within a short time a spurt of newspaper stories emanating from sources other than the WWB began to call attention to the situation, and board members considered that they had adequately handled the problem.[91]

In sharp contrast to the group's successes were its problematic efforts on behalf of the U.S. Navy. In May 1943 the Bureau of Aeronautics asked the board to publicize the fact that the navy had planes as well as ships and to encourage enlisted men to sign up for training as flight instructors and ground crew members, both essential but not glamorous jobs. The board appointed a committee under the chairmanship of Jack Goodman and journalist Paul Schubert, author of *Sea Power in Conflict*, but the WWB encountered obstacles almost immediately. Admiral Ernest King, chief of naval operations, frowned on generating publicity because he was afraid it might inadvertently provide valuable information to enemy nations. Another sore point was the navy's tradition of anonymity, which deterred writers from emphasizing the heroics of a single individual. Despite these problems committee members were able to achieve some success, and they sent an Advisory Council member, naval historian Fletcher Pratt, and eleven other authors on a five-day tour of navy bases to obtain material for informational stories and articles. Pratt agreed to write a book on naval aviation as quickly as possible, and four stories by Keith Ayling on the subject appeared in pulps published by Standard Magazines. However, the committee and the navy soon reached an impasse: the WWB could not convince military officials to release anything except material on the training of navy men and women, and publishers refused to use it since they had already printed information on the topic and needed a fresh angle.[92]

In the fall Admiral King took a stand that the WWB found unjustifiable and unforgivable. At the request of naval officers, the board had procured three writers including WWB member Carl Carmer to produce books on the submarine service. The authors had spent a good part of the year riding on subs in order to observe the dangerous jobs of crew members. Just as their works were about to be published, the navy ordered them suppressed on the grounds of security, even though the authors had worked with the consent and full cooperation of naval officials. Especially irritating to the board was the fact that all the material in question had already been published in newspaper and magazine articles. The WWB sent strong protests to King along with a letter requesting that he reconsider his decision. It was signed by a number of famous authors that the board had contacted. King made no response. A hard man who took a hard line, he had remarked on his appointment that when there was trouble, "They always send for the sons of bitches," and he obviously considered himself one of them.[93] The board next asked for some kind of financial compensation for the writers since their months of lost work had been at the navy's request. King, however, was unsympathetic and declined to recognize the problem.[94] One year later when the navy asked the board to stimulate interest in the job of air gunners, the WWB did not make much of an effort, mentioning it only in the *Bulletin to Cartoonists*, which had the smallest circulation of all its publications. In light of Admiral King's intransigence and the poor treatment its writers received, the organization's lack of enthusiasm was entirely justified.[95]

OTHER ISSUES

In February 1944 another assignment from the OWI and the Treasury fizzled through no fault of the WWB. The problem concerned strikes by industrial workers. The previous month Secretary of War Henry Stimson had expressed fear that "industrial unrest and lack of a sense of patriotic responsibility . . . has aroused a strong feeling of resentment and injustice among men of the armed forces."[96] While workers generally admired combat soldiers and sometimes thought of themselves as "soldiers of production," the reverse was not true. GIs were disgusted when they heard about highly paid civilians living in safety and comfort while they risked their lives on the battlefield for less pay.[97] In their eyes the strikers selfishly thought only of themselves instead of the common good. By bringing production to a halt, these workers and their labor unions had interfered with the war effort and threatened to disrupt national unity. While the government had considerable experience in propaganda aimed at motivating workers, it looked for assistance in the harder task of restoring consensus by minimizing the rift between soldiers and workers, both of whom played vital roles in the war.

The board promptly created a Labor Committee under chairman Jack Goodman to suggest ways to deal with the impasse. Members prepared the propaganda piece "What the Home Front Is Doing to Support the War Front" and distributed it to army orientation officers. The Scripts for Soldiers and Sailors Committee also prepared material demonstrating the contributions of those at home.[98] In yet another effort the WWB encouraged relatives and friends to inform soldiers stationed overseas about local activities to aid the war effort. LaFarge specifically addressed the wives of servicemen in *Army-Navy Woman* and asked them to include in their letters cheerful news about home-front support. The board's *Report* asked writers to make a similar suggestion in local media outlets:

"And can you help? It's easy. Write to your local paper and suggest in that letter that your fellow citizens write to their husbands and sons overseas the news about the War Bond Drives—the local news. Not the big, glittery, hard to understand figures. But what the town did, the village did. What crotchety old Mrs. Blankus bought. Tell them to put in a bit of positive good news to replace the negative bellyache that depresses. Good news that's true breeds good morale."[99] Quentin Reynolds echoed the plea in an article distributed through the *Brief Items* service, and magazine articles and newspaper columns quickly reiterated it.[100] For soldiers the board published "Private Joe Union" in *Brief Army Camp Items* over the signature of labor leader Walter Reuther. It encouraged former union members in the armed services to point out to their fellow soldiers that strikes back home were rare and less frequent than the current ones in Britain or those that had taken place during World War I.[101]

To generate other materials for the campaign, the board recommended that fiction writers focus on the hardships workers faced: putting in long hours of overtime until they were exhausted, trying to stretch their take-home pay to cover all their bills, living in cramped and uncomfortable housing, standing in long lines to make purchases, and so on. The WWB even made the ridiculous suggestion that writers depict war workers "in physical and dangerous combat with saboteurs."[102] No authors were able to produce plausible scenarios that working overtime compared to hours in a foxhole or that standing in long lines equaled ducking bullets, and the campaign went nowhere as the group should have foreseen.[103] The board concluded that any further publicity given to war workers would only highlight their salaries in comparison with the pay of soldiers and fixed-income groups. Members were afraid that calling attention to the issue might increase the hostility rather than dissipate it. In the end they decided to leave the problem alone although they did print a few more pieces in *Brief Army Camp Items*. "Who Is Labor?" gave impressive production statistics to demonstrate that workers at home were both loyal and energetic, and "Labor Is Fighting Too" cited a favorable Senate report on the strong contribution of industrial workers to the war. But the soldiers' resentment did not abate until after the war ended.[104]

In another effort, the board fought the censoring of reading materials for the troops overseas prior to the presidential election of 1944. The problem surfaced early in the year when Senator Robert Taft of Ohio and other Republicans became concerned that the Democrats in power might use their control over communication outlets to garner the soldiers' votes. In March Taft sponsored an amendment to the Soldier Voting Act to place sharp limitations on material sent to the troops at government expense. His amendment passed, prohibiting books and other materials designed to affect the results of federal elections by means of political argument or propaganda. Violations were punishable as crimes. The War Department, particularly the army branch, began to apply these regulations strictly, banning works such as the film biography *Wilson* and books like Charles Beard's *The Republic*, an analysis of the U.S. Constitution, and *Yankee from Olympus*, the biography of Oliver Wendell Holmes by Catherine Drinker Bowen. Either in an excess of zeal or in an attempt to demonstrate the absurdity of the law, the army even prevented the distribution of its own *Official Guide to the Army Air Forces* because the book contained a picture of President Roosevelt, who was running for reelection to his fourth term as the nation's commander in chief.[105]

The Council on Books in Wartime, an organization tied to the publishing industry, was the first to notice the problem since it supplied pocketbook editions to the troops. The Writers' War Board immediately joined it in launching a campaign against the censorship. When the facts became known, the public raised an outcry against the amendment sufficient to give Taft second thoughts. He claimed that the army was interpreting the provisions too strictly and agreed to meet with the council, the WWB, and the army on July 21. Opponents of the legislation suggested dropping the idea of criminal penalties and liberalizing the law so that books could be banned only if they were devoted in their entirety to obvious political propaganda, but Taft would not commit himself.[106] The New York writers saw no way to make him budge without an all-out blitz. They sent letters to 22 radio commentators and 156 newspaper and magazine book reviewers explaining the situation and asking for publicity. Several of the responses were prompt and pointed. Some took steps to form a nonpartisan front committee to advocate revision of the amendment. The WWB consulted the American Civil Liberties Union about the possibility of challenging the constitutionality of the rule. Advisory Council member Bernard DeVoto, editor of *Harper's Magazine*, wrote a stinging editorial on the issue. A number of other projects were in the formative stage when congressional action made further effort unnecessary. Faced with an increasingly aroused public, the Senate adopted a greatly liberalized version of the law, and the army ceased its strict prohibitions.[107]

In September 1944 overly optimistic army officials boosted the troops' morale by indicating that the war might end before Christmas. However, Germany did not formally surrender until the following May. Anticipating that day the United States and other countries planned parades and other events to celebrate the Allies' victory in Europe (V-E Day). The board, however, decided to mount a quick "Anti-V-E Day" campaign to remind Americans about all that remained to be done in the war against Japan. For a slogan they chose "Stay on the Job," which had both literal and figurative connotations. The WWB cautioned readers not to take a holiday from their jobs for a premature celebration and encouraged them to stay focused on the job of winning the war and securing a lasting peace. In a biting article in *Brief House Organ Items*, Paul Gallico compared Americans preparing to celebrate V-E Day to "a bunch of screwy college kids getting ready to paint the town red after the football team wins the big game." He added that even college kids did not buy red paint until after the game's final whistle and that the present conflict was "the most vicious, savage, ruthless war the world has ever known. And maybe there won't be any final whistle."[108] But these arguments were not widely publicized. The board confined its brief campaign entirely to its own publications. Perhaps members did not have enough time to contact their usual media outlets or did not want to take a public stand that contradicted the government's position, which supported the celebrations. Although the group made a valid point, the press and the public ignored its pleas, but the Department of Labor took notice. It requested the board's help with a brief burst of publicity to persuade war workers to remain at their jobs until all the fighting ended.[109]

Early in 1945 WWB members were brought up short by a forceful presentation from Gallico on the Battle of the Bulge (December 16, 1944–January 25, 1945), which seemed to be a serious setback for Allied forces. It indicated that Germany would not collapse as she had in World War I, and the board worried about the public's false perception that the war in Europe was close to an end. To keep war-related positions fully staffed until Japan surrendered, the writers decided to support the drive for a National Services Act that would conscript all able-bodied civilian workers including women and force them to remain on the job. Although the group had previously rejected the idea of drafting women to fill a WAC quota, members unanimously agreed to a stern memorandum proposed by Gallico stating that conscription was essential both for winning the war and for encouraging good relations between soldiers and civilians, who could share the common experiences of being drafted and patriotically serving their country. Grafton supported the idea in his nationally syndicated column. However, some board members who had not attended the meeting expressed doubt that Congress would pass the measure. Then the war news took a turn for the better as the German "bulge" was wiped out and Allied forces again rolled forward. The board continued to discuss the idea on occasion, but the proposal for an immediate campaign for national conscription was dropped because no urgent need existed.[110]

PROBLEMS OF RETURNING SOLDIERS

During the final year of the war the board began to address the difficulties that returning soldiers faced. As the military sent more and more wounded veterans home for treatment, the WWB made two efforts to help those in military hospitals in the New York area become reoriented to civilian life. It provided several speakers each month who brought patients up to date on current issues in the news. At Mitchel Field Hospital on Long Island the board developed a second initiative for wounded airmen beginning late in 1944 and continuing into the fall of 1945. WWB members regularly dispatched teams of writers to interview each patient and produce an article to send to his hometown newspaper. Local papers printed the vast majority of these stories, boosting the morale of the injured veterans and insuring that they received an understanding welcome when they returned home.[111]

In the summer of 1944 the board learned about another issue involving the healthcare of veterans after a visit from two prominent psychiatrists, Dr. George Stevenson, medical director of the National Committee for

Mental Hygiene, and Dr. Lawrence Kubie, husband of WWB volunteer Nora Kubie. They argued that the national rehabilitation program for the wounded was utterly inadequate, having improved very little since World War I. The two identified specific problems that needed to be addressed immediately to correct the situation and prepare for the influx of returning soldiers after the war ended. They also asserted that returnees could not receive the best care at veterans' hospitals because those facilities were plagued by incompetency and inefficiency. Although some veterans' groups recognized that civilian health centers had more to offer, they argued that their members should continue to be treated at military facilities where costs to patients were kept to a minimum. The war board created a Rehabilitation Committee under the chairmanship of Julian Brodie and began to publicize the need for better medical treatment and improved rehabilitative care for veterans. A subsequent request from the Surgeon General's office asking board members to publicize its proposed rehabilitation program provided additional impetus for this initiative.[112]

By the time that government request came in, the WWB had already begun to distribute and publicize the plan designed by Stevenson and Kubie, which had gained the support of a number of professional groups. It called for the psychological screening of all men released from the services in order to determine their mental fitness and aptitudes. It also proposed that the GI Bill of Rights be amended to provide for this screening. The information gathered would be made available to all rehabilitation agencies so that they could coordinate their efforts. The plan suggested relocating hospitals for veterans because many of them were not in large metropolitan areas where their staffs could benefit from the work of nearby centers of medical research and teaching. It advised gradually diminishing the distinctions between the facilities for veterans and civilians so that each would provide the same level of care. The two psychiatrists specified that employers and the general public would need to be educated about accepting returning veterans with both physical and mental disabilities. Their plan also advocated the establishment of a crash training program to provide adequate numbers of psychiatric social workers and psychiatrists to address the problems of returning soldiers.[113]

Publicizing the doctors' ideas, the New York writers made their usual contacts and promoted the campaign in WWB publications. From

October 1944 through June 1945 the board sent five editorials on rehabilitation to local newspapers around the United States. Large mailings about the plan went to magazine and newspaper editors, writers, and publishers, as well as to likely sources of assistance in the radio industry. All of these media outlets touched on the subject at some point. Although the WWB made no effort to tabulate the results of its activities, the group's files contain plenty of evidence. In one instance Green persuaded the producer of *The American Forum of the Air* radio show to conduct a debate on the merits of the GI Bill of Rights as it applied to rehabilitation. Dr. Kubie presented his plan while a representative of the American Legion had the uncomfortable duty of defending the status quo. The board also arranged for popular radio hostess Mary Margaret McBride to interview disabled veteran Howard Rasher about his experience with established rehabilitation procedures. It created a mild sensation, and thousands of letters poured into the network offices. The United Press syndicate sent a report about the interview to its affiliated newspapers, and the rehabilitation issue drew the attention of influential commentators Walter Winchell and Drew Pearson. National publicity and the public's reaction to it put pressure on the War Department. As a result changes were made in all phases of the rehabilitation program. Improvement was so marked that in June 1945 the board noted approvingly, "We're getting somewhere."[114]

THE END OF THE WAR

As the war wound down in 1945, the board started cutting back. Among the projects that it dropped was a publicity effort for the U.S. Coast Guard, which wanted to boost the morale of its members and give the public a greater appreciation of their contributions to the war by calling attention to their hazardous jobs such as operating barges in invasions. Early in the year the board agreed to contact its pool of writers about publicizing this branch of the military, but it never followed up after its original mention of the problem. In its final months the WWB rejected another 1945 request without giving it much consideration. The Army Air Corps asked the board to publicize the work of its Redistribution Center, a facility in Atlantic City that was virtually unknown. Periodically a small number of airmen and ground crew members had to be assigned to new positions for various reasons. Some were ill, wounded, had psychological problems, or were unsuited to their jobs. The morale of these individuals was often already low, and the public's mistaken impression of them as criminals or cowards made their situation even worse. The board sympathized with the plight of these soldiers, but it concluded that the problem did not affect enough of them to make a major effort. Even so, it found a spot for the commanding general of the Redistribution Center on a nationwide radio show so that he could present the need for greater understanding to a vast audience.[115]

The WWB sent out *Brief Army Camp Items* until the end of 1945, and its Committee on Scripts for Soldier and Sailor Shows supplied materials to the troops until the organization closed its doors in March 1946. Even at that time, members were still turning down inquiries from various branches of the military. The fact that the armed forces continued to seek the board's assistance indicates their high level of satisfaction with the group's accomplishments even though some of its campaigns were not successful. Despite their requests, however, the WWB ended its activities for the military after fighting in the Pacific ceased in August 1945. The group could reasonably claim that its work for American soldiers had had a significant impact. It had helped them through every phase of their service from recruitment to discharge and had demonstrated as much concern for their mental state as for their physical wellbeing. However, its campaigns to enlist young women made the board aware of its limitations. While societal mores were beginning to change as females entered the workforce to fill the wartime labor shortage, many Americans resisted the idea of women in the military, which seemed too big a leap. The Writers' War Board eventually conceded that no amount of propaganda could change traditional attitudes about the role of women before the end of the war, and it moved on to address other liberal issues.

CHAPTER 3

HOME FRONT PROPAGANDA

MOST OF THE Writers' War Board assignments lasted several months, but a few could be dispatched in a matter of days. Within a single week in the fall of 1942 the group quickly dealt with three requests for writers who had particular specialties. It sent the Board of Economic Warfare the names of authors familiar enough with German economics to prepare materials on the financial situation of the Axis nation, and it supplied the Office of Strategic Services with contact information on writers who might have photographs, maps, or accurate descriptions of foreign countries. At the same time it gave the Office of Civilian Defense a list of clergymen qualified to write about the role churches could play in defense.[1] In fact, most of the propaganda that the WWB generated was geared to the home front. The organization often acted as the needling voice in the conscience of Americans, whispering a litany: "Your country needs you; do the right thing; be a good citizen; help with the war effort; endure the hardships; work with others for the common good." Board members cooperated with a variety of government agencies in tackling problems from school absenteeism to inflation. One of its longest and most time-consuming campaigns involved the sale of war bonds for the Treasury Department, which held eight special "drives" including the Victory Campaign after the end of the war. All of these WWB domestic campaigns were intended to unite Americans in three efforts: funding the war, participating in government initiatives to address wartime needs and circumstances, and breaking down racial barriers that divided the nation.

FINANCING THE WAR

The government had two primary ways of funding the war: income tax revenue and bond sales. In 1942 Congress passed a new income tax law to generate more money. The legislation began the system of withholding taxes and required 10 million people to file for the first time. The Internal Revenue Service had made a hasty effort to publicize the problems, clear up misconceptions, and persuade the public to begin work on their tax returns well before the deadline because the new regulations and more complicated forms required greater attention. But the problem was more than it could handle, and the agency contacted the Office of War Information for assistance. On November 17, 1943, the OWI requested the board's help, and the WWB immediately responded. It embraced the "do it early" approach and worked to convince Americans that they needed to seek expert advice to complete the new tax forms.

Since war workers made up the majority of first-time filers, the board's connection with industrial house organs was particularly helpful. In an article for *Brief House Organ Items* entitled "Bergen Makes with Pay-as-You-Go," ventriloquist Edgar Bergen tried to explain to his acid-tongued and skeptical dummy Charlie McCarthy how the new withholding approach to taxation would impact his nickel-a-week allowance. Bergen got across the message that those who immediately sought the help of experts were, unlike Charlie, not dummies but the smartest people in the country.[2] The board told writers in its *Writers' War Board Report* that those who waited until March to begin work on their 1943 tax returns courted insanity. Economist and author Sylvia Porter warned the vast readership of the *Reader's Digest* that the upcoming tax blanks were the "most brutally complicated and unintelligible forms ever issued by any government to its citizens."[3] Even the readers of pulp magazines such as *Real Story* were doused with details about the stipulations of the new tax, and newspaper editors tucked information about it into empty spaces between columns.[4] No doubt the board's enthusiasm for this campaign was partly motivated by the fact that conservatives were among the chief critics of the new law. While the government's tax policy had always been a matter of public debate, the implementation of these new regulations caused no serious outcry because citizens knew that the war had to be funded.

During their first year WWB members put in more hours of work for the Treasury than for any other government department, mostly helping with the sale of war bonds.[5] Citizens could purchase these bonds in various denominations for less than their face value and redeem them ten years later for the full amount they were worth. Those who did not have enough money for a bond could buy savings stamps that cost as little as ten cents each. Although these stamps accrued no interest, a booklet full of them could be exchanged for a bond. The board received its first major assignment to publicize stamps and bonds about three months after the bombing of Pearl Harbor. One of its early activities involved setting up an essay contest for students on the question, "If either Franklin, Hamilton, Jefferson, Lincoln, or Lee talked to my school today about defense bonds, what would he say?" The WWB made an arrangement with newspapers in thirteen states to sponsor the competition through their state school systems and saw that the contest received widespread publicity in those areas. Student authors of the eight best manuscripts from each state received a prize, and WWB Advisory Council member Lewis Gannett of the *New York Herald-Tribune* selected a national winner whose essay was reprinted in many newspapers.[6] The board used similar contests to promote several other initiatives.

Within a short time the war board became involved in the Treasury Department's weekly radio program, *Treasury Star Parade*, which went to more than seven hundred stations around the country. The WWB Radio Committee came up with a number of scripts for the program but soon ceased to offer its assistance because Treasury officials would not provide the scriptwriters any compensation, even a minimal fee. That fall the department reconsidered its decision after it premiered *Treasury Bond Wagon*, an expanded version of the earlier radio show. Since it aired in prime time over the Mutual Broadcasting Company network, the Treasury Department wanted to use quality pieces that would attract attention. Chastened by its inability to locate appropriate scripts that were free, the department agreed to pay for the dramatic sketches, scripts, and comedy material that the WWB provided. The board also supplied all the commercials for the program and enlisted well-known authors to participate in it. To handle the workload, it organized a project committee that continued to operate into November 1942. The early shows were deemed a great success, and the board's relationship with the Treasury Department was harmonious.[7]

That changed after Treasury officials arranged for a third bond program on a rival network and decided to pay its writers higher salaries. In protest board members stopped working on *Bond Wagon*, an action that prompted the Treasury Department to accuse them of walking out on a government assignment. A meeting between the two parties did little to dissolve the acrimony. The show's producer aggravated the situation on November 21 when he junked the script that the WWB had prepared and allowed the guest star to insert pacifist comments that the board considered inappropriate. Although apologies followed, *Bond Wagon* was doomed. At the suggestion of the New York writers, the Treasury Department replaced it with yet another program that had a full-time staff, and the WWB went out of the radio production business.[8]

SLOGANS AND POSTERS

Despite this setback in its dealings with Treasury officials, the group continued to assist them with various projects including the bond drives. Each of the latter lasted for approximately one month and required special slogans and other publicity materials such as war posters to promote sales. In anticipation of the First War Loan Drive that was to begin on November 30, 1942, the WWB organized a Poster Committee in August under the able direction of co-chairmen Reeves Lewenthal, president of Associated American Artists, and art historian Thomas Craven. The group became adept at turning concepts into finished products. The first step was locating a suitable caption. Writers throughout the country produced over a thousand suggestions for the board, and the committee winnowed them down to a hundred or so. The next stage involved finding talented artists who could illustrate each in a memorable way. The committee interviewed thirty-nine and issued seventeen specific assignments. Deciding which of the posters to use was the final step. The group selected twelve of the seventeen to be printed although some of them were not used by the Treasury Department but were adapted for other government agencies that had requested similar advertisements. Once again the board had to deal with Treasury officials who balked at paying for the work. Fortunately, Abbott Laboratories, a private drug company, financed many of the WWB-inspired posters.[9]

In January 1943 the Poster Committee set a goal, assuring the board that "posters stimulated by the WWB will comprise the bulk of Government issued posters for general public distribution during the next four months."[10] To achieve that objective, the group worked with a number of agencies. Once the Graphics Department of the OWI shut down in June, the committee fielded even more requests for posters. In its *Second Annual Report* the board announced, "As accurately as can be determined from information on hand, approximately three-quarters of the generally distributed governmental posters during 1943 are products of the Poster Committee."[11] The following March Lewenthal informed the WWB that his committee had supplied slogans and posters for each of the six bond drives held up to that time. Some of the posters pictured wholesome Americans being attacked by a shadowy but sinister enemy. Others were more thoughtfully designed. One aficionado argues that many of these war posters were works of popular art which defined America, portraying the nation as a beacon of democracy.[12]

In 1942 the WWB helped to develop a poster that achieved phenomenal success. Created by Joseph Hirsch, it carried the caption "Till We Meet Again, Buy War Bonds" over the picture of a young soldier smiling and waving from the porthole of a ship. It appeared in newspapers and magazines, on billboards, and as letterhead stationery. At the instigation of Julian Street it was turned into a postcard given free of charge to servicemen overseas. With a printing of 14 million, it reached households across the nation as soldiers wrote home to their families and friends.[13] During the Third War Loan Drive (September 9–October 1, 1943) the Poster Committee contributed the slogan "Back the Attack." Although the War Advertising Council claimed responsibility for it, Street dismissed that assertion as "the typical automatic reflex of the huckster." He believed that the "WWB should . . . get the credit." The board asked George Schreiber to illustrate the ad, which depicts a grim-faced soldier advancing into battle carrying a rifle as American paratroopers drop from the sky. More than 3 million copies were distributed nationally. Board members also supplied two slogans for the Sixth Drive at the end of 1944 (November 20–December 16): "Invest in Invasion" by Franklin Adams and "If You Can't Go Across . . . Come Across" by Jack Goodman.[14]

BOND DRIVES

In fact the group participated in every World War II bond drive through December 1945, generating new ideas for each one. In 1942 its members wrote speeches for the War Bond Pledge campaign and worked on a movie short to boost sales. Paul Gallico and Jack Goodman wrote the script and Rex Stout narrated the film. For the Fourth War Loan Drive (January 18–February 15, 1944) the WWB convinced thirty writers to record personalized radio commercials written by Robert Landry and others. It also furnished the Treasury with a variety of written spot announcements over the signatures of literary notables including William Faulkner and Eugene O'Neill. Local merchants sponsored these squibs and local broadcasters across the nation read them on the air.[15] That summer the WWB prepared a "Handbook of Speeches" of varying lengths for local use in the Fifth Drive (June 12–July 8, 1944). Alan Green reported, "The Treasury Dept. informs us that the Handbook of Speeches . . . was one of the most successful bond-selling weapons they ever had."[16]

The previous year the board had helped develop a Treasury Department idea for another successful "weapon." On January 6, 1943, it set up an independent group composed of book publishers and librarians whose job was to schedule "Books for Bonds" rallies. Chaired by poet and WWB Advisory Council member Mark Van Doren, the Book and Author War Bond Committee was sponsored jointly by the board and various publishing houses. The WWB assisted it by recruiting at least two prominent writers to appear at each event. Both authors would devote an entire day to attending receptions, autograph sessions, school assemblies, and other meetings before speaking at the rally. The price of admission was the purchase of a war bond, and books signed by the participating authors were auctioned for more bonds. Often the rallies ended with the writers donating one or more of their original manuscripts to the local library. The clever idea for the events came from Julian Street. The committee procured the manuscripts and hired an organizer to arrange the details of each rally while the Treasury usually paid the authors and took care of additional expenses. The department also selected the host cities through its contacts with state and local War Finance Committees.[17]

The first Books for Bonds rally was held on an experimental basis in Allentown, Pennsylvania, in late February 1943 between the first and second bond drives. Van Doren served as master of ceremonies, and the WWB's Pearl Buck was the leading attraction. Successful far beyond anyone's expectations with bond sales of $804,000, this initial rally was followed by a series of similar ones across the country. The Treasury Department found to its astonishment that the author events produced better results than appearances by Hollywood stars. The WWB and the Book and Author Committee worked particularly hard on a rally held in Pittsburgh on February 1, 1944, during the Fourth War Loan Drive. It featured four writers: WWB member Clifton Fadiman, Advisory Council member Louis Bromfield, novelist Fannie Hurst, and Filipino diplomat Carlos P. Romulo. The event brought in the spectacular sum of over $32 million. In the spring of 1945 the Treasury Department took some of the responsibility of supplying authors as the WWB began to wind down its operations. Taken altogether, the eighty-three Books for Bonds rallies held from 1943 through December 1945 sold more than $188 million in bonds. The WWB felt that the rallies also succeeded in boosting the morale of local citizens and participating authors.[18]

"VICTORY" PROMOTIONS AND OTHER CAMPAIGNS

Throughout the war the government encouraged Americans to support the troops in a variety of ways. In 1942 the Office of Civilian Defense (OCD) enlisted the board's help in promoting the "Victory Homes" program. To win a prestigious V-Home sticker for display on their residences, citizens had to meet five criteria: (1) follow the instructions of the air raid warden; (2) conserve food, clothing, transportation, and health; (3) salvage essential war materials; (4) refuse to spread divisive rumors; and (5) purchase savings stamps and war bonds. The WWB dived into the campaign by preparing more than fifty spot announcements and jingles as well as several full-length scripts on the V-Homes theme. It developed kits for writers of radio programs aimed at housewives and arranged for speakers to appear on shows broadcast nationally. Through its publications the board urged writers around the country to see that V-Homes material ran in their local papers. It also asked them to produce magazine articles and stories for popular periodicals like *Home and Garden, Better Homes and Gardens, House Beautiful,* and *American Home.* Because of the board's perseverance, over twenty-five magazines carried information on the project. The Juvenile Writers Committee worked to see that thirteen periodicals designed for youth did their part too.[19]

The board was disheartened, however, when it discovered that much of its furious effort was wasted. For one thing, the OCD began the campaign much later than it had originally proposed, undermining the group's carefully timed publicity blitz. For another, the government agency bungled the job so that V-Homes stickers were not available in every part of the country when the campaign began. Local interest soon began to wane not only because of glitches in the campaign but also because enemy air raids never materialized. Critical of the OCD's lack of cooperation, Stout sent a letter to Director James Landis pointing out that the board's registered writers had done a great deal of work but that none of it had been used efficiently.[20]

A more successful program involved Victory Mail or "V-Mail." Beginning in June 1942 the government made an effort to cut down the bulk and weight of mail sent to and from servicemen so that more space on ships and planes could be reserved for war supplies. V-Mail letters were single sheets of paper with a place for writing on one side. The other side had to be folded into an envelope and addressed. As an added bonus the design made it easy for the government to censor the content and microfilm it for transportation abroad. After the microfilm reached its destination, the letter was enlarged, reprinted, and delivered to the addressee, who never saw the original. The OWI did not request the WWB's assistance in publicizing V-Mail until February 1944 when the space issue became more critical. It was surprised when board members declined its request, objecting to the brevity and impersonality of V-Mail communication. OWI officials spent months thereafter persuading the group of the merits of the idea, and the board finally agreed to help. Goodman contributed the slogan used throughout the publicity effort, "You Can Fly to Him in a V-Mail Letter," and the WWB's ever-active

Poster Committee arranged for the poster that became identified with the campaign.[21]

That year the board also supported the Department of Agriculture's "victory gardens" project, which encouraged citizens to grow some of their own food, and its members helped with the projects of a variety of other government agencies. For the War Manpower Commission board members secured feature articles about the labor shortage to send to local newspapers in the affected areas. Simultaneously they produced pieces urging women to apply for the vacant positions, and they arranged for Fadiman to speak in Baltimore at the first rally in the recruitment effort.[22] For the War Production Board the group promoted the salvage of essential war materials. Although the agency had originally asked the WWB for a short skit, the experienced propagandists advised against it: "Dressing up . . . war information in pseudo-dramatic form doesn't do the trick [and] is not worth the effort put into it either in terms of mass appeal, use or effect."[23]

The Office of Defense Transportation (ODT) was yet another government agency that benefited from the board's assistance. The ODT became concerned about unnecessary travel after the Allies invaded Normandy in June 1944. Because many Americans thought that the war would end soon afterward, some began to take vacations and leisure trips once again. Officials worried that a continued increase in leisure travel would completely swamp already overstrained transportation facilities, but they felt that rationing was not a feasible way to handle the problem. Instead they decided to mount a campaign to stop the trend. On June 21 Charles Prins of the ODT and New York mayor Fiorello La Guardia, who was helping to organize the initiative, held a meeting with WWB members. Prins asked them to encourage voluntary compliance by making an "intensified plea to the public to conserve travel."[24]

Board members immediately sent stories to newspapers in the New York area while they came up with additional approaches. The group knew that the government had already set up regulations to provide space for wounded soldiers on trains. Since no special arrangements had been made for other servicemen trying to return to their families, it decided to use the image of the stranded soldier to convey the ODT's message. The group played on the sympathetic feelings Americans had for their men in uniform in works like the poem "As You Were" by Berton Braley, who lamented that GI Joe "may find he can't get home / Unless you stay at home and let him."[25] In a *Brief Items* article Fadiman used a heavy dose of sarcasm to suggest that civilian travel might have to be curtailed: "Go ahead and travel. Have a fine vacation—that is, if while you're there you can stop worrying whether you're going to be able to get back or not. Go ahead and travel, it's a free country—IF you want to compete for your Pullman with a wounded soldier just back from France."[26] Humor worked too in articles like the one Weare Holbrook wrote for the Newspaper Enterprise Association (NEA) syndicate, "Why I Sit at Home with a Book—and a Blonde." The WWB eventually stimulated discussions on the problem by radio commentators Robert St. John, Cecil Brown, and Lowell Thomas, and it arranged several articles and editorials to mention unnecessary travel including a second Holbrook piece for the NEA, "There'll Always Be an Option."[27]

THE BLACK MARKET

During the war the sale of rationed goods on the "black market" posed a serious problem for the Office of Price Administration (OPA), which enforced price controls on a number of essential items. Black market vendors obtained these items through theft or fraud and sold them at inflated prices to buyers who did not want to give up their ration stamps. Such cash-only transactions allowed shoppers to obtain more than they were allotted since they could pick up supplies illegally and then use their ration stamps for legitimate purchases. Although it operated outside the law, the black market attracted more customers as the war wore on, especially in large cities. The OPA knew that it could not ask the War Advertising Council for assistance because of its ties to the business industry, which was not in favor of price controls. Consequently, it turned to the WWB for help with its campaign against black market trading.[28]

On August 29, 1943, WWB members Clifton Fadiman and Franklin Adams spoke at a kickoff rally in Bridgeport, Connecticut, that was broadcast over the Mutual network. In its own publications and in popular magazines the board addressed the problem and encouraged housewives to take a pledge that the OPA had written: "I will pay no more than top legal prices; I will accept no rationed goods without giving up ration stamps."²⁹ WWB-generated articles repeatedly emphasized the idea that any black market purchase was a blow to the war effort. Indeed, one of them compared the self-serving thinking of black market shoppers to the rationalization of alcoholics: "We can remind ourselves that Black Markets are a form of sabotage and that no amount of government planning can succeed without the individuals who can carry it out. The beautiful blind spot which keeps us from thinking of ourselves as the focal point—the feeling that 'this can't apply to me and this once can't harm anything'—is just another cozy sample of the theory that 'another little drink won't do me any harm.'"³⁰ By the spring of 1944 the OPA was satisfied that the black market had been cut to its irreducible minimum and gave substantial credit to the WWB.³¹

The only problem that remained involved the sale of gasoline. Illegal purchases of the fuel caused a loss of over 5 percent of the total supply for civilian use. Since this issue was critical, the OWI assigned an official to help the OPA, which soon decided to launch a crash campaign with the assistance of the WWB. The OWI official thought that an emotional appeal to the public might work: "What we need is something of the atmosphere of a crusade—or at the very least righteous indignation."³² To start the campaign, the WWB arranged for a press conference at the Hotel Commodore in New York on April 4. OPA officials Bryan Houston, deputy administrator for rationing, and Shad Polier, chief of the agency's Crime Enforcement Division, addressed fifty reporters and writers of magazine articles and radio scripts. The two explained that the situation was so bad that many drivers faced the loss of their gasoline allotment, which was closely monitored. They pointed out that it was impossible for a dealer to sell illegal gasoline unless he cooperated with criminals who stole ration coupons or printed counterfeit ones. They urged the writers to stress that any person purchasing black market gasoline was encouraging one of the largest and most dangerous rackets. The meeting had the desired effect. The following day all of the New York newspapers ran stories delivering the OPA message. The report in the *New York World-Telegram* carried the headline "Counterfeiters and Black Market Operators May Get It All." It warned that "unless the nationwide black market in gasoline is stemmed and counterfeiters and traffickers in that racket, including high school children, are apprehended the nation's A-card holders [nonessential drivers] may soon find themselves without any gasoline whatsoever."[33]

In another effort to stir up emotion, Gallico encouraged readers of *Army and Navy Woman* to "hurry down to the nearest chiseling garage or unscrupulous filling station and get your extra five or ten gallon quota of available gasoline because the criminal scum of the country is hungry. It has been a long time between juicy rackets. . . . Dope peddler, white slaver, kidnapper, extortionist, murderer and racket king have left their specialties to become a part of the gasoline black market."[34] A bitingly sarcastic article about the "civilian slacker" who proved how "smart" he was by living off the black market appeared in the *Saturday Evening Post*. *Scholastic* presented the case to high school students: "The racketeers who print and sell counterfeit gasoline coupons, [and] the car owners who buy coupons to obtain another supply of fuel, are no better than Nazi saboteurs."[35] Other warnings went out in pulp magazines, women's magazines, and publications aimed at automobile drivers.[36] Comic book writers also participated. The summer 1944 issue of *Blue Circle* took on the problem, and *Popular Comics* addressed it that fall. In both September and October the radio crime program *Gang Busters* used a story in which black market racketeers who sold gasoline were tracked down and imprisoned.[37]

Of course the WWB's publications carried articles on the campaign and suggestions about ways that writers might contribute to it. The board's editorial service sent out "Stop Thief!" by Robert Duffus in June. The OPA considered it to be especially effective, and it was widely reprinted. The *Bulletin to Cartoonists* stimulated several noteworthy cartoons on the subject including one titled "Gasoline for Pleasure." United Feature Syndicate distributed all of them nationally. In answer to the board's call for materials, at least two serial radio programs dealt with the issue, *Mr. Keen, Tracer of Lost Persons* and *David Harum*. The latter carried an extended story on the counterfeiting of gasoline coupons. In addition, many radio commentators took note of the situation on their regular broadcasts.[38] Injecting emotion into the campaign worked. By early 1945 government reports indicated that the amount of gasoline lost through the black market had fallen from 5 percent to a fraction of 1 percent. OPA officials again credited the WWB with a "major share" in this achievement.[39]

INFLATION AND SPENDING

In 1943 the board directly addressed inflation, a subject that it continued to publicize periodically throughout the war. On June 16, James Brackett, deputy in charge of the OWI's Economic Stabilization campaign, attended a WWB meeting to discuss the agency's "most elaborate and important program" against inflation.[40] He needed the group's help in (1) explaining the complex mix of factors that can trigger the problem, such as a sudden spending frenzy or a food shortage; (2) advocating the unpopular measures necessary to fight it including higher taxes and reduced spending, especially for scarce commodities; and (3) continuing the campaign as long as the danger to the economy remained. Brackett was aware that such a long-range effort would require both careful planning and sustained ingenuity, and he knew that the brief high-pressure advertising campaigns that the OWI and the War Advertising Council liked to use would not be sufficient for the job.[41]

The board immediately organized an Economic Stabilization Committee under the co-chairmanship of WWB member Rita Kleeman and Leon Shimkin, a Simon and Schuster executive. Its twofold task was to conceive of ideas for the campaign and to initiate and carry out anti-inflation projects. It not only instigated the production of several posters financed by life insurance companies and other businesses but also turned over many suggestions for programs and plays to the OWI's Radio Division, which handled the scriptwriting. Board members briefly considered attacking current government policies on inflation and on wage and price controls through a series of cartoons and articles; however, they ultimately rejected this approach on the grounds that they could not very well criticize the government if they were acting on its behalf. Instead they decided to mount an informational campaign using their regular media outlets.[42]

With the end of the fighting in view, many Americans who had saved money during the war were poised to spend it. Targeting housewives with purchasing power seemed to be the WWB's best move. One full-page picture of a headless woman published in *Harper's Bazaar* brought inquiries for reprints and department store displays. It bore a damning indictment: "This woman is the national nightmare. At the first scent of victory she walks out on her war job, walks into the shops. She buys by the dozens, yawns at inflation. . . . Multiplied by the thousands, she is draining the shops, cornering merchandise needed by others, shooting up prices, paving the way for post-war breadlines. She is the disgrace, the despair of America—this . . . selfish complacent little woman who has lost her head."[43]

At the instigation of the board, *Reader's Digest* produced "Let's Talk about Inflation" for several hundred clubs on its mailing list. The study guide stimulated discussion groups and was reprinted in *Independent Woman,* a magazine published by the National Federation of Business and Professional Women's Clubs. A story in *Thrilling Love* appealed to female readers of romance. The WWB also considered other audiences. High school students found an article on inflation in *High Road*, and two *Superman* comic strip sequences appeared on the subject. From facts furnished by the war board, Robert Ripley prepared a "Believe It or Not" panel on the effects of inflation for newspaper syndication. Committee co-chairman Shimkin arranged for banks and savings and loan associations to distribute material showing the economic advantages that would accrue to customers who left their money on deposit until well after the end of the war.[44]

At the OWI's request, the board attempted to persuade President Franklin Roosevelt to discuss inflation in one of his fireside chats. Failing in that effort, it secured the help of other famous people like singer Frank Sinatra, who spoke against excessive spending on his radio show. For the NEA syndicate the WWB supplied articles under the bylines of well-known individuals certain to attract attention. Comedian Jack Benny discovered that his notorious penny-pinching tendencies were now the epitome of patriotism, opera star Lily Pons discussed handling the problem as both housewife and artist, and author Booth Tarkington asked the nation, "Are You Choosing to Be Poor?"[45] Additionally the board publicized the work of an Ohio student with the unlikely name of Luette Goodbody. In 1943 she had founded at her high school an organization known by the acronym "BOND" for "Buy Only Necessities for the

Duration." WWB members arranged for her to attend one of their board meetings and were impressed by the young girl as well as by her idea. In early 1944 her photograph was carried in a major newspaper and a national magazine, and information about her organization appeared in several other publications. Public reaction to this publicity was so favorable that the board assisted in organizing other BOND groups for a time. Eventually the work became too much for both Luette Goodbody and the WWB, and they handed the job off to the Treasury.[46]

Around the same time the government launched a new program, "Planned Spending and Saving," and the board's Economic Stabilization Committee secured funding from bankers across the country for local advertisements encouraging area citizens to save. For this effort the WWB put articles in newspapers and periodicals geared to financial institutions and found prominent bankers who would agree to place their names on articles that the board provided.[47] The group also tried several different approaches to control American spending. One involved making writers aware that they had a "frightening influence on public behavior." When they described beautifully furnished homes or new mink coats, people had the urge to buy them. In view of the war, the board cautioned authors, "Don't get too fancy with your typewriter. Sell newly bought glamour short!"[48] In September 1944 the OWI asked the board to inform citizens that economic controls needed to stay in place because of the possibility that the United States would soon face another war. For once WWB members refused to touch the subject, which was certain to generate a wave of public pessimism. The group feared that such news might stimulate a resurgence of isolationism that could hamper war recovery and cripple international cooperation.[49]

Board members would have done well to reject another assignment from the OPA that they questioned from the outset. Less than two months before Germany surrendered, the agency began to worry that withdrawing price controls prematurely might trigger inflation. Even though most citizens considered the regulations to be unfair and onerous, both the OPA and the OWI believed that the controls helped the economy by keeping the cost of living down. The two asked board members to secure public support for continuing the system and for curtailing widespread cheating. The writers agreed to assist with the project even though they knew that convincing Americans to report violators would be a hard sell. The group placed campaign propaganda in its own publications and on several radio shows including *Now It Can Be Told*, which gave the issue full dramatic treatment. However, the WWB did not contact magazine editors, no doubt because it recognized that they would be loath to print such an objectionable message.[50]

In May the board's editorial service sent out "Help Wanted, Male and Female." The article acknowledged that the OPA had made mistakes, but it emphasized the point that cheating continued because ordinary citizens would not report those guilty of noncompliance.[51] The *Writers' War Board Report* encouraged writers to take that step: "While cussing out the OPA, are your neighbors themselves following the rules? Do they or do they not buy without points when they can pay above ceiling prices without protest or report or use the latest private detour to avoid the annoyances of decent community cooperation? Will you find out and tell us and let us pass the information on?"[52] This appeal immediately provoked controversy and came to no avail. The strongest attack on it came from conservative columnist George E. Sokolsky, who called it a "collector's gem of private Gestapo items." He continued, "I am neither a cop nor a snooper. Let those who like that kind of work engage in it, wear a badge and proclaim themselves for what they are. But the secret ones are just plain squealers and should be treated as such. . . . Don't tell the Writers' War Board anything. If you have something to tell, tell it to a cop." The WWB received less than twenty positive responses to its publicity effort; a greater number wrote to criticize the group's stand, and members dropped the brief, ineffective campaign.[53]

MAINTAINING THE NATION'S WELFARE AND SAFETY

The WWB not only pressed Americans to live up to their responsibilities as good citizens but also participated in campaigns to promote their well-being by addressing issues of health, education, security, and morale. In February 1944 the WWB, assisted by the Surgeon General's office, launched a campaign for the OWI against the spread of venereal disease, which had become an increasing problem under the changing social conditions of wartime. The purpose of the joint project was to educate the public about the dangers of the disease and its treatment. The board addressed the subject in its *Brief Items* publications with articles like "Know Your Enemy (Blonde, Brunette, or Redhead)." That piece contained the warning, "Any girl who is easy to make can be, and usually is, infected. Know your enemy and steer clear of her."[54] (Author Joseph Hirsh, husband of the WWB's Selma Hirsh, made no corresponding effort to warn women about men with VD.) The board had just gotten started when the campaign was virtually shut down after the Catholic Legion of Decency objected to an OWI documentary on the subject. The organization complained that the film violated the motion picture code, which stated that sex, hygiene, and venereal disease were not fit subjects for movies. Because of the protest the OWI decided not to distribute the work, and the War Advertising Council, which had promised to support the documentary, ducked for cover, fearing that businesses might receive unfavorable publicity or lose profits if the council took a stand. The WWB felt strongly that the project should continue, and members made tentative efforts to stifle the criticism by sending letters to the Motion Picture Producers and Distributors of America questioning the provisions of the code. They also tried to interest the *New York Post* and other newspapers in doing an exposé. Nothing worked. Eventually the board concluded that it did not have the time and resources to pursue the matter further, and members reluctantly dropped it.[55]

The WWB also participated in a "Back-to-School" Campaign that the Children's Bureau had asked the OWI to launch. During the 1943–44 school year attendance had dropped by more than 1 million, and 3 million students had found summer employment. Both educators and government officials began to worry that many teenagers would forego finishing high school in favor of finding jobs in industries that needed workers. The board sent the piece "Ninny" over the signature of Frank Sinatra to the newspaper syndicates and asked comic book publishers to help since their works were popular with teens. WWB member Carl Carmer wrote a widely praised article for *This Week* about his father, a school superintendent. Its message was potent: "No matter how much a fighting nation needs its men it should not be using its boys in jobs when they should be learning to live. If it does we lose the very thing we are fighting for."[56] Simon O. Lesser, program manager of the OWI, praised the board's efforts and was pleased with the outcome of the project: "I want you to know how conscious we are of your very substantial contribution to its success."[57]

Concerns about the nation's defenses and the safety of its people drove the government to notify Americans about the possibility of a Japanese invasion along the West Coast early in the war. Similar concerns about threats to the nation from inside its borders prompted the WWB to issue warnings about native fascists who denounced democratic ideals and racial minorities. The danger had come to the board's attention through the Friends of Democracy, another organization that Rex Stout headed. It had monitored extremist groups since the late 1930s and had made a collection of their subversive literature.[58] Using that resource, in 1943 the board prepared materials on American fascist organizations and mailed them to radio stations nationwide. Stout wrote "Are There Any Home-Grown Fascists?" and recorded it for broadcast. The November War Script of the Month was Norman Corwin's *To the Young*, an antifascist play that had originally aired on the author's radio program *This Is War*. Clifton Fadiman liked the writer's attitude: "Corwin hates fascism (domestic as well as foreign), knows why he hates it, and knows how to make you hate it, too. When I say hate, I mean hate, and not dislike or disapproval."[59]

Another problem that surfaced within the country had to do with the harm caused by idle gossip. At the request of the OWI, the board asked Americans to be careful about what they said in their casual conversations. Beginning in 1942 the Office of Civilian Defense had cautioned the public not to spread rumors that might divide the country. Two years later the WWB publicized the far more important admonition not to openly discuss facts about the war. The warning came after OWI officials obtained evidence that Germany and Japan had acquired valuable information simply by piecing together trivial bits of war news overheard by informants. Despite the best efforts of the Office of Censorship, sometimes parents, families, and close friends of soldiers were responsible for the unintentional leaks. An escaped American prisoner of war, Sergeant John H. Gardner, met with the board and left them stunned with his story. Even before his capture the Germans had compiled a complete dossier on his career in the armed forces by gathering isolated pieces of gossip. With the Allied invasion of Europe planned and American military operations underway around the globe, the problem was a serious one that needed to be addressed immediately.[60]

The OWI asked the board to use its regular channels to spread the "Don't talk!" message. The government was particularly interested in obtaining radio, newspaper, and magazine coverage. Through the services of WWB members Oscar Hammerstein and Hobe Morrison, on April 28, 1944, Gardner told his story on *The Kate Smith Hour*, one of radio's highest rated shows.[61] The board also placed "Pipe Down," a wry poem by Christopher Morley, in the *New York Times Magazine*. He cautioned readers to "leave the inside dope at anchor" because even the brief mention of an important fact might lead the enemy to sink a ship.[62] Paul Gallico wrote a novelette on the subject that ran serially for three months in *Cosmopolitan*. "Who Killed My Buddy" presented the story of a veteran who traced information leaks that led to the death of his fellow soldier. He learned that twenty well-meaning individuals had unwittingly provided German spies with telling facts.[63] WWB publications also carried articles on the subject including "Now Will You Stop Loose Talk?" by Gardner. Finally, committees that the Office of Civilian Defense had previously organized around the country received many of the board's materials on the subject so that they could address the problem locally.[64]

BOOSTING CIVILIAN CONFIDENCE AND MORALE

In 1942 the OWI asked the board to deal with a public relations issue. During the confusing period when the cabinet departments had scrambled to convert to a war footing, many Americans came to view the government as inefficient. Republicans who opposed Roosevelt's New Deal policies undoubtedly exacerbated the problem. The OWI was afraid that the misconception might eventually shake public confidence in the government's ability to handle the war. At the suggestion of the WWB, Gallico wrote and published a semi-humorous article in *Cosmopolitan* demonstrating that the government was a model of efficiency compared to the average American, who regularly engaged in time-wasting activities.[65]

To keep up civilian morale during the first year of America's involvement in the war, the OCD requested that the WWB supply materials on "the importance of every civilian's individual day by day activities" in order to "demonstrate, graphically and simply, that seemingly dull, routine efforts contribute to victory."[66] The board composed a speakers' manual that included brief addresses on subjects such as promoting community goodwill and joining a volunteer group. It also organized a Civilian Programs Committee to prepare short plays and skits for local groups to perform. For this endeavor WWB members worked primarily with radio writers who were used to meeting strict deadlines.[67] Rather quickly the committee put together a catalog of thirty-two short scripts that the OCD and the board distributed nationally by the thousands. One popular sketch was "Man Bites Carrot" by Ben Brady, a "fast moving piece of broad comedy on nutrition . . . that makes an important point."[68] Another argued that do-it-yourself home repair projects could help win the war. In "We the Tools" by Denis Halman, each performer portrayed a different implement such as a hammer, a saw, or a screwdriver. The OCD seemed pleased with these scripts, but the WWB believed that their propaganda message was too obvious and that they lacked impact because they dealt with boring daily routines. Despite its negative opinion the board continued to make them available throughout the war.[69]

In 1944 the group acted on its own to bolster morale at a critical time. That spring civilians and soldiers began to brace for the inevitable Allied invasion of Europe. Even though the exact date and place of the event were kept secret, the public knew what was coming, and an atmosphere of anxiety and apprehension prevailed on the home front as well as in the barracks. Board members took it upon themselves to do something unique to buoy public spirit and emphasize to Americans that home-front support was more vital than ever as ground troops fought to take territory from German control. They commissioned Pulitzer Prize–winning poet Edna St. Vincent Millay to write a prayer to be read over the radio once the invasion was announced.[70] "Poem and Prayer for an Invading Army" was recorded in advance by actor Ronald Coleman and broadcast over NBC radio on the evening of D-Day, June 6, when military forces from the United States, Canada, and Great Britain landed in Normandy, France. Millay insisted that the soldiers "must not go alone" into the metaphorical inferno of Europe without the full support of those at home: "You who have stood behind them to this hour, / move strong behind them now." The poet expressed the hope uppermost in the minds of most Americans, "Oh, let the battle, Lord, be brief, / and let our boys come home!" But she also voiced the fear that the soldiers "waited in the "anteroom / of Death, expecting every moment to be called by name."[71] According to a twenty-first-century *Washington Post* article, "millions of Americans pondered its meaning."[72] Even though it could not relieve public tension, the haunting poem identified the concerns of the entire nation and, in a sense, prepared Americans for the death and devastation of the final battles of the war in Europe.

EARLY EFFORTS TO PROMOTE RACIAL TOLERANCE

Of all its domestic campaigns, the WWB was most proud of its private initiative to combat racial prejudice. A cursory examination of the United States during the decades between the two world wars reveals the pervasiveness of racism and ethnic bias not only against blacks but also against Jews and other minorities as well as foreigners in general. The extent of the problem was such that black Americans prepared to march on Washington in 1941. That June Roosevelt was able to circumvent their plans by issuing a presidential order forbidding discrimination in defense employment and establishing a Fair Employment Practice Committee (FEPC) to deal with violators. Unfortunately, the committee was not given sufficient power and adequate funding to tackle the problem, and unrest steadily rose over the next two years until it climaxed in a riot in Detroit in 1943.[73] Looking back at the war years, historian John Hope Franklin summed up the situation of blacks in his classic study *From Slavery to Freedom*: "Experiences on the home front during the war drove the morale of African Americans to a new low."[74]

During the war WWB members became increasingly concerned about discriminatory practices on the home front and in the military. Their goals in fighting racial prejudice were similar to those of the "Double V" campaign initiated two months into the war by the outspoken *Pittsburgh Courier*, which had the largest circulation of any black newspaper in the country. The Double V effort—victory over fascism abroad and over racism at home—blossomed into a national movement among African Americans.[75] While WWB members were unaware of the campaign for some time and did not join it, their work to achieve racial equality ultimately won them plaudits from the *Courier*. In 1942, however, the New York writers failed to speak out against segregating black soldiers and segregating blood drawn from African Americans even though they opposed racism and wanted to unite all segments of the population in the war effort.

Despite that fact the WWB made a few efforts to improve race relations during its first year of operation. The War Script of the Month in September was *Brothers* by black poet Langston Hughes, who chronicled the heroic exploits of African American seamen. The first book the group chose to promote, Pearl Buck's *American Unity and Asia*, highlighted one of the effects of racial discrimination. The author pointed out that Japan exploited racial incidents involving Americans as a means of encouraging U.S. citizens of Asian and African descent to turn against those it referred to as "white imperialists." It publicized recently reported accounts of prejudice and discrimination in its short-wave radio broadcasts, leaflets, and other propaganda. Buck warned, "Every lynching, every race riot, . . . all our social discriminations are of the greatest aid to our enemy in Asia."[76] The media took note of Japan's interest in black Americans at the time, and some modern historians have argued that its efforts succeeded in several respects.[77]

The WWB also attempted to use more black speakers on the air through its contacts with the radio networks. The idea was to put them on interview shows without revealing their race until they identified themselves as African American in the course of the conversation. The fact that there are no further comments about this plan in subsequent board minutes probably indicates that it went nowhere. More characteristic of the group's involvement in the race issue was its attempt to encourage newspapers focused on African Americans to take notice of the war effort. Understandably most were more concerned about discrimination and civil rights violations at home than about the events in Europe. The WWB considered using positive reinforcement by asking national magazines to quote remarks on the war from these papers in the hope of encouraging the black press to include more commentary on the conflict.[78]

In December 1942 the WWB met with influential pastor and politician Adam Clayton Powell Jr., editor of the *People's Voice*. The activist had already written the magazine article "Is This a White Man's War?" in an attempt to stimulate African American support for the nation's involvement in the conflict: "The thinking Negro knows that if America loses the war, his plight as a Negro will be much worse than it is now. Under democracy, however poorly realized, the Negro does have a fighting chance."[79] Powell liked the idea of placing African American speakers on radio programs but insisted that, as a matter of pride, they be introduced as blacks. He emphasized the failure of national magazines and newspapers to carry stories on African Americans and urged the board to press for change on that front before pushing black papers to focus more on the war effort. WWB members conceded his point but took no immediate action. Nonetheless, their meeting with Powell undoubtedly made them more sensitive to racial issues, and the question that he had raised in the article troubled the group for the remainder of its existence.[80]

THE NEGRO SOLDIER AND THE RACES OF MANKIND

During the war several government agencies and private organizations had fought against anti-Semitism and promoted ethnic tolerance, but most of them had not challenged racial discrimination against African Americans because the problem was so entrenched and so polarizing. Undeterred, the board decided in February 1944 to begin an assault on prejudice against all races at a level that few other groups had attempted.[81] To monitor this private campaign it organized the Committee to Combat Race Hatred. Chaired by Robert Landry, it included Alan Green, Rita Kleeman, Margaret Leech, Jean Poletti, Hobe Morrison, and WWB volunteer Pat Selwyn Klopfer. Among its first activities was distributing a self-quiz to measure racist attitudes among the WWB's cadre of writers. A visit to the board by African American journalist Ted Posten the following month initiated other projects.[82]

As OWI racial adviser and head of the Negro Press section of its News Bureau, Posten asked the WWB for help in handling some problems that were not in the purview of the government agency. Although his office regularly sent information on African Americans in the war effort to a variety of media outlets, Posten was concerned that only the black press used the material. Because other papers, magazines, films, and radio programs generally ignored it, many citizens felt that blacks were not doing their part to achieve victory.⁸³ Posten was particularly disturbed by two instances in which government projects related to African Americans had been stymied. The Special Coverage Section of the U.S. Army Signal Corps had made a film entitled *The Negro Soldier* to document the role of blacks in the military. Although the War Activities Committee of the movie industry had agreed to distribute the Frank Capra production as widely as possible on request, the group had done nothing to publicize its availability and had scheduled no showings. Its only action was to request that the film be drastically shortened. Posten was also frustrated by the War Department. It had begun to distribute *The Races of Mankind*, a pamphlet about racial equality, to all branches of the armed services but had subsequently withdrawn the work.⁸⁴

The WWB committee promptly began to address these problems. Since the film industry had agreed to distribute *The Negro Soldier* through its War Activities Committee, the board began to publicize the film so that many individuals and groups would ask for showings. It sent mailings to columnists, schools, house organ publications, and movie reviewers urging them to stimulate interest in the film through their endorsements. The board also asked each of its registered writers to bombard local theater managers and newspaper editors with requests for showings. As in many instances involving the WWB's work, concrete results are difficult to demonstrate, but this effort seems to have met with success. By July 1944 the film was widely distributed, playing in hundreds of theaters in the New York City area alone. Many of the showings were free, but there was enough interest in the film to attract the attention of commercial theaters that had originally rejected it. Also, all incoming army recruits viewed the film as part of their orientation.⁸⁵ Positive reaction to it encouraged WWB members, who sent letters to five newsreel companies and seven movie producers asking that they present African Americans in a favorable light in their productions. Anticipating that they would not "depart from their usual story-lines," the board merely suggested that they place well-dressed, respectable blacks in the backgrounds of their shots and in small parts without being obvious.⁸⁶

The WWB also started to promote *The Races of Mankind* by Columbia University professors Ruth Benedict and Gene Weltfish, both students of the pioneering anthropologist Franz Boaz. Using simple language with cartoon illustrations, the pamphlet explained the scientific case against racism. The authors began with the observation that many different nations and "different physical types of men" were at that time involved in fighting the Axis nations, and they argued that differences between people had nothing to do with race but resulted from disparate economic circumstances and educational opportunities. As an example they pointed out that on some intelligence tests black and white northerners scored higher than black and white southerners. The authors clearly stated that southerners were the "inborn equals" of northerners but had lower scores because they had not been given the same opportunities.[87]

That reasoning was insufficient to quell the ire of southern congressmen, particularly Representative Andrew J. May of Kentucky, who wielded power as chairman of the House Military Affairs Committee. These lawmakers succeeded in persuading the War Department to ban *The Races of Mankind*. Chester Barnard, president of the USO, followed suit on February 14, having the pamphlet removed from USO centers on the grounds that its message was political. He asserted that his organization did not want to become involved in controversial matters because it served persons of many different beliefs. One month later Rex Stout sent him a letter of protest that explained the board's stand on the issue of racism: "Our disagreement is simple: *The Races of Mankind* is an educational pamphlet. . . . The Writers' War Board believes that the suppression of scientifically established facts concerning racial equality tends to the defeat of one of our outstanding war aims. We believe that interracial strife in our own communities is part of the war overseas and indivisible from it. We cannot combat the master race theory in Europe and appease it at home."[88]

Barnard replied immediately, citing "the element of dishonesty involved in taking the money and services of people and using it for purposes to which they did not agree." Stout dismissed this argument as "absurd and inadmissible."[89] In hopes of resolving the issue, members of the board met with Barnard on March 22, 1944, but he refused to change his mind even though the New York group argued that there had been no complaints about the USO having the pamphlet prior to Barnard's move against it.[90] The board began to pressure Barnard by publicizing the incident. On April 4 it sent its objections to fifty-four officers and board members of the USO, thirty-nine selected organizations, and twenty-four book reviewers. Included in each letter was a mimeographed copy of the entire Stout-Barnard correspondence as well as the pamphlet. Within two weeks Barnard received twelve letters of protest. One of the WWB editorials for April was "Exploding the Myth," a blast at the opponents of *The Races of Mankind*. When the Detroit USO center announced that it would defy Barnard and continue to distribute the pamphlet, board members sent letters to over 1,100 USO clubhouses and other organizations suggesting that they follow the Detroit example. Forty-one USO centers agreed to examine the work and then decide their position while nine others said they would either use it or promote its distribution immediately.[91]

The WWB did not stop there. It had *The Races of Mankind* made into a filmstrip entitled *We Are All Brothers—What Do You Know about Race?* and assisted its producer, New Tools for Learning of New York, in promoting its distribution. The filmstrip was eventually adapted into a comic strip as well. The board encouraged even wider dissemination of the information when it asked Benedict and Weltfish to write a dramatized version. In June the play, *Meet Your Relatives,* was distributed as the War Script of the Month to over seven hundred schools, radio stations, and educational organizations, and it was included in the WWB script catalog for further circulation.[92] Despite continuing attacks from individuals and groups such as the House Military Affairs Committee, which charged that the pamphlet was "communist inspired," thousands read *The Races of Mankind*. The controversy helped to publicize the work, and its title became something of a household phrase.[93]

THE CAMPAIGN TO COMBAT RACE HATRED

At its meeting on April 12, 1944, the board held one of its characteristic brainstorming sessions on its campaign against racial prejudice. Russel Crouse and Carl Carmer suggested that the group promote the Bill of Rights as a central theme of the initiative, and Alan Green proposed the idea of using a single individual as a "Messiah" to lead an onslaught against hate groups who profited from prejudice. Oscar Hammerstein and others objected that both measures would be too long-range to do much good. The consensus was that WWB members should work through their contacts and the board's committees to promote tolerance and to educate their colleagues in the publishing and entertainment industries about ways that they could help with the campaign. They considered this approach to be "a broadly and systematically conceived plan to enlist as many as possible of the media of communication on the side of an American unity [against racism] which will prevent the civil war now threatening this community."[94] While the WWB supported efforts to combat racism that were initiated by other organizations like the National Urban League, the National Conference of Christians and Jews, the Bureau for Intercultural Education of New York, and the American Council on Race Relations of Chicago, the board could offer them little assistance of any real substance because of its own heavy workload and limited budget.[95]

As part of its campaign the board worked on breaking down racism in several arenas. It defended the Indian Reorganization Act of 1934, which allowed Native Americans to manage their own affairs and restore their tribes and traditions. The board feared that repealing the legislation might cause the indigenous population to suffer even more discrimination and injustice.[96] In another initiative the WWB denounced some of the so-called Mothers' Groups such as the Mothers of Sons Forum and the National Blue Star Mothers of America. Despite their innocuous names, many of these antiwar organizations were xenophobic and racist. In the fall of 1944 the board sent a memorandum to writers, editors, and columnists exposing the pro-fascist leanings of such groups and their opposition to Russians, Britons, and Jews, to name only a few of their targets.[97] In one case the board went too far, decrying racism where there was none. In July it protested against two sentences in a *Time* article: "The U.S. citizen most likely to go to the polls next November 7 is an upper-income Northern male. He is college educated and over 40, Catholic or Jewish in religion."[98] The WWB claimed that the author was using connotations of intolerance "to imply that the November elections can and will be carried by the Jewish and Catholic vote." However, *Time* insisted that its staff had not had any agenda but had simply reported an unbiased survey in a straightforward manner, and the content of the article seems to bear out the magazine's contention.[99]

Discrimination in the workplace was another subject that the WWB addressed. On May 3, 1944, Malcolm Ross attended a board meeting to request publicity for the Fair Employment Practice Committee he chaired. He expressed concern that the agency had little power to treat problems proactively but depended on the complaints it received and on disputes in war industries that the president directed it to handle. He also asked the group to help him gain the cooperation of union members who resented the entry of black workers into skilled jobs that paid higher salaries. Noting the economic gains of African Americans, the OWI had reported the previous year a dangerous feeling among whites that "the Negro must be put in his place."[100] About three months after Ross's visit, a member of the National Council for a Permanent FEPC contacted the WWB about pressuring Congress to establish an ongoing system to address discrimination in the workplace.[101]

The board used its regular publications to spread the word about both initiatives. In May the War Script of the Month was *Is Fair Play Controversial?* by journalist Chet Huntley, whose name became a household word when he and David Brinkley anchored the NBC television evening news from 1956 to 1970. Set in a war plant, Huntley's fifteen-minute drama with four characters "shows that, when given equal opportunities, Negroes learn as rapidly as white people."[102] Duffus contributed three editorials: "Him Today—Me Tomorrow," "Fair Play on the Job," and "Fair Play Now—and Later." The first of these denounced discrimination "against Negroes, against Jews and other religious minorities, and against certain foreign-born groups." Dorothy Norman's "Making Democracy Permanent" was distributed in October. Also, a single paragraph promoting the FEPC in the *Writers' War Board Report* started a campaign in Massachusetts to retain the group as a government monitor.[103]

Board members secured writers for brief speeches on fair employment to be read over the public address systems in war plants across the country. The FEPC acknowledged the board's efforts as "some of the most effective cooperation we have received from outside supporters."[104] Later, as the fight over renewing the committee waged hot because powerful southern congressmen opposed any effort to assist African Americans, the WWB sent telegrams and letters to members of the House and Senate and to individuals and groups that might influence them. Board members used their contacts to promote a similar piece of legislation to establish a state FEPC in New York, the Ives-Quinn Bill, which passed in March 1945. Early in 1946, as the board was slated to go out of existence, the writers received more requests for assistance in the ongoing congressional fight to make the FEPC permanent. Although that effort failed and the federal agency closed its doors at the end of June, many state and local governments established FEPCs. These agencies and the U.S. Equal Employment Opportunity Commission, founded in 1965, continue to monitor the equal treatment of employees.[105]

The board unabashedly used the Fifth War Loan Drive to promote its campaign against racism. When Treasury officials asked its members for "special angles" on bond sales to use on radio shows, the WWB suggested that July 4 be established as a general tolerance day and created a slant to tie the issue of race to bond sales: "American boys abroad are living this American idea. They are all equal in the life they are living and the deaths they are facing. Bombs, torpedoes, and bullets are no respecter of race, creed, or color. Here at home we too are asked to make an all out effort. The responsibility for buying bonds and the privilege of buying bonds rests with each American citizen equally."[106] The writers outlined some ways that the media could support the tolerance theme. They used the NBC radio show *Mystery Theater* as one example: "This show dramatizes current mystery novels. A novel which contained the race tolerance ideas could be suggested to them for performance on July 4."[107] Although the board kept no record of whether or not its recommendations were followed, Julian Street observed that several programs that day used the WWB approach, and one quoted its theme verbatim.[108]

The board was particularly upset about an act of racial discrimination later that year against American servicemen of Japanese descent. On November 29 members of the American Legion in Hood River, Oregon, removed from their war memorial the names of sixteen local Japanese Americans then on active duty. Hobe Morrison apprised the board of the incident the following spring, and the group immediately launched protests. In March 1945 Clifton Fadiman wrote the editorial "Hood River Incident," and the *Writers' War Board Report* for April ran "An American Is an American Is an American," a short article praising the activities of loyal Japanese Americans and deploring racial attacks on them.[109]

The War Script of the Month for May was Millard Lampell's *Boy from Nebraska* about the homecoming of a Japanese American war veteran. The editorials distributed that month included "The Blood of Freedom" by Christopher LaFarge, a moving account of Japanese Americans who died defending the United States.[110]

BOOKS, BROADCASTS, AND OTHER TOLERANCE MATERIALS

To help with its campaign, the WWB promoted several books on racial tolerance. One was an interracial love story with a tragic ending for the black man and white woman. Written by southerner Lillian Smith, the novel takes its title from the antiracist song *Strange Fruit* that Billie Holiday made famous in 1939. The book sold well and received good reviews, spending several weeks on the *New York Times* fiction bestseller list in 1944. Board members plugged it through personal contacts and reviewed it favorably in WWB publications. When the work was banned from Boston bookstores in mid-March because of its language, they reacted quickly, feeling that the issue might simply be an excuse to suppress the theme of racial tolerance. They immediately sent telegrams of protest to Boston bookstores and to the local officials responsible for the ban. They also wrote to the sponsor of the *Kate Smith Hour* after the singer criticized the book on her radio show. When others wrote in echoing their comments, they dropped out of the argument. The group knew that the negative publicity would spur further public discussion of the book for some time.[111]

The WWB next turned its attention to *Earth and High Heaven* by Canadian novelist Gwethalyn Graham. A love story set in Montreal in 1942, it concerns the "polite" anti-Semitism a Jewish lawyer serving in the military and a young Protestant woman from a wealthy family must deal with in order to form a lasting relationship. Although popular magazines of the time had presented articles about anti-Semitism in Germany and had reported on the conditions that Russian troops found at the Majdanek concentration camp, they had not otherwise addressed the issue. Rita Kleeman reviewed the book favorably in her regular spot on the Radio Book Service of the National Council of Women, and the board took steps to see that *Earth and High Heaven* received the widest possible circulation. At the group's urging, *Collier's* magazine agreed to publish the novel in installments. Rex Stout subsequently sent a statement to its publishers on behalf of the board praising their "editorial forthrightness and simple honesty" in sanctioning the controversial theme.[112] In addition, it arranged for commentator Walter Winchell to compliment *Collier's* in his regular radio broadcast. Of course, the WWB utilized its own organs to promote the work, and Alan Green sent letters to a number of women commentators and to many members of the Advisory Council asking them to publicize it and to commend the magazine. In April 1945 Graham's book reached the top of the *New York Times* fiction bestseller list.[113]

The board also publicized a nonfiction work originally designed as an educational resource unit. *Probing Our Prejudices* by Hortense Powdermaker directly linked racial prejudice to Nazi barbarism and was an ideal fit for the WWB approach. The author described the work as "an attempt to help high school students become aware of their prejudices, to understand the nature, origin and effect of prejudices, and to suggest activities which can help reduce them."[114] Carl Carmer pointed out its value in an editorial, and the *Report* commended it. The group contacted women's commentator Martha Deane about giving a favorable review on the *Thursday Club* radio program and instigated written reviews in magazines including *Scholastic*, *Parents' Magazine*, and *School and Society*.[115] For younger audiences the Juvenile Writers Committee chose a series of books that made a forceful appeal for racial equality while providing enough entertainment to guarantee a wide audience. The WWB promoted them through mailings and radio reviews by committee chair Kleeman. For a time it even attempted to arrange a juvenile radio show to present books and propaganda messages geared to youngsters, but the program never became a reality.[116]

The WWB disseminated its message through radio broadcasts as well as books. In the summer of 1943 Mayor La Guardia organized a committee to plan a series of radio programs in the New York City area called *Unity at Home—Victory Abroad*. The Radio Committee of the WWB helped by supplying seven new scripts, two of them dealing with prejudice: *What's Wrong with Me?* by Eve Merriam, poet and author of children's books, and Langston Hughes's *In the Service of My Country*, which depicted different races working side by side during the building of a highway in Alaska. Both were later distributed as part of the War Script of the Month series.[117] The board also provided some scripts to the *New World a-Comin'* program produced by a local station. It was so effective that its sponsor, the YMCA, won a place on the "Negro Education Honor Roll for 1944" for presenting "the most forthright radio dramatization of Negro life and race relations on the air today."[118] One of the WWB scripts it aired was Mitchell Grayson's *There Are Things to Be Done*, a dramatization of a work of the same name by Lillian Smith. Both presented her powerful plea for her native South to break from its legacy of prejudice and discrimination, and both offered practical ways to promote the fair treatment of African Americans. The play became another War Script of the Month.[119] That fall the board enlisted twenty writers to create spot announcements opposing religious prejudice and racial discrimination. Offered free to every commercial radio station in the country, forty-five of them made it on the air.[120]

The board trumpeted its racial tolerance campaign in all of its regular publications. Among the first pieces that the board distributed in August 1943 when it began its monthly editorial service was "Democracy's Way with a Problem," an appeal for racial tolerance by editor Robert Duffus.[121] The following March he wrote about the dangers of prejudice in "Too Hot to Handle," and he included *The Races of Mankind* in the April mailing. In May board member Jean Poletti emphasized the stupidity of racial discrimination in "Blind Prejudice," and Robert Landry's "Bigotry Must Not Win the War" appeared in July. In November "We Discovered America" reminded the public of the diverse racial and cultural heritage of the United States. The final packet of WWB editorials that went out in December 1945 contained an article warning readers not to have "Open Mouths, Closed Minds."[122]

When members found a good speech on the topic, they frequently placed at least a summary of it in *Brief House Organ Items*. The December issue contained one written by prominent clergyman Harry Emerson Fosdick, "Will We Solve Our Negro Problem?" Many corporate publications carried the article, and it proved to be one of the most popular *Brief Items* pieces.[123] The first issue of *Brief Army Camp Items* in March 1944 included it, and two months later the publication ran "We Have

Racial Equity—Do You?" over the signature of actress Helen Hayes.[124] The *Writers' War Board Report* addressed the issue almost every month. One article equated racial stereotyping with bigotry:

> Writers play a considerable part in furthering the "old stock" swindle in picking out only Anglo-Saxon names for their attractive characters and marrying them only in Protestant churches and giving them only inferiority-emphasizing relationships to menial Negroes, ignorant working class Catholics, shyster or comic Jews, slovenly if picturesque Mexicans, and so on.
>
> In short, the time seems to have arrived for writers to stop shaking their heads about other peoples' race bigotry and examine their own very considerable contributions to it.[125]

Although board members encouraged authors, editors, and publishers to generate articles on racism for national magazines and other media outlets, they received little cooperation. While newspapers were willing to carry occasional editorials on the subject, most magazines shied away from the unpopular and controversial topic. In June 1944 one picture showing blacks and whites working together accompanied a Kleeman article on housekeeping in *Redbook*, and in April 1945 a single article on the need for tolerance appeared in the *American Legion Magazine*. An attempt to interest the NEA newspaper syndicate in a piece by Langston Hughes on discrimination against blacks in job placement fell through for the same reason.[126]

ENLISTING RADIO WRITERS IN THE CAMPAIGN

As a general rule WWB members preferred to educate and influence those who controlled the contents of radio programs instead of providing scripts for individual broadcasts. On May 31, 1944, they found an opportunity to sway industry insiders after Dan Golenpaul, producer of the radio quiz show *Information Please*, came to discuss the problems and possibilities of introducing racial tolerance into the fabric of commercial radio shows. He suggested that the group convince radio writers and advertisers that they could make money by attracting an audience interested in racial harmony.[127] Board members heard him out but were skeptical about his approach. Nevertheless, their talk with him spurred them to organize several meetings for radio writers on racial issues.

The first took place at Fadiman's New York home on June 15. Over twenty writers attended, and a few others sent their apologies. After Fadiman addressed the group, a frank discussion followed on whether or not to use a direct approach to combat racism. Scriptwriter Jerry McGill argued for it, condemning bigots and hatemongers like Gerald L. K. Smith, minister, politician, and radio personality: "We must expose our enemies, damn them and brand them. The Gerald Smiths change their lines from month to month. We must keep abreast of those changes and attack them all."[128] Others suggested a more subtle approach that paralleled the WWB's own point of view. At least one writer came away convinced. Goodman Ace, author and star of the popular radio show *Easy Aces*, wrote Fadiman, "Last night I was awakened to the cause . . . , and I am sure we can contribute something to the fight."[129]

The day after the gathering, a much larger, more formal meeting was held with fifty-four radio writers and sixty-five freelance authors. Stout addressed the group, urging them to incorporate the racial tolerance theme wherever possible rather than occasionally giving a blatant plug that the public might readily identify as propaganda. A few days later Green made a similar request in a meeting with eighteen editors of juvenile books.[130] The writers who attended the WWB meetings expressed interest in receiving additional material on race-related subjects. Accordingly, through the summer and into September the board prepared a series of special mailings for educational and propaganda purposes. One of the pamphlets was *They Got the Blame: The Story of Scapegoats in History* by Kenneth Gould, which examined the persecution of minority groups over time. Another was Henrietta Wireman's *By Different Boats*. It reiterated the idea that Americans are united as one people even though they come from many different places.[131]

The board also sent out *Negroes and the War*, an OWI pamphlet on the involvement of African Americans in the war and what they stood to gain by an American victory.[132] Because it had met with the same congressional opposition that resulted in the banning of *The Races of Mankind*, the OWI had chosen not to distribute it and had destroyed most of the copies, but the WWB was able to secure enough to use for its purpose. For radio programs aimed in whole or in part at the South, the board provided reprints of Lillian Smith's *There Are Things to Be Done*. The group also distributed scientific studies like *The Races of Mankind* as well as other materials on tolerance including a series of commercial advertisements put out by the Institute for American Democracy.[133]

One hiccup occurred when the writers of the radio program *Mr. District Attorney* tried to put the board's suggestions into effect in December. The storyline concerned a fictional outburst of racial antagonism in a school fomented by an advocate of "100% Americanism." Those who promoted this idea defined Americans as white Anglo-Saxon Protestants and viewed people of other ethnic groups and religious persuasions as "foreigners." The episode ended with the suggestion that the listening audience read *Probing Our Prejudices*. When the program received unexpected criticism, the WWB fought to counteract it by stimulating letters of approval to the show's producers and sponsors in order to insure continued treatment of the racial tolerance theme on the radio.[134] Luckily the negative response did not prove to be typical; in fact, the impact of the board's suggestions on some of the daytime radio serials was sufficient to be noticed in the *Des Moines Register*, which remarked on the increased "social consciousness" of the programs. The editorial ended with this affirmation: "Don't look now, but we suspect Rex Stout's Writers' War Board had a lot to do with this striking transformation."[135]

In the spring of 1945 the Radio Committee started the mailings once again, issuing a variety of new materials like the *ABC's of Scapegoating*, a pamphlet on the dangers inherent in singling out one or more segments of the population for blame and censure.[136] In a letter to the radio writers, Hobe Morrison reiterated the importance of the tolerance theme: "Because race and religious hatred is a weapon of our fascist enemies, because they are using it systematically and skillfully, not only to disrupt us in war, but also to divide us in the coming peace, it is one of the most vital issues of our time." He insisted that authors could play a critical role in the campaign: "Now more than ever, writers have an obligation to employ their craft in the fight against bigotry and for our cherished

American ideals. The board believes that radio writers without altering or impairing the honesty or entertainment value of their programs are in a unique position to do this."[137]

EXPLOITING THE COMIC BOOK CONNECTION

In December the board reiterated the plea it had made to radio scriptwriters, this time urging comic book publishers to weave racial tolerance material into their stories: "While your readers cannot be expected to accept heroes or heroines belonging to minority groups, it is possible to give subsidiary characters Jewish names or depict them as Negroes, etc. Above all, along the line of racial hatred, stereotypes should be avoided. The Catholic should not be portrayed as superstitious, the Jew avaricious, humble, aggressive, or the Negro as a menial or comic."[138] The Comics Committee was notably active in the board's endeavor against racism, helping to develop a series of newspaper cartoons attacking vicious rumors about minority groups. Drawn by political cartoonist Eric Godal, *Don't Listen to Him* featured characters like "The Destroyer," who "eggs on his followers by blaming their trouble on innocent scapegoats, Negroes, Catholics, Jews, or foreign born—an old Hitler trick. His goal is riots and confusion—power for himself." Some five hundred newspapers wrote to the WWB to obtain the free mats of this series.[139]

Other committee projects involved overseeing the development of one article and two stories on the tolerance theme in 1944 for the winter edition of *Comic Cavalcade*. The article "Filipinos Are People" distinguished "good" East Asians from the "bad" Japanese. In the story "A Tale of a City," superhero Green Lantern confronted a racist during the Christmas season. Touting the xenophobic slogan "100% Americanism," the villain had attacked Jews and had taken control of several women's committees that resembled Mothers' Groups. Green Lantern triumphed over the anti-Semite and his evil ways with the assistance of black and white men dressed as street corner Santa Clauses.[140]

Another story, "A Ride in the Sky [The 99th Squadron]," features Hop Harrigan, a fictional pilot who is "America's Ace of the Airways." He undertakes a mission with a group of African American pilots who are part of the Tuskegee Airmen. Harrigan converses with an arrogant Nazi general as they take him to be incarcerated in a prisoner of war camp. First Hop informs the German that his life is in the hands of a Jewish pilot named Izzy Epstein. Then he shows the general three movies about the work of the 99th Squadron. Impressed with the first film, which shows American planes shooting down Luftwaffe aircraft, the Nazi comments, "Those pilots of the 99th must be . . . no doubt men of a superior race." To the shock of the German the next movie shows the black members of the squadron disembarking from their planes. The third film documents the fact that the general's own plane was shot down by the 99th before his capture. Finally, the racist discovers that his life was saved after the crash by blood transfusions from two soldiers, one Jewish and the other African American. Hop sarcastically concludes the sequence by telling the Nazi, "So much for your 'superior race' nonsense." The Hop Harrigan story also appeared in the *CIO News*, a publication of the Congress of Industrial Organizations with a circulation of half a million.[141]

A second triumph for the Comics Committee was a brief biography of black heroine Sojourner Truth. Although the WWB had some trouble preparing the article, it appeared in the summer of 1945. At first the board tried to solicit assistance from the National Association for the Advancement of Colored People, but the organization apparently offered no help.[142] Next the group contacted M. C. Gaines, the publisher of *Wonder Woman Comics*, and suggested that the former slave was an appropriate subject for one of the "Wonder Women of History" segments included in the magazine. Gaines provided the WWB with a draft that met with its general approval, but to insure that the piece hit the right tone, the writers sent it to the New York State Bureau for Intercultural Relations. Helen Traeger of that agency responded with a blistering critique. She argued that the panels "inspire repugnance" by perpetuating stereotypes associated with "illiteracy and ridicule." She further criticized the story for its inclusion of the word "nigger" and for its portrayal of one slaveholder as kindly. Chastened, the WWB and Gaines made the suggested revisions.[143]

While these comic book presentations show progress in the fight against racial prejudice and indicate the WWB's sincerity and commitment to the campaign, they also reveal the limitations of the board's vision and, perhaps, the extent of what they could achieve in the mid-1940s.

Sojourner Truth is able to succeed, but even the revised essay on her life implies that she could not have done so without the help of white people sympathetic to her cause. Furthermore her story introduced no other African American character. The article on good and bad Asians, which Fadiman called a "fine job," did not distinguish between Filipinos and Japanese. Because both groups were stereotypically depicted with bright yellow skin and buckteeth, American soldiers could not identify the Filipino hero until he spoke in broken English. As for the story entitled "A Ride in the Sky [The 99th Squadron]," none of the Tuskegee Airmen appeared with hero Hop Harrigan or had a speaking part. Readers saw them only as small figures on a movie screen. In addition, the Jewish pilot was no more than a disembodied voice from the cockpit.[144]

THE MYTH THAT THREATENS AMERICA

Carrying out one of the board's most important projects in 1944, the Committee to Combat Race Hatred sponsored a study to gather convincing evidence of racial prejudice in the media. During the summer the Bureau of Applied Social Research at Columbia University agreed to survey and analyze all of the media—motion pictures, stage plays, radio programs, magazine articles, cartoons, newsreels, and advertisements—produced that year. Evaluators specifically checked to see how frequently writers and editors used racial stereotypes such as the "avaricious Jew" and the "lazy Negro." The results of the Columbia University survey, said to be "the most comprehensive . . . ever attempted," supported the contention of the WWB that writers of the time often reinforced common misconceptions in their depictions of minority characters.[145]

The WWB committee then considered the most effective way to use the unimpeachable data to change the status quo, and it came up with the idea of putting on a show for an audience composed of almost six hundred of the leading writers, editors, publishers, illustrators, artists, and technicians in the entertainment and communications industries. The board persuaded top-notch authors and entertainers to participate in the dramatic, antiracist sketches and songs. Recognizing the difficulties of presenting such a production to a sophisticated and discerning audience, the members debated how to handle it. Some argued that the event should present a serious exposition of factual data while others thought a less heavy-handed approach would be more acceptable. The final script was something of a compromise between the two factions, and it worked almost to perfection.[146] Those who attended learned about racial stereotyping and became indoctrinated with the WWB's ideas on dealing with prejudice. Green correctly regarded the program as one of the best demonstrations of the board's ability to marshal assistance from the ranks of the rich and famous and as "one of the most lastingly useful things" that the group ever accomplished.[147]

Drama critic, author, and war correspondent John Mason Brown served as master of ceremonies and narrator of *The Myth That Threatens America* on January 12, 1945, at the Hotel Barbizon Plaza in New York City. After an opening address by Stout, a carefully prepared "Education Please" quiz was presented as a takeoff on Fadiman's popular radio show *Information Please*. The panelists included playwright Moss Hart, editor and author Carl Van Doren, publisher and columnist Bennett Cerf, and striptease artist Gypsy Rose Lee, who had become a campaigner for racial tolerance. They answered questions such as "What percentage of the American population is not native, white, Protestant?" The answer, which surprised the audience, was 55.3 percent.[148] An overview of the Columbia survey results as well as some basic information was delivered in this fashion. According to the show-business trade paper *Variety*, the panel gave a "sock" performance.[149]

The event included the song "Free and Equal Blues" performed by actress Benay Venuta and speeches by anthropologist Margaret Mead, associate curator of the American Museum of Natural History; Eric Johnston, president of the U.S. Chamber of Commerce; and bestselling nonfiction author John Roy Carlson. Mead's approach was educational: "We must think of the American people as composed of people of all types in the world—tall and short, light and dark, with thin features and with broad features." Johnson made an appeal to pragmatism in "Prejudice Is Bad for Business." Carlson asserted that racial discrimination in America was dangerous in a speech entitled "It Can Lead to Civil War."[150] Christopher LaFarge gave the closing remarks.

One reviewer observed that the evening "hit its peak" with "Ol' Man Author," Oscar Hammerstein's parody of his 1927 hit "Ol' Man River."

Using humor to criticize writers for perpetuating racial and cultural myths, a quartet of stereotypical characters introduce themselves. While Irishman Mike, who wears a bright red wig, may not be very smart, he likes to fight, drink, and eat potatoes. As a Jew Ben is a "scheming scamp" who loves money and blintzes. Black Eb'nezer is a happy guy who spends his time stealing chickens and playing craps. Angelo rounds out the group as a gun-toting, bank-robbing gangster who eats garlic and spaghetti. The four have several complaints:

We are as old as the Mississippi,
Stereotyped as inferior men.
We are condemned to be dumb and dippy:
Angelo, Mike, Eb'nezer, and Ben. . . .

We are the men of amusing races,
Fated to be eternal jokes.
Dialect men with amusing faces,
Never are we like other folks.[151]

As stereotypes they feel that they "need a corner to go and die in," but they must continue to exist as long as the writers' "harmful foolin' / It keeps on droolin' along." Their refrain emphasizes the song's main theme. The four characters will never have individualized, well-rounded personalities as long as "Ol' man author, / He keeps on writin' us wrong!"[152]

The production was a big success. The *Variety* reviewer complained only that the periodic levity of the master of ceremonies was out of keeping with the serious nature of the material presented. He summed up, "The application of showmanship in the all out effort to battle 'The Myth That Threatens America' was a wise one and the whole idea of directing it at a few hundred who have the power to mold public opinion ties in with the WWB program to mobilize its own."[153] Landry, chairman of the Committee to Combat Racial Hatred, later stated, "This may well have been our absolute high point of massed impact upon opinion makers."[154] The Hammerstein song was publicized and widely reprinted. Its distribution became one of the board's race tolerance projects. The group considered the results of the event to be so good that repetitions of the complete show were planned. Although duplicating the original performance was impossible since it had an all-star cast, the basic script that Hammerstein had arranged and directed was utilized in subsequent shows both in the United States and Europe. The board also distributed to the public a similar production. It included some sections of the original program that could easily be delivered by local performers.[155]

The board decided to compile and publicize the shocking data gleaned from the Columbia University survey so that the media industry and individual writers could use it as a baseline to measure improvement. Accordingly, WWB member Jack Goodman ghostwrote a twelve-page pamphlet entitled *How Writers Perpetuate Stereotypes*. Using the survey results, he ranked each type of media in the order of its use of stereotypes. On a comparative basis plays were ranked best although even some of them portrayed stereotypical characters. They were followed by novels and then motion pictures. Worst by far were short stories. Goodman presented impressive evidence to explain his rankings. The Bureau of Applied Social Research at Columbia had surveyed 185 short stories from popular magazines. The group found only sixteen black and ten Jewish characters and "subtle disparagement of minorities was noted throughout.... 'Heart' motivations such as love, marriage, affection, patriotism, idealism, and justice were attributed to Anglo-Saxon characters."[156] On the other hand, non-Anglo-Saxons had "head" motivations like power, dominance, self-interest, and the acquisition of money. Goodman concluded, "Anglo-Saxons received better treatment than minority and foreign groups: in frequency of appearance, importance in story, approval and disapproval, status and occupation, and in traits."[157] Once the WWB's *Report* publicized it, hundreds of writers asked for a copy, and the board honored each request.[158] While the results of the study were certainly no news to black and white radicals who had been making similar assertions for at least ten years, it was a major event that brought the issue into the literary mainstream. The importance of the survey can be judged by the fact that it is still cited in footnotes and bibliographies in the twenty-first century.[159]

CHAMPION OF MINORITIES

Late in March 1945 the U.S. Department of Justice requested that Robert Landry's committee assist with a special event to reduce prejudice against foreign-born citizens. The national celebration of "I Am an American Day" was set for May 20, 1945. The board publications promoted it in several articles like "Thank You, Americans," ostensibly written by recently naturalized actress Ingrid Bergman. It ran in the April editions of *Brief House Organ Items* and *Brief Army Camp Items* and appeared later in *Photoplay* magazine. The Joe Palooka cartoon in both versions emphasized the theme as well. The WWB editorial for May included a statement of support for the celebration by committee member Jean Poletti, and the *Report* that month contained an article praising the virtues of naturalized citizens under the title "How about an Oath for Old Citizens?"[160]

The group also supplied scripts on the theme. Because board members felt that their registered writers did not have enough time to produce new ones, they turned to two plays previously distributed in their War Script of the Month series: *These Are Americans* by Chet Huntley and Ernest Martin and *Foreigners Settled America* by Gretta Baker. The former is a fact-based story about the contributions of Mexican Americans to the United States, and the latter concerns two young people, one who is a first-generation American and another whose ancestors arrived on the *Mayflower*. Both learn that all Americans could correctly be termed "foreigners." The board promptly sent the scripts to the Justice Department, which rushed them out quickly so that local performers could rehearse them for presentation on May 20. In an associated project the WWB secured Claude Rains as the principal speaker for a large "I Am an American Day" outdoor rally in Springfield, Massachusetts. The actor, who had become a naturalized American citizen in 1939, gave an address written for him by board member Alan Green. It went over so well that the Springfield Mayor's Committee worked to have it entered in the *Congressional Record*. Finally, the WWB Radio Committee took quick action to insert the "I Am an American" theme into radio spots for the Seventh War Loan Drive (May 14–June 30, 1945) then being held.[161]

In the fall of 1944 Rex Stout had asked the most active WWB members to identify the group's major objectives from that point until the end of the war. They ranked bringing the war to a successful conclusion first, but most of them said that the achievement of racial tolerance should be second. Christopher LaFarge explained that even though the campaign against prejudice would extend far into the future, the board considered it a major problem "because it is in a dynamic state and may go boom in our faces any day now."[162] Consequently, even as the WWB wound down its wartime activities, it continued to emphasize racial tolerance, especially in its war scripts. In February 1945 the board issued Ben Kagan's *Scapegoats in History*, which was based on Kenneth Gould's *They Got the Blame*. Two other previously mentioned plays, *There Are Things to Be Done* and *Boy from Nebraska*, went out in March and May respectively. The October script was Arnold Hartley's *Dr. Hopkins' Atomic Bomb*, a documentary about the danger to democracy inherent in the American educational system, which frequently demonstrated prejudice against minority groups. The War Script of the Month series ended in December with *Hate, Incorporated* by Caye Christian, a direct attack on racial hatred and the people who profit from it.[163]

Considering the other campaigns that the WWB had to juggle simultaneously, the group's effort to condemn racial hatred was probably as extensive as it could be. Members regarded it as one of the board's most significant projects even though it was not large in scope, did not produce much controversy, and did not develop as a major campaign until 1944. By then the group had come to believe that the situation had reached emergency levels. They were no doubt persuaded by increasing evidence of racial animosity such as the 1943 race riots and the prevalence of domestic racist propaganda. In his private meeting with radio writers, Clifton Fadiman had spoken of the "organized race hatred which may soon drive this country into civil war."[164] If the situation did not prove to be quite that catastrophic, the need to promote racial tolerance was unquestionable. In July 1945 the outspoken *Pittsburgh Courier* paid tribute to the WWB as "one of the greatest champions of racial and religious minorities."[165] In retrospect this pioneering effort may well represent the group's greatest long-term contribution to America's liberal democratic culture.

Overall the domestic campaigns in which the Writers' War Board participated had a high rate of success, and they helped to shape the domestic culture of wartime America by focusing the public's attention on uniting in a common cause. With the assistance of a variety of government agencies and private groups, the board urged all Americans to faithfully carry out their jobs, abide by federal regulations such as rationing and price controls, and financially support the country's war effort. Their propaganda reinforced the policies of the Roosevelt administration and encouraged a "can do" attitude. The board's own campaign to curtail prejudice achieved a significant reduction in the media's portrayal of stereotypical characters, and it encouraged African Americans and other minorities to rally behind the nation as it focused on achieving victory over fascism. It also made writers more aware of the impact they had on national attitudes from changing spending habits to accepting women in the workplace to questioning discriminatory practices and long-held prejudices. The uncertainties of wartime disrupted traditional ways of thinking and acting and created an opening for new points of view that the WWB eagerly exploited.

CHAPTER 4

PROPAGANDA ON AMERICA'S ALLIES AND ENEMIES

THE UNITED STATES recognized that it could not win the war without the cooperation of its allies, and in 1942 almost fifty countries outside the Axis block formed the United Nations. This military alliance developed humanitarian programs and served as the foundation of the present-day international peacekeeping organization of the same name. Since most Americans knew little about other countries, several groups including the Writers' War Board began an informational initiative to promote understanding. Their job was twofold: they worked with members of the foreign press to see that the United States and its soldiers had a good image abroad, and they designed materials for civilians at home on each of America's major allies. Board members wanted to insure international cooperation not only to bring the war to a successful conclusion but also to lay a good foundation for a postwar organization that could prevent other worldwide conflicts. Ongoing relief efforts also demanded the cooperation of the United States and its global neighbors. An article in the *Writers' War Board Report* explained that meeting the needs of war-ravaged populations that did not have adequate food, clothing, and shelter was not only "simple humanity" but also "good, selfish common sense" because desperation might breed chaos.[1] In addition to these projects, the WWB participated in several campaigns to promote hatred for America's enemies. The group did not often target Japan because its members felt that the surprise attack on Pearl Harbor had done a better job of arousing animosity for the Japanese than any organization could have achieved.[2] Although the board occasionally vilified Japan and its leaders, most of its propaganda focused on the brutality of the Germans as a whole.

PROMOTING THE ALLIES

In 1942 the Office of Civilian Defense and the Office of Facts and Figures requested the WWB's help with a special event to recognize America's allies. In conjunction with Flag Day on June 14, the two government agencies planned to celebrate United Nations Day by honoring the flag of each American ally at ceremonies held across the United States. Well in advance board members recruited prominent writers to produce works for the occasion. One script by Erik Barnouw went to radio stations, and the WWB widely distributed two others, a play by lyricist Otto Harbach and an outdoor pageant by playwright Maxwell Anderson. The success of the board in arranging for top-flight material in this instance helped to establish its reputation for quality assistance delivered on time.[3]

The day before the event President Franklin Roosevelt established the Office of War Information. When the agency was put in charge of handling United Nations Day the following year, it turned to the board once again. The group's newly organized Committee on Speeches and Speakers promptly arranged for several addresses including one each from radio writers Ruth Gordon and Theodore Ferro. The War Script of the Month Committee marked the occasion with a play on international organization that it distributed in June, Michael Greenwood's *Reminder to the Free*. Four board members contributed other scripts. Oscar Hammerstein authored and staged *Hitler Had a Vision*, a pageant performed in Washington before a distinguished audience. Russel Crouse and Robert Colwell combined their talents on a dramatic presentation entitled *An American's Progress*, which received nationwide distribution. In addition, Alan Green wrote part of a script for an event held at Radio City Music Hall in New York.[4]

The WWB produced a number of other materials for United Nations Day as well. Rex Stout and Samuel Grafton each wrote a speech that the American Legion Women's Auxiliary aired on a network broadcast it sponsored. Board members Stout, Grafton, Colwell, and Landry as well as author Ruth Jordan and playwright Elmer Rice prepared editorials on the subject that went to 750 local newspapers. These pieces met with such a positive reception that the WWB decided to begin its monthly editorial service. The New York writers got the idea for their *Brief House Organ Items* in much the same way. After the group instigated articles on United Nations Day, the OWI sent them to several thousand major corporations, and many of the in-house publications of those companies reprinted them. The results were sufficiently impressive that the board took note and began its monthly publication for house organs in July. The board also received help from twenty authors around the country who wrote materials for distribution in their local regions. The OWI considered the June 1943 celebration a major success and was impressed by the "exceptionally effective" work of the WWB.[5]

That year the group participated in several other projects to inform Americans about the Allies. The United Nations Information Office asked the board to prepare a pamphlet on the European governments forced into exile. Around the same time the U.S. Office of the Coordinator of Inter-American Affairs requested that WWB members arrange for a series of pamphlets to stimulate hemispheric understanding and unity, each of them on a different Central or South American country. The board developed both sets of materials for the government to print and distribute to schools, clubs, churches, and the like. To promote global cooperation from every angle, the WWB tried to appeal to all citizens including children, teenagers, and young adults. The group contacted author Herbert Zim about writing an article for the yearly update of a children's encyclopedia, the *Book of Knowledge Annual 1943*, and he contributed "The Price of Freedom." The WWB also asked its Comics Committee for assistance that summer. After the small group met with representatives of comic book publishers, a new story sequence emerged. Beginning in September 1943 and continuing in subsequent issues Street and Smith publishers introduced in the *Air Aces* comic book the "Four Musketeers," who represented the four major Allied nations. Although each musketeer was vulnerable alone, together the four were unbeatable.[6]

To further encourage global understanding, WWB members felt that they could not pass up the opportunity to promote a book by Wendell Willkie. In 1942 the former Republican presidential candidate had spent more than six weeks making a well-publicized trip around the world as Roosevelt's representative, stopping in North Africa, the Middle East, the Soviet Union, and China. Willkie chronicled his travels, meetings with world leaders, encounters with native citizens and American soldiers, and impressions of America's allies in *One World*, which offered a strong plea for a postwar world organization. He was such a prominent figure that he needed little assistance in arranging interviews and obtaining comments on his book, which became an instant bestseller. Nevertheless, the board helped persuade the Council on Books in Wartime to adopt the volume as one of its "imperative" books, an honor that brought Willkie's work and his cogent arguments even more recognition.[7]

Despite its efforts, the board was aware of latent American hostility toward three important allies: China, the Union of Soviet Socialist Republics, and Great Britain. It publicized Pearl Buck's *American Unity and Asia* not only because the book condemned racism in the United States but also because it helped to enlighten the public about China and India. Working in collaboration with the Council for Democracy, in 1942 the board sent a copy to every member of Congress and arranged for radio commentary on it.[8] The following year the WWB generated pressure for the repeal of the Chinese Exclusion Act of 1882, which prevented virtually all immigration to the United States by the Chinese, who found it discriminatory and offensive. The *Writers' War Board Report* carried a brief article advocating reversal of the law, and the board asked J. C. Furnas, a writer for the *Saturday Evening Post*, to persuade the magazine to print an editorial on the subject. Congress repealed the act on December 17, 1943.[9]

Board members also made a sincere effort to promote America's second most important ally, the Soviet Union, but they did not achieve much success because the public was suspicious of communism and of Joseph Stalin's dictatorship. Nevertheless, the group persisted. One of its first projects began with a cable that arrived in July 1942 from Alexander Fadeev (also spelled Fadeyev), a staunch Stalinist who served as secretary of the Union of Soviet Writers, an organization he had helped to found.[10] It was fairly large since membership in it was a prerequisite for publication. Fadeev requested a variety of materials to show the people of the USSR what the United States was doing about the war. He proposed that the Soviet writers send similar material in exchange, thus increasing mutual understanding. WWB members were delighted to have this opportunity for partnership with fellow writers, and Robert Landry and Jack Goodman immediately assembled an appropriate collection of pamphlets, books, films, short stories, poetry, and radio scripts about the war. In return the Soviet writers provided the WWB with a series of cabled reports containing atrocity stories, war literature, commentary on Soviet life in wartime, and the like. The board had them translated and got a considerable number of the pieces into print.[11]

The two groups continued to send more material back and forth throughout 1942 and early 1943, but the quality of the items the WWB received began to decline after the first batch. The board was unable to use statistical reports and other materials cleared by Stalin's censors because they held little interest for American audiences. In June 1943, when repeated requests by the WWB for more human-interest stories went unfulfilled once again, Stout informed the Russian writers that the use of their work was insufficiently widespread to warrant the expense and trouble of further cables.[12] Two other board efforts to promote the Soviet Union in 1942 and 1943 fizzled even before they got off the ground. Believing that the Germans would win the Battle of Stalingrad, the WWB prepared an elaborate tribute to the Russian heroes. It was to be aired when the city surrendered; however, Russian troops held off the Germans, and the tribute never saw the light of day.[13] The following year the Soviet government gave its approval for twenty Russian war heroes to tour the United States, and the WWB established the Russian Committee under the chairmanship of Goodman to handle preparations for the trip. After it had made several arrangements, the Russians inexplicably canceled the trip.[14]

Despite these setbacks, the board did what it could to foster American support for the Soviet Union. In March 1943 it selected as a War Script of the Month Sandra Michael's *My Brother Lives in Stalingrad*, a story of the wartime sufferings of the Russian people. The board also asked dramatist Robert Ardrey to ghostwrite a brief first-person biography of seventeen-year-old gunner Konstantin Konstantinov, who received some media attention when the vessel he worked on came to the United States to pick up munitions and medical supplies for Russian War Relief. As a soldier in the Red Army he had received an award for valor after being wounded four times. Novelist Booth Tarkington, yet another author in the WWB's stable of Pulitzer Prize winners, composed a letter to him about ways the United States and the Soviet Union could work together to defeat the Germans and build world peace. The two compositions were published together in September 1943 in *Boys' Life*.[15] The following June *Brief Army Camp Items* carried the article "Why We Must Get Along with Russia" signed by Joseph E. Davies, former American ambassador to the Soviet Union. The July War Script of the Month continued the theme with Norman Rosten's *Concerning the Red Army*, which chronicled the valiant deeds of Russian soldiers.[16]

Early in 1945 the WWB became disturbed by public opinion polls that showed (1) only 10 percent of Americans were well-informed about Russia; (2) most Americans identified Russia with communism, which they disliked; and (3) approximately one-third of the U.S. population thoroughly distrusted the Soviets.[17] The board promptly revived the Russian Committee that had been dormant since the failure of the War Heroes Tour. It prepared material for each of the WWB publications to use as the war in Europe drew to a close. William Nelson wrote a speech entitled "Why the U.S. and Russia Must Be Friends," and WWB member Alan Green produced another one along the same lines, "Not Just Allies—Friends." He also composed the April 1945 editorial "Bad News for Mars," which emphasized American-Russian cooperation. The May War Script of the Month was *Death and Dr. Burdenko*, partly written by pro-Soviet journalist Walter Duranty, who had lived in Moscow for more than a decade and was familiar with the accomplishments of eminent neurosurgeon Nikolay Burdenko, who was born in 1876 to Russian peasants. It presented a highly favorable picture of the development of Soviet Russia from the tsarist days of the doctor's childhood to its development as one of the major Allied nations in World War II.[18]

In addition, the committee arranged for the promotion of the 1945 book *These Are the Russians* by *Life* magazine correspondent Richard Lauterbach, and his favorable article, "Russians Are People—and a Lot Like Us," appeared in *Brief House Organ Items* in May. Designed to stimulate a feeling of kinship between the people of the United States and the Soviet Union, it claimed that the two had a similar fondness for gadgets, speed, sports, jokes, and material progress. Lauterbach included gratitude in his recitation of Russia's virtues: "Every Russian I met was fully aware how much American help meant to their nation when things were black in 1941–42." He reported two other observations that were just as certain to win the approval of most Americans: "There has been a real rebirth of religious feeling in Russia. . . . The desire for peace is firm and deep too." His concluding statement was one of the WWB's main contentions: "Americans and Russians have cooperated well in fighting a war against Fascism and oppression: there is no reason why they can't remain good friends and fight together for peace and plenty."[19]

The board felt that it should not only praise the Soviets but also defend their government against two often-repeated accusations. One had to do with its failure to enter the war against Japan and the other with its refusal to allow United States forces to use Siberia for their base of operation in the Eastern Theater. In his June 1945 editorial "Russia in the Pacific," Robert Bellaire, a United Press correspondent who covered the Pacific war, asserted that the Soviet Union could not possibly have entered the war against Japan because her troops were busy stopping the German invasion of their country. Furthermore, he believed that the Soviet Union had done the United States a favor by keeping American troops out of Siberia, and he argued that the Russians had forced a large contingent of Japanese soldiers to remain stationed in the area, far away from Americans fighting in the Pacific:

> The fact that our use of Russian bases against Japan would have inevitably opened a new fighting front hundreds of miles in length, far from Allied sources of supply and conveniently near to Japan's is the best argument in favor of Russia's past policy. . . . By waging merely a war of nerves against Japan, Russia has accomplished for the Allies all that could have been accomplished under the circumstances. By never making it clear whether they intended to move against Japan before Germany's defeat, Russia forced Japan to concentrate millions of her best troops along the Siberian frontier where they were unable to interfere with our 6000 mile march across the Pacific.[20]

Pro-Soviet material distributed by the WWB through periodic mailings either relentlessly complimented the Soviet people or defended their government's war policies. Even with the early stages of the Cold War underway in December 1945, the board continued to present Russia in a favorable light. The final issue of *Brief Army Camp Items* that month contained a piece by George Fielding Eliot, who found the lifting of Soviet censorship on news dispatches to be "a step in the growth of confidence."[21]

PROMOTING GOOD RELATIONS WITH THE BRITISH

Anti-British feeling was another matter. Although Great Britain was America's most important ally in World War II, the public could not help but remember that the British were the villains in America's struggle for independence. For that reason the board decided to focus on publicizing the contribution of the English to the war effort. Just as WWB members began to feel that they were making headway in their campaign, a leading American literary figure publicly disparaged the British in September 1942. Before a speaking engagement in Toronto, novelist Theodore Dreiser made headlines by complaining that Winston Churchill "has no intention of opening a second front. He's afraid the Communists will rule the world so he does nothing except send thousands of Canadians to be slaughtered at Dieppe. He didn't send the English. They stay at home and do nothing. Nothing!" He chastised the British for their "unbelievable gall and brass" and admitted, "I would rather see the Germans in England than those damned aristocratic, horse-riding snobs there now. The English have done nothing in this war thus far except borrow money, planes, and men from the United States. . . . They are lousy."[22] Board members, who were both surprised by the author's comments and concerned about the effect they might have, immediately struck back. They recounted British heroics and castigated Dreiser, suggesting that his remarks were treasonous: "Not being lawyers, we do not know whether Theodore Dreiser's utterance was treasonable in the legal sense, but certainly our enemies would pay him well for his disservice to our country's cause. We profoundly regret that an American writer of Mr. Dreiser's eminence should thus insult and offend our allies and commit so shameful an act of sabotage against our government and people."[23]

Stung, the author wrote a letter to the WWB asserting that what he had said was misinterpreted. However, his blustery note was more accusatory than apologetic. He charged WWB members with "servility to British Toryism"; declared that they had "set themselves up as prosecutor, court, and jury and condemned me to the newspaper hell prepared for the anti-capitalistic class"; and demanded that they make a public apology.[24] The group considered the demand absurd since Dreiser argued in the same letter that British Tories were "more responsible than anyone else" for bringing on the war and claimed that he saw no difference between Churchill's colonial policy and Hitler's firing squads.[25] Board members made no reply, but the objections they had raised earlier triggered sharp criticism of Dreiser by other writers. It eventually forced the eminent author to write a public letter of explanation to the Authors' League of America.[26]

To improve the image of America's allies, especially the British, the board formed a United Nations Committee in December 1942 under the chairmanship of first Paul Gallico, then Jack Goodman. The group considered but rejected several ideas for spectacular one-time events and ultimately decided to ask writers and commentators about composing material "to develop a better understanding of the English both as human beings and as brave allies." Gallico elaborated further, explaining that the authors did not have to focus on the British. As an example, he suggested a scenario involving American soldiers: "Stories which will bring home to the civilian population the fact that at any moment the lives and safety of their sons may depend upon the friendship, the courage, and the intelligence of a soldier of the British Empire, or a Russian, or a Chinese, might bring these same civilians into a more cooperative mood."[27]

In the spring of 1943 the WWB placed in *Collier's* "The Clark and the Clurk," a title that refers to the British and American pronunciations of the word *clerk*. The story highlighted the friendship that quickly developed between a British soldier and an American GI.[28] Several other pieces appeared along the same lines. Gallico even arranged with cartoonist Ham Fisher for his character Joe Palooka to be rescued by an Englishman from one of his periodic plights.[29] The board, which carefully monitored the materials that it disseminated about Britain, also decided to check the literature that the British sent to the United States to determine whether it struck the right tone. Members critiqued several British Broadcasting Company radio broadcasts and read issues of *Britain*, the magazine published by the British Information Service. Afterward they forwarded their comments and suggestions through the proper channels.[30]

By the end of March the United Nations Committee felt that the need for combating anti-British sentiment had diminished, and it largely confined its role to fulfilling specific requests dealing with the country.[31] However, during the summer the WWB made a quick effort to promote a book soon to be published, *The Making of Modern Britain* by John Bartlet Brebner and Allan Nevins, who joined the board's Advisory Council that year.[32] The *New York Times* saw the book's theme as "Two Countries—One Heritage" and quoted Nevins, "Civil liberty and free political institutions—these are the inestimable heritage which Great Britain has bequeathed to our age and the ages to come."[33]

PRO-AMERICAN PROPAGANDA

WWB members provided several services to the Overseas Branch of the Office of War Information. In 1943 it requested short articles describing the activities of American educational and philanthropic institutions for distribution abroad. The board contacted fifty foundations and organizations to collect useful information and quickly passed on the material. The group also located writers who could prepare radio scripts in one or more foreign languages, and it notified qualified writers about other OWI-Overseas needs.[34] While the government agency regularly provided foreign magazines and newspapers with factual war information, it was not equipped to handle the flood of requests from these outlets for special material on Americans and their country.[35] In March 1943 the OWI asked the WWB to furnish at least one major article per day by a well-known author on one of the topics it provided. Board members agreed to help but warned that they could not supply the number of articles requested; still, they created a Special Assignments Committee. With Advisory Council member Joseph Wood Krutch as chairman, the group immediately began to provide the Overseas Branch with three or four pieces per week.

It procured excellent articles including "Life in a Boom Town" by John Dos Passos, "Walt Whitman and the Common Man" by Mark Van Doren, "What America Means to Me" by Pearl Buck, "The New England Town Meeting" by R. P. Tristram Coffin, "Political Cartoons" by Rollin Kirby, and well over one hundred others.[36] The OWI informed the board that these articles had appeared in as many as two thousand newspapers around the world. More realistically, the head of OWI-Overseas assured Stout, "A single article from a member of the Writers' War Board may be translated into a dozen languages, published in the press of twenty-five to fifty nations, and used in a variety of languages on OWI shortwave radio around the world." The files of the WWB contain proof of this assertion. The article by Buck, for instance, appeared in translation in an Egyptian paper on September 30, 1943, and ran in the Icelandic newspaper *Morgunbladid* the following day.[37] Although the board worked hard on the project, the Overseas Division dropped it in December 1943. The WWB committee received a few subsequent requests for technical articles, but they did not pursue them since they felt that the government's own experts could best fill them.[38]

Apart from that effort the WWB supplied material to a few British publications over the course of the war to encourage the English to develop a positive view of their U.S. ally and of American soldiers stationed at bases in their country. Paul Gallico and Russel Crouse accepted an extended assignment, alternately writing a weekly column for *Parade*, which was distributed to British military personnel. The columns gave insight into the lives of ordinary Americans and highlighted their interests. One of Gallico's contributions was a 1,500-word piece explaining the importance of sports in America. For several months the two authors continued their column until the OWI decided not to waste their talents on a relatively limited market.[39] Another board project involved putting together the entire June 1944 issue of *The Studio,* an English art magazine. Under the direction of Thomas Craven, co-chair of the Poster Committee, the group assembled articles and prints giving an overview of the history of American art and its cultural contributions.[40]

The WWB began its most concerted effort to publicize the United States in Britain after OWI official Herbert Agar attended its meeting on January 6, 1943. He presented a proposal from British and American officials to produce a new monthly British magazine called *Transatlantic* to inform the English about American life, culture, and character. The British government was willing to finance much of the venture by providing the salaries of the London staff and paying for the articles, which would be written by Americans. The OWI did not want to be involved in the project for two reasons: it did not have the personal contacts to deliver the prominent writers that would be best for the job, and it did not want the venture to have any official connection to the U.S. government. The agency asked the WWB to serve as the magazine's editorial board and procure material for each issue.[41] Both Edward Wood, Lord Halifax, British ambassador to the United States, and John G. Winant, U.S. ambassador to Britain, encouraged the group to undertake the task.[42]

Negotiations ensued, and the board agreed to carry out, insofar as was possible, the suggestions of the London editors and the members of the OWI-Overseas office in London, primarily Agar. All material would be submitted first to Ferdinand Kuhn, an OWI official in Washington, who could consult with the New York writers about any problems or necessary revisions. The OWI would pay all expenses incurred on the American side such as office rent, cable fees, and the like. The WWB established a *Transatlantic* Committee with Margaret Leech taking the demanding position of chair. It continued to operate under her leadership throughout the rest of the war. After some debate Geoffrey Crowther, who had been the prewar editor of the well-respected British publication *The Economist*, was selected as overall editor, and Penguin Press agreed to print the slick-looking magazine.[43]

The first issue in September 1943 carried Crowther's statement about the aim of the periodical and made reference to the words that Winston Churchill used when he addressed the United States Congress in December 1941: "The purpose is very serious and very ambitious. It is to assist the British and American peoples to 'walk together in majesty and peace.' . . . The temple of peace will need many pillars and buttresses. But the keystone of the arch is British-American co-operation."[44] In the September and November issues, Crowther gave an explanation of the WWB and its role in the preparation of *Transatlantic*. He acknowledged his close collaboration with the group but stated in no uncertain terms that the board was primarily responsible both for conceiving ideas for the periodical and for finding writers to carry them out. Both Crowther and the OWI could veto material, but in practice they rarely did. In a real sense *Transatlantic* became another WWB publication, albeit a much more sophisticated one than the others it produced.[45]

The board made no attempt at overt propaganda in the publication but presented general information and sometimes amusing anecdotes about America. Among the regular columns were "Washington Letter" by veteran journalist Roscoe Drummond and "State of the States" by Carl Van Doren and others. A sampling of original pieces written specifically for *Transatlantic* indicates a wide range of topics including history ("The Writing of the American Constitution" by Allan Nevins and "American Folklore" by Carl Carmer), description ("The Intermountain West" by Bernard DeVoto and "The Deep South" by Hamilton Basso), entertainment ("The New York Theatre" by Howard Lindsay and "The Intelligent Britisher's Guide to Baseball" by Gallico), American attitudes ("Public Opinion Polls" by Frederick L. Allen, "Big Newspapers" by Henry Pringle, and "What Has Happened to the Gangster?" by Stanley Walker), and occasionally one or two on the war ("Bradley: A Freehand Sketch" by Quentin Reynolds and "Thoughts Thought as Goebbels Burbles" by humorist Ogden Nash). A variety of articles were also reprinted from other sources: "Raisins" by William Saroyan; "Ships That Grow on the Prairie" by journalist James Reston, head of OWI-London; "The Declaration of Interdependence" by Wendell Willkie; and "The Atlantic Community" by Walter Lippmann.[46]

The magazine was well received by British critics, and each issue sold out completely since circulation was limited to fifty thousand copies because of the wartime paper shortage. The quality of the articles was sufficiently high that several were reprinted in British and American digest magazines including *This Month* and *Reader's Digest*. Despite these signs of success, board members were never satisfied that *Transatlantic* had the influence they desired. They gave no thought to halting publication, however, and worked on the magazine until the end of 1945.[47] *Transatlantic* was so popular that it continued even after the British government withdrew its subsidy and the board ended its involvement. Circulation finally ceased in the summer of 1948.

RELIEF EFFORTS

In 1943 the Writers' War Board began to help America's allies by working with several private agencies including Russian War Relief, Yugoslavian War Relief, and the United China Relief Fund. It also furnished speeches, radio material, and articles such as a piece for *This Week* on the dire conditions in Greece. Recognizing the critical need, sixteen war-related philanthropic organizations including the USO combined to launch the National War Fund (NWF) that summer, and board members produced slogans, radio speeches, and inspirational magazine articles to publicize the $125 million fundraising campaign. In October President Roosevelt addressed the nation about the importance of giving to the NWF, and the WWB arranged an original radio script by Forest Barnes that was broadcast one month later.[48] In addition, the board supported the relief work of artist Harold Weston. Haunted by scenes of famine that he had witnessed in the Middle East after World War I, Weston founded a Washington-based nonprofit called Food for Freedom in 1943, and he was a major force behind the United Nations Relief and Rehabilitation Administration (UNRRA), which President Roosevelt prompted the Allies to establish. It went into operation on December 1, 1943.[49]

Weston believed that food properly used could shorten the war and lay a foundation for peace. He urged Americans to sacrifice some of their personal comforts in order to feed and clothe the needy in war-torn countries both during the conflict and for several years thereafter. Food for Freedom began to stimulate food production and encourage conservation in the United States in order to insure that adequate supplies were readily available to those impoverished by the war. On May 19, 1944, the activist visited the offices of the WWB to ask for help with the work of both Food for Freedom and the UNRRA. The entire board met with him on June 14. At the time Weston was frustrated because the United States had not yet adopted an official policy on providing food for those liberated from Axis control. He was also upset about unjust accusations lodged against the UNRRA concerning its allocation of funds and the adequacy of its food supplies. Believing that most Americans did not understand the dire situation abroad, Weston wanted to see more publicity about those left destitute and starving by the war. He said that stockpiling was necessary to make sure that supplies were not depleted, and he argued that it should begin immediately even if it meant tighter rationing of American goods.[50]

The WWB offered to help both agencies build up stockpiles for distribution and established a Food and Relief Committee with Henry Pringle as chairman in Washington and Alan Green as acting chairman in New York. On July 24, 1944, Green and Clifton Fadiman along with Selma

Hirsh of the WWB's Washington office called on Herbert Lehman of the UNRRA to determine how the board could generate favorable publicity for the organization he headed. Lehman, who was the target of much of the criticism of the UNRAA in the United States, was gracious but not enthusiastic. He doubted that the group could offer any effective assistance, but he mentioned three areas where publicity would be welcomed: acquainting Americans with the UNRRA and its purposes, preparing them for the continuation of food rationing, and selling them on the need for rationing clothing as well as food.[51]

Despite Lehman's discouraging response, the WWB decided at its meeting on July 26 to move ahead on what Green called "as difficult a propaganda problem as it has ever seen." He bemoaned the fact that Americans "are in no sense aware that the stability of Europe and consequently the future peace of the world depends mostly upon the success of the Relief and Rehabilitation Program. To make them aware of this is not enough, but they must also be prepared to accept continued rationing and imposed sacrifices for a considerable time after the end of hostilities." Members decided that the work of the UNRRA was so critical that they should publicize it even though they had received no official government request to do so.[52]

As an initial step the Food and Relief Committee held a "Food Dinner" in Washington on August 31. Among the guests were representatives of each agency involved in feeding the people of Europe including Lee Marshall, director of food distribution for the War Food Administration, and General E. G. Gregory, quartermaster general of the U.S. Army. Addressing the group, Pringle emphasized the need to prepare the American public for continued rationing of food.[53] At one time war board members had considered a "Scaring the Bejesus out of Them" campaign to warn the public about frightening situations that might occur if wartime controls were not maintained, but they eventually rejected the idea.[54] Instead they decided to protest the easing of rationing in light of European shortages and the lack of stockpiles in this country. Pringle complained to Chester Bowles, head of the Office of Price Administration, about the situation. Bowles acknowledged that he personally agreed with the WWB's point of view and urged its members to proceed with their campaign. He also suggested that the writers put pressure on the War Food Administration, which had ultimate authority in the matter.[55]

The board had little trouble in dealing with the government agencies, but it ran into problems with the UNRRA. The organization had no clear-cut statement of policy about what area to emphasize—relief, recovery, or rehabilitation—and which countries to help. Those decisions had been left to its council, which met periodically. The Allied agency was also crippled by staffing issues and stymied by the requirement that its efforts be subordinate to military considerations. Without enough help or guidance, the organization ended up dragging its feet on working out the logistics of feeding Europe.[56] As a consequence the board was unable to offer an already skeptical public specific details about how their donations would be used.

The effort was hit even harder by several newspaper and magazine stories about surpluses and stockpiles of food in the United States. Not convinced that these stories were accurate, the WWB writers doggedly plunged ahead with their campaign, but such reports cast doubt on their credibility. In fact, while staples like meat, butter, coffee, and sugar were sometimes in short supply, other items were periodically unavailable because of erratic deliveries, not inadequate supplies.[57] In addition, the conflicting initiatives of two government agencies had contributed to the problem. While the U.S. Department of Agriculture worked to decrease stockpiles in order to avoid postwar surpluses that might adversely affect the income of American farmers, the Food Administration took measures to hold on to additional supplies to increase domestic pork production.[58]

The board's Food and Relief Committee made personal contacts to persuade influential food distributors to help explain the food problem to the public, and the WWB arranged a press conference in Washington on behalf of several relief agencies including Food for Freedom. It also prepared and sent to newspaper columnists and radio commentators a collection of materials about the problems of providing food and relief to liberated countries. The packet included an authoritative article written for the board by Lester "Mike" Pearson, future Nobel Peace Prize winner and Canadian prime minister. As chairman of the UNRRA's Interim Committee on Food and Agriculture, which collected supplies to distribute, he discussed the long-term aspects of feeding Europe and the necessity of maintaining food production in the United States.[59]

The board publications also championed the cause of the "eating war." In its January 1945 issue the *Writers' War Board Report* asserted that food shortages would continue because American soldiers on the battlefield required regular meals as they liberated more and more of the hungry and starving who also had to be fed. The article admonished all authors to join in the effort: "Wherever and whenever you can, pound home the idea that a meatless dinner or a butterless piece of toast are weapons and that relaxation of rationing before the war is ended and the relief job completed will be a defeat inflicted by too many soft civilians and too-greedy food industrialists."[60] A similar message had been delivered in the December 1944 editorial "Food for Friends" by Alan Green and Margaret Widdemer, Pulitzer Prize–winning poet. Other articles appeared in *Brief House Organ Items*.[61] By its standards the board's campaign was not large, but Weston was convinced that it played a significant role in focusing public attention on the problem and persuading the War Food Administration to institute stricter rationing procedures.[62] The group considered it a modest success.

In January 1945 the WWB began to publicize another part of the relief effort, the United National Clothing Collection, which obtained used but wearable items to send to those liberated from German control. The board arranged for some thirty well-known individuals to plug the initiative so that it could use the appeals on the radio and in various publications. Several members participated as well as actors Humphrey Bogart and Fredric March; columnist Elsa Maxwell; dramatist Clifford Odets; and writers Cornelia Otis Skinner, Jan Struthers, Booth Tarkington, Sinclair Lewis, and Fannie Hurst.[63] "Their Sunday Best," an editorial distributed in March and April, was carefully written so that each newspaper could easily insert a local reference.[64] The entire *Bulletin to Cartoonists* for April was devoted to the subject, and the *Writers' War Board Report* promoted it as well. In November the board wrote an editorial for the Victory Clothing Drive, the campaign that succeeded the Clothing Collection.[65] The board continued its relief efforts into 1946, providing publicity materials to relief agencies free of charge even after the war.

DENOUNCING JAPAN

None of the board's campaigns were as vehement, sustained, and controversial as its campaign against the German enemy. The WWB rarely mentioned Italy and the other Axis nations nor did it spend much time on Japan since that nation had stunned Americans with its surprise attack on Pearl Harbor and had made them obsessed with annihilating the Japanese people and their centuries-old culture.[66] A January 1943 poll showed that five times as many Americans advocated complete extermination of the Japanese as of the Germans.[67] With little knowledge of Japanese history, religious beliefs, or customs, many in the United States mistrusted their fellow citizens of Japanese descent and made them the targets of insults and racial intolerance. In an effort to contain the fear of invasion that pervaded the West Coast, Roosevelt signed an executive order on February 19, 1942, giving military authorities in the area permission to intern both Japanese immigrants and Japanese American citizens.[68]

Forced to leave their homes, their jobs, and most of their possessions, more than 100,000 of them spent the war confined in camps. Such was the level of animosity toward Japan that the WWB continued to give it short shrift until 1944 when it developed a few minor campaigns and published some pieces of anti-Japanese propaganda. The Speech Committee listed only two addresses on Japan in its catalog: "Our Enemy—Madame Butterfly" and a commentary on Japanese atrocities called "A Story from the Pacific." That spring the board placed an article by Wallace Irwin in the *American Legion Magazine* that argued for the unrestricted bombing of the country without regard for its cultural or historical landmarks.[69]

In January a "high government official" made an urgent plea to Stout and Fadiman that the WWB arouse hatred against Japan's god-emperor. Because his request was not in line with the thinking of other policymakers who believed that Hirohito might one day prove useful to the Allies, he asked to remain anonymous. Honoring that request, neither Stout nor Fadiman revealed his name when they presented his suggestion to the board.[70] Members were skeptical about taking the assignment but formed a committee on Japan chaired by Christopher LaFarge. After its favorable recommendation, board members began an anti-Hirohito campaign even though it required them to oppose the State Department publicly. Like the unnamed official, they believed that the peace settlement should hold Hirohito responsible for his country's military actions and punish him accordingly.[71] The October edition of the *Report* explained their position: "A group of government advisers and consultants on the policy level, headed by a high official of the State Department, want no hair touched on Hirohito's head. They say the Japanese regard him as divine, so we should preserve him, in order to use him—to lead the Japanese into and along the path of righteousness. But what if he is not divine to us? He either leads the Japanese or he doesn't. If he does, he led them to Pearl Harbor and Bataan."[72]

When Prime Minister Hideki Tojo seemed on the brink of losing power about one month after the under-the-table request, board members saw an opportunity to shift American hatred from the reviled prime minister to Hirohito. Green suggested that the board prepare a file of political cartoons, short pieces, editorials, and scripts aimed at the emperor, and it immediately put out a call in order to have them ready to print as soon as Tojo departed.[73] With his usual bluntness Stout explained the slant that the board wanted: "We say nuts to the state department policy saying Hirohito is a nice little boy and that we can count safely on dealing with him some day. In the not too distant future Tojo will probably have a great fall. We think it would be well to accustom Americans to the idea of selecting Hirohito as a symbol of Japanese iniquity when Tojo is gone."[74] Tojo, however, managed to retain his position until July. By that time the board had already begun its campaign against the emperor. In April it had distributed the editorial "Hirohito Must Go," which suggested that the Allies remove him once Japan surrendered.[75] Shortly afterward the WWB members temporarily suspended the campaign, which was not a top priority, because they needed to deal with some critically important projects related to the war against Germany. These distracted them to such an extent that they let Tojo's removal from office go by unmarked.

When they returned to the campaign, Goodman expressed concern that he and other board members knew little about Japan. The writers agreed to educate themselves on the nation and its culture and asked LaFarge to prepare a bibliography of books and articles for their use.[76] At their board meeting on September 6, 1944, Stout encouraged the group to plunge into the anti-Hirohito campaign without delay. He believed that the war in Europe might end before winter came, and he wanted to prevent any slump in America's war fervor against the Japanese when Germany surrendered. But nothing concrete was decided since WWB members disagreed about how to attack Hirohito and foment increased public hostility toward him.[77]

Two weeks later Robert Eunson, an Associated Press correspondent who had recently witnessed the fighting in the Pacific, came to urge the group to publicize Japanese atrocity stories. He felt that the government had not made Americans aware of many gruesome incidents that occurred early in the war for fear that the accounts would discourage recruiting for the armed forces and would dampen the morale of soldiers stationed in the Pacific, particularly those in the Army Air Forces whose comrades were victims of some of the worst atrocities. Since Americans were now accustomed to the brutalities of war, Eunson argued, they needed to know about the dreadful stories, which still might have shock value.[78]

The board attempted to obtain the release of these incidents but failed miserably because of government buck-passing. A suggestion to Army Chief of Staff George Marshall that accounts of documented Japanese atrocities ought to be published brought only a referral to the Department of War. Secretary of War Henry Stimson said that his department favored the release of such stories "provided that the reports have been substantiated and such releases are consistent with military security."[79] Secretary of the Navy James Forrestal agreed but pointed out that the board would first need clearance from the State Department, which was currently involved in delicate negotiations. Secretary of State Edward Stettinius would only say that his department would consider the matter, but he refused to set a time frame for its decision.[80] Flummoxed, the board turned to Elmer Davis, director of the OWI, who finally killed off the idea by pointing out the dangers of such a campaign. Because German atrocities in the First World War had been demonstrably exaggerated, he argued that the board would have to make certain that the reports of Japanese brutality were correct and admitted that locating documented evidence could prove difficult. Furthermore, he said that publicizing the accounts might cause the Japanese to treat American prisoners of war more harshly or might encourage Japan to circulate false reports of American atrocities.[81] Ordinarily such arguments would not have kept the WWB from moving ahead with the project, but in this case it could not do so without the assistance of the government. Since no department was willing to cooperate, the board had to drop the matter.

In November the *Writers' War Board Report* included "A Japanese Quiz for Writers," a piece that resulted from the board's reading of Japanese history. Among the questions were, (1) "What would have happened to Hirohito if he had refused to sign the Declaration of War against Great Britain and the United States?" (2) "How many Japanese Emperors have been assassinated?" and (3) "What extremes of Japanese policy have used the Emperorship as justification of their excesses?" The board concluded, "If you can answer these after looking them up, you've begun to know something about (a) Japanese history and (b) what we shall have to do with Hirohito or his successor after victory."[82] Aside from printing anti-Japanese articles in its own publications, the board did not make many efforts to place similar materials in other media outlets.

One exception was a series on Japan that the WWB agreed to handle for *American Legion Magazine*. In a letter to China-based journalist J. B. Powell, who had promised to write one of the articles, Clifton Fadiman emphasized the idea of a hard peace for Japan. He and his fellow board members believed that a vocal group of American businessmen, missionaries, and others was certain to call for appeasement:

> The marks by which the movement may be recognized are (1) the attempt to put over the "gangster theory" (it is a military clique that is causing all the trouble); (2) the urging of the claims of Hirohito to retain power . . . ; (3) a "stable" Japan is necessary to offset the preponderating population of China; (4) if we are going to do business in the Far East there is no sense in destroying a good customer; (5) the missionary folks, in particular, will take the line that some of the Japs are awfully nice people, particularly those converted to Christianity.[83]

Powell's article "After We Have Occupied Japan" appeared late that year, and in January 1945 Carl Crow's "The Emperor Must Go" came close to restating the editorial "Hirohito Must Go," which the WWB had previously published.[84]

One other outlet that the board used to disseminate its anti-Japanese propaganda was comic books. It asked writers, artists, and others working in the genre to portray Japanese soldiers realistically rather than picturing them as bumbling stooges or as super-human monsters. The board specifically objected to one popular representation of Japan as "The Claw," a Godzilla-like creature. Alan Green complained, "The comics are drumming up a lot of hate for the enemy but usually for the wrong reasons—frequently fantastic ones (mad Jap scientists, etc.). Why not use the real reasons—they're plenty worthy of hate!"[85] M. C. Gaines and Sheldon Mayer of All-American Comics, who had worked with the WWB previously, were willing to create an entire issue on Japan, but they did not want it to be criticized for showing racial intolerance. They proposed a scenario that involved a fictional antifascist underground movement in the enemy nation. The storyline promoted sympathy for the Japanese by falsely indicating that some of them opposed fascism and by portraying a young Japanese woman in a favorable light. Horrified by the plot, Fadiman demanded that the "bad" story be "committed to the flames." He asserted, "Our attitude toward the Japanese must . . . be more stringent."[86] Gaines and Mayer eventually dropped the project because they could never come to a meeting of the minds with the members of the WWB.

The anti-Hirohito campaign was suspended again in late 1944 and early 1945 because of events in Europe. Even though Germany's defeat was months away, the board felt that it should concentrate its efforts on suggesting a peace settlement that would last. For that reason its emphasis on Japan disappeared from WWB publications. In its public announcements the board was unusually circumspect about the reason for switching its focus, saying only that it was studying Japanese history and the Japanese government "in order to be in a position to clarify that issue."[87] After Germany surrendered, the WWB made some effort to return to its attack on Hirohito. The *Report* for June conceded that most writers had "laid off" the emperor during the war because they felt that attacking him might increase Japanese fanaticism and make a martyr of the man considered to be a Japanese god. The newsletter cautioned its readers that the imperial system would have to be destroyed in order to protect future generations of Americans. Simultaneously, the board sent out the editorial "Why Coddle Hirohito?" by Robert Bellaire. The June 1945 *Brief Army Camp Items* carried the harshest material. Jimmy Young, a former Tokyo news correspondent, called the emperor "a number one war criminal" and expressed the hope that he "is executed and that his body will be put on public display at Nanking, China." Millard Price's July editorial "Shall We Let Japan Off Easy?" called for the unconditional surrender of the nation.[88]

The board prepared a kit of materials on Japan that it sent to editors, writers, and commentators on July 9. Along with a few pieces about Japanese atrocities was "A Statement Concerning the Emperor of Japan" by Far East expert Edgar Salinger. He had written background material for the board's campaign at Stout's request and had submitted his eleven-page document in October 1944, but the group chose not to release it until after Germany surrendered. Salinger gave a hostile examination of imperial history and attacked the idea that Allied forces should not harm Hirohito because he was a religious symbol who might be persuaded to support a democratic government in postwar Japan. While Salinger acknowledged that "the Emperor of Japan is the central personage about whom the entire Japanese government revolves," he argued that Hirohito should be targeted. The author believed that the collapse of Hirohito's reign would immediately weaken Japan's military forces: "Destroy the . . . symbols of national unity, the bonds which unite a people to defend sacrosanct ideals, and the fanaticism and will-to-fight suffer corresponding diminution." He said that ending "the God-Emperor cult" would also promote lasting peace since the Japanese could no longer follow the dictates of their revered leader or the traditional customs he represented.[89]

The document basically reflected the sentiments of the war board, but its members rejected Salinger's suggestion that the emperor's palace be bombed for practical reasons. If the United States announced that it intended to kill Hirohito and failed, it would be humiliated in the eyes of the Japanese. Furthermore, the board recognized that killing the emperor would not put an end to the god-emperor cult because Hirohito had a twelve-year-old son who would immediately succeed him.[90] After this brief spurt of activity the group abandoned its campaign against Japan, America's only remaining foe. Within a month the United States had dropped two atomic bombs on the country, and Japan unconditionally surrendered on September 2, 1945.

THE CAMPAIGN AGAINST GERMANY

The WWB mounted its Nature of the Enemy Campaign against Germany with alacrity, determined to ignite as much hatred for the Germans as Americans had felt for the Japanese since Pearl Harbor. Rex Stout acknowledged, "Our chief concern is Germany because only a minority of us are under any delusions regarding the Japanese, while a large majority of us still believe that the Germans are on the whole people of good-will temporarily misled by the Nazi gangsters."[91] Most Americans agreed with the board that Germany posed a greater threat to world peace than Japan. A *Fortune* survey published in February 1942 indicated that 47.5 percent felt Germany to be more of a menace than Japan compared to only 10.2 percent who considered Germany less of a menace. Despite that fact, 62.4 percent of Americans were more interested in the fight against Japan. They wanted the United States either to disregard the war in Europe and concentrate all its efforts on beating Japan or to provide some aid to Britain while remaining focused on Japan.[92] In a 1943 poll 57 percent of the population believed Japan to be the greatest military threat to America and 62 percent thought that the Japanese had always wanted war. Only 21 percent thought that the Japanese could become good world citizens in the postwar era. In contrast just 22 percent said that the people of Germany had always wanted war while 32 percent of Americans surveyed believed that Germans disliked war and could become good world citizens. These numbers are surprising in light of the fact that American troops had fought Germany less than twenty-five years before.[93]

The first WWB attempt to stir up anti-German feeling was a rather curious effort to generate material for the newspaper syndicates. The group requested that well-known mystery writers produce appropriate "quotes" about the nature of the enemy from the viewpoint of their fictional heroes. For example, Stout's detective Nero Wolfe commented on the possibility of hurting bystanders when cracking down on German and Japanese sympathizers. Wolfe argued that the risk must be taken: "How . . . can we sensibly avoid harassment of the innocent when we are out after the two most murderous gangs in all history? . . . Pfui! . . . I say go after them! Lock them up or shoot them."[94] The group launched a far more successful effort in August 1942 when members of the Poster Committee asked writers for captions and attention-grabbing designs to use on posters that emphasized the sinister nature of German and Japanese troops: "Don't pull your punches. Bring the cruelty of the Nazi or Jap home to the suburban housewife, to the Midwestern farmer, to those Americans who, no matter how patriotic, are actually untouched by this battle for survival. . . . Make them realize we can lose this war and what will happen if we do." To make certain the writers understood what it had in mind, the Poster Committee included one of Goodman's ideas: "Picture: Several bodies just after they have been shot and firing squad is just marching away. Caption: Severance pay—the Fascist way?"[95] Hundreds of ideas poured in. Eventually the committee selected seven that had the greatest impact—all but one featured German soldiers. These were illustrated and sent to the government for printing and distribution. Although the WWB planned an exhibition of the posters, the event apparently never took place.[96]

In April 1942 the board began its first major propaganda campaign against Germany at the behest of the recently founded Council on Books in Wartime, which wanted to commemorate the anniversary of the massive book burning that had taken place in Germany almost a decade before. Shortly after Hitler rose to power, the Nazis had published a list of forbidden books and authors. In support of government censorship, members of the German Student Union destroyed some 25,000 volumes in a single conflagration on May 10, 1933. Chester Kerr, chief of the Book Division of the Office of Facts and Figures, had suggested the commemoration at the council's meeting on March 24.[97] Board members agreed to help because they felt that the shocking event clearly indicated the evil nature of the German people. They asserted that "the burning and banning of . . . books" had been "as symbolic as the Crucifixion itself," and they called the action "a declaration of war, a war against mankind, waged by that part of mankind that wishes to be less than itself."[98]

WWB members formed a committee chaired by Bennett Cerf of Random House to handle the project. The committee and Kerr believed that a radio dramatization of the event might be the most effective approach, and the WWB contacted Pulitzer Prize–winning author Stephen Vincent Benet, who had already written a powerful indictment of fascism in his 1940 novel *Nightmare at Noon*. For this occasion he created the verse drama *They Burned the Books*, which included imaginary laments from the authors whose works were destroyed shortly after Hitler took power nine years before:

Nine! Nine iron years of terror and evil!
Nine years since a fire was lighted in a public square in Berlin.
Nine years since the "burning of the book!" Do you remember?
Write it down in your calendars, May 10th, 1933,
And write it down in red by the light of the fire.
These are people who work by fire.[99]

A member of the committee, network official Orin Tovrov, set up the nationwide broadcast over NBC's Red Network on Monday, May 11, 1942, from 10:30 to 11:00 p.m.[100] The successful program provoked such a reaction that the WWB arranged for repeat performances and saw that the script was published in book form. Abridged versions appeared in *Scholastic* and the *Saturday Review of Literature*. It was also used as the first WWB War Script of the Month. Sent to radio stations and schools all over the country, it was performed in local venues throughout the war. The council praised the play, remarking that those who heard the broadcast "called it the best radio program which ever issued from the Council on Books in Wartime."[101] It was subsequently translated into other languages for transmission over OWI-Overseas shortwave radio. Most of those who participated in the project gave the WWB primary credit for organizing and publicizing the event.[102]

The group sponsored a number of other activities for the commemoration as well. A second play, *The Nature of the Enemy* by Tovrov, presented a broad indictment of the Germans that did not focus solely on state censorship. Designed for easy presentation at the local level, it went to 210 radio stations. The board also mailed hundreds of letters publicizing the anniversary and encouraging 130 commentators and columnists around the country to mention the event. Their correspondence generated a "fair response" including a strong statement from popular radio commentator Raymond Gram Swing. Letters sent to the presidents of American colleges and universities suggested that appropriate ceremonies be held in conjunction with the event, and at least a few of them took action.[103]

In addition, the WWB prepared lists of banned books to assist bookstores and libraries in setting up displays on the subject and arranging local commemorations. After Stout and Fadiman addressed a meeting of the council on "Books as Weapons in the War of Ideas," that title became the slogan for the campaign. Stout soon gave a speech about the May 10 observance at the annual convention of the American Booksellers Association, and other board members made similar presentations to a variety of groups.[104] According to the U.S. Holocaust Memorial Museum, thousands of commemorations took place in 1942 and 1943. For the tenth anniversary of the date, board members kept their involvement to a minimum, having a host of other assignments. However, they sent out more than a thousand postcards asking writers to publicize the event around the nation, and they allowed the council to use the materials the WWB had originally compiled.[105]

The next board effort to vilify the Germans proved to be one of the major propaganda successes of the group's existence. It was occasioned by a Nazi atrocity in early June 1942. On May 27, SS General Reinhard Heydrich, one of the major architects of the Holocaust who had achieved notoriety as "Hitler's hangman," was ambushed in Czechoslovakia. He died on June 4. Five days later the Germans began to level the small Czech village of Lidice in retaliation. Suspecting that it had provided refuge to the assassins, German troops executed the town's adult male population and took most of its women and children to concentration camps, prisons, or institutions where many were subsequently killed. Some women became servants in German homes, and a few of the children were placed with families connected to the SS so that they could be reared as Germans. All of the houses in the village were looted and burned. On June 10 the Germans boasted that they had erased the village from the map.[106]

The WWB viewed the massacre as an ideal means of focusing Americans on German brutality. The board appointed a committee under the chairmanship of Fadiman to preserve the memory of Lidice and to keep it in the public eye. Alan Green and Rita Kleeman were among the more active members. The first official directive of Elmer Davis, head of the newly established OWI, ordered the federal agency to cooperate with the WWB in its Lidice campaign. Three OWI workers became members of the Lidice Committee, which held its first meeting on June 26 and promptly set up specific propaganda guidelines. The aim of the campaign was "not so much to arouse sympathy as the emotion of horror to be followed by the emotion of anger. Thus the net effect will be militant and aggressive." Fadiman's committee was not interested in emphasizing the nationality of the victims but in using "Lidice . . . as a symbol. Whenever possible this symbol is to be used as a method of further uniting the United Nations."[107]

The group immediately decided to form a "front" committee with a roster of influential members and sponsors. Known as the Lidice Lives Committee, it would appear to do the work for purposes of publicity, but all of its actions would remain a function of the WWB.[108] The board chose as chairman Joseph Davies. Over one hundred foreign dignitaries and prominent Americans sponsored the group. Among them were Russian ambassador Maxim Litvinov, physicist Albert Einstein, motion picture magnate Samuel Goldwyn, and three Supreme Court justices. Since disgust over the massacre was widespread, few declined to become involved, but British playwright George Bernard Shaw was one exception: "I am not such a mischievous fool as to waste time in preserving the memory of atrocities of which we are equally guilty. They are better forgotten."[109] Eventually 110 individuals became members of the Lidice Lives Committee, and its formation was formally announced on September 21.[110]

While the front group was being established, Fadiman's Lidice Committee continued to refute the Germans' contention that they had erased Lidice from the map. At its first meeting members decided to rename a small American town in its memory. For the purpose they found an unincorporated village called Stern Park Gardens on the outskirts of Joliet, Illinois. Originally a federal housing project, it was largely populated by Czechs who agreed to the name change. Acting at the instigation of the board, the *Chicago Sun* obtained the necessary consent, and the WWB committee took charge of arranging nationwide publicity for the ceremony. After the announcement about the renaming appeared, a favorable editorial in the *New York Times* concluded with the statement, "We need tanks, planes, and guns. We need symbols, too."[111]

The event took place on July 12 before a crowd that Fadiman estimated to number 35,000, and it was broadcast overseas as well as coast to coast. Principal speaker Wendell Willkie delivered the kind of message that WWB members wanted to hear. After reading the official German announcement of the extermination of Lidice, Willkie said, "Let us here highly resolve that the memory of this little village of Bohemia now resurrected by the people of a little village in Illinois will fire us, now and until the battle is over, with the iron resolution that the madness of tyrants must perish from the earth so that the earth may return to the people to whom it belongs, and be their village, their home, forever."[112] Colonel Vladimir S. Hurban, Czechoslovak minister to the United States, also spoke, and Fadiman served as master of ceremonies. Messages from President Roosevelt, Vice President Henry A. Wallace, and Dr. Edvard Beneš, Czechoslovakia's president in exile, were read to the audience. Colonel Hurban lit an eternal flame on a granite shaft monument dedicated to the Czech village. In addition to radio coverage, the event received photographic, newsreel, newsmagazine, and front-page newspaper attention.[113] The board considered the publicity to be excellent. In fact, a *New York Times* editorial made the point that the WWB wished to emphasize: "We may in the meantime remember that what Hitler [did] to the men, women, and children of Lidice, Czechoslovakia, he would do to those of Lidice, Ill., or of any American town if he could."[114]

Much encouraged, the Lidice Committee began to look for other places to rename. After considerable frustration and difficulty, a second ceremony was arranged in Mexico. On August 30 the farm village of San Jerónimo changed its name to Lidice in an event broadcast throughout the United States. Aside from the Mexican and South American dignitaries who made addresses, Vice President Wallace impressed the crowd by speaking in both English and Spanish. He asserted, "As symbols of the unbreakable spirit of the common man, Lidice in Mexico and Lidice in the United States are immortal." The board characterized the amount of attention in the Mexican and South American press as "astonishing," and the ceremony received full coverage in the United States.[115]

An attempt to arrange a similar ceremony in Canada was unfortunately bungled by local authorities. With the assistance of the premier of Quebec province, who was a Lidice Lives Committee sponsor, officials had agreed to rename the town of Frelighsburg. Fadiman announced the event in Washington, and his committee began to prepare for yet another publicity blitz. Unfortunately, no one had thought to ask the inhabitants of Frelighsburg about the name change, and, as it happened, they objected to it strenuously. The provincial government and Fadiman's committee had no choice but to back down. Although they eventually succeeded in naming a Quebec township for the Czech village, the event brought little publicity.[116] The last ceremony directly inspired by the committee took place in June 1943, the first anniversary of the atrocity. A locality near the Brazilian city of Rio de Janeiro took the name Lidice in an appropriately large and well-publicized ceremony.[117] Although a few other places around the globe held similar events, the WWB was not involved in them.

The board's actions stimulated memorials to the Czech village in several art forms. Sculptor Jo Davidson created a statue entitled *Lest We Forget* that depicts a village citizen determinedly facing his Nazi executioners as his wife and child look on. On October 12, 1942, Davidson presented the work to the Lidice Lives Committee at the American Associated Artists gallery in New York. Actress Madeleine Carroll accepted it on behalf of the group, and many prominent New Yorkers attended the ceremony, several at the board's suggestion. After its initial showing the sculpture went to places around the United States where, in Fadiman's words, "it will do the most good."[118] Painter-cartoonist William Gropper also memorialized the massacre as did several other artists, and the WWB widely promoted their efforts. The Colonial Bank and Trust Company in Rockefeller Center displayed many of the works along with a model of the memorial monument in Illinois, and the WWB saw that the exhibit toured other cities.[119] Filmmakers and playwrights made use of the massacre also. In October Paramount Pictures produced *We Refuse to Die*. Although the studio did not consult the Lidice Committee during the making of the one-reel movie, Fadiman's group arranged for the film to be adapted by Justin Herman into a radio play of the same name, and it helped procure a top-line cast. New York station WNEW and its affiliates broadcast the drama on October 25, three days after the release of the documentary. That December the board issued the play as a War Script of the Month.[120]

Other memorials appeared in verse. Poet and novelist Robert Nathan wrote "Lidice," which was read at some of the ceremonies and received a full-page spread in the Sunday magazine supplement *This Week*. It was, however, a little mild for the taste of some board members.[121] In complete accord with the WWB propaganda line was the dramatic poem *The Murder of Lidice* by Edna St. Vincent Millay. Although Millay had never before written poetry to order, the WWB's request was so persuasive that she agreed to take on the task: "I knew I should not be able to draw one contented breath unless I tried to do the job."[122] Her biographer considers it "astonishing" that Millay was able to write anything at this time considering her drug addiction, but her powerful poem probably drew more public attention than any other single project of the Lidice Committee.[123]

Presented as a radio drama, *The Murder of Lidice* had a cast of nine headed by distinguished actor Paul Muni. The performance before an overflow crowd was broadcast nationwide on the NBC network at 10:30 p.m. on Monday, October 19. It was simultaneously sent to Hawaii, Alaska, Australia, and New Zealand via shortwave radio, and a Spanish translation was made available to most of South America. The next day delayed broadcasts went to the British Isles, the Middle East, and Brazil. Independent radio stations received transcripts, and listeners were able to hear several rebroadcasts. Poet and critic Alexander Woollcott introduced the lavish production and served as master of ceremonies. Maestro Frank Black of the popular *Cities Service Concerts* radio show composed special music for the event and conducted the orchestra.[124]

Although Millay's hastily written poem dripped with sentimentality and lacked depth and finesse, it was well designed to fit the WWB purpose of revealing the evil nature of the enemy personified by Heydrich the Hangman:

Heydrich the Hangman howls tonight,
He howls for a bucket of bubbly blood—
It may be man's or it may be of woman,
But it has to be hot and it must be human!

Millay began by picturing the people of Lidice and their idyllic life, which was shattered in June 1942 by the early morning arrival of German troops. She related how the soldiers went from house to house, pulled the two hundred men from their beds, and executed them in the village square. In her graphic account the Germans brutally killed several of the dogs too by kicking them to death.

> Oh, many a faithful dog that day
> Stood by his master's body at bay,
> And tugged at the sleeve of an arm outflung;
> Or laid his paws on his master's breast,
> With panting jaws and whimpering cries,
> Gazing into his glazing eyes
> And licking his face with loving tongue;
> Nor would from his master's body depart,
> Till they kicked in his ribs and crushed his heart.

The poet recounted the events that followed the massacre. The soldiers razed the village and carried away the women and children, leaving nothing in their wake.

> The women and children out to the square
> They marched, that there they could plainly see
> How mighty a state is Germany!—
> That can drag from his bed unawake, unaware,
> Unarmed, a man, to be murdered, where
> His wife and his children must watch and see;
> Then carted them off in truck and cart
> Into Germany, into Germany,—
> The wives to be slaves of German men;
> The children to start life over again,
> In German schools, to German rules,
> As butchers' apprentices;
> And hail and salute the master-mind
> Of Hitler, Butcher of Human-kind.

In the final stanzas Millay again played on each reader's sympathy by depicting Lidice as a lifeless child. The poet ended her work with the warning that the United States would become a target if Americans did not stop Hitler:

The whole world holds in its arms today
The murdered village of Lidice,
Like the murdered body of a little child,
Innocent, happy, surprised at play,—
The murdered body, stained and defiled,
Tortured and mangled, of a helpless child!

And moans of vengeance frightful to hear
From the throat of a whole world, reach his ear—
The maniac killer who still runs wild— . . .

Careless America, crooning a tune:
Catch him! Catch him and stop him soon! . . .
Or will you wait, and let him destroy
The village of Lidice, Illinois?
Oh, catch him! Catch him, and stop him soon!
Never let him come here![125]

Despite the shortcomings of the poem, the board felt that it was "one of the finest pieces of true propaganda to come out of the war." The *Newsweek* reviewer mentioned the poem's dramatic "challenge to freedom-loving people." The *Christian Science Monitor* called it "war propaganda of the right kind." *Theatre Arts* reported that the program was so effective that it greatly increased enthusiasm for radio as a medium for drama due to the "emotional impact on the audience reported over and over again. . . . There is no doubt that it was the theme of the poem and the poet's dramatic attack on that theme that created the effect." Finally, the *Variety* reviewer described the poem in glowing terms, claiming that it was "the most eloquent piece of righteous wrath heard on this side of the ocean in the war. It had the intensity of a blast furnace, the scorn of a trial lawyer, the mood-building power of a Beethoven symphony. . . . Seldom has the gangster mentality of Prussianism been so cleverly exposed, so scathingly detailed in all its offensive arrogance and practical cruelty. . . . [Millay] produced an indictment with philharmonic orchestration."[126]

Life magazine printed it in full, Harper and Brothers published it as a pamphlet with a foreword by the WWB, and Columbia Records issued it in a three-disk collection. The 1943 MGM movie *Hitler's Madman* on Heydrich's assassination and the Nazis' quick retaliation opens and closes with lines from Millay's poem. Despite the general praise it received, critical comments about the poem were unfavorable. In a particularly harsh review in *Common Sense*, Harry Brown claimed Millay made a "mockery" of the atrocity by "bad writing and bad taste."[127] Ignoring the emotional impact of such timely pieces of poetic propaganda, modern critic Paul Fussell cites Millay, Benet, and Nathan as examples of writers who produced "patriotic drivel" because they were "persuaded that the war effort required the laying aside of all normal standards of art and intellect."[128] Millay herself was dissatisfied with the poem and considered it "merely propaganda." She hoped that it would be "allowed to die along with the war that provoked it."[129] WWB members, however, were far more interested in the poem's use as a propaganda tool than in its literary merit, and the work unquestionably produced the effect they desired. One critic has recently argued that the poem "might have been up to that point the most widely circulated poem of the twentieth century."[130]

Government agencies became interested in the story. Treasury officials who were preparing to start their first war bond drive on November 30 saw the razing of the village as an excellent reason for the public to support the fight against German brutality. They set aside the week of September 13–19, 1942, as Lidice Week, and the Brief Items Committee furnished slogans and radio material for the special emphasis. Fadiman's group helped prepare a pamphlet on the atrocity for the OWI to distribute at home and abroad.[131] By the end of October the Lidice Committee felt that the propaganda value of the story had been sufficiently explored. It began to cut back its activities so as not to destroy Lidice as a symbol by being too heavy-handed, particularly since its projects had inspired numerous imitators. The front committee continued to operate for a short while but was officially dissolved in March 1943. The entire propaganda effort was achieved for an expenditure of only $450 including travel expenses. Fadiman was pleased with the successful outcome: "The word Lidice has meaning; it crops up continually and our record of achievements has been praised by responsible Office of War Information officials as one of the most effective single pieces of propaganda since the war started."[132] Ironically the involvement of the Writers' War Board in this effort is not acknowledged on the website of the village of Lidice, now a suburb of Crest Hill, Illinois. While the area still bears a plaque explaining its name change in 1942, the original monument was vandalized in 1995.

The Lidice campaign was such a success that the New York group had the opportunity to repeat it two years later. In retaliation for a guerilla raid on German troops occupying Greece, the soldiers of the Reich entered the small village of Distomo on June 10, 1944, and machine-gunned to death 218 people. In recognition of the massacre, concerned Americans formed the Committee for the Rebirth of Distomo under the chairmanship of dramatist Maxwell Anderson. Hoping that the WWB would participate in their activities, leaders of the group consulted Green, one of the principal movers behind the Lidice Committee. Feeling that Americans were becoming numb to this type of atrocity story, he advised against it. Although he did not specify his reasons, three factors probably figured into his assessment. First, the Lidice campaign had shock value in 1942 that the destruction of Distomo did not. Second, news of the Holocaust had been circulated by 1944 and proof of the German extermination of millions of Jews was beginning to surface. The killing at Distomo paled in comparison, Third, after Distomo the Germans issued no statement proudly proclaiming that they had erased the existence of the Greek village from the map. The board agreed with Green but decided to provide some materials for the new effort. "Distomo—Successor to Lidice" was one of the WWB editorials for September 1944, and the WWB helped the Distomo Committee enlist some well-known authors to produce commentaries on the atrocity for the newspaper syndicates. The public's reaction to the committee's work was unenthusiastic, however, and the board felt justified in its decision not to recycle the Lidice campaign.[133]

The most surprising fact about the board's persistent campaign to stir up feeling against the Germans was its reluctance to chronicle early atrocity stories about the Holocaust that would have bolstered its argument about German cruelty and encouraged Americans to hate them.

The WWB specifically stated that it intended to make "judicious . . . use of . . . atrocities," but its reasoning is unclear.[134] Maybe its self-imposed mandate grew out of the board's caution about printing falsified accounts as the Committee on Public Information did in World War I. Perhaps board members found the reports from the concentration camps too extreme to be credible. Even so, sometimes they ignored well-documented instances that involved hundreds of victims. They may have felt that the accounts were too gruesome for the public to believe or that anti-Semitism was so strong among some Americans that the incidents would not have the desired effect. Then again the writers might have thought that the public had become inured to atrocity stories after their Lidice campaign. Whatever their thinking, WWB members remained uncharacteristically silent as evidence mounted in 1942 about what would later be known as the Holocaust.

Beginning in 1943 the board wove occasional accounts of the persecution of European Jews into their propaganda. In cooperation with the Polish Information Center, the WWB mailed several authenticated German atrocity stories to its Advisory Council and to selected writers who might mention them in articles and other propaganda pieces. The board also requested comments from its pool of writers about the terrible accounts, and it received a variety of quotations and manuscripts to use as well as evidence of the inclusion of some of the material in local outlets. In February 1943 the popular magazine *American Mercury* carried "The Extermination of the Jews," which decried the systematic slaughter of 2 million individuals of all ages up to that time. The article was divided into two parts, Ben Hecht's emotionally charged "Remember Us" and a fact-based analysis by Eugene Lyons called "Horror Unlimited." Simultaneously *Reader's Digest* published Hecht's piece in abridged form.[135] It depicts several of the atrocity stories the WWB sent out including this incident, which is touchingly related by a victim who speaks from the grave:

> In . . . Szczucin in Poland on the morning of September 23, which is the day . . . for our Atonement, we were all in our synagogues praying God to forgive us. All our village was there. . . . Above our prayers we heard the sound of the motor lorries. They stopped in front of our synagogue.

The Germans tumbled out of them, torches in hand, . . . [and] set fire to us. When we ran out of the flames, they turned machine guns on us. They seized our women and undressed them and made them run naked through the market place before their whips. All of us were killed before our Atonement was done. Remember us.[136]

The mailings on German atrocities appeared throughout the war whenever the board felt it had something that was newsworthy. Early on the organization made and distributed one thousand copies of the article "Axis Crimes—Don't Let Them Happen Here," which had appeared in the magazine supplement of the *Philadelphia Inquirer* on October 22, 1942. The text was accompanied by a series of gory pictures that were among the first solid pieces of proof about the Holocaust. The WWB was disappointed when the material did not cause any appreciable outcry.[137] In April and May 1943 the board augmented newspaper accounts of the revolt by Polish Jews. It also distributed *The Battle of the Warsaw Ghetto* by Morton Wishengrad as a War Script of the Month. A respected scriptwriter of over one hundred programs produced by the Jewish Theological Seminary, Wishengrad had access to detailed information about the massacre of approximately thirteen thousand Jews that had taken place less than six months before the publication of his drama. His stark and brutal script focused on the Nazis' relentless response to the Jewish resistance.[138]

No indication of personal anti-Semitic feelings appears in the board's records, but there are a few curious references that might suggest them. In December 1942 when reports of atrocities against Polish Jews began to emerge, Clifton Fadiman urged WWB writers not to emphasize them from the Jewish angle but to describe the victims as Poles. More than a year later he told Dorothy Thompson that he did not despise the Germans "for their murder of the Jewish people" but rather for "the profoundly evil system they have elected to live under."[139] The statement seems to indicate racial prejudice, but it might instead reflect Fadiman's fear that latent anti-Semitism among Americans would lessen animus against the Germans rather than strengthen it should the board decide to emphasize their brutal treatment of European Jews. Professor Alvin Goldfarb, the son of Holocaust survivors, remarks, "It was easier to muster sympathy for the war effort by emphasizing the sufferings of generalized nationalities rather than focusing on the specific atrocities perpetrated against the Jews." He believes that the WWB was "unlikely" to have harbored anti-Semitic feelings.[140] However that may be, the quick Russian takeover of the Majdanek concentration camp in Poland on July 24, 1944, marked a turning point. The camp was captured almost intact, and the pictures and grisly accounts of what troops found there provided irrefutable evidence of exploitation and massacre far beyond what the WWB had presented to the general public. The board began to publicize newspaper accounts of the unparalleled horror and successfully urged the *Reader's Digest* to publish them. W. H. Lawrence, who condensed the accounts for the well-known magazine, labeled Majdanek "the most terrible place on earth." Filled with details of mass executions and individual cruelties such as instances of Jews burned alive, it went out in November to the *Digest's* vast audience.[141]

During the war WWB members worked hard to pull America's allies closer and to condemn the nation's enemies. While they devoted little time to China, they did an excellent job of solidifying America's relationship with the English and improving the image of the United States in Great Britain. Their activities to promote understanding of the Russians, however, led nowhere, and American attitudes about the communist nation further deteriorated as soon as the war ended. The board's halfhearted initiatives against the Japanese were more of an afterthought than a concentrated effort. The group knew that Americans detested Japan and needed little encouragement to denounce its people and their leaders, demand the country's unconditional surrender, and require harsh peace terms. From the beginning Germany was the group's main target. The WWB was successful in getting its campaign against the country off to a good start with both the book-burning commemorations and the Lidice ceremonies. Less than a month after the Illinois event board chairman Rex Stout began his weekly radio program *Our Secret Weapon* to refute German propaganda. The board described it as "a forward step in the development of a psychology of hate in this country."[142] The use of the term *hate*, which had never before appeared in the WWB minutes, was portentous. In 1943 Stout introduced the word as a topic of public debate and inadvertently changed the tenor of the group's campaign against Germany.

CHAPTER 5

THE CONTROVERSIAL HATE CAMPAIGN

THE NATURE OF the Enemy Campaign launched by the Writers' War Board was only one component of its virulent attack on the Germans, which might be called the "hate campaign." Although WWB members never referred to it in that way, the word *hate* began to appear with some consistency in their propaganda materials beginning in 1943. This campaign expanded over time and continued even after Germany surrendered. It had four major aims that the group considered crucial to victory and world peace: (1) exposing the brutal nature of the Germans, which violated the codes of civilized behavior and human decency; (2) promoting hatred for all German citizens, not only the Nazis; (3) condemning dangerous and infectious ideas like fascism and pan-Germanism, which emphasized German superiority and nationalism; and (4) supporting harsh peace terms to prevent Germany from mounting a third global conflict. Rather quickly the WWB met with opposition in addressing these goals, but the board persisted and met with some success. Even so, the hate campaign brought public criticism of the group from some of its Advisory Council members and its affiliated writers and caused three WWB members to offer their resignations, each of which was declined.

When board members began their propaganda war against Germany, they found that they could not capitalize on anti-German feelings generated by America's participation in World War I. During that conflict German immigrants and German American citizens had faced discrimination, and German language newspapers in the United States had endured harassment. Americans threw out some of the German words that had entered their vocabulary so that "liberty sausage" replaced *hamburger* while *sauerkraut* became "liberty cabbage." Even the Lutheran Church, long supported by the German government, had come under suspicion.[1] However, after the end of the Great War, attitudes shifted. By the time Germany declared war on the United States in 1941, the majority of Americans had mentally separated Hitler and his political party from the rest of the population. They blamed the Nazis for misguiding German citizens and for invading other countries. In their eyes ordinary Germans were intelligent, industrious people whose traditions and accomplishments they knew and respected. This distinction between Nazis and Germans disturbed WWB members, who thought it might lead Americans to question the conduct of the war or otherwise hamper the Allied effort. In fact, an early subject of debate concerned the possibility of harming innocent bystanders in the fighting. Determined to convince the public that Nazis and Germans were one and the same enemy, the board began its propaganda campaign even though poll after poll indicated that the task would be an uphill climb. One survey in June 1942 revealed that a mere 6 percent of Americans felt that the chief enemy in the war against Germany was the German public; 79 percent held that the German government was to blame.[2]

Since the WWB wanted to stress the brutality of all Germans, it repeatedly disparaged the idea of the "good German" and tried to stamp it out. The term might refer to a German who actively opposed the Nazis or to one who passively followed government regulations without harming anyone. In the eyes of many Americans these Germans were not guilty of wrongdoing. Louis Nizer's article "What about the Good Germans?" appeared in the second issue of *Brief Army Camp Items*. It addressed the concern that a harsh peace settlement would hurt all Germans including those who had opposed the Nazis. Nizer, a brilliant New York lawyer, contended that virtually no "good" Germans existed and that the entire population of the nation should be punished for her brutal and aggressive actions. The November 1944 issue of the same publication carried another article on the theme, "True Justice for the Germans" by Nobel Prize–winning Norwegian author Sigrid Undset. It reiterated Nizer's conclusion.[3] The December 1944 editorials contained Alan Green's "Maybe It's Just Some Guys Named Schmidt," which quashed the idea that the ordinary German might be a thoroughly likeable human being.[4]

In September 1942 WWB members established an informal Committee on Creating a Stronger Feeling against the Enemy. Unofficially they referred to it as the "Get Tough" Committee or the "Goddam Truth" Committee or, even more accurately, the "Truth and Hate" Committee, but it never reached the stage of formal organization. Although its name regularly appeared in the group's internal memos, the board's published reports made no mention of it.[5] Chaired by Jack Goodman, its members included Clifton Fadiman, Carl Carmer, Robert Landry, and Margaret Leech. Their main activities involved giving speeches around the East Coast. During the fall Goodman spoke in Pittsburgh; Bridgeport, Connecticut; and three cities in New York—Syracuse, Flushing, and New York City.[6] Others on the board tried different approaches to convince Americans that hatred was a just and indispensable weapon, but some of their projects did not pan out. One was an attempt to sponsor a full-page newspaper advertisement about Nazi atrocities. Board members immediately sought the signatures of a host of prominent individuals but were unable to secure enough names and had to give up the idea. They also tried to arrange a series of radio talks by influential Americans on the nature of the enemy. These were to be given on the Kate Smith program, and well-known people like Wendell Willkie and Alexander Woollcott agreed to give addresses prepared by the WWB. However, the network shortened the length of Smith's airtime before arrangements could be finalized. Subsequent scheduling difficulties made it impossible to find enough time for the speakers, and the board eventually dropped this effort as well.[7] Soon Goodman's committee ceased to function altogether. Its demise was not so much a reflection of failure as a testament to the fact that the Nature of the Enemy Campaign was vitally important to the board as a whole. WWB members saw no need for a specific group since all of them worked on the initiative continually.

As the board expected, opposition to its call to hate surfaced immediately. Members of the religious community complained that it defied the biblical admonition, "Love your enemies, bless them that curse you, do good to them that hate you, and pray for them which despitefully use you, and persecute you" (Matt. 5:44). Officials in the Roosevelt administration expressed concern that targeting all German citizens might hinder peace negotiations and adversely affect efforts to promote international cooperation after the war.⁸ Several writers took a stand against the hate campaign at a PEN dinner in late October 1942. The group, which had invited Rex Stout and Clifton Fadiman to report on the board's work, listened politely to their presentation about the ongoing projects of the Lidice Lives Committee. Then the two speakers called on the international writers' organization to generate an active hate against Germany's entire population. After an objection by literary historian and critic Henry Seidel Canby, who had been one of the most active members of the WWB's Advisory Council during the early months of its existence, a shouting, table-pounding discussion ensued. Writer Arthur G. Hayes called the board's position "hysterical," but Fadiman held his ground, insisting that he knew of "only one way to make a German understand and that's to kill them and even then I don't think they understand."⁹ The debate emphasized the controversial nature of the hate campaign and indicated the arguments that could be lodged against it. WWB members soon found concrete evidence that the general public would have as much trouble accepting their call to hate as the PEN members. Polls continued to show that most people were reluctant to hold ordinary Germans accountable. A National Opinion Research Center survey near the end of 1942 found that a majority of Americans did not blame the German population at large for war atrocities.¹⁰

Appalled by the pervasiveness and the persistence of such attitudes, WWB members determined to present their arguments even more forcefully despite the fact that additional criticism was certain to follow. They found encouragement from a surprising source—the government. Leo Rosten of the OWI attended the board meeting on November 11, 1942, and reported off the record that his agency would welcome pressure to force it and the State Department to identify the enemy as the entire German population rather than the Nazis alone.¹¹ Officially, however, OWI directives continued to state that the majority of Germans should be portrayed as victims.¹² Thereafter, as the board continued to press the issue of German guilt, it appeared once again to be out of sync with the government's viewpoint even though it was not. The military establishment also concurred with the board, and Allied commanders from Great Britain and the United State stirred up animosity toward the enemy whenever they could. In November General Lesley James McNair, American infantry commander, made a nationally broadcast speech in which he taunted his troops, "You are going to get killing mad eventually—why not now?" Similarly, the U.S. Army in Algiers ordered its commanders to "teach their men to hate the enemy."[13]

HATEMONGERING

Late in 1942 Paul Gallico composed "Slant on Hate," an internal document intended to clarify the attitude that the WWB wanted to cultivate. From a twenty-first-century perspective it seems rabid, berating the enemy as less than human. Despite the fact that his father had immigrated to the United States from Italy, Gallico denounced Italians as well as Germans and Japanese. He contended that Americans should "hate, abominate and abhor the enemy, Nazi, Wop and Jap, with a loathing that grips us night and day." He not only described the feeling of all-consuming hatred but also explained its necessity in war, stating unequivocally that no citizen could look favorably on the country's enemies, their "brats," or their customs without dire consequences: "To say that they are human like ourselves, but misled, is to send a bullet whistling through the body of some American." He continued,

> We must . . . cultivate black anger, bitterness and loathing at the thought of [the enemy]. His presence on earth must stink in our nostrils like carrion. We must bend our minds not to educating, winning or reforming him, but to wiping him out. We must learn to distill and spew forth a venom that is more powerful and deadly than his and trust in God for the saving of our own souls. For without this hatred there will be nothing for us to save and none of us will survive.[14]

The group discussed Gallico's strong and uncompromising statement at length and decided to use it as a working memorandum. Although no objections appear in the minutes, WWB member Carl Carmer asserted twenty-five years later that it would be "unfair" to say that the statement represented the majority feeling. While agreeing that certain members "had become for individual and personal reasons as hysterical as the statement indicates," he was "positive from my knowledge of the personnel of the group that these extremists were not in the majority." He was, furthermore, "certain . . . that the Board did not release this [document] as in any way identified with its own feelings."[15] The records of the WWB, however, do not bear out Carmer's memories. Many believed that reviling the enemy was essential to winning the war.

With the approval and support of the board, Stout published a controversial article entitled "We Shall Hate, or We Shall Fail" in the *New York Times Magazine* at the beginning of 1943. Disregarding his upbringing as a Quaker, the author observed that the biblical command to love is an ideal to strive for rather than a practical rule by which to live, and he argued that Americans should not be so repulsed by the word *hate* that they would refuse to curb the violent actions of the Germans. He felt that hatred was the proper response to "their savage attack upon the rights and dignity of man, . . . their ruthless assault on the persons and property of innocent and well-meaning people, [and] their arrogant and insolent doctrine of the German master race . . . , by which [they] justify their contempt of all other people and their domination of other countries by force." Stout further charged that it is not possible to hate cruelty and injustice without hating those who are cruel and unjust: "A man who tells you he hates evil but not the doer of evil is kidding either you or himself and in any case is gibbering." According to the WWB chairman the only acceptable motive for destroying evildoers is hatred: "To kill them while pretending to love them is dishonest, to kill them and remain emotionally indifferent is abhorrent, and to kill them with an assumption of the attributes of God is inadmissible." Stout also discussed the issue of hating some Germans but not others and admitted that he felt no shame about hating all Germans, even those who were not Nazis. He believed that their failure to stop Hitler "through lack of courage or conviction" was responsible for "plunging the world into this filthy swamp of destruction, misery, and hatred." Finally, to those who saw hatred as inevitably harmful, Stout declared,

> It is not true that if we hate the Germans now we are helping to fill a reservoir of hate-poison that will infect the future beyond all hope of antisepsis. On the contrary. If we do not hate the Germans now, we shall inevitably fail in our purpose to establish the world on a basis of

peace. If we do not see the evil clearly enough to hate it as it deserves, which means, make no mistake, hating those who do or tolerate the evil, the temptation will be irresistible, at one point or another, to compromise with it instead of destroying it.[16]

Within four days the newspaper received a number of letters, almost all of them opposing Stout's views. One expressed fear that hatred would interfere with the technical efficiency of American soldiers; another protested that Stout was "going Nazi" in order to conquer Nazism. Yet a third emphasized Christ's refusal to express hatred on the cross and ended with the comment that the Nazis "know not what they do."[17] Stout replied to these letters, reemphasizing the points he had made and concluding that the letter writers "are as well meaning as anybody else, but they are incapable of facing the ugly facts regarding our enemies."[18] On January 31 the *New York Times Magazine* published the rebuttal article "Hate Is Moral Poison" by Episcopal theologian Walter R. Bowie. He stated, "Mr. Stout's argument runs to an indiscriminate ferocity," and claimed that the author's words "would twist this war away from any hope of a decent result." He said that soldiers used "costly courage" in fighting the enemy, but only "professional pamphleteers" needed to get their "emotional release" from such hatred, which he called a "sort of insanity." He concluded, "The truth is that wars are not won by dosing people up with a lot of synthetic hatred. They can be lost that way, as Hitler will find out."[19] Undaunted, Stout replied that such men as John Brown, William Lloyd Garrison, Oliver Cromwell, and Martin Luther were "powerful and effective haters" who "knew quite well that hate is not always a moral poison; it may be and sometimes is a moral necessity."[20]

In comparison to Gallico's internal memorandum Stout's published article seems tame, but negative responses immediately came from Catholic newspapers, the Federal Council of Churches, and members of the general public. A number of these sources described the chairman's views as "appalling."[21] His argument found only occasional supporters like the individual who asserted, "There is ever a need for good hatred."[22] The atmosphere of dissension continued to grow and soon invaded the board. When Stout suggested in a WWB meeting that minority opinions be suppressed in the interest of time and unity, Goodman immediately offered his resignation. Given the fact that Stout was a trustee of Freedom House, an organization that championed freedom of speech, his comment was totally out of line. The board quickly affirmed Goodman's right to object and rejected his resignation.[23] Despite the fact that this foray into the public forum had brought controversy, neither Stout nor the majority of the board backed off.

As part of their hate campaign on March 4, 1943, WWB members met with radio commentators Cecil Brown, John Gunther, Larry LeSeuer, George Fielding Eliot, and others who could suggest subtle changes in the wording and tone that radio broadcasters used to present war information. The list that they compiled and subsequently sent to radio stations across the country included the following items:

- Use *German* for *Nazi* except where specific reference is made to the Nazi party.
- Use *enslaved* for *occupied* whenever reference is made to territory held by the Germans.
- Use *liberated* or some synonym for *occupied* whenever reference is made to territory won by any of the United [Allied] Nations, including Soviet Russia.
- Use . . . *murder* for *execute* (when it is a question of Germans killing civilians).[24]

When such changes in wording were incorporated into the scripts of a variety of programs on each network and repeated several times every day, they eventually affected the public's attitude and outlook. For example, Americans who reacted negatively to the idea that they needed to endure hardships *for the duration* of the war, which seemed endless, might not mind so much if they heard that they had to hold out *until victory*, a goal that dangled before them like a coveted award. The WWB list also encouraged radio broadcasters to play on the emotions of their listeners by using atrocity stories and connecting fascist leaders to the brutal actions of their regimes. Announcers were instructed to refer to Francisco Franco not as the fascist head of the Spanish government but as "the head of the party that has sworn to exterminate one third of the male Spanish population."[25] About six months before Germany surrendered, the group added one final suggestion: "Use *genocide* when referring to German crimes." Many broadcasters complied with these requests including radio commentator and newspaper journalist Walter Winchell, whose column appeared in two thousand papers and had a readership of 50 million.[26]

Every WWB committee and publication contributed to the hate campaign in some way. "Around the Cracker Barrel," a recurring column in the *Writers' War Board Report* and some issues of the *Brief Items* publications, offered an informal discussion of materials the Nazis circulated as part of their psychological warfare program. The issue of June 1, 1944, disdainfully mentioned a German group rumored to exist: "Well, boys, they're starting early. The report has reached this country that the Nazis have already formed a new organization, the Black Party, to take up the cause of National Socialism after the war. . . . Apparently they no more intend to give up after this war than they did after the last war. What do we do about it? Give 'em a nice, easy, negotiated peace? Or fight on till we teach 'em all a lesson they'll *never* forget?"[27] Another column that appeared periodically in the monthly *Report* and regularly in *Brief House Organ Items* was "Take Your Pick." It contrasted provocative quotations from prominent Germans with the remarks of well-known Americans. In May 1944 the column presented a denunciation of democracy from Hitler's *Mein Kampf*: "A majority can never replace a man. A majority always represents both stupidity and cowardice. There is no principle so wrong as the parliamentary principle." Set against the Führer's words was a brief observation by Abraham Lincoln: "No man is good enough to govern another without the other's consent."[28] Board publications often promoted some special emphasis on the hate theme. In March 1944 "How to Tell a Fascist" by Cecil Brown appeared in the inaugural issue of *Brief Army Camp Items*. It offered a checklist that anyone could use to identify Americans sympathetic to the Nazi viewpoint. The article was later put in pamphlet form for general distribution and was published in *See* magazine. In the January 1945 *Bulletin to Cartoonists*, Fadiman called for drawings on the subject "Hitler or No Hitler—Doesn't Make Any Difference."[29] The Führer having survived an assassination attempt the previous July, the board decided to argue that Germans would adhere to their goals even if their leaders changed as the war in Europe wound down.

The board promoted anti-German material in a variety of other publications too. *Real Life Comics* printed Lorraine Beim's "A Loaf of Bread" and Sigrid Schultz's "The Story of Fritz." The latter, which ran in its March 1945 issue, is the true account of an eleven-year-old German boy who saw his friends turn into brutes after Hitler came to power. One day they beat him unconscious during recess because his mother was Jewish. None of the teachers came to his rescue, and no one was punished for the crime even though Fritz suffered brain damage and could no longer recognize his parents. Both stories were to be part of a series on German atrocities that Standard Comics had proposed the previous summer, but it never materialized even though the WWB responded eagerly and recruited a number of writers. The publisher accepted only those two pieces and then dropped the idea, possibly because Germany's surrender was then imminent.[30]

Plays written under the auspices of the WWB addressed the hate topic also. In December 1942 the War Scripts of the Month Committee distributed Janet Brandus's *The Nazi*, which presented the board's view of the German character. In June 1944 it mailed two more scripts on the malevolent nature of Germans and their prospective fate, *Judgment* by Norman Williams and *Der Führer (and the Great Lie He Borrowed)* by Max Ehrlich. The August script was *War Criminals and Punishment*, an adaptation by Richard McDonough of parts of the George Creel book of the same title, which detailed the brutality of German and Japanese officials and recommended stern punishment for them. Although board members had declined to promote the 1944 work because it was poorly written, they found a way to use its message for propaganda purposes. The October Script of the Month, *Promise vs. the Deed* by William K. Clarke, was also based on Creel's book.[31]

The Committee on Speeches and Speakers helped the campaign by preparing addresses denigrating Germans. In 1942 these included "The Nature of the Enemy" by Green and a Fadiman piece, "Who Is Our Enemy?" The latter identified America's foe as "the man on the street of Berlin or Tokyo—because of his basic nature."[32] One of the first messages the Assignments Committee sent to writers after its establishment in January 1943 concerned the "Decade of Death." The group encouraged authors to emphasize the devastation Hitler had caused during his ten years in power as they made public appearances, addressed audiences, and wrote articles for publication.[33] For firsthand accounts about Germany the board turned to several journalists who had served as overseas correspondents. Quentin Reynolds, Robert St. John, and others presented U.S. Army orientation lectures detailing German brutality. The committee also secured speakers for private organizations like the National Press Club, which heard Paul Gallico deliver an address on the often deplorable treatment of Americans and others in German prisons.

ANTI-GERMAN BOOKS AND OTHER PUBLICATIONS

A large part of the board's hate campaign was the promotion of books that revealed the malevolent nature of America's enemies or validated the board's position in some other way. In his 1943 work *The Hidden Enemy: The German Threat to Post-War Peace*, expatriate Heinz Pol acknowledged the menace posed by Nazi fascists and identified pan-Germans as an unrecognized, insidious danger. Referring to the ethnocentric nationalists as the "Nazis behind the Nazis," Pol traced their history over two generations, tying their attitude of superiority and destiny to Germany's long drive for unification, achieved in 1871. Although the pan-Germans did not formally organize until 1890, Pol argued that they had driven their countrymen to achieve glory, power, and conquest by instigating conflict after conflict long before that time. Whether they joined the Nazi Party when Hitler came to power or simply acquiesced to his leadership, the pan-Germans remained focused on imperialism, Pol insisted, and their views permeated all levels of German society.[34]

Another notable book that the WWB publicized was *Under Cover: My Four Years in the Nazi Underworld of America* by journalist Avedis Derounian, an Armenian immigrant who used the pseudonym John Roy Carlson. It became the number one nonfiction bestseller in 1943, at least partly because of the board's efforts, which were augmented by the Friends of Democracy (FOD) and Freedom House. The book's subtitle indicates the author's emphasis on sensational details: *The Amazing Revelation of How Axis Agents and Our Enemies within Are Now Plotting to Destroy the United States*. Working for the FOD, Carlson infiltrated a number of right-wing groups, twenty-two of which he specifically identified in his work.[35] WWB members also had high regard for Richard M. Brickner's *Is Germany Incurable?* A psychiatrist, Brickner contended that

Germany exemplified in its past and present actions traits comparable to those of a paranoid individual. He used medical terminology in asserting that its future actions could be predicted by studying the behavior patterns of people diagnosed with the condition. Brickner proposed a plan to "cure" Germany by reeducating its citizens.[36]

Other books that received board attention that year included *Black Mail* by Henry Hoke. A pioneer in the use of the relatively new and "distinctly American . . . selling tool" called "Direct Mail Advertising," Hoke claimed to expose a Nazi "conspiracy . . . to convert Direct Mail . . . into an instrument for destruction" by sending fascist material to individual homes.[37] Another volume was *Germany Will Try It Again* by Sigrid Schultz, who had lived in Germany for twenty-five years. She traced the origins of the Second World War to a secret plot concocted by the pan-German general staff of the army before the end of the First World War, and she suggested that a similar plot was underway to prepare for a third war.[38] *The Thousand Year Conspiracy: Secret Germany behind the Mask* makes a similar argument. Author Paul Winkler asserted that Nazism was the latest manifestation of a secret society that had its origins in the thirteenth century. He contended that the aggressive attitude of the German people had arisen during the "First Reich" of Otto the Great, German king and Holy Roman Emperor from 936 to 973.[39]

The board criticized two books that did not adhere to its views and tried to prevent the public from reading them. One was Rosie Goldschmidt Waldeck's *Meet Mr. Blank, the Leader of Tomorrow's Germans*. The WWB first contacted the G. P. Putnam firm to persuade it not to publish the book, arguing that its assessment of possible postwar German leaders did not take into account the group's dictum that all Germans were responsible for Germany's actions. When Putnam issued the book anyway, board members successfully stimulated disparaging reviews to curb sales and discussion.[40] The WWB had a similar problem with *Germany: A Short History* by George W. Schuster and Arnold Bergsträsser. Despite the fact that members found the work to be too sympathetic to its subject, W. W. Norton published it, and the board gave it the same treatment that the Waldeck book had received the previous year.[41]

When one of their own recommended selections encountered criticism, WWB members launched a special effort to save it. At first Brickner's

Is Germany Incurable? received the usual support with favorable quotes from prominent people. Stout discussed it and praised it in a *New York Times Magazine* article, and Carmer arranged for Brickner to appear on the radio program *Author Meets Critic*. However, in the *Saturday Review of Literature* a panel of six prominent individuals, including philosopher Bertrand Russell and psychologist Erich Fromm, attacked the book and challenged its premise.[42] In order to refute their criticism and to reestablish the credibility of the book, the board instigated an authoritative rebuttal. It obtained a long letter signed by Dr. Lawrence Kubie and five other psychiatrists, who reaffirmed Brickner's argument as "wholly valid," and the organization saw that the *Saturday Review* published it.[43]

The board also used comic books to deliver its hate message, but it had a problem with the way that these illustrated works presented Germans. As Clifton Fadiman observed, they often depicted enemy troops as pushovers who were easily fooled, and they identified only Nazis as the enemy without blaming the rest of the German population.[44] Accordingly, correspondence went out to writers and illustrators of comic strips and comic books from *Terry and the Pirates* to *Superman*. The board urged them to give the Germans realistic treatment and suggested several war themes and storylines that reflected its concerns.[45] Although the letters initiated some changes, board members felt that the comics could have done more to deliver the right propaganda message.

In the summer of 1944 M. C. Gaines and Sheldon Mayer of *All-Star Comics* made their first contact with the WWB about helping to produce an issue. The board jumped at the chance to portray the German menace and chronicle the adventures of the Justice Society of America. This group of super heroes included Green Lantern, Flash, Hawkman, Wonder Woman, The Atom, Dr. Mid-Nite, and Johnny Thunder. When an early version of the script blamed the Nazi leadership alone for Germany's actions, Stout, Gallico, and Green demanded a change and worked on the revision. WWB executive secretary Frederica Barach brought Mayer up short in a letter: "The emphasis on leaders who tricked their people into war strikes entirely the wrong note from the Board's point of view. Emphasis should be rather that the people were willing dupes and easily sold on a program of aggression."[46] Mayer conceded the point, and the board was well pleased with the outcome. WWB members fretted over a title, coming up with a number of suggestions including "Goosestepping through the Centuries" and "Germany, Bully among Nations." As editor, Mayer eventually settled on "This Is Our Enemy," which they accepted.[47]

The spring 1945 issue of *All-Star Comics* identified Germany as "a degenerate nation whose people throughout the centuries have always been willing to follow their military leaders into endless, bloody but futile warfare." In the story members of the Justice Society move back through time from the 1400s to the 1920s, encountering Germans from different eras who have one thing in common: all of them are ruthless warmongers. Even the dim-witted Johnny Thunder, whose super hero status derived solely from his ability to summon the powerful creature Thunderbolt, grasped the point: "I have learned the truth that for many centuries Germanic rulers and military leaders have led a willing people into war after war." Pleased with the storyline, which emphasized that German barbarism could only be stopped through the use of force, the WWB attempted to get an extra paper ration for the publication but did not succeed. Even so, six hundred thousand copies of the issue were printed, and estimates at the time suggested that they would reach several million readers as they were passed around.[48]

The WWB also urged members of the film industry to depict Germans negatively. They opposed any effort to make Hitler seem ridiculous, however, because they did not want to distract from the seriousness of the nation's purpose. Fadiman said, "It is very true that a sense of humor is one of the most valuable possessions; and I am of the opinion that we should resume our exercise of it when the peace is won."[49] To steer filmmakers in the right direction, the board used its "bombs" or "duds" movie reviews beginning in April 1943 with the first issue of its *Report*. The group developed a fourteen-point checklist and deducted points if films portrayed (1) "Hitler and the Nazis as our chief enemy, instead of the German people"; (2) "the Germans as an innocent people misled by Hitler and the Nazis"; (3) "any German or Japanese as a sympathetic character"; (4) "any former cultural achievements of the Germans or Japanese"; or (5) "any of the United [Allied] Nations in an unsympathetic light."[50] The board also used a carrot-and-stick approach. It made an effort to promote films that supported its viewpoint but worked against those that did not. When the New York writers heard about a movie that delivered the wrong message, they sent letters to its producers requesting a change. Usually their comments arrived before or during filming, but on occasion they did not learn about objectionable content until after filming had wrapped up. Even at such a late date, they did not hesitate to inform filmmakers about their concerns.

One movie that they backed was a fictional account of Reinhard Heydrich's assassination released in April 1943. As usual, they obtained favorable quotes on *Hangmen Also Die!* from well-known people. The propaganda ploy stimulated interest despite the fact that most of the prominent individuals who plugged the film had never seen it but had simply given the WWB permission to use their names. Because the board's tactics proved effective, Fadiman could report, "Frequently the film producers have been quite cooperative."[51] A special WWB promotion in late 1944 involved the March of Time film *What to Do with Germany?* Based on Louis Nizer's book of the same title, this twenty-minute documentary showed scenes from concentration camps and explained that killing hundreds of thousands of Jews and other minorities could give German Aryans a biological victory even if they lost the war. It then discussed the necessity of imposing harsh peace terms.[52]

Board members arranged for key figures from the press and radio to attend one of four previews of the film that it set up in New York. On behalf of the WWB Henry Pringle hosted a special showing in Washington attended by over one hundred diplomats, press representatives, and government officials. Subsequently the Treasury and State Departments arranged their own previews. The board included quotes from prominent writers in advertisements of the film, and a special notice of its New York showings appeared in *Variety*. The board gave the film a four-bomb rating in its *Report* and asked writers around the country to mention it favorably whenever possible. In January 1945 *Brief Army Camp Items* published "Sanity—German Style," a reiteration of the film's major arguments, and radio commentator Gabriel Heatter broadcast Nizer's idea that the Nazis planned to achieve a biological victory.[53]

A DITTY, SOME DOGGEREL, AND OTHER PROPAGANDA

Although a number of World War I songs like "Over There" and "Pack Up Your Troubles in Your Old Kit Bag" were memorable enough to last long after the conflict, the same cannot be said of the majority of World

War II songs.[54] Nevertheless, the WWB found a satirical piece by Noel Coward that proved to be an excellent vehicle to convey its arguments. The group premiered the song in a fifteen-minute radio program over the NBC network on November 23, 1943. "Don't Let's Be Beastly to the Germans" used humor instead of fear to ridicule the notion of showing Christian charity to a nation that had torn the world apart with two wars in less than thirty years. It also debunked some popular notions that the board had repeatedly denounced: the idea that the Germans did not deserve a hard peace because they had been helplessly manipulated by their leaders and the idea that Hitler and the Nazis were the only ones to blame for the country's vicious actions. In jaunty words Coward facetiously suggested that the peace settlement would provide a good opportunity for the Allies and the Axis nations to kiss and make up:

Don't let's be beastly to the Germans
When our victory is ultimately won,
It was just those hasty Nazis who persuaded them to fight,
And their Beethoven and Bach are really far worse than their bite!
Let's be meek to them,
And turn the other cheek to them
And try to bring out their latent sense of fun.
Let's give them full air parity
And treat the rats with charity
But don't let's be beastly to the Hun![55]

The equally sarcastic second verse compared the Germans to gangsters with guns and pointed out that they had "been a little naughty to the Czechs and Poles and Dutch" by invading their countries. It blithely suggested that they needed to regain confidence: "Let's help them feel they're swell again / And bomb us all to hell again, / But don't let's be beastly to the Hun!" The song had caused considerable controversy in Britain after its original performance in July. Some literal-minded individuals mistakenly believed it to be a pro-German piece while others objected to its real meaning, which is evident both in the metaphors comparing the Germans to rats and gangsters and in the ridiculous notion that the Allies should help them make more bombing raids. In reaction British radio executives withdrew it, and American publishers prevented its circulation in the United States.[56]

Primarily at Fadiman's urging, the WWB obtained the rights to broadcast the song. In a letter to scriptwriter Frank Sullivan, he explained what the board wanted: "The script should be light, make fun of the pious folks who want us to be sweet to the Germans both now and after the war, and should explain enough about the song to get over to the old lady from Dubuque that it is ironical and not meant to be taken seriously. . . . All I know is that this is a wonderful chance to put over our propaganda with plenty of chocolate syrup, and we must not muff it."[57] Fadiman opened the program with an explanatory preamble to make certain that the song could not be misunderstood. Sarcastically he said, "If the Germans have murdered millions of their fellow men it was all done in a spirit of innocent fun. . . . We must not blame the poor darlings of the master race. . . . Let's have no mistake about it; this song is satiric, tongue-in-cheek and bludgeon in hand."[58] Next came the American debut of Coward's song by Broadway star Celeste Holm, and finally Fadiman read an added verse that he had written on assignment from the board. It mentioned "the German master race" and said that the Allies would be "a bunch of saps" if they followed the example of the Good Samaritan. The show proved to be highly successful, and several hundred recordings of the presentation were sent to radio stations across the nation.[59]

Editorials that the WWB distributed in February 1944 utilized Coward's song to caution Americans not to have soft hearts and short memories. In March a plug for Schultz's *Germany Will Try It Again* was mixed with a statement about the possibility of another war if the peace settlement did not place enough restrictions on Germany. In his August editorial "Preparing for 1964," Rex Stout envisaged future German plots. That September Fadiman contributed "Recipe for Civil War," an exposé of American fascist movements as well as a promotion for the book *Black Mail*. The October editorials included ". . . But the German General Staff Goes on Forever" by Joseph Jackson and "Don't Say We Weren't Warned" by Alan Green, both of which reiterated the WWB's point of view about a possible third world war.[60]

The board also organized a project to send letters signed by prominent people to newspaper editors throughout the United States. Although they varied in style and content, all supported one or more contentions of the hate campaign. As it often did, the WWB agreed to handle the writing if the individuals gave their consent and furnished their letterhead stationery. Among those who took advantage of the offer were authors Channing Pollock and Booth Tarkington and self-improvement expert Dale Carnegie.[61] The participation of such people insured a fairly high rate of publication. Among the letters printed in the *Indianapolis Star* and other local newspapers was one from board member Franklin P. Adams, who managed to couch the WWB message of hate in a bit of doggerel:

Some people "pity the poor Germans."
    I hate 'em.
Some "turn the other cheek" in sermons.
    I hate 'em.
Pity for them I haven't got:
I do not pity them a jot.
I mean the whole pan-German lot.
    I hate 'em.[62]

A similar poem of his appeared in the June 1944 issue of *Brief Army Camp Items*:

The Germans hate the U. S. A.
    They hate all people who are free.
Easter they hate and Christmas Day.
    They don't like you; they dislike me.
They have a hundred daily hates.
    They scream, they holler, and they curse.
And this citizen of the U. S. A.
    Hates them immeasurably worse.[63]

Aside from letters WWB members either wrote or inspired magazine articles to promote all aspects of the hate campaign. Beginning in June 1944 they placed six "tough propaganda pieces" in different issues of *American Legion Magazine*, which went to 1.3 million veterans. Contributors included John Kieran, Paul Gallico, Sumner Welles, and J. B. Powell.[64] William Shirer's article "Soft Peace = World War III" emphasized the wholehearted support of the German people for the conquest of much of Europe. In "White-Washing the Nazis" prominent historian Allan Nevins attacked revisionists who argued "that Germany, after all, was no more to blame for World War I than France or Britain" and claimed that they had already begun "waving the first whitewash brushes at the war guilt of the Nazis."[65] Articles on similar topics appeared in a host of magazines. For example, the Allies that liberated Holland had not completely routed Hitler's forces from the country before Christopher LaFarge published an article in *Cosmopolitan* describing German brutalities there.[66]

ATTACKS ON THE WWB

Beginning in January 1944 one controversy after another surfaced, miring the WWB in criticism from within as well as without. Left-wing columnist Milton Mayer fired the first volley. In 1942 he had earned some notoriety with his deliberately provocative *Saturday Evening Post* article "The Case against the Jew" in which he predicted, "The post-war collapse [into anti-Semitism] will remind a bitter and bewildered nation that 'the Jews got us into the war.'"[67] Writing two years later in *Common Sense*, he got the board's attention when he described its members as a group of haters intent on "transform[ing] the American people into mad dogs."[68] The WWB believed that his article "The War Guilt of Fadiman Kip" had two underlying purposes: to cripple the hate campaign and to disparage the board's ideas about harsh peace terms for Germany such as the dismemberment of the nation. Mayer insisted that a stringent peace settlement was certain to be as unfair as the Versailles Treaty of 1919 and, in a rather convoluted argument, concluded that it would ultimately bring "new Hitlers" to power: "I am not saying that the dismemberment of Germany, or the enslavement of Germans to rebuild France and Russia will be unjust. I am saying only that if, when this war is won, we feel unjust, we will then feel guilty, and in the terror of our guilt, real or imagined, we will allow new Hitlers to relieve us of our guiltiness by committing new enormities."[69]

Mayer sprinkled his mean-spirited article with insults, referring to Stout as "Jack the Rip" and depicting "Kip and Rip" as two horses with

Rip "prancing proudly in front" and Kip "trotting pathetically behind," mindlessly following Stout's lead.[70] Fadiman replied to Mayer, an old acquaintance: "There is nothing to say about your completely insane and completely untrue vicious attack on me except to tell you privately what a larger number will soon know publicly—that you are a first-rate son of a bitch and that I hope to have the opportunity very soon of making the point to you more clearly and more personally."[71] Deciding that his presence might now be detrimental to the board, Fadiman resigned, but the other members of the group persuaded him to remain.[72] In April Mayer returned to the attack in another *Common Sense* article, "Are Japs Human?" He referred to board members as "maniacs" and complained about a suggestion that the WWB never made: "Those members of the Writers' War Board who want to sterilize all Germans are premeditating an atrocity, and yet the time will come when we will all say that they, the Bloody Writers, should be forgiven because they were momentarily crazy even in their premeditation."[73] In August Mayer took another swipe at the organization, linking Stout with Father Charles Coughlin. The Catholic priest had attracted a large nationwide following by spouting isolationist, racist, neo-fascist views on his weekly radio program. Mayer considered both men to be experts in hatred.[74]

Three months after Mayer's first article denouncing the WWB, more criticism came from political scientist Carl J. Friedrich, a longtime rival of the board chairman. In 1941 Stout had pushed the German-born Harvard professor out of the antifascist Council for Democracy because of Friedrich's contention that the Nazis alone were our enemies, not the German people. The professor privately acknowledged, "I didn't like Rex and he didn't like me."[75] Writing in the *American Journal of Sociology* in March 1944, Friedrich stated, "Perhaps the most marked forms of undemocratic, pro-Fascist mentality are today to be observed in certain traditionally liberal circles when they discuss the treatment of the enemy. The Writers' War Board is permeated with such influences." He further incurred the group's wrath by contending that Germany was changing: "According to most competent observers, Germany is headed toward a genuine democratic revolution, a revolution that was artificially delayed by all sorts of factors."[76] Stout, who enjoyed verbal sparring, replied to the editor, "That the Writers' War Board is permeated by pro-Fascist influences, without offering a shred of evidence to support the charge, is inexcusable." He taunted the author, "I challenge Mr. Friedrich to name ten, or even two, competent observers . . . who believe Germany is headed toward a democratic revolution."⁷⁷ While Friedrich let most of his arguments stand with no rebuttal, he made one correction, blaming his comment about the WWB's "pro-fascist mentality" on a typographical error and stating that he had intended to use the adjective "pre-fascist" instead. Elsewhere he criticized the OWI and the WWB for the "informational strategy" of blaming all Germans, even though the former never did so publicly. He argued that the Germans were misguided and declared, "The enemy whose will to fight must be broken are the Nazis themselves."⁷⁸

Another organization that Stout headed, the Society for the Prevention of World War III (SPWW3), published a full-page advertisement in the *New York Times* that occasioned additional criticism of the WWB. It denounced a group of German expatriates, many of them well-known, well-educated professionals who were in the process of forming their own organization, the Council for a Democratic Germany (CDG). Both the SPWW3 and the WWB suspected that they might be pan-Germans that intended to use the CDG to try and soften the terms of the peace settlement with Germany when the time came. The ad that appeared on April 22, 1944, cautioned the public not to be deceived by the "political exiles" forming "a so-called council of democratic Germans" and vehemently argued, "We have been fooled once by a so-called German 'democracy.' Must we be fooled again? This is no time for Americans to work on the manufacture of a device for Germany's escape. It is time to teach Germany and the German people the only lesson they apply to others, the only lesson they understand: Force."⁷⁹ This propaganda effort may have made some people wary, but it had little effect on the CDG. Less than two weeks after its publication, the newly formed group began to operate under the leadership of theologian Paul Tillich. He praised its German-born members, many of them experts in their fields, and asserted that they "might best be able to create a democracy in Germany" during the postwar period.⁸⁰

But the strong condemnation of the CDG did not fail to provoke one public response: renewed criticism from *Common Sense*. It insisted that the ad showed "an attitude toward democratic organizations that is shared by Goebbels and Himmler. . . . It is virtually incitement to lynching." Presumably written by editor Sidney Hertzberg, "The Shame of American Writers" castigated not only Stout and the SPWW3 but also the WWB: "Under . . . Rex Stout the Writers' War Board has . . . acquired an ideology. Mr. Stout is the heart of the Writers' War Board and Mr. Stout's heart seethes with hatred for all Germans." As evidence Hertzberg cited Stout's writings and complained that most of the books promoted by the New York group in 1943 and 1944 were "indiscriminate condemnations of the German people, or lend themselves to this view."[81]

Admitting that the WWB had clout, Hertzberg charged that its chairman used media outlets to espouse racism, and he denounced American writers for acquiescing to Stout's leadership:

> The influence of the Board is far-reaching. It has direct access to all media of mass communications. It cooperates with various official agencies. . . . Rex Stout, the mystery writer, is not important. But Rex Stout, Chairman of the Writers' War Board is—because he can use his position to pose as the spokesman of American writers, and because he can use his position to gain access to publications and radio stations through which he can reach millions with the propaganda of hatred and vengeance. . . . There is a danger that we will come through this war victims of rampant racism—hating the Germans as Germans, crying for blood vengeance. If we do, the fault will lie partly with American writers who, by their silence, are condoning an international vendetta now being carried on in their name.[82]

Hertzberg ended his diatribe with a call for protests by American writers, WWB members, and OWI director Elmer Davis. Without waiting for their responses, the editor contacted several of them and published their replies in June. Davis said that the WWB's private announcements had no official status; however, speaking as a private citizen, he expressed support for the board, calling attention to German barbarism and the willingness of "non-Nazi" Germans to go along with Hitler. Davis called on them to prove that they were different: "It is about time the good Germans did something."[83]

A few writers either backed Stout or took a neutral position about his actions. Poet and educator Mark Van Doren said, "Rex Stout has my full sympathy and support. . . . You have invited me to make a protest. Very well, I protest against the lack of candor and common sense in your report and against the poisonously sentimental nonsense by Milton Mayer which you have printed." Author Struthers Burt, who agreed with the WWB, objected to Hertzberg's vocabulary, especially "the use of such terms as 'racism' etc. in this discussion. Stout does not hate the Germans because they are Germans, he hates them, as I do, because they have endorsed evil, and because for many generations they have subscribed, save for a few great men and women, to evil doctrines." William McFee and Louis Bromfield largely concurred, but John P. Marquand, who saw no harm in Stout's expression of private views, questioned the mystery writer's mention of his position as WWB chairman. Henry Seidel Canby, caught in the middle as a member of the WWB Advisory Council and as a sponsor of the CDG, agreed with Stout that all Germans were responsible for their history. However, he found some of Stout's remarks "impractical, unpolitic, and fundamentally absurd." Editor-author Frederick Lewis Allen disagreed with Stout. Nevertheless, he felt that the issue was "not vital" and should not be used to discredit the "manifold and useful services" of both Stout and the WWB.[84]

No doubt to Hertzberg's delight the majority of the writers were critical of Stout, sometimes condemnatory. Their comments reveal dissatisfaction with some of the board's views and its tactics. Literary critic and historian Alfred Kazin did not mince words: "It is sickening that the war, and some of the most important political problems of our time, should be exploited by a detective-story writer, puffed up with letterheads and nominal official 'contacts' when so many honest writers are silent." Two historians expressed their disgust. Carl Becker called the views of the WWB "romantic and deluded," while William Henry Chamberlin said the elementary facts of recent European history would repudiate Stout's ideas. He referred to Stout as a "noncombatant" whose "hatemongering outbursts . . . with their bad history and bad logic and inverted racism are a direct challenge to every member of the Writers' War Board." One of the editors of the *New York Herald-Tribune* expressed consternation: "I fail to see how any self-respecting writer can serve on the Writers'

War Board under Mr. Stout's chairmanship." Others described Stout and the members of the WWB with adjectives like "pernicious," "infantile and effeminate," and "ignorant and immoral." They characterized the group's beliefs as "rubbish," "idiocy," and a "shameless betrayal of the truth." A particularly strong condemnation came from literary critic Granville Hicks:

> As one who receives material from the Writers' War Board, I know that the situation is rather worse than your editorial suggests. Month after month writers are urged to preach hatred of the German people not only in their books and articles but also in anonymous paragraphs to be distributed by the board and in speeches that are to be ghost-written for delivery by persons of influence. I believe that the Writers' War Board should be repudiated by both the Authors' League and the Office of War Information unless Mr. Stout can demonstrate that he is speaking for the majority of American writers and for the government.[85]

All WWB members who attended the board meeting on May 17 signed a letter to *Common Sense* rejecting Hertzberg's views as "largely based upon falsehood." To support their leader, they made it clear that he never spoke as WWB chairman without their approval although he had the right to express his own opinions under his own name on his personal stationery.[86] Hertzberg seems to have deliberately misinterpreted the board's reply in his follow-up editorial, "The Points at Issue."[87] Reviewing his work later that year, Hertzberg proudly claimed, "On the subject of postwar Europe, perhaps our most useful achievement was the destruction of the notion that Rex Stout's hatred propaganda against Germany represented the sentiment of American writers or even of the handful of writers on the Writers' War Board of which Stout is chairman."[88] Ironically, less than a year after the political left denounced the board, the political right attacked it on the same grounds. In January 1945 conservative columnist George E. Sokolsky asked how Americans could prevent another war "if we go on ever-lastingly hating sixty million Germans and Japanese. . . . When Rex Stout and the Writers' War Board [condemn these people], they do mischief, well intentioned perhaps, but nonetheless senseless and vicious."[89]

COMPOSING A POSITION STATEMENT

Sidney Hertzberg's comments had no immediate impact on the board. Before their meeting on May 17, 1944, adjourned, members approved without change a script that Christopher LaFarge had written for a broadcast in cooperation with the SPWW3. It reiterated the board's long-held views: "What good Germans do you expect to find still in Germany? You will find none. You will find only those who can be led and led again to war, to rape, to murder. Remember this, the Nazis are but Germans."[90] However, the unrelenting criticism that the board received eventually began to concern its members. They feared that if their pool of writers became hostile to their views, the WWB's ability to produce material would quickly diminish. Believing that the group's stance might have been misunderstood, Stout suggested at the May 24 board meeting that the WWB draw up a formal statement of its position on the German question. Only a few months before the group had had no difficulty in agreeing on three principles to guide peace negotiations with Germany: that the defeated country be treated justly with no vindictiveness, that her citizens understand the totality of their defeat and its consequences, and that the Allies take all steps necessary to prevent a third world war. Since a majority of the board members thought along the same lines, Stout assumed they would have little trouble in agreeing on a plan concerning the disposition of Germany, but he was profoundly wrong.[91] He had no inkling that the issues involved would generate internal disagreement and embroil the WWB in even more controversy.

Board members appointed Stout and Fadiman to handle the job of writing their position statement since the two were hardliners who took the strongest stand. To identify issues that were most problematic, Alan Green created a questionnaire that he asked the two of them to answer. He gave the same form to two moderates, Jack Goodman and Russel Crouse. Green hoped that the four responses would help Stout and Fadiman distinguish between superficial differences of opinion and serious ones.[92] Despite Green's efforts, several objected when the two presented their draft on May 31. Some considered the statement emotional rather than objective and wanted to revise its arguments. Goodman, for instance, did not like the overtones of racism and the implication that the German people as a whole espoused pan-Germanism. Others wanted the document to specify that the problem with Germans lay in the circumstances of their culture, not in their genes.[93] Stout and Fadiman immediately got to work again. On June 7 the board formally adopted their revised statement. Although Goodman declined to vote, he was finally persuaded to add his name to the document. Those who were absent received a copy within a week, and all signed it except columnist Samuel Grafton. He basically agreed with it but questioned "some points of political theory." Realizing the importance of a unanimous vote, he offered his resignation, but the group declined it.[94]

The WWB soon sent the five-page statement to its Advisory Council along with a sharp denial of the most extreme charges against it: "The Writers' War Board has on occasion been accused of advocating such absurd measures as sterilization and extermination in dealing with the German problem. These charges are either dishonest or irresponsible, or both." As before, the board asserted in its revised document that all Germans were to blame for their country's conduct during the war. Members dismissed as irrelevant the idea that taking a hard line against Germany would punish the innocent with the guilty: "The German people, as a political unit . . . cannot be absolved from war guilt. They have accepted some actively, some passively, Pan-Germanism as a political philosophy and as a cultural standard for many years. . . . If our sympathy for an innocent minority prevents us from dealing effectively with the guilty majority . . . we are convinced it will lead to another world war."[95]

The board's statement gave special emphasis to pan-Germanism and identified several of its manifestations in German history. It contended that all of the major German political parties in 1931 had been "colored by pan-Germanism" and reiterated its suggestion that German-born members of the newly established Council for a Democratic Germany might be pan-Germans working to undermine an unconditional victory over Germany. Even though the CDG opposed Hitler, WWB members argued that pan-Germans had a strong connection with Nazis: "Nazism is merely a recent manifestation of Pan-Germanism which for a century has been the prevailing political doctrine in Germany and has determined the attitude and purpose of German foreign policy. The two basic characteristics of Pan-Germanism have been and are (a) the belief that the Germans are a master race, and (b) the conviction that the master race Germans should and will dominate the world. The Nazis differ from other Pan-Germans only in method (both strategy and tactics), not in fundamentals of doctrine and objective."[96]

Because the WWB felt that pan-Germanism would continue to pose problems long after the war, the group argued that the reorientation of the populace toward democracy could not be assured until it was proven over a period of years. The WWB statement ended with a brief list of guidelines for the postwar treatment of Germany including

1. In the alleviation of suffering the victims of German aggression have a claim on us prior to that of aggressors.
2. The severity of our treatment of Germany shall be no greater and no less than is necessary to convince the Germans that the master-race theory will not work and that Pan-Germanism and militarism lead inevitably to disaster.
3. Every encouragement should be given all Germans who have proved themselves not in sympathy with Nazism and Pan-Germanism to obtain and maintain control and leadership of the German government.[97]

While the majority of Advisory Council members agreed to sign the document, a significant number dissented. Henry Seidel Canby, Dorothy Canfield Fisher, Louis Adamic, and Walter Edmonds raised objections. Even more critical comments came from Lewis Gannett, who was sufficiently disturbed not only to send a letter to the board but also to attend its next meeting to express his views in person. He questioned the propriety of issuing any kind of statement on the matter and was particularly concerned about the board's "malicious" attack on the CDG. He felt that the board associated the new organization with pan-German views "in a manner that verge[d] on sheer dishonesty."[98] He also argued that the Nazis differed from other Germans in ways more far-reaching than mere methodology. Gannett left the meeting after threatening to resign from the Advisory Council if the document were published as written. Carl Carmer led a successful move to have the name of the CDG removed from the statement and the focus of that section broadened but not weakened.[99]

The most serious objections came from Dorothy Thompson, a journalist well acquainted with the issues. She had served as a newspaper correspondent in Berlin before her expulsion from Germany in 1934 on Hitler's personal order. She had criticized the Third Reich relentlessly in her popular newspaper column and radio broadcasts and had made suggestions about the postwar treatment of Germany in her 1942 book *Listen, Hans*. Although Thompson was a personal friend of both Rex Stout and William Shirer, she disagreed with some of their views. She argued that the German people were more Hitler's victims than his supporters, and she believed that a strong anti-Nazi movement had developed in Germany.[100] For those reasons she had begun to write against the hate campaign in the fall of 1943, but she had pulled her punches by keeping the name of the WWB out of her comments.[101] Consequently, the group was not surprised to receive her letter condemning its position statement and refusing to sign the document: "It is as a whole an insult to my intellectual integrity. . . . I protest against this statement being put out as representative of the thought of American writers." She went on to challenge the competence of the board to speak on German history and the right of the group to provide guidance to other writers and the public on highly controversial questions. Like Gannett, she strongly opposed the attack on the CDG.[102]

When Thompson posted her letter to the board, she simultaneously dispatched a memorandum to her colleagues on the Advisory Council. It condemned several of the board's main points and charged, "This statement so clearly reflects the views of the Society for the Prevention of World War III that it looks as though the latter organization, which has many vehement opponents amongst patriotic writers and especially among liberals, has captured the Writers' War Board and turned it into an instrument for its own propaganda."[103] In July board members considered how to respond to Thompson but took no action. They rejected a quick reply written by Stout that called her a "German apologist" and a "liar." Stout disapproved of their failure to answer her criticism, but his fellow members remained mute on the point.[104]

Rumors of the board's internal dissension surfaced after a heated public debate on postwar policy at Town Hall in New York City on June 12. Stout and Advisory Council member Mark Van Doren represented the hardline view while Thompson and journalist Louis Fischer argued for a more moderate approach.[105] Two weeks later nationally syndicated columnist Leonard Lyons wrote, "A revolt is brewing at the Writers' War

Board as a result of Rex Stout's statement on 'What to Do with Germany.' Dorothy Thompson, William Shirer, Lewis Gannett, Henry S. Canby have registered dissents and eight resignations may follow."[106] The board authorized a reply to Lyons informing him (1) that the group, not Stout, wrote the statement; (2) that Thompson, Canby, and Gannett were not WWB members even though they served on its Advisory Council; and (3) that Shirer had signed the document. The board also agreed to draw up a reply to the letter Thompson had sent to the Advisory Council, but at the next meeting they backed off once again.[107]

One week later, with Stout absent from New York to write another Nero Wolfe mystery, the board seemed unsure of its position. On further examination Margaret Leech and others had decided that the use of the term "pan-Germanism" was, historically speaking, an oversimplification. Board members withdrew the document until they obtained advice from experts in the field. Charles Cole of Columbia University, Edward Earle of the Institute for Advanced Study at Princeton, Bernadotte E. Schmitt of the University of Chicago, and Frederick L. Schuman of Williams College rejected the board's comments on pan-Germanism, especially its contention that Nazism was an outburst of pan-Germanism, and they disapproved of some of the historical examples that were cited to indicate its influence over time.[108] When the board met on July 12, more disagreement ensued until the group accepted the suggestion of Luise Sillcox that the document be entirely rewritten omitting any mention of pan-Germanism.[109]

Although the newly revised document was about a page longer than the board's previous statement, it reflected the same basic attitude toward Germany that the WWB had always maintained. At its July 19 meeting the board approved it. Subsequently all the members signed the statement including Samuel Grafton, who had rejected the earlier version, and Stout, who had opposed the second revision. The group tried to avoid any implication that it espoused a racist viewpoint, made no mention of the CDG, and replaced most references to pan-Germanism with historical evidence of what it called the nation's "will-to-aggression":

> The German Will-to-Aggression has expressed itself *practically* in a series of aggressive wars. Naming only those within the last century, there were the Danish War of 1864, the Austrian War of 1866, the

Franco-Prussian War of 1870, the First World War of 1914, and the Second World War of 1939.

The German Will-to-Aggression has expressed itself *ideologically* in a series of closely related movements and systems of thought. These movements and systems of thought have at various times been designated as "Prussianism," "Junkerism," "Nordicism," "Militarism," "Kaiserism," "Pan-Germanism," and the theory of Master-Race Germans pre-destined to dominate the world. They culminate in that German version of Fascism known as Nazism.[110]

As before, the new statement went out to the sixty-four current members of the Advisory Council. Forty-four signed it including three who had objected to the previous version. Marquand and a few others who basically supported the statement still wondered about the propriety of taking a position at all.[111] Of the twenty who did not sign, thirteen failed to answer the correspondence from the war board and may have been abroad or otherwise indisposed. Out of the remaining seven, one claimed ignorance and felt disqualified to pass judgment; four objected to the statement on principle; and two, novelist Edna Ferber and dramatist George S. Kaufman, thought it was too easy on the enemy. Kaufman had supported the original version but complained about the final document: "Not a word about the punishment of the guilty. . . . I am for the liquidation or banishment of all Nazi officials. . . . The problem of Hitler youth calls for a better psychologist than I am. These evil little bastards are beyond changing, according to those who have encountered them. I am for their deportation from Germany and for their settlement on some distant island."[112]

But the debates did not end. In her column of August 9, 1944, Thompson used the unsuccessful generals' revolt against Hitler the previous month as a springboard to attack the WWB and its view of German history once again. She believed that the revolt destroyed all notions of the German tradition of devotion to aggression, which the WWB perpetrated. The following day another columnist attacked her arguments.[113] In the August issue of its *Report*, the board reemphasized its position but downplayed the controversy over hatred of the enemy: "A great many people hate the Germans and say so. A great many others think it wrong to hate. Don't let us get mixed up in this irrelevant debate. Let us concentrate on the importance of *fearing* the Germans. Let us fear what they believe about themselves and have always believed—[that] they are the destined masters of the world."[114] That fall the board attempted to publish its controversial position statement in *Life*, but the magazine turned it down. *Look* next declined to publish the document because its staff members were in the process of formulating their own plan. The peace proposal they eventually produced was similar to the board's and even borrowed some of its phrasing, citing the group.[115] The WWB revision finally saw publication on November 1, 1944, when it went out with the *Report*. The *New York World-Telegram* summarized the statement, and several other papers printed it in whole or in part after the board released it to newspaper editors early in 1945.[116]

Board members never wavered from their convictions, and they continued to censor or suppress works that did not align with their views. In early June they prevented the *Ladies Home Journal* from publishing an article entitled "The Rehabilitation of German Universities after the War" because it suggested that the educational system of the Axis nation had some good qualities. According to Stout the group's influence was sufficient to have it dropped.[117] During the same month Fadiman disparaged an article by expatriate Hermann Rauschning that had appeared in the *New York Times Magazine*. In a letter to the editor that had board approval, he referred to the piece as "pan-German propaganda" from "an ex-Nazi using as a blind his supposed disillusionment with his former boss."[118] The WWB member also criticized the *New York Herald-Tribune* article "Many Reich Women Seen Favoring U.S." by Dorothy Dunbar Bromley on the grounds that it promoted the wrong kind of peace settlement.[119] In August the WWB sent protests to the Fellowship of Reconciliation because that organization objected to the massive bombing of German cities. However, members praised works that supported their views. One individual they recognized was the editor of *The Protestant*, who argued against a soft peace.[120]

MORE BAD PUBLICITY

On August 17, 1944, Stout lost an opportunity to address a nationwide audience on Edwin C. Hill's radio program about the board's view of the German problem. While the bad publicity that the board had received may not have been a factor, it could not have helped. CBS officials called the script he had prepared a controversial "plea for a very hard peace" and insisted that he present the opposing view with equal force. Stout refused and declined the network's subsequent offer to give him fifteen minutes of noncommercial airtime at another hour. The board considered a public protest against CBS but decided not to offend the network because it was an important channel of communication. Instead it instigated a *Variety* editorial that criticized CBS, questioning the fairness of its decision and asking whether Hitler should be granted equal time with Stout. Even though the board called attention to the issue, it was able to maintain a cordial relationship with the network.[121]

The fall brought additional problems as Milton Mayer, Dorothy Thompson, and the Council for a Democratic Germany weighed in once again. Mayer made his now customary slap at the writers, referring to them as one of the groups that would have to be kept in hand at the end of the war to prevent them from "torturing, castrating, or exterminating" Germans.[122] Thompson took a more reasonable swing at the WWB: "It cannot possibly be intelligent tactics" but "Rex Stout and associates and many others [like Lord Robert Gilbert Vansittart] have been furnishing Goebbels with . . . the only propaganda with which he can hope to unite despairing German forces to continue the war to the death."[123] In Thompson's view, calls for a harsh peace from people like Stout and Vansittart, former British undersecretary for foreign affairs and chief diplomatic adviser to the British government, gave the Germans no incentive to surrender. For example, Vansittart had vehemently argued that the entire German military and industrial complex be permanently destroyed. Although there may have been some truth in Thompson's argument, Stout immediately denounced the charge as "fantastic" and offered his resignation to Freedom House. Both he and Thompson had been among its founders and most ardent members, and she served as its president at the time. In turn the journalist proffered her resignation, but the organization refused both after several days of public dispute. Tempers calmed after Thompson declared that she had nothing personal against Stout and invited the WWB chairman to dinner, but the rift remained.[124]

In November theologian Reinhold Niebuhr, vice chairman of the CDG, waded into the controversy. He circulated a letter stating the position of his organization: "We believe it possible to demonstrate to the American people that there are helpful and democratic forces in Germany which ought to be encouraged and supported."[125] It caused an uproar among board members, who designated Paul Gallico to send an open letter in reply. He called Niebuhr's statements "untrue" and "apologetic" and argued that no forces in Germany could be supported or encouraged without hindering the Allied military effort. The CDG responded that Niebuhr's comments concerned a postwar program and did not affect the conduct of the war.[126]

Around the same time unexpected opposition arose from Robert L. Duffus, who had handled the board's editorial service since its inception. He declined to write any other pieces on the German question because of his convictions: "I don't believe in a race theory for Germans any more than I do for Americans, English, Chinese, or Jews; I don't believe we can punish the innocent-meaning children and some others—without bringing on what we want to avoid; I think we have got to make a settlement that will seem just to the Germans themselves ten years from now."[127] In reply Stout agreed that Duffus should not write what he did not believe but argued that the group did not advocate a race theory or enslavement.[128] Duffus never formally resigned his WWB position, but he did not participate in any of its activities after he submitted the editorials for November 1944.

CONTINUING THE ANTI-GERMAN CAMPAIGN

To keep Americans from having a softhearted reaction to Germany's defeat, which seemed imminent in the fall of 1944, the WWB focused once again on the heinous nature of the German character, widely publicizing atrocities that had recently come to light. In January 1945 the War Script of the Month was Mortimer Frankel's *The Dead Are Not Liars*, and the *Report* carried excerpts of a personal account from an unnamed author who had witnessed German brutality firsthand. He found the population to be "rotten from top to bottom" and warned, "Don't let anybody tell you about the Germans being really nice people at heart.... They practice the most unthinkable varieties of civilian looting, torture, and everything else."[129] Germany's unconditional surrender on May 8,

1945, did not stop the WWB's hate campaign lest Americans begin to sympathize with their former foes. In his June editorial "The Shock Is Late" LaFarge wondered why Americans were surprised when they heard about the extent of the Germans' persecution and slaughter of Jews and their inhumane treatment of many prisoners of war:

> Did no one stop to consider that if you train the cream of your university youth (long, long before Hitler) to fight duels for the scars that were honorable on their faces, you were creating Lublin camp? . . . Did no one ever stop to consider that the extermination of the Jews of Europe by the Master Race would lead straight to the starved skeletons of French, Polish, Russian, British and American prisoners of war?
>
> Why are we shocked now? . . . Germanism has merely reached its logical and inevitable conclusion. . . . Dachau, Lublin, Vught, Stalag 9—all the horrible list—these are but the end results, foretold—long before Hitler, long, long before V-E Day.[130]

In order to prove the authenticity of the atrocity stories, the WWB promoted two army films, *Your Job in Germany* and *German Atrocities Unexpurgated*. Both were composed of selected clips from official documentaries filmed during the liberation of concentration camps and other sites of German horrors. The board arranged with the army pictorial service to show them in one sitting to a select audience. Then WWB members urged the group, virtually all of whom had been shocked and horrified by the pictures of starvation and death, to send letters to Secretary of War Henry L. Stimson asking that the films be released to the general public. A number of the viewers complied. The board also dispatched letters about the films to almost two hundred newspapers throughout the country asking them to request public showings. Newspaper clippings referring to multiple showings are included in the WWB files.[131] At the time many had difficulty believing that the Holocaust stories were real events rather than propaganda pieces circulated for effect. The films provided convincing proof, allowing Americans to see for themselves the emaciated bodies of the living and the dead.

The summer of 1945 saw the last surge in the board's anti-German activity. In July Gallico's editorial "The Neatest Trick of the Month" blasted those who had praised Germans for treating American prisoners of war properly while ignoring the horrors that continued for years in their concentration camps.[132] Arnold Hartley's War Script of the Month, *Loving Cups for Murderers*, also chided Americans, emphasizing how easily they could be misled and how quickly they could forget: "This gullible American . . . sucker . . . really believed the . . . German propaganda [lie] that Germans didn't want to conquer the world. That Germany just wanted to save the world from Bolshevism. . . . Is it any wonder that the Germans are boasting they haven't lost the war—that this is only an interlude before we all join up to jump the Russians. Aren't [the] newborn anti-Nazis spouting the old Hitler line? Are we forgetting already?" Hartley insisted that places of torture like the concentration camps were not "the sadistic playgrounds of a few perverted Nazis" but "a deliberate German—repeat German—policy." He gave a nod of approval to calls for the mass execution of the guilty. His play ended with a request urging audience members to send postcards or letters giving their opinions about how to handle Nazi generals, German prisoners of war, and others including wealthy industrialists who helped effect Germany's plans of conquest.[133]

The strange title of Hartley's play, *Loving Cups for Murderers*, referred to what he called American "politeness to murderers and hangmen." He specifically mentioned the treatment of Reichsmarschall Hermann Göring among others. After the man who was Hitler's second in command surrendered to Brigadier General Robert Stack, he was allowed to bathe, change his uniform, eat a hearty chicken dinner, give a Nazi salute, and shake Stack's hand. In January William Shirer had informed the board about his firsthand observations of similar cushy treatment that German detainees received in American prisoner-of-war camps in Europe. He reported that they often had better food and clothing than the troops of America's ally, France. Although democratic literature was forbidden in the prisons, Shirer found that Nazi propaganda was blatantly circulated and that hard-core Nazis ran the camps. Angered, the board agreed to demand more supervision and stricter policies at the facilities and organized a Prisoner-of-War Committee under the leadership of Alan Green.[134] Before it was able to act, however, congressmen who had been informed of the issue made charges of scandal, and the

Senate began to investigate the allegations. Realizing that news reports would keep the public sufficiently informed without its help, the board dropped the campaign.[135]

That summer the WWB also denounced a German who had opposed Hitler just as it had previously criticized the motives of anti-Nazi German expatriates who were members of the Council for a Democratic Germany. After *Time* magazine praised Martin Niemöller as "the only German whom Christians everywhere had respected," Green attacked the leader of Germany's Lutheran Confessional Church in his editorial "The Pastor Couldn't Fool the GI."[136] From the outside Niemöller seemed to have a sterling record. After publicly denouncing the Führer, he had spent eight years in confinement, four of them in a concentration camp. At the end of the war he was considered a possible German leader.[137] But Green questioned his suitability. He pointed out that Niemöller had served as a submarine commander in World War I and had made "repeated" attempts to enlist in World War II. He identified the Lutheran as a supporter of Hitler who had remained in the Nazi Party "until Hitler attacked the church." He further condemned the clergyman for his imperialistic views: "He preached Anschluss [the German takeover of Austria] from his pulpit; he preached Germany's right to the Sudetenland, the Ukraine, and other sections of non-German central Europe. In other words, he was a confirmed and potent pan-German."[138]

Green maintained that Niemöller received no ill treatment as a prisoner of the Reich and was neither starved nor beaten during his internment in Sachsenhausen camp. The WWB member considered the question, "Who reserved him and what for?" Green contended that the German high command, unsure of Hitler's victory, had "not place[d] all its eggs in the Nazi basket" but held "other leaders in reserve, men of different outward stripe but of a similar inward political heart. Pastor Niemöller is one such reservist." Green's article included a statement that Niemöller had made at a news conference in Rome: "It may be that Germany can become democratic, but you have got to face the fact that the German people are not adapted to the sort of democracy which exists in Britain and the United States. The German people . . . like to be governed; they like to feel authority." Green asserted that Niemöller's comments implied "that the new Germany must in basic principle be no different from the

Germany of Bismarck, the Germany of Kaiser Wilhelm, the Germany of Hitler."[139] His provocative editorial brought a nationwide attack against Niemöller. Even Eleanor Roosevelt, who had been widowed less than a month before Germany's surrender, called the Lutheran minister "a dangerous pan-German . . . looking down at us Americans."[140]

At least one national publication identified the WWB article as the sole source of the attack on Niemöller. In an unsigned editorial written or authorized by managing editor Paul Hutchinson, *Christian Century* called Green's attack a "mixture of plain untruths and unwarranted inferences" and complained that the war board "blankets the nation" with its editorials. The magazine pointed out that Green had offered no proof that Niemöller was a member of the Nazi Party or that the German high command had held him in reserve as a future German leader. It suggested that Niemöller acted under compulsion when he made repeated attempts to serve in World War II and excused Niemöller's comment about the Germans' love of authority, arguing that the press conference in Rome had been conducted under "hostile conditions" and that the reporters had not clearly understood his situation. After quoting some of Niemöller's supporters, the magazine demanded to know why the board had targeted the Lutheran leader.[141]

The argument of the *Christian Century* drew replies that attributed the board's attack against Niemöller to "pathological hate" and to the influence of the SPWW3.[142] In the WWB's response Stout cheerfully admitted responsibility for the WWB editorial, adding, "We attacked Niemöller only as a proposed leader of the German people into the way of democratic decency, and we had ample documentation for that attack." Stout cited two documents from the late 1930s, a letter to the editor of *Christian Century* by Ewart Edmund Turner and an article in *Atlantic Monthly* by Hutchinson. The board chairman quoted Hutchinson: "Niemöller had been (and is) a fanatical German nationalist. . . . Eventually he enrolled as a member of the Nazi party. . . . If Germany is to go forward, it can no more go through Niemöller than through Hitler."[143] Stout's rejoinder was devastating. Hutchinson could do little except assert that Niemöller was now a different man. He characterized Stout's comments as "superficially clever, but misleading."[144] This exchange did not end the controversy over Martin Niemöller, which went on long after the WWB ceased to exist. For more than a year some unbiased researchers with no strong preconceptions looked into the matter using different sources of information, and they reached much the same conclusion that Green and Stout had.[145]

Another attack on German anti-Nazis for which Stout was partly responsible came in the form of an article in the *Saturday Review of Literature*. In "German Apologists and the German Record," Lewis Mumford reviewed several recent books on Germany written by exiles. Stout had requested the piece, telling Mumford that no one had "pointed out that [the exiles] are apparently part and parcel of an organized pro-German propaganda movement exactly similar to that which began directly after the close of the first World War."[146] Mumford, who followed Stout's suggestions closely, referenced the attitude of Americans who became so sympathetic to the Germans after World War I that they overlooked evidence that Germany was preparing for another conflict. He warned, "Even the most carefully documented volumes bear the common taint of German apologetics: covertly or openly, they seek to lessen the world's sense of Germany's guilt, to soften her punishment, to diminish the term of military occupation, to transform the Black Record into a grey one, and to lose the greyness itself in a picture of an international twilight in which all cats are of the same color." Mumford attacked three illusions about Germany that the exiles fostered in their writing, refuting each one and asserting instead that (1) Germans were different from other Europeans "in . . . background, . . . culture, [and] . . . purposes"; (2) better treatment of Germany after World War I would not have prevented her aggression in World War II; and (3) no dichotomy existed between good and bad Germans since the population was homogeneous.[147]

The Writers' War Board fundamentally believed in equality and repeatedly fought against stereotyping people of different cultures and races. Nevertheless, they made an exception for the population of Germany, which they pigeonholed into two groups. One consisted of arrogant, violent, and untrustworthy Germans set on conquering the world, and the other contained weak citizens who followed the lead of the aggressors without challenge or protest. The board considered both groups responsible for Germany's actions. Whether or not board members recognized the contradiction in their thinking, it never bothered them, no doubt because they remained focused on the goal of defeating Germany and sapping its military might.

By the time the nation surrendered, the hate campaign had drawn more criticism than the board received on all of its other projects combined, but the group's enthusiasm for attacking the Axis nation and its people never changed. The board's argument that there were no "good Germans" seems extreme, as does its call for harsh treatment of all Germans, but some modern scholarship has found both positions defensible.[148] More than twenty years after the war six board members—Paul Gallico, Alan Green, Rita Kleeman, Robert Landry, Margaret Leech, and Rex Stout—continued to think that they had acted correctly in dealing with the issue even though they were publicly criticized. Only Clifton Fadiman, always the most image-conscious, brazenly denied that he ever advocated hatred. Both Stout and Green expressed no doubts whatsoever and made no apologies. Each of the two admitted in separate interviews that he continued to hold strong feelings against the Germans and was convinced that Germany "would try it again" even though by that time both West Germany and Japan were America's allies in the Cold War.[149]

CHAPTER 6

SHAPING THE PEACE

As the scent of victory in Europe grew stronger, Writers' War Board members escalated their campaign to promote harsh peace terms for Germany, fearing that the country would mount a third world war if left unchecked. Like many other groups the writers proposed a peace plan to publicize their ideas about suppressing Germany and preventing a repeat performance. Recognizing that lasting peace could not be achieved without the cooperation of large and small nations around the world, WWB members encouraged Americans to develop an international perspective and to support the proposals of the multinational conferences held in 1944 and 1945. What the group envisioned was a global government with an executive department, a world legislature, and a judiciary branch. It would have jurisdiction over all countries and people, and its military force would have enough power to suppress warring states. In order to establish such a government and insure its effectiveness, every nation would have to relinquish some of its power and commit to permanent membership. The board thought that the devastation caused by two world wars and the prospect of enduring peace would motivate each country to do both, and it was sorely disappointed when it realized that nation-states were not willing to do either. In the end board members supported the only viable option, a weak organization of independent nations with no power or authority to enforce lasting peace.

Throughout its existence the WWB was concerned that isolationists, pro-fascists, German sympathizers, and others might forestall its plans. A mid-1942 survey indicated that three out of every ten Americans would favor a peace negotiated with the leaders of the German Army even though the outcome might leave the military establishment in a good position to resume its conquests later.¹ Some were willing to negotiate a peace settlement with the Nazis immediately instead of waiting for victory and dictating the terms of peace. One contingent thought that ousting Franklin Roosevelt and his liberal cronies was the answer. Many bought into the pervasive notion that the war in Europe could end with a quick set of compromises once Adolf Hitler and some high-ranking Nazi leaders were removed from office. Isolationists who opposed the concept of international cooperation tried to foment distrust among the Allies to break up the United Nations alliance. They specifically zeroed in on the USSR as a country that could not be trusted. Several anticommunist groups did not want to work with the Soviets in a peacekeeping organization.² Concerned, the government unofficially encouraged the board to suppress these ideas or root them out, and the WWB repeatedly returned to that task.

In 1943 and 1944 board members promoted five works that outlined harsh peace terms for Germany. One of their selections was *Lessons of My Life* by British statesman Robert Gilbert, Lord Vansittart. Upon its publication in 1943, the book had stirred up a storm in British circles, where it was called "the most sweeping condemnation of the German people ever made by a literate man."³ The board praised it as the "ablest, wittiest, most solidly documented demonstration in English of the inadvisability of making any distinction between Germans and the Nazis."⁴ After tracing the history of Germany from the sixteenth century to World War II, Vansittart produced evidence that German citizens had steadily grown more aggressive. To deal with this long-term problem, he advocated the occupation of Germany—perhaps for generations—until the Allies were able to eradicate the country's traditions, complete its demilitarization, and reeducate its citizens.⁵ Similarly, in *How to Treat the Germans* (1943), expatriate Emil Ludwig observed that only the strictest postwar treatment with no conciliations had any chance of disabusing the Germans of the conviction that they were entitled to rule all other nations.⁶

Another WWB favorite was *The Time for Decision* by Sumner Welles, former undersecretary of state and prominent foreign policy adviser to President Roosevelt. Welles examined the history of German expansion and argued that the only way to prevent the country's continued growth was to dismember it. Welles suggested that Poland take over a portion of eastern Germany and advocated dividing the rest of the German state into three countries that would be integrated into one economic union. He also presented a comprehensive plan for a world organization. As was its habit, the board mentioned the work in its own publications, scheduled radio interviews for Welles, and sent display materials to bookstores. Members scored a major coup when they arranged for the work to be the primary selection of the Book of the Month Club in August 1944. Clifton Fadiman, a member of the club's editorial board, was largely responsible for securing the honor, though he received assistance from his colleagues on the board. Welles's book went to the top of the *New York Times* bestseller list with over half a million copies sold. The author reprised his thesis for the board's *Brief Army Camp Items* and wrote a seven-hundred-word article that the WWB placed in *American Legion Magazine* that fall.[7]

Two previously mentioned books took an even harder line on the postwar treatment of Germany. In *What to Do with Germany* (1944) Louis Nizer suggested scrapping the country's educational system, dismantling its war industries, getting rid of its metals and other war resources, and making Germany pay reparations.[8] Heinz Pol's "very stimulating, even . . . disturbing" book, *The Hidden Enemy: The German Threat to Post-War Peace* (1943), offered a more extreme solution.[9] Pol wanted to "eliminate" three groups: (1) "all persons who . . . played any leading and responsible part in the . . . Pan-German parties and their organizations"; (2) "all intellectuals who, Nazi or merely 'nationalist,' paved the way for Hitler and as propagandists supported the Third Reich"; and (3) "all Nazi criminals," which he identified as 3,000 to 5,000 party leaders and government bureaucrats as well as 150,000 to 200,000 "intermediate leaders." He estimated that the "great purge" might wipe out as many as half a million Germans, but he thought the executions were "absolutely necessary" to stop German imperialism even though many people would find them "utterly repugnant." He further argued that the millions of Nazis who survived should be segregated, kept under surveillance, restricted to certain types of employment, and barred from voting and from holding political office.[10]

The Society for the Prevention of World War III (SPWW3) took an even tougher stand. Headed by hardliner Rex Stout, the group included three other WWB members as well as a few outspoken German expatriates and several long-term critics of the World War I peace settlement like George Creel. Although the SPWW3 supported the board's push for a hard peace settlement, it independently called for the execution of 1.5 million Germans. When that hair-raising proposal drew accusations of racial hatred, the society's German-born members—Emil Ludwig, T. H. Tetens, and Friedrich Wilhelm Foerster—vociferously denounced their native country in hopes of deflecting some of the criticism.[11] Stout himself had come down hard on the Germans in late 1942. Speaking on his radio program *Our Secret Weapon* on September 27, he condemned them for opposing democracy and suggested that killing them by the millions might be the only way to secure peace: "The chief difficulty to any peace in this world is not the momentary, spasmodic vices of the Nazis but the inherent anti-democratic traits in the German character. We must . . . convince them that the only way to get along in this world is to cooperate with democracy. . . . If we can only convince them by killing twenty million of them, we must do that."[12]

THE MORGENTHAU PLAN

In 1944 the WWB was drawn to a plan devised by Treasury Secretary Henry Morgenthau Jr. It called for the relocation of German industrial machinery to any liberated country that requested it and suggested that the rest be destroyed. All mines would be closed and large land holdings divided into small farms. The Germans would receive no relief supplies, and nothing would be done to sustain their economy. Since the defeated nation would have no means of paying reparations either immediately after the war or in the foreseeable future, none would be demanded.[13] Secretary of War Henry Stimson and Secretary of State Cordell Hull immediately opposed Morgenthau's plan. Stimson believed that taking stringent measures against Germany would make the task of governing it after the war more difficult while Hull's concern was more immediate. He was convinced that the Germans would hold out as long as possible if they knew their country would receive harsh treatment after they surrendered. He objected to the plan because a longer war meant a higher death toll.

Although Roosevelt agreed with Stimson originally, he signaled a change in his attitude by asking Morgenthau to accompany him to the Quebec Conference in September 1944. There Roosevelt and British prime minister Winston Churchill initiated a statement of intent that embodied the secretary's suggestions.[14] But Morgenthau's triumph was short-lived. When leaks to the press disclosed some of the terms of his plan, the public objected, and Roosevelt backed away from taking such a strong stand.[15] Many newspapers, magazines, and radio commentators were hostile to Morgenthau's plan, and they reported that it had caused dissension between cabinet members and the White House. The German propaganda machine picked up the story and used Morgenthau's suggestions as a threat to motivate German forces to continue to fight. Roosevelt feared that Thomas Dewey, his Republican opponent in the November presidential election, might make its provisions a campaign issue.[16]

In late September Secretary Morgenthau sought the board's help. He knew of its public stand in support of a harsh peace and was aware of its record of successful propaganda campaigns for the Treasury Department and other government agencies. During a meeting with Fadiman, he requested that the group do whatever it could to counteract the adverse reaction to his ideas. Fadiman promptly contacted Stout, who immediately sent a telegram to Roosevelt on behalf of the board. He argued that the president should not veer from supporting a harsh peace for Germany because his waffling might make the public question the government's conduct of the war as well as its postwar plans.[17]

By way of reply the administration invited Stout and other WWB members to Washington for a briefing, presumably to reassure them about the president's position. On September 28, twelve of the writers met with Robert Sherwood of the OWI's Overseas Branch. He too asked the group to do everything possible to counteract the unfavorable publicity about the Morgenthau plan, particularly that fomented by Republicans and other anti-administration forces involved in the presidential campaign.[18] At their October 4 meeting, board members decided that they did not have enough time to change the attitude of the public about the need for a harsh peace before the November election; however, they enthusiastically began to consider ways to promote the Morgenthau plan.[19]

Since the proposal had received so much bad press, the WWB's first step was to disguise it under the name "Security Plan." Next the writers launched the Reparations and Security Campaign in coordination with the SPWW3. Its dual purpose was to disparage the demand for war reparations and to promote Morgenthau's hardline ideas. On October 5, 1944, Stout strongly attacked the concept of reparations on the radio program *Town Meeting of the Air*. His comments elicited a letter of thanks from Morgenthau, who thought he saw a favorable trend in public sentiment. He offered his "compliments on your vigorous and convincing appearance on the Town Hall program last night. The impression here is that 'our' side had all the best of it."[20] However, the president continued to be cautious. Although he had invited Stout to come to Washington to discuss the plan, Roosevelt postponed the invitation in mid-October. The White House told the WWB chairman that the meeting would be rescheduled after the election, but no record indicates that it ever occurred.[21] In fact, Roosevelt's administration never took an official position on the peace settlement.

The WWB devoted much of its effort during the first six weeks of the initiative to drawing up a memorandum that delineated the differences between the two approaches. Based on a draft by Fadiman, "Notes on Current Thinking on Post-War Germany" presented the proposals of the reparations school: large payments from Germany over approximately five years, the punishment of Nazi criminals, an end to Germany's manufacture of planes and weaponry, Allied control of German armaments still in existence, and the loss of a few German territories. In order for Germany to acquire the funds to make such payments, the WWB pointed out, the United States and its allies would have to rebuild her heavy industries. Such assistance would give Germany full employment and prosperity while businesses in the victor nations receiving German goods would suffer from unemployment. Once Allied control ended, Germany would have both the political autonomy and the new equipment to start another war.[22]

Instead the board promoted the Security Plan, which "is interested in one thing: to make the world safe from further German aggression. . . . It therefore purposes to destroy German autonomy as presently constituted, without denying the German people a livelihood." The group listed its three main components: (1) splitting off industrial areas including the Ruhr and Saar as well as parts of East Prussia, Upper Silesia, and the left bank of the Rhine River; (2) dividing the remainder of the country into two states; and (3) encouraging light industries such as textiles and agriculture while moving all heavy industries to other areas of Europe. A secondary goal of the plan was to inculcate democratic ideas by reeducating the population. No mention was made of the execution of the Nazis, which adherents felt would be a useless expenditure of effort and time because it would achieve little. In fact, they feared that it might satiate the public's demand for justice and retribution to such an extent that it would mitigate the Allies' postwar treatment of Germany.[23]

The memorandum asserted that the Security Plan provision to relocate Germany's industrial complex would not cause the economy of Europe to suffer or force German citizens to become peasants. The document also addressed concerns about the Soviet Union. It noted that the Security Plan, unlike the Reparations School, based its propositions on the assumption "that Russia intends to be a non-aggressive power after its present legitimate claims have been satisfied."[24] The WWB argued that demonstrating trust in the Soviets would reassure them about America's postwar intentions. Board members approved the memorandum on November 15, and five days later it went to members of their Advisory Council; one hundred or so directors of industrial corporations; and seventy-five editors, columnists, and commentators who might be sympathetic to the plan. Subsequently the SPWW3 and a Philadelphia organization that promoted the United Nations used "Notes on Current Thinking on Post-War Germany" to prepare their own materials on the peace settlement.[25]

Unfortunately, the board could not convince *Look* or *Collier's* to publish the memorandum or to include articles that presented its arguments, particularly those that disparaged the idea of reparations.[26] The WWB notified influential reporters and commentators and used its own publications to address the issue. Its *Report* carried "If He Yells for Reparations, He's Giving a Helping Hand to World War III," which warned readers about playing into the hands of the Germans: "a) The Germans *want* to pay reparations—because they can't pay them unless we lend them money to rebuild the plant. b) They *want* a few thousand Nazis hung—so that our indignation will thus expend itself—and so that we will assume the remaining Germans are 'good' Germans. c) They *want* us to 'control' German armaments—because they know that sooner or later it is human nature to relax those controls."²⁷ Stout wrote an article for *Brief Army Camp Items* and produced two editorials that the board sent to newspapers on its mailing list, "The Reparations Booby Trap" and "What Do We Want?" The latter argued that it would be easy to dismantle German industries still operating after the Allied bombing if all the machines that Nazi troops had stolen from other countries were returned to their rightful owners.²⁸

THE WRITERS' WAR BOARD PLAN

At Paul Gallico's suggestion the WWB decided in December to develop its own plan for dealing with Germany, one that was more comprehensive and detailed than the Security Plan.²⁹ The board listened to the views of its members before deciding its stand on each item by majority rule. Although virtually none of the votes were unanimous, no rancor surfaced due to differences of opinion. The slow procedure allowed the group to consider each issue carefully and modify its stance if necessary. Several supported the punishment of war criminals. In Gallico's words,

> It is most important that the arrest, trial, and execution of members of the German Gestapo and Reichwehr involved in torture and manslaughter of European people be continued over a period of years until the job is done, and that the "innocent little men" who were just carrying out orders be punished as severely as the higher ups who planned and gave the orders. The more German homes into which this punishment reaches, the more it will be remembered. This needs to be said to the American people as not taking place for revenge but for future protection.³⁰

Samuel Grafton advocated the exile of at least 100,000 members of the Nazi bureaucracy and insisted that it be a condition of the armistice. Robert Colwell agreed with Gallico but wanted to prosecute more Germans, claiming that all of them were "war criminals and must be treated as such" because "some 99% of [them] went on record as supporting the current regime." However, Alan Green argued that the punishment of war criminals should "be generally avoided." He felt that taking action against "only a few would suggest that those punished were the guilty and the rest of Germans were innocent."[31] To handle charges against members of the military, the group called for the establishment of tribunals composed of representatives of the Allied forces.[32]

A few topics were not so difficult to handle. Members generally supported the reeducation of Germans, and Colwell expressed his belief that "such tenets as racial equality, human decency, etc. can eventually be taught."[33] As Morgenthau had suggested, board members advocated a ban on reparations and the complete demolition of Germany's industries. Although they said nothing about dividing the country, they did not oppose taking some of its peripheral territories. Their plan specified that the Germans would receive relief assistance only after all other countries were adequately supplied. To help rebuild the nations Germany had occupied, they permitted the use of German labor battalions. Since board members believed at the time that the Germans had taken steps to increase the Aryan birthrate, they stipulated that German men could be detained outside the country for up to five years in order to hold down population growth. They suggested that Germans should regain their political autonomy gradually over time, beginning with referenda on matters of local government. The question of when such autonomy would take effect was to be determined by a vote of all the Allies.[34]

After going through the lengthy process of creating their plan, WWB members elected not to seek the consent of the Advisory Council but to publish their proposal in the board's *Third Annual Report* released in January 1945.[35] A few questioned the propriety of issuing it without the administration's sanction since the WWB received a government subsidy, but most considered the timing critical. Winston Churchill, Franklin Roosevelt, and Joseph Stalin were scheduled to meet at a Russian resort on the Black Sea early the next month to decide the terms of the peace settlement. In January the board helped to stimulate interest in the conference and generate thoughtful public discussion about possible peace terms by sponsoring a contest in *See* magazine for the best essay on the topic "What to Do with Germany after the War."[36] At Yalta the leaders determined that both Germany and its capital, Berlin, would be split into four zones of occupation, each controlled by one of the major allies: the United States, Britain, the USSR, and France. They also agreed to prosecute Nazi war criminals and to exact reparations in the form of forced German labor. When the results of the Yalta Conference became known, the board concluded that the Reparations and Security Campaign had accomplished as much as it could and dropped the project.[37]

THE CALL FOR A WORLD ORGANIZATION

Even more important than the board's plan for dealing with Germany after her defeat was its effort to shape a postwar peacekeeping organization. By the end of the group's first year of operation Rex Stout observed that the WWB already considered "that its primary concern was no longer the military war, rather the problem of organizing the world for peace, and presenting the necessity of participating in world affairs to the American people."[38] The board felt that an international organization was necessary to handle a host of postwar problems such as addressing security issues, organizing relief efforts, rebuilding war-torn areas, restarting agriculture and industry, and reconfiguring the global economy. The group believed that it was time for a true world government to have ultimate authority and enforce peace. Well before Pearl Harbor, Stout had advocated a global police force: "The time may come—I hope it does, and the sooner the better—when nations will be willing to surrender enough of their sovereignty to permit the establishment of an effective world police."[39] The board eventually talked Fawcett Magazines into introducing a new comic book character in 1944. "Radar, the International Policeman" appeared in thirty issues, most of them in the Master Comics series.[40]

In June 1943 the WWB distributed Howard Fast's *Tomorrow Will Be Ours* as a War Script of the Month. Board members considered the play a clever piece of propaganda because the playwright drew an analogy between the struggle to unite the countries of the world that lay outside the Axis alliance and the difficulties the thirteen colonies had in joining together to establish the United States. Fast insisted that disagreements among the nations were no greater than those among the colonies in 1776.[41] The drama implicitly downplayed the problems involved in dealing with the Soviets, which concerned many government officials and private citizens. The board made use of Fast's comparison when it prepared and sponsored a CBS radio program the following month in cooperation with Wendell Willkie. *The Declaration of Interdependence* aired on July 4, 1943. *Tomorrow Will Be Ours* inspired much of the radio script prepared by WWB members Russel Crouse and Robert Landry. Fredric March narrated the program, and Willkie gave a speech emphasizing two major points: the peoples of the world must work together to win the war and the peace, and the nations of the world are tied together so that what happens to one country affects all countries. Willkie expressed the firm conviction that Americans would decide "by overwhelming majority" to choose equality for everyone everywhere rather than either "narrow nationalism" or "international imperialism." He argued that the former would "inevitably [mean] the ultimate loss of our own liberty and the certainty of recurring wars," while the latter would mean "the sacrifice of some other nation's liberty and the same certainty of war."[42]

Beginning in 1942 when board members conceived their idea for maintaining peace around the globe, they faced problems in convincing people at home and abroad that every nation should give up some of its authority in deference to a world government. They knew that American isolationists would strongly resist the idea, but WWB member Margaret Leech raised another issue. She thought it impolitic to give gratuitous advice to other nations, and she urged the board to focus on readying the United States to take its part in world affairs.[43] Soon the WWB had to return its attention to the war as the action on several fronts escalated later that year, but America's postwar participation in a global organization became an increasingly important part of the group's activities from that point onward.

When Republican senator Joseph Ball of Minnesota introduced a resolution calling for the immediate establishment of a world organization with policing powers in March 1943, the WWB quickly threw its support behind the legislation and congratulated each of the four senators who sponsored the bipartisan bill—Harold Burton (R-OH), Carl Hatch (D-NM), Lister Hill (D-AL), and Ball. The board joined a number of other organizations in promoting the resolution under the leadership of George Fielding Eliot, but the bill failed to pass in October. The group then helped to strengthen a resolution by Texas Democrat Tom Connally. More general in nature, it proposed that the United States "join with free and sovereign nations in the establishment and maintenance of international authority with power to prevent aggression and to preserve the peace of the world." The Senate adopted it on November 5.[44] One year later the board promoted a book by Kenneth W. Colegrove, *The American Senate and World Peace*, which considered a problem that could endanger the establishment of an international organization. Reflecting on the circumstances that doomed American ratification of the Treaty of Versailles after World War I, Colegrove declared that the requirement for a two-thirds majority of the Senate to approve treaties was outdated and undemocratic. He suggested that the stipulation be removed or bypassed before legislation on a postwar world organization came up for consideration because he feared it might not win approval otherwise, but his argument brought no change.[45]

In 1943 the board began to present the topics of international cooperation and world organization in its publications, and the number of these articles steadily increased as the end of the war drew nearer. In June the first issue of *Brief House Organ Items* carried a Stout article emphasizing the need for an organization of nations, "The Post-War World." The following year two articles in *Brief Army Camp Items* repeated the theme in simple language designed to appeal to a broader audience. One was "The Price of Freedom" signed by Fredric March and the other was "United We Stand" by news commentator H. V. Kaltenborn.[46] The board also added to its catalog several war talks designed to show Americans the necessity of world union. The most requested was "The Simple Idea" by Christopher LaFarge.[47] Many of the speeches described the problems of creating a peace settlement that would last and the rewards that could be reaped from postwar negotiations: "Peace Is a Result, Not an Accident," "We're Smart Enough to Win a Peace," "We Must Plan," "Let's Do It Better This Time," "Can We Trust Our Other Allies at the Peace Table?" and over a dozen more.[48]

In July 1943 the board dispatched Carl Carmer and children's book author James Marshall to argue for world federation on New York radio station WHN, which held a forum on the question, "Should the United [Allied] Nations Enter into a Regional Federation or into World Federation?" On August 10 the board provided two outspoken pro-Soviet speakers to a well-regarded nationwide radio program called *American*

Forum of the Air. Journalist Walter Duranty and Arthur Upham Pope, vice president of the National Council for American-Soviet Friendship, supported the affirmative in a discussion of the topic, "Can America and Russia Work Together?" For an October 1943 radio show commemorating the anniversary of Freedom House, the WWB obtained a moving drama that had previously aired. Norman Corwin's *Untitled* recounted the way a young soldier lived and the things for which he died, most notably the chance for permanent peace. The WWB later added the play to its script catalog, one of many on the need for lasting peace.[49]

That fall the organization began a publicity effort connected with the Opera Victory Rallies. These weekly programs of less than fifteen minutes took up one of the intermissions during the Saturday afternoon Metropolitan Opera live radio broadcasts, which aired from December 1943 to early April 1944. The theme for the rallies was "The Road to Lasting Peace," and the topic the following season was "The Fight for Lasting Peace." The brief programs may well have reached the largest audience of any WWB activity. Henry Souvaine, general manager of the Metropolitan Opera, estimated the number of listeners for each broadcast to be between 8 and 12 million in the Western Hemisphere.[50] Board members secured prominent individuals to deliver speeches for nine of the twenty-four programs. They carefully supervised the preparation of each address and provided writing assistance as needed in order to insure that the speaker covered the subject adequately and that the material accorded with the group's thinking. As they put it to one speaker, "Neither we nor the Metropolitan Opera Guild are laying down any vigorous 'line' but we are assuming that all our speakers take for granted certain simple presuppositions: (a) The United States has definitely rejected isolationism or semi-isolation as a national policy, (b) International cooperation is possible and necessary: peace is a process not a condition. It must be continually fought for."[51] An extreme example of the WWB's control over the content of the rallies occurred when they wrote a speech for World War I hero General John J. Pershing, persuaded actor Orson Welles to read it for him on the air, and then belatedly contacted Pershing to obtain his agreement for the address to be delivered in his name.[52]

Usually the group was not so high-handed. In December 1943 the board arranged for a speech by Jan Masaryk, the vice premier for the

Czechoslovak government in exile. In "The Aggressor Nations," he detailed German atrocities and presented a frightening picture of what the German way of life meant for occupied countries. He strongly advocated the dissolution of the Nazi Party.[53] On January 8, 1944, Wendell Willkie urged Americans to press for closer cooperation with other nations. He commented that the Moscow, Cairo, and Teheran conferences, all of which had been held during the previous two months, were occasions that had brought the leaders of the major Allied nations to work together. He emphasized the need for the public to demand further cooperation in order to achieve lasting peace:

> We have reason to believe we have established effective military coordination and cooperation of the four great allies. But we also have reason to believe that we have not as yet produced sufficient political and economic and moral understandings. The force of the people's opinion was responsible for the very fact that the conferences took place and for such progress as has been made thus far. The people must now assert their opinion clearly to bring about those political understandings which alone can make real the great principles for which we fight.[54]

Vice President Henry Wallace gave the rallies' presentation on April 1, 1944. He asserted that the American people "want a peace which means the destruction of the ideas and systems which created dictatorship and . . . are overwhelmingly for a peace which can be enforced under international law which has definite authority behind it."[55] Because the board believed that this series found a particularly thoughtful and presumably influential audience "ready to listen to serious speeches," it took responsibility for every one of the Opera Victory Rallies in the 1944–45 season.[56] They included an address by John W. Davis, 1924 Democratic candidate for the presidency, who believed that the United States could play a major role in helping the proposed international organization succeed. He declared that the country should "make available to the security council on its call . . . armed forces, facilities and assistance necessary for the purpose of maintaining international peace and security. It is cheap insurance if it will work. It can never work unless America joins in the effort. Can we make an agreement to contribute so many airplanes, so many ships, so many guns and men when the council calls for them? To my mind, the answer . . . is 'Yes.'"[57]

While the reasoned arguments of prominent individuals found a vast erudite audience during the opera broadcasts, WWB members also sought a visceral approach that would appeal to the masses. They looked for an image that would immediately convey the devastating consequences of another war if peace could not be maintained. In late summer 1944 board members produced a car card for display on buses and other means of public transportation in New York City. The poster showed five infants—one Asian, one black, and three white—under the caption "Must They Die in World War III?" The answer printed under the picture was "Yes: Unless you work now for a lasting peace after victory." Americans United for World Organization (AUWO), led by journalist Ulrich Bell, distributed them, but a problem soon surfaced. For some reason John H. Delaney, chairman of the city's Board of Transportation, refused to allow the cards on subways. The board brought pressure on him by sending letters of protest to the *New York Times* and asking radio commentator Walter Winchell to comment on the situation. Although Delaney never backed down, a number of other cities reacted to the controversy by requesting car cards. The posters soon appeared in San Francisco, Philadelphia, St. Louis, and Portland, Oregon, even though some citizens in each area objected. Board members were never sure whether opposition to the posters stemmed from racial prejudice or isolationism, but they were inclined to believe the latter because they knew that a substantial minority of Americans disapproved of an international peacekeeping organization. Nevertheless the New York writers felt that the majority would support it, and they continued their propaganda efforts with the help of both government agencies and private groups like the AUWO.[58]

THE PLEDGE FOR PEACE

None of the board's work to promote the idea of a global organization was as successful as the "Pledge for Peace" campaign that extended from 1943 through the spring of 1944. Fadiman wrote the original document in 1942, and the entire board subsequently discussed and thoroughly revised it. Its purpose was twofold: "to state in the smallest possible compass the irreducible minimum requirements for a serious effort to organize the world for peace" and to secure widespread support for an international organization by having Americans sign the document and send it to their senators and representatives.[59] For six weeks beginning in early May 1943, the WWB discussed the pledge with some 150 writers including those on its Advisory Council. Members carefully considered whether the document espousing liberal democracy should be general or specific in nature and pored over matters of semantics and length as well as content. Without controversy the board unanimously passed the pledge and agreed to move forward with its promotion and distribution throughout the United States. The only concern was one Clifton Fadiman raised, that "the more widely this pledge is publicized the more open the board will be to attacks from the right, based on the fact that we are engaged in propaganda."[60] To promote its pledge, the WWB organized a front group just as it had done in the Lidice campaign. The Pledge for Peace Committee, chaired by Supreme Court Justice Owen J. Roberts, had a membership of fifty-six prominent individuals, most of them writers. Historian Douglas Southall Freeman and William Allan Neilson, retired president of Smith College, served as vice chairmen, while bestselling author Margaret Culkin Banning took the position of secretary. Carl Carmer orchestrated the committee's activities from behind the scenes, and its executive director, Ruth Hays Friend, a WWB volunteer, did much of the actual work.[61]

The pledge made its official debut on Armistice Day, November 11, 1943. The board arranged a reception at the Hotel Willard in Washington, DC, for representatives of the press and other interested citizens. Justice Roberts delivered the principal address, and Carmer spoke briefly before Fadiman read the "admirably worded document" aloud.[62] It was composed of eight propositions, the first of which stated, "To save myself, my children, and my fellow-beings from inevitable destruction in future wars, a world organization shall be formed." The other stipulations added details. The organization was to be composed of countries not connected with the Axis nations. Those few were to be accorded probationary status until they became full-fledged members. No country could join without agreeing that it would never again wage war and would never withdraw from the organization. Its mission was to maintain global peace by wiping out "economic and political imperialism," and it would have an international police force to implement its regulations. The first of these policies would be to take necessary precautions against Germany and Japan to prevent a third global war. Signees pledged "loyalty to the human race along with, but not conflicting with, my loyalty to my own country."[63] The board printed enough copies of the pledge to supply as many as any individual, group, school system, or business requested.[64]

The *Brief House Organ Items* issue of November 22, 1943, provided a version of the pledge written in simplified language with illustrative examples that the uneducated could comprehend, and the board encouraged corporate publications to disseminate it to industrial employees. The November and December issues of the *Writers' War Board Report* asked writers to promote it in their local areas. One of the editorials sent out in October heralded the pledge as a "Prescription for Peace," and the following month "A Four-Square Peace" called on the Soviet Union, Great Britain, China, and the United States to advocate world organization. In January 1944 Rex Stout's editorial "The Bugaboo of Sovereignty" anticipated possible objections to the pledge.[65] The committee did its part to see that the document was publicized in popular periodicals and on the radio. The Pledge for Peace appeared in *Parents' Magazine*, *Mechanix Illustrated*, *True Confessions*, the *Women's League Outlook*, and a bulletin of the *Veterans of Foreign Wars*, to name only a few.[66]

The board helped publicize the document widely. On May 30, 1944, Fadiman plugged the pledge on the Imogene Wolcott radio show and the WWB sponsored a nationwide broadcast that featured an address by Justice Roberts to the United Nations Council of Philadelphia. On June 13 Carmer made a pitch on the Adelaide Hawley show, and on June 30 Fadiman had a coveted session with the "First Lady of Radio," Mary Margaret McBride. In each case the show's host signed the pledge on the air. According to the board's tabulations the McBride program alone brought in requests for over ten thousand copies.[67] Members of many local groups that supported a postwar international organization helped to put out the word, not only discussing the pledge and signing it but also circulating it on their own. It was preached from pulpits, analyzed in college classrooms, posted on bulletin boards in factories, and distributed by a traveling library in Iowa. Farm, church, civic, business, and labor groups made use of the pledge. The wide range of activities organized across the United States to promote it impressed WWB members.[68]

Within a short time opponents of the pledge began to present their arguments. In an editorial in May 1944 the *Philadelphia Record* strongly objected to the requirement "that Americans should give up forever their independence by renouncing . . . (a) the right to withdraw from any world organization; (b) the right to make war against anyone." The article pointed out that if Americans "tried to fight in defense of their rights the other nations would be bound to jump on them and fight them. . . . America thus would no longer be a nation once its government signed that pledge." The WWB was caught off guard since the paper had generally supported the board's positions, especially those against a soft peace for Germany. Board members found the author's final comments particularly exasperating: "The committee not only threatens to undermine all the progress we have made toward world collaboration but sizes up as exactly the kind of organization which Col. Robert McCormick [publisher of the isolationist *Chicago Tribune*] visioned in his dreams. Here is what the isolationists have longed for: a committee of earnest well-meaning people with a big figure at the front to whose extreme proposals they can point as typical of what world collaboration means."[69]

The board invited David Stern, publisher of the *Record*, to come to New York to discuss the editorial. After Stout, Fadiman, and Friend met with him, they dismissed his objections as unwillingness to abrogate U.S. sovereignty covered over with a framework of rationalizations.[70] Syndicated columnist Philip Wylie, another opponent of the pledge, accused board members of being ingenuous:

> They are good people and they wish to do good. None more. Some of them think they are realists. But in truth they are sentimental people. And they are not practical people.
>
> I am talking about writers on the "writers' war board" who have recently given the world a brand new pledge for peace. The writers' war board is quasi-official. Its pledge for peace will be widely disseminated. Perhaps millions will sign it. And everybody who signs it will think he has done something for world peace. But this pledge will not

help peace any. And it may even harm the minds of some of its signers by giving them, once again, the tragic illusion that high resolve and dotted lines will keep us out of war in the future.[71]

Despite such arguments, the group considered its campaign successful. The August 1944 *Report* gloated, "Strong support for the Pledge for Peace is sweeping from coast to coast."[72]

THE DEBATES OVER THE DUMBARTON OAKS PROPOSALS

In the summer of 1944 the Allies began a series of meetings to shape the economy and political structure of the postwar world, and the board concentrated on doing what it could to influence their decisions. WWB members supported the proposals of three conferences that sponsored international cooperation. The first was held over a three-week period in July 1944 at Bretton Woods, New Hampshire. It involved 730 delegates from 44 Allied countries who met to consider future financial concerns. Among its accomplishments was the establishment of the International Monetary Fund and the World Bank to help with the enormous costs of reconstruction. The new organizations were also designed to prevent a recurrence of the slowdown in global trade that had occurred during the 1930s after some nations set high tariffs on outside goods and others followed suit.[73] The members of the WWB knew little about financial matters and waited until its proposals came up for ratification in Congress before promoting them.

They focused primarily on the two other meetings, one held a month later in Washington, DC, at Dumbarton Oaks and another that took place the following spring in San Francisco. At Dumbarton Oaks representatives of China, the Soviet Union, Great Britain, and the United States met to outline what was to become the United Nations. Their deliberations were held in two sessions from August 21 to October 7. The following spring the UN Charter was drawn up at the San Francisco Conference, which 850 delegates attended from April 25 to June 26, 1945. WWB members worked to inform the public about the plans under consideration in both of these meetings and encouraged acceptance of the new global organization. Even though they had always advocated a powerful world government, they realized that it did not have the support of enough nations to make it a reality, and they backed the much weaker organization instead. They were especially concerned about several thorny issues that the delegates faced such as the extent of veto power of the major Allied nations designated as permanent members of the Security Council. Despite those obstacles, Americans had a general feeling of optimism about establishing an organization that included a majority of the nations around the world.[74] Since Congress prohibited the OWI from any involvement in promoting the conference proposals, the board's efforts to inform the public about them were critically important.

Once the Dumbarton Oaks proposals became public in late September 1944, WWB members struggled to decide whether to endorse them or to demand amendments that would provide a stronger world organization more in keeping with their own ideas. They wavered back and forth, changing their opinions at least three times, but they never openly opposed the propositions. At first the board members decided to make an all-out effort to promote the proposals, and they promptly sent a memorandum urging the WWB's pool of writers, Advisory Council members, and other influential individuals who had signed the Pledge for Peace to advocate the Dumbarton Oaks agreements. Concerned that Congress might refuse to approve it because it did not give the senators veto power over Security Council activities, the group stated emphatically, "The Pledge for Peace which you signed states that the authority of the world organization shall be made effective and irresistible. Certainly it will be neither; instead it will be futile and impotent, if its decisions will be subject to ratification by the legislatures of member nations."[75] To assure recipients that American interests would be protected without such a veto, the board reiterated the facts: "Decisions can be made only with the concurrence of all four delegates of the major powers and two of the remaining [seven] delegates [on the Security Council]. . . . Thus no such decisions can be made and no pressures, sanctions, or force applied without the approval of the U. S. delegates."[76]

But second thoughts crept in. At the group's October 11 meeting the board heard from four members who had separately studied the results of Dumbarton Oaks. Alan Green, Rex Stout, Christopher LaFarge, and Clifton Fadiman each reported that he had found "dangerous loop-holes and omissions which largely cancelled out its good points." The board decided that every member should examine the proposals carefully.[77] The WWB soon heard from historian Lewis Mumford, who also believed the Dumbarton Oaks agreement needed improvement. He objected to the board's approach and sent a letter to Stout accusing the group of "flabby tactics" in accepting battle on the enemy's terms:

> You single out the weakest provision of the Dumbarton Oaks project, that which would ruin the effectiveness of any organization for peace because it would make possible for a single one of the four powers to block action when it pleases. . . . Instead of working to correct this defect you are actually putting it forward as one of the talking points for the Dumbarton Oaks arrangement on the very ground that would make it attractive to every American isolationist, namely that we could at any time escape responsibility and wreck with a single vote any contemplated international action.[78]

His comment caused the group to swing against accepting the proposals as they stood. Stout's reply to Mumford was candid: "I have been wrestling with my soul and now agree completely with you. If we settle for Dumbarton Oaks as it now stands we will be participating in another swindle."[79]

At the board's next meeting the OWI and a few pro-UN organizations asked for help in preparing a brief and readable summary of the Dumbarton Oaks proposals. A long debate ensued with some WWB members arguing that it would not be possible to write about Dumbarton Oaks without admitting that the proposals had no substance. Others felt that criticizing the proposals put the board "in the position of playing Senator [Henry Cabot] Lodge," who had opposed President Woodrow Wilson. In 1919 Lodge successfully used the technique of proposing amendment after amendment to block Senate approval of the Treaty of Versailles ending World War I because he objected to a provision that would make the United States part of the League of Nations, an organization that Wilson strongly supported. Fearing some similar action to block acceptance of the 1944 proposals, the WWB eventually decided to label Dumbarton Oaks "a start in the right direction," but the group noted that much remained to be done. Despite this ambivalence, the board arranged for Stout to write three pieces, each one geared to a different audience.[80]

His widely distributed "Questions and Answers about Dumbarton Oaks" was a rather simplistic but vaguely favorable account of the results of the conference. Stout posed the question, "Is this [new organization] sure to prevent wars?" and gave a practical rather than patent reply: "Not necessarily. But if we really mean it when we say we want no more wars, here is our chance to make a real start on a set-up that will get us what we want if we work at it." Study kits on the subject distributed by the Women's Action Committee for Victory and Lasting Peace contained the second Stout piece, "The Primer of Dumbarton Oaks." The board also sent this more simplified version using a question-and-answer format to soldiers, war plant workers, and various organizations. At the end of the year Stout restated the issues once again in "Test for Dumbarton Oaks." A more critical study, it indicated the weak points of the conference proposals by comparing them with the terms of the Pledge for Peace. Stout asserted that the stipulations were unclear about the treatment of the Axis nations and their admission to membership. Furthermore, some items in the pledge were not included in the agreement. For instance, the Dumbarton Oaks proposals did not require every nation to renounce its right to make war or to abolish economic and political imperialism. Because members could secede, the WWB chairman argued that the "authority of the world organization" could be neither "effective" nor "irresistible" as the pledge had specified.[81]

The board included "Test for Dumbarton Oaks" in its *Third Annual Report* and sent the editorial to all members of Congress, almost 200 army orientation officers, recipients of the *Report*, 350 editors of periodicals, 182 cooperating peace organizations, and other groups including religious societies, agricultural associations, libraries, and Pledge for Peace clubs. It mailed copies to anyone requesting them, and put them in 1,150 kits on the Dumbarton Oaks proposals prepared under WWB auspices for use in schools.[82] The group received a number of responses to the article, the majority of them favorable. Senator J. William Fulbright of Arkansas complimented the board: "I am certain that by presenting these discussions to the people of the country you are doing a very fine work. It certainly is necessary to enlighten and inform our people on our foreign relations."⁸³ Among the hostile comments were accusations that board members had stifled any chance for world organization by demanding instant perfection.⁸⁴

In addition to the three documents by Stout, board publications and standing committees promoted the Dumbarton Oaks proposals. In December 1944 the *Bulletin to Cartoonists* encouraged its recipients to present the proposals creatively. The Committee on Speeches and Speakers wrote a number of addresses and arranged for their delivery by prominent speakers like actress Florence Eldridge. She drew audiences at a Carnegie Hall rally on April 25, 1945, and at several other venues. For radio broadcast Jack Goodman and Robert Cenedella of Decca Records prepared recordings explaining the provisions of the Dumbarton Oaks agreement. The board also contacted writers Nick Carter and Martin Stearns about preparing a series of radio dramas on the proposals for the OWI.⁸⁵

At the instigation of the board, war correspondent Edgar Ansel Mowrer sent a letter to Secretary of State Edward R. Stettinius Jr. in December asking about the direction the WWB should take: "How can we Americans who support the Dumbarton Oaks proposals best aid you who have to negotiate them? By accepting the proposals as written and urging approval on them as they stand, or by criticizing them as insufficient and insisting that you obtain something better?"⁸⁶ Stettinius was clear: "Needle us like Hell. Ask for the maximum. We shall do much better at the coming conference if we are backed by an American public that is yelling for the strongest, most perfect organization conceivable. Then if we only get 80% of what you are asking for it will still be a victory for us all."⁸⁷ His reply was circulated to board members, the WWB Advisory Council, the Pledge for Peace Committee, and other cooperating groups. Encouraged, they kept up their call for a more powerful world organization. Although the New York writers attempted to obtain a similarly strong statement from Stettinius for publication, they were unsuccessful.⁸⁸

Despite the secretary of state's remarks and their own deep conviction that their approach was correct on principle, board members continued to have doubts. At their meeting on March 7 Alan Green made an argument to stand behind Dumbarton Oaks without reservation on the grounds of political expediency. He believed that there would be no second chance for international union in the foreseeable future if the proposals were defeated. He thought "Test for Dumbarton Oaks" had delighted isolationists and others who did not want a global organization because Stout's comparison indicated revisions that might be made to improve the agreement. Green believed that amending the proposals was dangerous because the process could delay their passage and perhaps defeat them. After deliberating the WWB acknowledged the validity of his view and agreed to support them as they were.[89]

But Green's change of heart did not settle the argument, and the board soon reversed itself again, this time at the behest of Archibald MacLeish and his special assistant, future presidential candidate Adlai Stevenson, both of whom attended the board meeting the following week. In his relatively new position as assistant secretary of state for public and cultural relations (now public affairs), MacLeish asked for assistance in setting the stage for the upcoming international conference in San Francisco that would formally establish the United Nations. Even though the State Department had endorsed Dumbarton Oaks, both MacLeish and Stevenson agreed with Stettinius that the WWB should fight for a stronger set of proposals. All three wanted problems with the propositions to be made public while the opportunity to change them still existed.[90]

Noting that Americans were ready as never before to plan for world security, MacLeish declared, "Now is the psychological moment to fortify this emotional conviction with an intellectual understanding of the problems involved and the practical possibilities for achieving the desired goals." Calling on the writers to go after what they believed in, Stevenson observed, "Public opinion is often ahead of official action; such thinking often results in advancing the center."[91] This was music to the board's ears. Again the pendulum swung as members received encouragement from the administration to go beyond official policy. The WWB agreed to give all possible help to the State Department, and the group reasserted its stand for a world organization that had greater power.[92]

THE BRETTON WOODS CONFERENCE

That month the board's attention was temporarily diverted as Congress began to consider whether or not to ratify the Bretton Woods proposals that would establish the International Monetary Fund (IMF) and the World Bank. Since both of these organizations focused on cooperation among the nations of the world, congressional approval of them could pave the way for the upcoming San Francisco Conference to work out the details of a global peacekeeping body. Alan Green pointed out that failure to pass the agreements might send a negative message to the delegates set to meet in California, making them feel that their work would be futile because it had no chance of approval in the United States. The board knew that it would have to work fast to encourage congressional approval of the two new financial institutions before the San Francisco Conference began, and members quickly compiled a list of ideas for the brief campaign. The group decided that it would not attempt to persuade the public of the excellence of the agreements because they were too complicated to explain in a short campaign. Acknowledging that the board had no expertise in banking and finance, members did not attempt to address the concerns of opponents of the World Bank and the International Monetary Fund about either economic policies or the issue of isolationism. Instead the group determined to sell Bretton Woods as a token of America's willingness to participate in international organizations.[93]

Working at remarkable speed, within three days board members distributed "Bretton Woods—A First Step to Lasting Peace" written by Alan Green but slightly revised by Samuel Grafton. This document, which the board internally referred to as the "clarion call," was mailed to a number of newspaper columnists and radio commentators as well as the Pledge for Peace Committee and the board's Advisory Council. It opened with the alarming statement, "The fate of national security—the possibility of any international security organization coming into being in our lifetime—may be decided within the next few days." It contended that viewing the agreements as complex matters of economics instead of initial steps in the drive toward international organization would doom the establishment of a global peacekeeping group: "The essential fact about Bretton Woods has nothing to do with economics. Its most essential fact is that the San Francisco Conference will meet only a few weeks after the American Congress accepts—or rejects—Bretton Woods. If the San Francisco Congress convenes in the knowledge that our Congress has rejected Bretton Woods . . . , then there is little use in reaching any international agreement with American delegates because of the non-ratification of our Congress." Claiming that the Bretton Woods proposals were worked out by experts and that opponents were trying to amend them to death, the board concluded, "If you believe in the cause of a world organization, be it Dumbarton Oaks or some other variety, use all your influence to urge the passage of Bretton Woods *without change*."[94]

The board launched its campaign at a special dinner meeting on March 19, 1945, attended by a group of individuals who could help with the promotion. In his *New York Post* column Grafton said that the Bretton Woods agreements were simply a matter of stabilizing currency and should be quickly accepted. His remarks brought a flurry of attention from the New York press. Drawing on both the "clarion call" and the Grafton article, the *New York Herald-Tribune* sarcastically referred to Clifton Fadiman, Franklin Adams, and Russel Crouse as "outstanding monetary experts" and complained that the board's oversimplification prevented serious consideration of the complex financial matters and their long-term effects.[95] A *New York World-Telegram* editorial was even more critical. It attacked the group and its methodology while paying unwilling tribute to the extent of its influence. It identified the WWB as "a pressure group that could become very dangerous to the country. They have direct contact with more people than any other, and they have the confidence of the great majority of them. They may not know how to throw the balls but they certainly know how to roll them."[96]

To generate even more publicity for the Bretton Woods agreements, board members duplicated the efforts they had made for the Dumbarton Oaks proposals. They arranged for favorable mention by radio commentators and correspondents Walter Winchell, Cecil Brown, J. W. Vandercook, and William Shirer. Orson Welles recorded another informational plug prepared by Decca Records executive Robert Cenedella and the board's Jack Goodman. The WWB set up interviews on the shows of Mary Margaret McBride and Martha Deane. On March 25 Stout appeared as a guest on the nationwide program *Report to the Nation*. The board also assisted in an April 30 broadcast on Bretton Woods on the Mutual Network. It was conceived and written by the WWB's counterpart, the Hollywood Writers' Mobilization. LaFarge and Green hastily wrote the speech "Road to Peace—Under Construction" for wide distribution. The board prepared kits with background material on the conference that included the speech as well as "Bretton Woods—A First Step to Lasting Peace."[97]

The *Report* ran a short article partly based on "Road to Peace," and *Brief Army Camp Items* carried the speech under the byline of Dean Acheson, chief American delegate to Bretton Woods. WWB member Jean Poletti addressed a Brooklyn rally and Florence Eldridge spoke at several others. The group wrote a brief summary of the symbolic importance of Bretton Woods called "Recipe for World War III" and mailed it to over 1,300 influential figures. The WWB asked them to send letters or telegrams to their congressmen and made similar appeals to many others. The entire campaign, a typical WWB performance, took place within six weeks of its inception. At that time the board learned that the Bretton Woods agreements would not come up for a final vote until after San Francisco. WWB members felt that they had done all they could in such a short period, but they continued to face criticism.[98] For example, college president N. S. Byrd said the board had no business asking the public to support Bretton Woods without knowing what the legislation did.[99] The point was reasonable, but the WWB did not stop to answer such comments since it needed to begin its United Nations campaign before the San Francisco Conference convened on April 25.

THE SAN FRANCISCO CONFERENCE

Delegates at the California conference made no significant modifications to the Dumbarton Oaks agreements, and the United Nations Charter they signed on June 26 set up guidelines for an international organization that was not the powerful world government that the WWB had hoped to achieve. Each nation was to retain its sovereignty, and the great-power veto remained in place. The board was disappointed but decided to give the United Nations its unconditional endorsement, fearing that the Henry Cabot Lodge technique of adding amendments to it might kill the UN. In cooperation with the American Association for the United Nations (AAUN), the WWB arranged for the presentation of a play by Norman Rosten over the Mutual Broadcasting network on April 27. *They Shall Be Heard* was a generalized call for world unification as well as a plea for a strong organization of nations that not only set the stage for the San Francisco proceedings but also promoted the WWB campaigns on Dumbarton Oaks and Bretton Woods. In May the board set up another production of the drama over WNYC in New York, and the following month it distributed the play as a War Script of the Month.[100]

Through the efforts of Jean Poletti, the Hummert Radio Agency, whose founders have been described as "broadcasting's most prolific producers," agreed to send out regular nonpartisan appeals for Americans to express their views on the United Nations Charter by writing to their local newspapers and senators.[101] The WWB enlisted CBS news analyst Ned Calmer to write radio scripts on the charter that were distributed to local stations by the AAUN. Board members wrote spot announcements that the Americans United for World Organization (AUWO) recorded. They persuaded McBride to conduct a weekly interview on the charter and supplied guests like Robert Sherwood, Carl Van Doren, and Pearl Buck. The group also encouraged a number of radio commentators to promote the charter and mention it prominently.[102] In May a short article in the *Writers' War Board Report* entitled "Keep Special Issues away from San Francisco" asked readers to create an atmosphere in which the conference would have a chance to succeed. It pointed out that delegates were "tackling history's greatest problem. This problem is to maintain peace in the world. It must, of necessity, restrict itself to a very general and overall plan. [Attendees] will . . . draft a document for world peace which will be flexible enough to admit all ways in which international, national, group or racial tensions may be eased. They cannot begin to consider, in this particular conference, each and every problem. Give them a chance."[103]

The WWB stepped up its campaign to generate public interest in the proceedings as the final month of negotiations began. On June 11 it held a special meeting of some thirty prominent individuals including *Saturday Review* editor Norman Cousins, a strong advocate of world organization, and Freedom House official William Agar. Members asked for favorable publicity in all media outlets during the period that the charter was under consideration. The board agreed to arrange public addresses on the subject and furnished speakers to several dozen rallies, most sponsored by peace groups such as AUWO. Effective public speakers in the

WWB and its Advisory Council assisted in this enterprise.[104] The board also targeted specific states. Soon after the conference started, members privately obtained from Secretary of the Senate Leslie Biffle the names of members likely to vote against the charter. Then they began special propaganda efforts in the home states of those legislators with the help of several peace organizations that circulated materials and called for public meetings on the UN.[105]

During that month the WWB dispatched to individuals and organizations hundreds of kits that contained outlines of letters to newspapers and senators, plans for working through community groups, and five speeches of varying lengths advocating the United Nations, some intended for educated audiences and others for less sophisticated listeners. These were "Why We Need the San Francisco Charter" by Norman Cousins; "Take Your Place at the Peace Table" by Edward Bernays; "Our Chances of Avoiding World War III" by Robert Landry; "Comparison with the History of the U. S. Constitution" by Florence Eldridge and Nina Bourne; and "Why the U. S. and Russia Must Be Friends" by William Nelson. Also included were the text of the charter, a series of questions and answers prepared by the Woodrow Wilson Foundation, an illustrative chart, and "Toward the Peace," a collection of related documents. The WWB added two pieces by Rex Stout—a summary of the charter and "The United Smiths," an idealistic article that explained the purpose of a global peacekeeping organization in simple, persuasive, optimistic language. Stout acknowledged that few thought world peace was possible since they considered war to be a fact of life. But he argued that they were wrong because throughout history people have gradually expanded "the area within which bloodshed is not permitted." Stout contended that this expansion would continue until there was no area for fighting and all places on the earth would be at peace.[106]

Once the delegates ratified the UN charter, its approval by the U.S. Senate seemed assured. Nevertheless, the *Writers' War Board Report* told readers, "It's Up to You from Here on In." WWB members strongly believed that American public opinion would determine whether the senators worked to strengthen the document or refused to challenge it.[107] In May *Brief House Organ Items* ran the feature "Let's Buy It" over Eldridge's signature. It encouraged widespread support: "It is up to us to see the United Nations through to a start . . . even if it isn't perfect to start with." The following month the WWB editorial "The Course of True Love" attempted to calm fears about minor disagreements among the great powers. Some Americans thought the rifts could become so serious that they might deter the establishment of the organization or render it ineffective. The July *Bulletin to Cartoonists* was entirely devoted to suggestions for portraying the San Francisco Conference.[108] That month the UN campaign ended as the WWB prepared to shut its doors, but the organization continued to fulfill the commitments it had already made.

Even though the organization that emerged from the San Francisco Conference proved to be the disappointment that the WWB members had feared, the writers can hardly be faulted for their pragmatic decision to work for its establishment rather than lose the possibility for greater international cooperation. Although the group had identified the major weaknesses in the UN charter, they did not anticipate the biggest obstacle to the work of the new organization: the split between Russia and its allies, the so-called Cold War. From a twenty-first-century perspective, the pro-Soviet propaganda the board generated on behalf of the government seems both ill-advised and naive. Within a year of Germany's surrender Winston Churchill called attention to the intransigence and insular nature of the Soviet bloc in his March 1946 "Iron Curtain" speech. The widening schism between communism and the Western democracies made the peace process to end World War II complicated and slow. While WWB members did all they could to insure international cooperation and peace, they were not able to achieve either goal to their satisfaction. The work they did on their Pledge for Peace, their "Notes on Current Thinking on Post-War Germany," and their peace plan produced no definite results. Still, their propaganda efforts helped to insure the establishment of the United Nations even though the OWI was not allowed to participate in the debate.

In the summer of 1945 the United States, Great Britain, France, and the Soviet Union divided Germany and its capital into zones of occupation. The peace talks that began a year later specified that the Axis nations pay reparations, which the board had fought. In the end there was no peace settlement comparable to the Treaty of Versailles that all of the major belligerents signed. The Allied Control Council, the military authority in occupied Germany, set up some policies similar to those suggested by the board and others. It sharply limited the German steel industry and attempted to reduce the German standard of living to depression levels.[109] It also began an aggressive de-Nazification process in schools and professions. In November the prosecution of Nazi criminals in Nuremberg began and continued for almost a year. However, the trials had the effect that Green predicted. They caused Americans to believe that the guilty had been punished and that other German citizens were not at fault. The de-Nazification initiatives soon sputtered to a halt.[110]

In 1953 the London Agreement on German External Debts took effect, helping the nation's economy recover rapidly, just as the WWB had feared.[111] It reduced the remainder of Germany's reparations payments and many of its other debts. As a result the nation's industry revived so fast that within ten years, "people were already talking about the German economic miracle."[112] In 1949 the country joined the North Atlantic Treaty Organization and began to rebuild its military forces. Germany was reunited in 1990, and it made its last reparations payment in 2010. Although some of the suggestions of the board for a harsh peace settlement were enforced for a time, they did not prevent Germany's quick comeback. Its recovery, however, proved advantageous in the Cold War confrontation with communism. That conflict encouraged greater international cooperation and silenced the isolationists.

CHAPTER 7

REFLECTIONS ON THE WRITERS' WAR BOARD

IN A CABLE to the members of the Writers' War Board on December 31, 1943, the presidium of the Union of Soviet Writers hailed the American authors as "comrades in arms" and commented on the similar role of the two organizations: "Never has the lofty role of literature been so clear as in this war. . . . We soldiers of the pen are more clearly than ever aware of our duty to fuse our words of truth with language of fire and steel so that they shall call to struggle and smite the enemy. . . . Let us devote all our abilities, and all our efforts to hasten the hour of complete victory over Hitlerite tyranny and to secure . . . enduring peace and progress."[1] Their words must have resonated with the board members. Confident of their abilities and of their cause, the majority of the influential men and women on the WWB were devoted to their volunteer work for the organization and approached it as enthusiastically and relentlessly as soldiers mounting an attack. No other explanation can account so well for the thousands of hours they logged making contacts, giving speeches, focusing on board projects at the expense of their own work, and—always—writing, writing, writing for one campaign or another.

Julian Street Jr., the Treasury consultant who first stimulated the creation of the group, also thought of its members as soldiers of a kind. He admitted that he was astounded by their output and remarked that they had "turned in a truly superb job" that was "impressive." He acknowledged the organization's help to his department throughout the war: "In one way or another the Writers' War Board . . . served practically every promotional section of the War Finance Division."[2] He credited those on the board for being "amazingly generous with their talents" and argued that they deserved thanks along with the soldiers on the battlefront: "No professional group on the home front has worked more consistently or more unselfishly for the war effort. The highest paid writers in the country have worked long hours, frequently anonymously and without any pay of course, on government wartime needs. . . . So often they don't even get thanks. I honestly think they have been magnificent. Sure, I know about the guys in foxholes. I'll admit they rate the highest. But my hat's off to these authors, too."[3]

THE DEMISE OF THE WWB

Beginning in January 1945 both the OWI and the WWB considered dispensing with the board's governmental subsidy after Congress began to question the expenditure. With the war in Europe coming to an end, the members of the Writers' War Board knew that they would be forced to shut down their operations soon. The OWI had made that fact clear more than six months before the Germans surrendered. In October 1944 it distributed a memorandum canceling most of the government's wartime publicity endeavors and announcing the institution of postwar programs immediately following Adolf Hitler's defeat. The WWB had protested, arguing that the notice was premature and unwarranted since fighting in the Pacific was certain to continue after the Germans laid down their arms; however, the board's argument did not convince the government agency to alter its plans. Despite the OWI's intransigence, WWB members continued to send out their publications, work on their committees, and proceed with their campaigns, particularly those on the terms of peace and the establishment of an international organization. However, they were very selective about the new assignments they accepted. Anticipating that the board would soon go out of business, they began to make arrangements to halt or transfer all of their activities, leaving the anti-German campaign in the capable hands of the Society for the Prevention of World War III and the Friends of Democracy. Although the writers felt that many of their projects were necessary and should continue, they were realistic about what they could accomplish in the short time left to them. The board's subsidy ended in June 1945, and the OWI itself went out of business on September 15. Even so, the board continued to function on its own through the summer. As late as mid-September WWB members were persuading celebrities like Jimmy Stewart, air force pilot and popular film star, to participate in the Victory War Loan Drive that fall (October 29–December 8).[4]

After it lost its subsidy, the WWB scrambled for funding. It became for a short time the Writers' Board of the Friends of Democracy.[5] In August the group dropped that affiliation and reorganized as a private organization called simply the Writers' Board.[6] The former WWB finally succeeded in acquiring the financing it needed, but it had to close its Washington office. The organization continued to publish the *Writers' Board Report* through March 1, 1946, and to send out scripts for troop camp shows. While it worked on completing a few assignments left from its days as a quasi-government group, it mounted a handful of new campaigns as a strictly private organization. Not surprisingly, it also returned to some of its old battles. Its members identified two primary objectives, promoting racial harmony and arguing for a harsh peace settlement. Rex Stout acknowledged that its "main purpose was to combat 'the myth that the United States is and should remain a White Protestant Anglo-Saxon country.'"[7] In the last two months of 1945, members briefly revived their anti-German mantra. They recruited prominent people to express their opposition to a soft peace with Germany and offered to prepare a letter for each individual who agreed to participate. Once they submitted the signed documents to newspaper editors across the country, however, they made no follow-up effort.[8]

In December the Writers' Board launched a quick campaign to save an appropriations bill to partially fund the United Nations Relief and Rehabilitation Administration (UNRRA). The Emergency Non-Partisan Committee for Relief to Liberated Areas made the urgent request, and the board immediately responded. Although failure to pass the legislation immediately would break the agency's supply chain, Congress seemed unlikely to act because some members questioned the UNRRA expenditures. More importantly, the Senate was set to adjourn for Christmas. The board sent information about the issue to ten radio commentators and hastily prepared an editorial. "A Conscience for Christmas" went to 1,300 newspapers on December 12. It suggested that the legislators would not be able to have a merry Christmas if they realized that their haste to get home would condemn thousands of people to starvation: "Unless the . . . $150 million is appropriated before Congress recesses, Senators will have killed men, women, and children as surely as if they had snatched the food with their own hands from the plates of the destitute."[9] The board also conceived a plan to gain the sympathy of Americans and publicly blackmail members of Congress. It obtained a large number of pledges from writers and professional men and women to fast on Christmas Day if Congress did not approve the necessary funds before it recessed. Press releases were prepared for Sunday, December 23, and full publicity was about to begin when word came that the Senate would pass the bill, thus ending the brief campaign.[10]

By early 1946 most of the WWB publications had stopped, and all but one or two of its committees had ceased to operate. Even though its members were convinced that the United Nations was far too weak, they felt so strongly about the need for a worldwide peacekeeping organization that they began one final effort to modify it into a true world government. In February they circulated a petition asking President Harry Truman to restructure the UN. The New York writers believed that the world situation was desperate enough to justify such a drastic change. Since there was no defense against the atomic bomb, they feared that a nuclear attack could wipe out humanity unless a global government took immediate preventative steps.[11] But their effort came far too late, and it received no response. Despite its plans for other projects, the Writers' Board officially dissolved on April 1, 1946, after approximately eight months.[12] Both its funding and its outlets for disseminating propaganda had begun to dry up. Without the impetus of war, the media industry had no compelling reason to give space and time to the initiatives of the Writers' Board, which had lost its government connection.

More than three years later several former members felt compelled to continue their fight for a strong world organization. In July 1949 they established the Writers' Board for World Government. Its members included Rex Stout, Clifton Fadiman, Alan Green, Oscar Hammerstein II, Russel Crouse, Christopher LaFarge, and Margaret Leech as well as a number of authors who had served on the WWB's Advisory Council or had otherwise worked closely with the board: Norman Cousins, Mark Van Doren, Henry Seidel Canby, Dorothy Canfield Fisher, and Robert

Sherwood. Since the strength of the United Nations fell considerably short of what the WWB had wanted, the members of this new group were not surprised by its essential ineffectiveness. Nevertheless, they continued to think that world federation provided hope for lasting peace if individual nations were willing to grant it sovereignty. Their organization carried on the work of the WWB by advocating a strong world government for more than two decades.[13]

CRITICISM OF THE BOARD

Over the course of the board's existence, a variety of charges were lodged against it. These ran the gamut from accusations that it was communist-oriented to claims that it used fascist techniques. Most of these vituperative attacks were made in haste and had no basis in fact. However, a few merit examination. The group was sometimes criticized for masquerading as a government agency. Writer John Patric claimed that the board misled authors into believing that its requests were official assignments. He complained, "Is not my point the ... worse [that] the Writers' War Board is not actually a government agency, but a quasi-government owned agency, ... which leaves writers unable to decide which is which?"[14] Board members were proud of the WWB's status as a private agency that operated outside the government's authority, but they did not hesitate to imply or state outright the board's close ties to the government if that connection could be used to their advantage. Although this practice may have seemed deceptive to Patric and others, it accurately reflected the group's intimate working relationship with official agencies such as the OWI and the Treasury Department.

Ironically, some who valued the WWB made the opposite argument. They worried that the board might fall too closely under the government's control. In practice the group did not engage in public attacks on official agencies or their employees, and it never obstructed the work of the administration although it occasionally took a stand against one policy or another, usually at the government's unofficial request. The WWB chose to forego making such denunciations not because the government required its allegiance or because it feared losing its OWI subsidy but because the organization was committed to promoting consensus.

Skeptical or adverse commentary would only have served the conservative opponents of democratic liberalism. For the same reason board members did not criticize President Franklin Roosevelt in public.[15] They believed that raising doubts about the country's leader was a luxury that could wait until peacetime. In their view condemning his actions would do little good and might undermine the nation's unity of purpose. If the board disagreed with one of the government's positions, it simply refrained from participating in any activities related to the issue. Fortunately, as WWB member Robert Landry put it, "We were on the same general wave length" as the Roosevelt administration.[16] Obstruction would have been foolish since members believed that the government was generally on the right track. The only real chance they had of influencing it was to take a stand before officials made a policy decision, but they did not often have that opportunity.

A few writers including Advisory Council member John Steinbeck had the mistaken notion that the WWB was a secretive organization that not only attempted to dictate what authors should write but also inserted insidious propaganda into America's reading material. These charges are unfounded. In fact, the WWB made every effort to publicize its existence and its function among government agencies and private organizations that might need its services and among media outlets that the board regularly used to promote its campaigns. It recounted its activities in three annual reports to the writers of the country. Almost eight thousand copies of the last one were sent out in May 1945.[17] Unfortunately, because the WWB ceased to operate as a quasi-governmental body in the summer of 1945, it never issued an annual report for the final year of the war. Although its annual reports are self-laudatory on occasion, they detail the work of the organization and provide evidence that the group had no authority to dictate its will. Its primary job was to help with the government's propaganda efforts and to enlist writers to produce materials for the campaigns of various federal agencies. The board not only circulated its reports privately but also saw that they were summarized in the *New York Times*, *Variety*, and *Publishers Weekly*. In addition, it issued periodic statements to the news media on particular projects, and it tried to answer all inquiries about its operation and activities fully and frankly, even acknowledging disagreement among its members at one time or another.

The false perception of the board as a secret organization may have resulted in part from its attitude of self-effacement. Outside its own publications and periodic letters to its wide-ranging contacts, the name of the WWB rarely appeared in connection with its propaganda. Presenting the information to the public was far more important to the board than receiving credit for its work. Demanding recognition or insisting that materials be printed verbatim might have delayed their use, and the board did not want to do anything that would hinder the chances of publicizing its messages. Furthermore, by insisting that its name be attached, the WWB could have offended the many writers who supplied materials for its frequent campaigns. Although an author, publisher, or radio broadcaster might occasionally mention the group's involvement, the board neither required nor sought recognition.

Some Washington officials also thought of the WWB as a secret society because it refused to permit the general circulation of its minutes through government channels.[18] Members considered a number of items at their weekly meetings aside from their activities on behalf of the government. Understandably they did not wish to supply OWI personnel with comprehensive information about their private campaigns or the projects they were working on for nongovernmental organizations. During one discussion of whether or not the board should develop its own radio program, some board members had expressed reservations about exposing the group's "propaganda mechanism," but most were not concerned about keeping their tactics a secret, and the matter never came up again. In fact, the group did not hide any of its activities. It routinely sent a full accounting of all its campaigns as well as complete copies of its minutes to the upper echelon of OWI officials.[19]

Another accusation periodically made against the WWB was that it did not confine its efforts to war activities but intervened in party politics on the side of the Roosevelt administration and Democrats in general.[20] That argument seems to be bolstered by the fact that many of the opponents of the WWB were conservative Republicans who favored isolationism. They included Senator Robert A. Taft of Ohio, Representative Hamilton Fish III of New York, and former president Herbert Hoover. The board felt such animosity toward Hoover because of his open hostility to Roosevelt's foreign policy that it declined a government request to ghostwrite an article for him.²¹ Roosevelt critics also pointed to a supposedly nonpartisan WWB campaign to encourage citizens to register and vote, noting that it was suspiciously similar to Democratic Party efforts in support of Roosevelt's fourth term.²²

Most of the board's work with the Roosevelt administration was apolitical, focusing specifically on the effort to win the war while maintaining unity at home. All who served on the WWB were careful to dissociate themselves from the group when they engaged in partisan activities. Such was the case when Rex Stout and Margaret Leech assisted with Roosevelt's fourth-term campaign and when Jean Poletti led Democratic Party organizations for women. The members of the board included both Republicans and Democrats, and many of them had fought isolationists long before Pearl Harbor. Furthermore, the liberal New York writers had a close working relationship with Republican Wendell Willkie. In 1944 Stout attended a news conference announcing the Draft Willkie Committee, and WWB members Clifton Fadiman, Russel Crouse, and Samuel Grafton were among a group that publicly urged Willkie to run.²³ As a whole the WWB never helped candidates, and any political effects of their work must be considered indirect and incidental.

A fifth charge leveled against the WWB members is that they were racially biased. The board's historical documentation of the so-called German will-to-aggression is reminiscent of the type of "evidence" once used to demonstrate the inferiority of African Americans. The group's advocacy of hatred for Germany and its argument that Germans were aggressive, arrogant, and intrinsically evil appears in striking contrast to its stand against racial intolerance and stereotyping in the United States. Even though board members steadfastly denied espousing any racist theory about Germans, the group's hardliners—Stout, Fadiman, Paul Gallico, William Shirer, and Alan Green—believed that all of the population, even expatriates with records of opposition to Hitler, were part of the problem because they were reared in an atmosphere of pan-Germanism.²⁴ Most on the board had strong convictions about racism. Fighting discrimination in the United States while condoning it in regards to Germans indicates an unnerving inconsistency. Certainly combating Germany in two twentieth-century global conflicts accounts for much of the group's anti-German belligerence, but the issue divided the group and its Advisory Council so deeply in 1944 that they were barely able to retain a united front. According to Stout, the WWB looked on World War II as "a moral crusade" and believed that almost everyone shared its feeling that "there was something intolerably evil loose in the world."[25] Once the conflict ended, the strong anti-German views of the five hardliners continued even though expressing such feelings was no longer acceptable. Gallico complained, "When the war was still going full blast, . . . it was . . . permitted to hate fascists, the Nazi, German, Jap, and Argentine brands, without being stigmatized as a 'liberal' in the pregnant quotes."[26] Others on the board took a more moderate view.

Finally, in early 1945 political philosopher Hannah Arendt contended that the anti-German campaigns in World War II launched by various groups were failures because they merely duplicated the work of the Committee on Public Information in World War I. She charged that World War II propaganda had "lost much of its inspirational power" and was "no longer effective." Since some of the atrocity stories circulated in the earlier war proved to be false, she was not surprised that many Americans did not believe reports about the Holocaust. She concluded, "The result of the revival of the *German problem* is therefore negative."[27] Her comments were not directed specifically at the WWB but at all organizations engaged in disseminating anti-German material; however, the board would certainly have taken note of her assessment although no reference to her appears in its files. A twenty-first-century historian has made a similar charge, asserting that the board's campaign for a harsh peace was a failure too. However, he admits that the WWB was able to generate a large measure of ill will toward Germany within government and media circles close to the end of the war.[28]

UNIQUE POSITION AS A QUASI-GOVERNMENTAL AGENCY

Regardless of these criticisms, the WWB was primarily a private propaganda agency that served the needs of the government. In his classic 1927 study of propaganda in World War I, Harold D. Lasswell defined the word as "the control of opinion by . . . social communication" and identified its purposes in wartime: "During war much reliance must be placed on propaganda to promote economy of food, textiles, fuel, and other commodities, and to stimulate recruiting, employment in war industries, service in relief work, and the purchase of bonds. But by far the most potent role of propaganda is to mobilize the animosity of the community against the enemy, to maintain friendly relations with neutrals and allies, to arouse neutrals against the enemy, and to break up the solid wall of enemy antagonism."[29] All of the board's activities fall into the first four duties that Lasswell mentioned. It devoted no time to arousing neutrals and overcoming enemy antagonism because it directed its propaganda primarily to Americans on the home front. Despite the fact that the group had no formal training in propaganda, as writers, journalists, and advertisers they knew how to persuade. Fadiman impressed Julian Street early on by working singlehandedly for an entire day in December 1941 to compile over one hundred activities for selling war bonds that "included everything from ideas for comic strips to slogans for chewing gum wrappers."[30] Fadiman and many of the other board members had learned propaganda techniques from reading about the work of the Committee on Public Information in World War I and from participating in the interventionist organizations that sprang up in the United States after Germany invaded Poland in 1939.

Before America entered the war, groups like the Committee to Defend America by Aiding the Allies and the Fight for Freedom Committee had given future board members the opportunity to develop their arguments against both isolationists and fascists, hone their debating skills, practice public speaking, and discover ways to make their ideas appealing to all segments of the population.[31] These organizations engaged in a number of activities that the board later adopted. Their members collected statements from prominent people; wrote letters to newspapers and members of Congress; formed a speakers' bureau that arranged for public addresses; distributed nationwide ready-to-print newspaper features, inspirational pieces, editorials, and cartoons; promoted appropriate books, stage plays, and radio scripts; and prepared and disseminated various types of propaganda. Board members also came up with some highly successful ideas of their own including the Lidice renaming ceremonies and the Pledge for Peace effort. Other tactics of the group included inserting "war pages" into books published between 1942 and 1946. Similar inserts carrying the group's propaganda messages were included in some of the programs of New York theater productions during the war.[32]

The work of the first official propaganda agency in the United States undoubtedly had the greatest impact on the interventionist groups and on the Writers' War Board. In fact, two of the board's own campaigns—its emphasis on the malevolent nature of the German enemy and its promotion of world government—were strikingly similar to those of the Committee on Public Information twenty-five years earlier. Although the CPI operated for just over two years and was heavily criticized for its high-handed approach and false or misleading reports, it blanketed both the United States and Europe with an astounding amount of material and inundated American newspapers with editorials and columns of information about the war. It made use of cartoons, pictures, store displays, and posters for wide distribution. No radio broadcasting system existed during the Great War, but CPI chairman George Creel organized the next best thing, a nationwide group of "four-minute men" who delivered CPI-supplied speeches on various topics. He also used motion pictures to disseminate government propaganda and sent materials to schools, churches, women's clubs, and labor organizations.[33]

The WWB followed Creel's lead. Like the CPI, the board cooperated with other federal agencies and the armed services in carrying out a variety of campaigns from recruiting for the military to helping the Treasury Department sell war bonds. Although they did not go as far as Creel did, board members also tried to censor or downplay opposing viewpoints when they could. Because of the CPI's unpopularity after the war and the controversial reputation of its chairman, however, the Writers' War Board felt that it should distance itself from Creel even though the government agency he headed had pioneered many propaganda techniques. While Creel expressed interest in the board's projects and often enthusiastically agreed with its positions, the group did not invite him to be a member or promote his 1944 work, *War Criminals and Punishment*. However, Creel served on the board's Advisory Council, and the WWB arranged for the publication of one of his articles and commissioned two scripts based on his book.[34]

To avoid the mistakes of the Creel committee, as soon as the Office of War Information began to operate in June 1942, Congress enjoined it not to meddle in controversial issues and limited its functions. Conservative Republicans and southern Democrats did everything they could to keep it from issuing propaganda that supported the administration's liberal agenda by confining it to a "strategy of truth" and directing it to relay only factual information to the public about war-related concerns.[35]

These restrictions on the OWI created an opening for an organization such as the Writers' War Board that could fill government requests and address liberal causes without cloaking its messages in the guise of factual information. The WWB quickly developed as a valuable adjunct to the OWI because its activities were neither regulated nor monitored. The government found the board useful in a number of ways. It could handle assignments that the closely watched OWI dared not tackle, and it could promote a position that the administration advocated but could not take publicly. The OWI and the administration secretly supported the board's condemnation of the entire German population even though both took a more conciliatory approach officially. The board's other private government assignments included denigrating Emperor Hirohito, attacking isolationists and others opposed to an international organization, and criticizing the Dumbarton Oaks proposals as insufficient.

The WWB presented other advantages as well. First, its members had the expert knowledge and contacts to make use of all the communications media. Second, its reservoir of talented writers insured that its propaganda would be both convincing and palatable. They skillfully intermingled slanted subject matter with entertaining material in articles and other works. Third, the WWB could engage in controversial polemics without involving the government. The OWI in particular did not have to worry that its reputation for objectivity would be compromised. As board member Robert Landry later put it, "I think we broke through a lot of taboos, did many things the government wanted done and could not itself do. . . . The government was slow; we were fast. They were timid; we were bold. They used official gobblygook; we had some wit. World War II was strangely unemotional and needed a WWB to stir things up."[36] A recent social history of Americans in World War II notes that government agencies used popular culture to support the war effort and maintain morale. The WWB was one of the most successful agents in that effort, inserting propaganda into popular media without attracting much notice.[37]

SOCIAL AND POLITICAL SIGNIFICANCE

As a group of volunteers assisting an official propaganda organization while simultaneously engaging in its own campaigns, the Writers'

War Board was similar to both the Vigilantes and the National Board for Historical Service that gave assistance to the Committee on Public Information in World War I and pursued their own initiatives. As a quasi-governmental agency, the WWB has no precedent in American history. It influenced America's wartime domestic culture by shaping what people read and heard and thought. In concert with other government agencies and private organizations, it promoted unity of purpose and focused the nation's attention on the attainment of two goals: winning the war and securing lasting peace.[38] The writers improved troop morale, urged compliance with wartime restrictions on the home front, encouraged cooperation among the Allies, and supported government initiatives. But the group also kept some lofty ideals in mind, pursuing liberal causes even when congressional Republicans and southern Democrats attacked some of Roosevelt's policies and made repeated attempts to suppress political liberalism. The WWB tackled the highly charged issue of racial prejudice. It made decision makers in the media industry aware of the pervasiveness of racial stereotyping in printed materials, radio broadcasts, and films, and it encouraged them to avoid oversimplistic characterizations. Achieving lasting peace through international cooperation was another ideal of the board, which sought to keep the citizens of every nation safe from future global wars that were certain to be even more destructive than World War II.

The Lidice renaming ceremonies and the board's popular Books for Bonds rallies testify to its successes. But the WWB could not always achieve its goals. Its members were especially discouraged by their inability to attract women into military service, and they were troubled when their exhortations to hate the entire population of Germany created internal dissension as well as negative publicity. They were even more distraught when they were not able to achieve a genuine world government with enough power to subdue aggressive nation-states. Still, they supported the United Nations organization, hoping that it would continue to promote internationalism and work to address global problems. Writing in 1946, Gallico expressed his disillusionment in bitter words: "Any line about the kind of world we hoped to make out of this war has a hollow ring today. I guess at the time I wrote [1944], . . . I was actually naïve enough to believe that this time it would be different."[39] Other board members were undoubtedly equally disheartened.

Government agencies and private groups that sought the board's assistance often returned to ask for its help on other projects. They valued its work, which was also acknowledged on several occasions by the press. The Writers' War Board was such an influential group that it is astonishing to find that it has remained relatively unknown for more than seventy years. At one time it billed itself as "the focal point of a group of American writers, several thousand in number, who have offered their talents to the Government for the duration of the war," and Rex Stout argued that the board "was the best instance in a violent conflict of the organized use of writing abilities to help the fight."[40] In November 1944 the OWI asked for an estimate of the number of words American authors had written for the war through the WWB. Stout came up with the figure 7 million, and Alan Green thought it might be closer to 7.5 million. But both were educated guesses made in the absence of firm data.[41] Estimating the number of propaganda pieces that the board generated might be even more difficult because the works varied in length from books to slogans and because much of the group's output was never credited to the board.

The failure to recognize the Writers' War Board and its contributions may stem from a number of factors. First, the board frequently worked behind the scenes in arranging for authors to write materials, sometimes anonymously, for various projects. Individual pieces can rarely be traced back to the board. A second reason might have to do with its emphasis on placing subtle propaganda in a variety of forms in many different outlets. WWB members sought no public acknowledgment and were pleased when their works were not recognized as parts of a concerted effort to persuade the public. The claim that advertising "dominate[d] domestic war propaganda" cannot be considered definitive without a thorough examination of the slanted materials that the WWB and other organizations produced in every type of written and spoken form.[42] The board's lack of recognition might also be due to the group's penchant for giving famous people credit for its work in order to attract the greatest amount of attention to WWB causes. Since most board members were famous in their own right, they had no need to aggrandize themselves or their organization. Their greatest achievement was their ability to generate action through their collective influence, knowledge, and connections in New York and Washington, DC. The board utilized all of the media outlets available to it and gave particular attention to those that regularly reached millions of Americans: daily newspapers, popular magazines, radio programs, in-house publications of large corporations, comic books, and the like. Its own publications went to those in the communications industry who could immediately disseminate its propaganda. These newsletters also kept authors around the country informed about the board's current and future projects so that the writers could augment national stories and campaign topics by contributing letters, articles, speeches, and the like to media outlets and civic groups in their local areas. That ploy created a boomerang effect, making local authors feel that they were contributing to the war and tying area residents more closely to global events. The Writers' War Board could never have funded all the works its writers produced, but by serving as a clearinghouse, it could put writers in touch with those that needed slanted material on a particular topic and were willing to pay for it.

Roosevelt's administration considered the WWB so useful that it did not give any thought to dropping the board's subsidy even when financial constraints forced the OWI to cut some of its departments. In serving the cause of liberalism and internationalism, in covertly helping the Roosevelt administration publicize the views it could not openly advocate, and in producing government propaganda that permeated American media outlets and brought citizens together to support the fight against fascism, the Writers' War Board won more than the admiration of government officials and federal agencies. It earned a place in history as an influential force in American society during World War II.

NOTES

WORD ON SOURCES

THE RECORDS OF the Writers' War Board in the Manuscript Division of the Library of Congress provide the main source of information about the organization. Stored in 144 containers and 2 scrapbooks are files dealing with the group's correspondence, committee work, publications, and so on. Also helpful in producing this initial study of the WWB were the Rex Stout Papers at Boston College. While far less extensive, that collection has an almost complete set of board minutes whereas the organization's official records contain mostly excerpts. However, the latter include many issues of *Brief House Organ Items* and *Brief Army Camp Items from the Writers' War Board*. Those missing may be found in other repositories. For example, the 1944 summer issues of the *House Organ* publication are part of the Harold Moore Collection in the West Virginia State Archives in Charleston. The New York Public Library probably has the most extensive collection of the group's monthly newsletter, the *Writers' War Board Report*. Several issues are located in the WWB records in the Library of Congress, but they are scattered in many containers. The board's three annual reports are not included in those extensive records but are in the book collection of the Library of Congress.

There is no complete set of all of the editorials and scripts that the WWB distributed, but approximately fifty titles of Script of the Month plays may be found on the Worldcat website (search terms: Writers' War Board Script of the Month). To indicate the extent of the board's influence and the wide distribution of its editorials and articles, the author has intentionally cited both national and local newspapers around the country as well as popular magazines.

ABBREVIATIONS

- Board Minutes: Since some minutes of the board have slightly different titles, all of them have been given a single designation to avoid confusion.
- Editorial Service: This resource found in the Writers' War Board Records consists of a series of internal WWB documents with different headings and dates that give the titles of editorials and the board members who agreed to write them. Most of these documents use the term "Editorial Service."
- n.p.: not paginated
- SP: Rex Stout Papers (MS 1986–096), John J. Burns Library, Boston College, Chestnut Hill, Massachusetts, followed by a box number (e.g., SP46 refers to box 46 in the collection)
- *War Speeches:* Like the *Writers' War Board Script Catalog*, the list of WWB speeches was revised many times as new items were added. This study uses the most complete, if undated, edition in the Writers' War Board Records with descriptions of thirty-six speeches and the title of one other penciled in. The catalog was originally distributed as *A List of War Speeches Available for Clubs, Business Organizations, Radio Stations, etc., Prepared by the Writers' War Board.* Two versions, including what appears to be the last, bear the generic name *Material on the War Procurable from the Writers' War Board.* To distinguish these speeches from the other kinds of propaganda the board circulated (such as editorials and scripts), this list is referenced as *War Speeches,* an accurate description although not the actual title of the later issues.
- WR: Writers' War Board Records, Manuscript Division, Library of Congress, followed by a container number (e.g., WR106 refers to container number 106 in the collection)

Introduction

1. Lewis Gannett, "Books," in *While You Were Gone: A Report on Wartime Life in the United States,* ed. Jack Goodman (New York: Simon and Schuster, 1946), 459–60.

2. This summary is drawn from Lynne Olson, *Those Angry Days: Roosevelt, Lindbergh, and America's Fight over World War II* (New York: Random House, 2014).

3. Porter Emerson Browne, "The Vigilantes: Who and Why and What They Are," *Outlook,* May 8, 1918, 67–69.

4. Ibid.

5. J. Franklin Jameson, "Historical Scholars at War," *American Historical Review* 21 (July 1917): 831–35; Mildred Jane Orr, "Historians at War: The National Board for Historical Service, 1917–1919" (M.A. thesis, Louisiana State University, 1966), iv–v, 64.

6. Orr, "Historians at War," v, 9–28. See, for example, National Board for Historical Service, *Opportunities for History Teachers: The Lessons of the Great War in the Classroom* (Washington, DC: Department of the Interior, Bureau of Education, 1917).

7. Harold A. Wolff to WWB, October 6, 1942, WR13; Frederica Barach to Henry Pringle, February 27, 1943, WR13.

8. James R. Mock and Cedric Larson, *Words That Won the War: The Story of the Committee on Public Information* (Princeton, NJ: Princeton University Press, 1939), vii.

9. Nancy Snow, *Information War: American Propaganda, Free Speech, and Opinion Control since 9–11* (New York: Seven Stories, 2003), 50–52.

10. George Creel, *How We Advertised America: The First Telling of the Amazing Story of the Committee on Public Information That Carried the Gospel of Americanism to Every Corner of the Globe* (New York: Harper and Brothers, 1920), 5.

11. Ibid., 117; Stewart Halsey Ross, *Propaganda for War: How the United States Was Conditioned to Fight the Great War of 1914–1918*, 2nd ed. (Joshua Tree, CA: Progressive, 2009), 240, 249–50; Thomas J. Fleming, *The Illusion of Victory: America in World War I* (New York: Basic Books, 2003), 120.

12. Creel, *How We Advertised America*, 47; Ross, *Propaganda for War*, 227.

13. Alan Axelrod, *Selling the Great War: The Making of American Propaganda* (New York: Palgrave Macmillan, 2009), 218–19.

14. Brett Gary, *The Nervous Liberals: Propaganda Anxieties from World War I to the Cold War* (New York: Columbia University Press, 1999), 77.

15. Allan M. Winkler, *The Politics of Propaganda: The Office of War Information, 1942–1945* (New Haven, CT: Yale University Press, 1978), 70–71.

16. Obituary of Edward Bernays, *New York Times*, March 10, 1995; Bernays, *Propaganda* (New York: H. Liveright, 1928), 9–10.

17. "Debut of a Pledge," *Writers' War Board Report*, December 1, 1943.

18. Executive Office of the President, Office of Government Reports, U.S. Information Service, *United States Government Manual, Spring, 1942* (Washington, DC: Government Printing Office, 1942), 64; Rex Stout to Selma G. Hirsh, March 5, 1942, WR6; Selma G. Hirsh to Hollister Noble, September 3, 1943, WR126.

19. Rex Stout to Hirsh, March 5, 1942, WR6; Henry Pringle to Frederica Barach, May 5, 1942, WR127; Barach, letter to author, July 19, 1968.

20. Stout, quoted in "Minutes of the Meeting of Representatives of the Writers' War Board, Deputies and Program Managers of OWI, February 11, 1944," WR8; Bureau of Public Inquiries, Office of War Information, *United States Government Manual, Fall, 1942* (Washington, DC: Government Printing Office, 1942), 618; Dorothy Ducas to Ulric Bell, May 11, 1942, Records of the Office of War Information, Book Division, Historical Records 1944–45, Record Group 208, box 1695, National Archives, College Park, MD.

21. Stout to Mrs. William R. Butler, June 5, 1942, WR94; Stout to Melvyn Douglas, May 21, 1942, WR6.

22. Theodore Strauss, "Douglas of the OCD," *New York Times*, May 31, 1942; Stout to Douglas, May 21, 1942, WR6.

23. "Minutes of the Meeting of Representatives"; Stout, letter to author, June 15, 1968; Clayton D. Laurie, *The Propaganda Warriors: America's Crusade against Nazi Germany* (Lawrence: University Press of Kansas, 1996), 64–65.

24. Gardner Cowles Jr., letter to author, March 4, 1969; Board Minutes, February 14, 1945, SP47; Winkler, *Politics of Propaganda*, 17–18.

25. Leo Rosten, letter to author, March 14, 1969.

26. Winkler, *Politics of Propaganda*, 62–71.

27. Ibid., 71, 62–65; Inger L. Stole, *Advertising at War: Business, Consumers, and Government in the 1940s* (Urbana: University of Illinois Press, 2012), 112–16.

28. Bureau of Public Inquiries, Office of War Information, *United States Government Manual, Summer, 1944* (Washington, DC: Government Printing Office, 1944), 94; Rex Stout, interview by author, August 14, 1968.

29. WWB, *Second Annual Report* (New York: WWB, 1944), 13; Selma G. Hirsh to Hollister Noble, September 3, 1943, WR126; Elmer Davis, "Report to the President," 61–62, Davis Papers, container 10, Manuscript Division, Library of Congress, Washington, DC.

30. Oscar Schisgall to Rex Stout, February 25, 1944, WR52.

31. Stout to Schisgall, February 29, 1944, WR52.

32. Stout, letter to author, June 15, 1968; Leo Rosten, letter to author, March 14, 1969.

33. See, for example, Selma G. Hirsh to WWB, March 8, 1943, WR127.

34. Hirsh to Frederica Barach, March 8, 1943, WR127; obituary of Hirsh, *New York Times*, February 25, 2010.

35. Clifton Fadiman, letter to author, February 17, 1969.

36. Franklin D. Roosevelt, quoted in Richard W. Steele, "The War on Intolerance: The Reformulation of American Nationalism, 1939–1941," *Journal of American Ethnic History* 9 (Fall 1989): 14.

Chapter 1: The History and Function of the Writers' War Board

1. [Edmund J. Linehan], *A History of the United States Savings Bonds Program*, 50th anniversary ed. (Washington, DC: Department of the Treasury, 1991), 11–12.

2. Julian Street Jr., "High Lights of My Work with Writers and Artists for the Treasury Department: November 1, 1941 to January 31, 1946" (unpublished manuscript), November 22, 1946, 2, 4, Peter Odegard Papers, Franklin D. Roosevelt Presidential Library, Hyde Park, NY.

3. Ibid., 2; "Julian Street Jr. Appointed Secretary of MOMA," Museum of Modern Art, press release, April 17, 1939, https://www.moma.org/momaorg/shared/pdfs/docs/press_archives/478/releases/MOMA_1939_0009_1939-04-14_39414-9.pdf.

4. Street, "High Lights of My Work," 4, 2.

5. "Julian Street Jr. '25," Memorials, *Princeton Alumni Weekly*, September 13, 1995, https://paw.princeton.edu/memorial/julian-street-jr-'25; "Miss N. Vanderlip Is Engaged to Wed," *New York Times*, February 5, 1927.

6. Street, "High Lights of My Work," 12, 7, 85.

7. Ibid., 12; Rex Stout, interview by author, August 14, 1968. Since the author of this study did not become aware of Street's report until recently, he did not question Stout about the discrepancies between the two versions.

8. More information might be gleaned from the Authors' League minutes now located in a warehouse in Queens. Unfortunately, none of those files are organized.

9. Street, "High Lights of My Work," 13.

10. Rex Stout, interview; Stout, letter to author, June 15, 1968; Russel Crouse, "Writers and the War," *The Writer*, September 1944, 267–68; Stout, quoted in "Minutes of the Meeting of Representatives of the Writers' War Board, Deputies and Program Managers of OWI, February 11, 1944," WR8.

11. Stout, letter to author, June 15, 1968; Street, "High Lights of My Work," 13, 3, 12.

12. Clifton Fadiman to Bennett Cerf, May 2, 1942, WR5.

13. Biographical information on Rex Stout throughout this chapter is drawn from John McAleer, *Rex Stout: A Biography* (Boston: Little, Brown, 1977).

14. At the Bouchercon Convention, the world's largest gathering of mystery novel enthusiasts, Agatha Christie won over Stout, Raymond Chandler, Dashiell Hammett, and Dorothy L. Sayers. Tom Walker, "Mystery Writers Shine Light on Best: Bouchercon 2000 Convention Honors Authors," *Denver Post*, September 10, 2000.

15. Quoted in Robert Van Gelder, *Writers and Writing* (New York: Charles Scribner's Sons, 1946), 219.

16. "Help for Britain Debated on Radio: Stout Appears on Radio Show," *New York Times*, November 25, 1940; McAleer, *Rex Stout*, 279.

17. Mark Lincoln Chadwin, *The Hawks of World War II* (Chapel Hill: University of North Carolina Press, 1968), 168, 179; McAleer, *Rex Stout*, 279, 288–90; Stout, interview.

18. "The Stout Ire," *Newsweek*, October 30, 1944, 48–49.

19. McAleer, *Rex Stout*, 293.

20. *America First—Nazi Transmission Belt* (Kansas City, MO: Friends of Democracy, 1941), 1. For more information on the Friends of Democracy, see Thomas Howell, "Kansas City's Crusader: Leon Birkhead and the Fight against Fascism," *Missouri Historical Review* 110 (July 2016): 237–59.

21. Chadwin, *The Hawks of World War II*, 209; "Sharp Responses Made to Lindbergh," *New York Times*, April 25, 1941; John Bainbridge, "Rex Stout: The Quaker Who Is Heckling Hitler," *Look*, February 23, 1943, 42–46.

22. Rex Stout, *The Illustrious Dunderheads* (New York: Knopf, 1942).

23. Quoted in "Stout Nearly Causes a Riot at Fish Rally," *New York Times*, November 3, 1944.

24. Chesly Manly, "Writers' War Board Aids Smear Campaign," *Chicago Tribune*, June 4, 1942.

25. McAleer, *Rex Stout*, 305–6.

26. Ibid., 329, 372–73, 484; "Society for the Prevention of World War III Records, 1945–1972," Columbia University Libraries Archival Collections, http://www.columbia.edu/cu/lweb/archival/collections/ldpd_4079604/.

27. McAleer, *Rex Stout*, 301.

28. Bainbridge, "Rex Stout," 42, 45–46.

29. Frederica Barach to Dr. Richard M. Brickner, July 27, 1944, WR12; "Eight U.S. Writers Tour Fronts as Army Air Forces' Guests," *New York Herald-Tribune*, March 23, 1945.

30. Barach, letter to author, July 19, 1968.

31. Alan Green, interview by author, August 8, 1968.

32. Quoted in McAleer, *Rex Stout*, 301.

33. John Chamberlain, "Fadiman for the Millions," *Saturday Evening Post*, January 1, 1941, 27. Sally Ashley, *F.P.A.: The Life and Times of Franklin Pierce Adams* (New York: Beaufort Books, 1986), 214; obituary of Clifton Fadiman, *New York Times*, June 20, 1999; Rex Stout, interview; Alan Green, interview.

34. Fadiman to Stout, June 12, 1944, WR8.

35. Board Minutes, December 27, 1944, SP47.

36. Hugh Fordin, *Getting to Know Him: A Biography of Oscar Hammerstein II* (New York: Da Capo, 1986), 211; Francis S. Wickware, "Oscar Hammerstein II," *Life*, May 29, 1944, 98–110.

37. Alan Green, interview.

38. Rex Stout, interview; Wickware, "Oscar Hammerstein, II"; Oscar Hammerstein II, *The Complete Lyrics of Oscar Hammerstein II*, ed. Amy Asch (New York: Knopf, 2008), 256, 259; WWB, *Second Annual Report* (New York: WWB, 1944), 28.

39. Lucy E. Cross, "Howard Lindsay and Russel Crouse," *Masterworks Broadway*, 2015, http://www.masterworksbroadway.com/artist/howard-lindsay-and-russel-crouse.

40. *The Good Earth* by Pearl Buck received a Pulitzer Prize in 1932, and John P. Marquand's *The Late George Apley* won in 1938.

41. Buck to Rex Stout, July 12, 1943, WR109.

42. WWB, *First Annual Report* (New York: WWB, 1943), 4; Board Minutes, February 21, July 11, 1945, SP47; obituary of Jean Poletti, *New York Times*, March 1, 1974; *Second Annual Report*, 28; WWB, *Third Annual Report* (New York: WWB, 1945); obituary of Robert Colwell, *New York Times*, June 27, 1967.

43. John Hersey, introduction to Barbara W. Tuchman, *The Book: A Lecture Sponsored by the Center for the Book in the Library of Congress and the Authors' League of America* (Washington, DC: Library of Congress, 1980), 9; obituary of Luise Sillcox, *New York Times*, June 29, 1965.

44. Hersey, introduction, 7.

45. Crouse, "Writers and the War," 267; Rex Stout, quoted in "Minutes of the Meeting of Representatives"; Stout, interview; Alan Green, interview.

46. "Writers' War Committee Questionnaires," WR6; "Summary of WWB Activities—September, 1942," WR8; *First Annual Report*, 3–6; *Second Annual Report*, 2–4.

47. F. F. Kelly, review of Rita Halle Kleeman, *Gracious Lady*, *New York Times Book Review*, October 20, 1935, 14; Durward Howes, ed., *American Women: The Official Who's Who among the Women of the Nation*, vol. 2, *1937–38* (Los Angeles: American, 1937), 372, 625; obituary of Kleeman, *New York Times*, May 17, 1971; Kleeman, letter to author, March 14, 1969; Rex Stout, interview.

48. *First Annual Report*, 16; "Summary of WWB Activities—September, 1942"; Board Minutes, November 18, 1942, February 10, 1943, SP46.

49. Lyn Harrington, *Syllables of Recorded Time: The Story of the Canadian Authors Association, 1921–1981* (Toronto: Simon and Pierre, 1981), 211; Board Minutes, November 11, 1942, SP46.

50. Board Minutes, April 21, 1943, SP47.

51. Larry Cephlar and Steven Englund, *The Inquisition in Hollywood: Politics in the Film Community, 1930–1960* (Berkeley: University of California Press, 1979), 187–88; Board Minutes, September 27, 1944, SP47; Lewis Gannett, "Books," in *While You Were Gone: A Report on Wartime Life in the United States*, ed. Jack Goodman (New York: Simon and Schuster, 1946), 460.

52. Rex Stout to Pauline Lauber, July 20, 1942; Lauber to Stout, August 26, 1942; John Howard Lawson to Stout, December 22, 1942; Stout to Lawson, February 1, 1943, all WR125.

53. Crouse, "Writers and the War," 268; *First Annual Report*, 3–6; *Second Annual Report*, 2–4; Martha McCleery to James Fisher, March 5, 1943, WR125; form letter about forest fires circulated to fifty writers, April 1, 1943, WR13.

54. Board Minutes, May 19, 1943, SP47. Since the minutes contain many reports of failures and negative results, positive statements made in private to the group may be taken at face value.

55. Copies of the *Magazine War Guide* and the *Magazine War Guide Supplement* are located in Records of the Office of War Information, Book Division, Record Group 208, box 1700, National Archives, College Park, MD. Some issues of both publications are located in WR52.

56. *First Annual Report*, 8; Patti Clayton Becker, *Books and Libraries in American Society during World War II: Weapons in the War of Ideas* (New York: Routledge, 2005), 118.

57. *Second Annual Report*, 4–5; *Third Annual Report*, 4; "Summary of the Writers' War Board Activities for the Month of November, 1944," WR81.

58. "Home-Front Pledge Campaign," "Will You Write Something for Us?," "The WAC Recruiting Committee," "War Songs," and "Racial Tolerance Series," all in *Writers' War Board Report*, September 1, 1943; Jane Grant to Rex Stout, June 6, 1945, WR124.

59. Obituary of Jane Grant, *New York Times*, March 17, 1972; William Grimes, obituary of Nina Bourne, *New York Times*, April 14, 2010.

60. *Third Annual Report*, 1; *First Annual Report*, 4. Other members of the board's Advisory Council are listed in the *Second Annual Report*, 29.

61. *Brief House Organ Items from the Writers' War Board*, May 1945, cover, WR36; November 25, 1943, 1, WR35.

62. "Memorandum on the Activities of the Committee on *Brief Items*," WR6; *First Annual Report*, 14–15; Jack Goodman, form letter to writers, January 7, 1943, WR6.

63. *Third Annual Report*, 45; "Minutes of the Meeting of Representatives."

64. Board Minutes, June 2, 16, 1943, SP47; Julian Brodie to Marjorie Denton, November 29, 1943, WR6; Gypsy Rose Lee, "About Those War Bonds," *Brief House*

Organ Items, June 15, 1943, WR6; Rex Stout, "The Post-War World," *Brief House Organ Items*, June 15, 1943, WR6.

65. WR6 contains copies of articles attributed to prominent individuals and some clippings from publications that carried them. Bing Crosby's piece, for example, appeared on December 13, 1943, in *The Weekly Turnstile*, a publication of the Piggly Wiggly grocery store chain.

66. *Third Annual Report*, 4–5; *Second Annual Report*, 13.

67. "Report on Results of *Brief House Organ Items*," August 10, 1943, WR6; "Report on *Brief House Organ Items*," December 30, 1943; January 31, 1944, both WR6; *Third Annual Report*, 4.

68. *Third Annual Report*, 4; *Brief Army Camp Items from the Writers' War Board*, March 1944–December 1945 (missing complete issues of March and April 1944, and May and October 1945), WR35 and WR36.

69. Board Minutes, March 15, 1944, SP47; "We Are Not Keeping Military Secrets" and "Can We Glamourize Economy?" *Bulletin to Cartoonists*, May 3, 1944, WR12; *Third Annual Report*, 5; Board Minutes, August 2, 1944, SP47; Frederica Barach to Karl Knecht, October 23, 1944, WR12. Knecht, cartoonist for the *Evansville (IN) Courier*, sent the WWB clippings that show how he plugged their war themes.

70. Sutherland Denlinger to Chester Kerr, May 5, 1943; Denlinger to WWB, May 5, 1943; Selma G. Hirsh to Charlotte Hatton, August 3, 1943, all WR57.

71. Hirsh to Hatton, August 3, 1943, WR57; *Third Annual Report*, 5–6; "Editorial Service," WR57; Frederica Barach to Robert L. Duffus, July 9, 1943, WR57.

72. "Editorial Service."

73. John Burnham to WWB, January 11, 1944, WR57.

74. "Omigosh! What an Idea," *Lubbock (TX) Morning Avalanche*, October 17, 1944.

75. Frederica Barach to Robert L. Duffus, September 15, 1944, WR62.

76. *First Annual Report*, 25; *Third Annual Report*, 6; "Summary of Writers' War Board Activities—September, 1942"; Carl Carmer to King Features Syndicate, August 25, 1942, WR6; Board Minutes, June 7, 1944, SP47.

77. "War Scripts of the Month Selections," WR21; "Summary of WWB Activities—September, 1942"; *First Annual Report*, 27–28; *Second Annual Report*, 15, 27; *Third Annual Report*, 7, 31; Robert Landry to the Philadelphia Fellowship Committee, November 19, 1945, WR21. Several scripts are located in WR136–40.

78. "War Scripts of the Month Selections"; "Summary of WWB Activities—September, 1942"; Erik Barnouw to Louella Hoskins, January 18, 1943, WR21; *First Annual Report*, 27.

79. *First Annual Report*, 24; *Second Annual Report*, 10; Frederica Barach to WWB, March 10, 1943, WR13; "Report to Date on the Activities of the Committee on Speeches and Speakers, November 5, 1943," WR13; "Minutes of the Meeting of Representatives."

80. *Second Annual Report*, 10; *Third Annual Report*, 7; "Summary of WWB Activities for November, 1944"; Alan Green to Jane Tibbett, September 15, 1943, WR13; "Report to Date on the Activities of the Committee on Speeches and Speakers."

81. *War Speeches*, WR136; Stout, quoted in "Minutes of the Meeting of Representatives."

82. Cecily Geyelin, "Check List [of ways to promote books]," November 13, 1944, WR10.
83. Carl Carmer, ed., *The War against God* (New York: Henry Holt, 1943).
84. Humphrey Bogart to Clifton Fadiman, September 7, 1944, WR10.
85. Geyelin, "Check List"; Board Minutes, October 20, 1943, SP47; *Second Annual Report*, 12.
86. Rex Stout to William Sloane, June 19, 1945, WR115.
87. Clifton Fadiman to W. W. Norton, September 2, 1944, WR81; Board Minutes, October 6, 1943, SP47.
88. Robert Colwell to Rex Stout, October 21, 1942, WR12.
89. Clifton Fadiman to William Fadiman, April 24, 1944, WR12; Carroll Carroll to Fadiman, September 22, 1944, WR21.
90. "Movies," *Writers' War Board Report*, September 1, 1943.
91. David O. Selznick to Rex Stout, April 23, 1945, WR12; "Movies," *Writers' War Board Report*, August 1, 1944.
92. Frederica Barach to Clifton Fadiman, July 13, 1944, WR11.
93. George H. Roeder Jr., "Censoring Disorder: American Visual Imagery of World War II," in *The War in American Culture: Society and Consciousness during World War II*, ed. Lewis A. Erenberg and Susan E. Hirsch (Chicago: University of Chicago Press, 1996), 46–70; Clayton R. Koppes and Gregory D. Black, *Hollywood Goes to War: How Politics, Profits, and Propaganda Shaped World War II Movies* (Berkeley: University of California Press, 1987), 66–68, 87, 112, 141.
94. Frederica Barach to Henry Pringle, August 15, 1942; Ellen Tannenbaum to Selma G. Hirsh, August 28, 1942, both WR6.
95. Alan Green, interview; "The Writers' War Board: What It Is and What It Does," in *Second Annual Report*, 2–6; *Third Annual Report*, 2; Franklin D. Roosevelt, "Fireside Chat," December 9, 1941, in John T. Woolley and Gerhard Peters, The American Presidency Project, http://www.presidency.ucsb.edu/ws/?pid=16056.
96. Frederica Barach, letter to author, July 19, 1968; Green, interview. For an example of the board's brainstorming, see Board Minutes, January 26, 1944, SP47.
97. The spelling and punctuation used here appear in the Francis Scott Key manuscript in the Maryland Historical Society collection posted on the Smithsonian Institute website: amhistory.si.edu/starspangledbanner/pdf/ssb_lyrics.pdf; *First Annual Report*, 24.
98. Rex Stout to Kate Smith and Ted Collins, October 21, 1942; Frederica Barach to Mary Little, October 27, 1942; Barach to WWB, October 24, 1942, all WR13; Barach to Selma G. Hirsh, October 16, 1942, WR130.
99. Stout, letter to author, July 5, 1968; *Second Annual Report*, 25–28; *Third Annual Report*, 28–31; Clifton Fadiman, letter to author, February 17, 1969; Christopher LaFarge, "What Is the Writers' War Board?" November 1944, WR93.
100. *First Annual Report*, 13–28; *Second Annual Report*, 25–28; *Third Annual Report*, 28–31.
101. Frederik Stromberg, *Comic Art Propaganda: A Graphic History* (New York: St. Martin's, 2010), 42; Paul Gallico to Frederica Barach, August 22, 1942, WR8.

102. Dwight Jon Zimmerman, "The Comic Books Go to War: The Entertainment Industry at War, Part I," *Defense Media Network*, 2017, https://www.defensemedianetwork.com/stories/the-comic-books-go-to-war; John Morton Blum, *V Was for Victory: Politics and American Culture during World War II* (New York: Harcourt and Brace, 1976), 36.

103. Frederica Barach to George Marcoux, June 16, 1943, WR11.

104. Lee Server, *Danger Is My Business: An Illustrated History of the Fabulous Pulp Magazines* (San Francisco: Chronicle Books, 1993), 62–65.

105. *First Annual Report*, 22.

106. Faith Baldwin to Rex Stout, September 9, 1943; Stout to Baldwin, September 14, 1943, both WR8.

107. Board Minutes, May 13, July 22, 29, 1942; February 3, 1943, all SP46.

108. "Script Writers" (radio episode with Katharine Seymour interview from the NBC Blue Network program *Behind the Scenes*), January 12, 1941, Old Time Radio Downloads, http://www.oldtimeradiodownloads.com/drama/behind-the-mike/script-writers-1941-01-12; Katharine Seymour and John T. W. Martin, *Practical Radio Writing: The Technique of Writing for Broadcasting Simply and Thoroughly Explained* (New York: Longmans, Green, 1938); *First Annual Report*, 22–23, 25; Stout, interview.

109. "Biographical/Historical Information," Hobe Morrison Papers, Billy Rose Theatre Division, New York Public Library; Hobe Morrison, letter to author, September 5, 1970.

110. "R. J. Landry to Join CBS," *New York Times*, November 25, 1942; obituary of Robert Landry, *New York Times*, May 25, 1991.

111. William L. Shirer, *Berlin Diary: The Journal of a Foreign Correspondent, 1934–1941* (New York: Knopf, 1941), 591–93; Shirer, *The Nightmare Years, 1930–1940* (Boston: Little, Brown, 1984), 601–9.

112. "WWB Radio Script," WR32; Katharine Seymour to Rex Stout, June 1, 1943, WR32.

113. Paul Gallico, *Confessions of a Story Writer* (New York: Knopf, 1946), 3–16; Gallico, letter to author, March 17, 1969.

114. Dean Flower, "Christopher Grant LaFarge," *Dictionary of American Biography, Supplement 6, 1956–1960*, ed. John A. Garraty (New York: Charles Scribner's Sons, 1980), 355–56; "Pacific Front, Fiction Division," *Newsweek*, July 24, 1944, 97–100.

115. Phillip D. Beidler, "Yankee Interloper and Native Son: Carl Carmer and Clarence Cason: Unlikely Twins of Alabama Exposé," *Southern Cultures* 9 (Spring 2003): 18–35; J. K. Hutchens, "On an Author," *New York Herald Tribune Book Review*, November 20, 1949.

116. Obituary of Robert Colwell; "Advertising News and Notes," *New York Times*, April 12, 1946; "Robert Talcott Colwell," *Who's Who in the East*, 2nd ed. (Chicago: A. N. Marquis, 1948), 367.

117. Al Silverman, *The Time of Their Lives: The Golden Age of Great American Book Publishers, Their Editors and Authors* (New York: St. Martin's, 2008), 256; Alan Green, interview; Grimes, obituary of Nina Bourne.

118. "Ad Man's Holiday," *Publishers Weekly*, December 5, 1936, 2207–8; Alan Green Collection, Howard Gotlieb Archival Research Center, Boston University,

http://archives.bu.edu/collections/collection?id=122075; obituary of Robert Colwell; Green, interview. Colwell's play *Strictly Dynamite* was made into a 1934 movie starring Jimmy Durante. Using the pseudonym Roger Denbie, Green and Brodie wrote "Love on the Run," a 1932 *Cosmopolitan* short story that was released as a motion picture four years later with Joan Crawford and Clark Gable. In 1937 a story by Goodman and Albert Rice (penname of publisher Albert Rice Leventhal) was made into the movie *Meet the Missus*, starring Victor Moore and Helen Broderick.

119. The fact that Margaret Leech was the widow of Ralph Pulitzer, son of the newspaper publisher who established the Pulitzer Prizes, had no bearing on her two-time selection as winner since the awards have always been administered by Columbia University.

120. Ashley, *F.P.A.*, 129–31, 225; "F.P.A.," *Time*, April 4, 1960, 55–58.

121. Albert Deutsch, "Crusading Columnist," *New Republic*, September 13, 1943, 368; Rex Stout, interview.

122. Robert Klara, "How the Ad Council Turned the PSA into a Powerful Engine for Social Change," *Adweek*, March 21, 2011, www.adweek.com.

123. Wendy L. Wall, *Inventing the American Way: The Politics of Consensus from the New Deal to the Civil Rights Movement* (Oxford: Oxford University Press, 2008), 108.

124. Frank W. Fox, *Madison Avenue Goes to War: The Strange Military Career of American Advertising, 1941–45* (Provo, UT: Brigham Young University Press, 1975), 3, 23–41, 92–95; Robert Griffith, "The Selling of America: The Advertising Council and American Politics, 1942–1960," *Business History Review* 57 (Autumn 1983): 388–412; Koppes and Black, *Hollywood Goes to War*, vii, 48–81, 323. See also Mark H. Leff, "The Politics of Sacrifice on the American Home Front in World War II," *Journal of American History* 78 (March 1991): 1296–1318.

125. Fox, *Madison Avenue Goes to War*, 66.

126. Ibid., 53; Inger L. Stole, *Advertising at War: Business, Consumers, and Government in the 1940s* (Urbana: University of Illinois Press, 2012), 71–120.

127. "Minutes of the Meeting of Representatives."

128. "OWI Domestic Branch, Book Division, as of June 2, 1943," Records of the Office of War Information, Book Division, Historical Records 1944–45, Record Group 208, box 1695, National Archives.

129. Wheeler Sammons Jr., "Frederica Pisek Barach," *Who's Who of American Women* (Chicago: A. N. Marquis, 1958), 1:79; Barach, letter to author, July 19, 1968; Rex Stout, letter to author, June 15, 1968; Stout, interview; Street, "High Lights of My Work," 17.

130. "OWI Domestic Branch, Book Division"; Selma G. Hirsh to Hollister Noble, September 3, 1943, WR126; Barach, letter to author, July 19, 1968.

131. Hirsh to Noble, September 3, 1943, WR126; Barach, letter to author, July 19, 1968.

132. "The Writers' War Board Financial Report Year Ending December 31, 1942," WR127.

133. "OWI Domestic Branch, Book Division."

134. See, for example, Board Minutes, January 26, 1944, SP47; Alan Green, interview; Rex Stout, interview.

135. Board Minutes, February 14, 1945, SP47. A list of budgeted items for 1944 and projections for 1945 can be found in National War Agencies Appropriations Bill for 1945: H.R. Hearings before the Subcommittee of the Committee on Appropriations, 78th Cong., pt. 2 (1944), 263:

	1944	1945
Personal services	$14,756	$17,100
Travel	300	1,260
Transportation	425	500
Communication	2,568	3,000
Rent and utilities	3,926	3,926
Printing and binding	22	24
Special projects	5,037	4,500
Other contractual services	757	900
Duplication supplies and materials	458	0
Equipment	103	0

136. Rex Stout, letter to author, June 15, 1968.

137. Oscar Schisgall to Elmer Davis, April 13, 1944, WR52.

138. Rex Stout to Joseph Wood Krutch, July 11, 1945, WR105.

139. Pola Stout, form letter [1943]; Pola Stout to Mrs. Harold Lehman, June 17, 1943, both WR15.

140. "Current WWB Committees and Continuing Projects," October 1943, WR8; Robert Landry, letter to author, September 28, 1970.

141. Board Minutes, November 8, 1944, SP47.

142. Isidore Lipschultz to Rex Stout, May 22, 1944, WR128; Board Minutes, April 21, 1943, SP47; "Biographical Note," Isidore Lipschultz Papers, 1937–75, 2001.117.1, U.S. Holocaust Memorial Museum, Washington, DC, https://collections.ushmm.org/findingaids/2001.117.1_01_fnd_en.pdf.

143. Alan Green, interview.

144. McAleer, *Rex Stout*, 307–8.

Chapter 2: Propaganda for the Military

1. "Dogs for Defense," *Writers' War Board Report*, May 15, 1943; Faith Baldwin, "Taffy at War," *Cosmopolitan*, October 1943, 14.

2. Assignments Committee, form letter to writers, March 12, 1943, WR13; "Dogs for Defense."

3. "Army Air Forces Slants," WR27; Frederica Barach to Selma G. Hirsh, April

10, 1942, WR6; "Summary of Writers War Board Activities—September, 1942," WR8; WWB, *First Annual Report* (New York: WWB, 1943), 14.

4. "Army Air Forces Slants."

5. Ibid.

6. "Dorothy Thompson," *Pittsburg Post-Gazette*, February 1, 1961.

7. "Typical Jobs Accomplished by the Writers' War Board for the Army Air Forces," October 13, 1942, WR26; "Columnist Visits Langley Field," *Daily Press* (Newport News, VA), April 26, 1942.

8. Howard Fast, "Joe Levy," *Young American*, December 9, 1942, 8; William Fay, "We Fly for Freedom," *Elks Magazine*, October 1942, 21–22. According to WWB records, a story by Fannie Heaslip Lea for female readers appeared in *Popular Love* around the same time. Frederica Barach to WWB, WR26.

9. Maxine Davis, "Flying Is Safe," *Woman's Home Companion*, October 1942, 100–101; Margaret Case Harriman, "Went on Cutting Bread and Butter," *New Yorker*, July 25, 1942, 34–45; W. L. White, "Boys Who Fight the Subs," *New Republic*, April 20, 1942, 536–38, republished as "The Boys Who Keep 'Em Down," *Reader's Digest*, May 1942, 1–5; White, "To the Four Far Corners," *Atlantic*, July 1942, 9–13. White also published *They Were Expendable: An American Torpedo Squadron in the U.S. Retreat from the Philippines* (London: H. Hamilton, 1942) and *Queens Die Proudly* (New York: Harcourt, Brace, 1943) on the Boeing B-17 Flying Fortresses and their crews in the Pacific.

10. "They Keep 'Em in the Air," *Look*, January 26, 1943, 25; Frank J. Taylor, "1000 Men Are Coming on Tuesday," *Saturday Evening Post*, September 19, 1942, 18, 36, 39; Harold E. Hartney, "Gong for the Victory Round," *American Legion Magazine*, October 1942, 46–50; Harold Titus, "Commandos of the Air," *Country Gentleman*, November 1942, 11, 60–61; Vincent Sheean, "We Can Win in the Air," *Look*, October 6, 1942, 24–25.

11. Paul Gallico, "Bombardier," *Saturday Evening Post*, August 15, 1942, 46, 24; "Typical Jobs Accomplished."

12. Thomas Glynn, "We Blast U-Boats," *American Magazine*, October 1942, 121–22; "Typical Jobs Accomplished."

13. Ed Churchill, "America Builds the Best Air Force in the World," *Look*, June 2, 1942, 11–17; Baldwin, "Change of Heart," *Collier's*, May 27, 1944, 11–13, 52–54; June 3, 1944, 16–17, 27–29; June 10, 1944, 20–21, 33–35; June 17, 1944, 27–31; June 24, 1944, 27–40.

14. Keith Ayling, *How Every Boy Can Prepare for Aviation Service* (Garden City, NY: Garden City Publishing, 1942).

15. "Typical Jobs Accomplished"; John McAleer, *Rex Stout: A Biography* (Boston: Little, Brown, 1977), 314; John Bush Jones, *The Songs That Fought the War: Popular Music and the Home Front* (Lebanon, NH: University Press of New England, 2006), 218. Copies of some songs are located in WR26.

16. *First Annual Report*, 14; Rex Stout, letter to author, June 15, 1968; Stout, interview by author, August 14, 1968; Alan Green, interview by author, August 8, 1968;

Frederica Barach, letter to author, July 19, 1968; "Report on Army Air Forces Campaign, October 29, 1942," WR26.

17. "Army Aviation Cadets," *Writers' War Board Report*, December 1, 1943.

18. "Army Air Forces Cadet Recruitment Committee—Final Report of Progress, April 20, 1943," WR29; Frederica Barach to Edward Thomas, April 22, 1943, WR29; Rita Weiman, "He Wants to Fly," *Liberty Magazine*, March 25, 1944, 14–15; Phil Stong, "Don't Talk about Love," *Saturday Evening Post*, April 29, 1944, 9–13, 46–54; May 6, 1944, 28–29, 58–62; May 13, 1944, 32–33, 71–79; May 20, 1944, 32–33, 72–78, 81–83; "Fledged in Florida," *Rotarian*, December 1943, 44–46; Milton Caniff, "Terry and the Pirates," *New York Daily News*, February 2–4, 1944; "Air Force Aviation Cadets," *Ranch Romances*, April 1944, 72.

19. "War Reporting, 1942 Style," *Saturday Evening Post*, November 7, 1942, 4. For a general account of the PQ16 convoy, see Michael G. Walling, *Forgotten Sacrifice: The Arctic Convoys of World War II* (Oxford: Osprey, 2012), 124–50. Mark O'Dea to Alden Chester, June 1, 1942; Edna Ferber to WWB, August 30, 1942, both WR40; *First Annual Report*, 3; Ferber, "Lifeboat," *Cosmopolitan*, September 1942, 28–29, 94–96; Robert Carse, "We Fought Through to Murmansk," *Saturday Evening Post*, November 7, 1942, 9–11, 59–63; November 14, 1942, 16–17, 40–42, 46–48; November 21, 1942, 28–29, 46–50; Carse, *There Go the Ships* (New York: Morrow, 1942).

20. S. Edward Roos, "I Ride the Hell Ships," as told to Frederick C. Painton, *American Magazine*, December 1942, 22, 128.

21. Board Minutes, January 5, 1944, SP47; Mark L. Evans, "Lawrence H. Gianella (T-AOT-1125) 1986–," Naval History and Heritage Command, January 20, 2016, https://www.history.navy.mil/research/histories/ship-histories/danfs/l/lawrence-h—gianella—t-aot-1125-.html.

22. Frederica Barach to Mark O'Dea, January 7, 1943, WR40; "Summary of Writers' War Board Activities—September, 1942"; *First Annual Report*, 13.

23. Robert Carse, "The Young—The Hardy Are Needed," *Bakersfield Californian*, August 11, 1944.

24. "Merchant Marine Recruitment," WR20; Board Minutes, August 2, November 22, 1944, SP47; Rita Halle Kleeman, "The Captain Lost His Leg," *Saturday Evening Post*, September 16, 1944, 111; D. Kelly Scruton, "Sports Scraps," *Sedalia (MO) Democrat*, August 20, 1944; Al Laney, "Views of Sport," *New York Herald-Tribune*, September 1, 1944; Franklin Pierce Adams to Bill Corum, August 15, 1944, WR20; Bill Stern, "Their Secret Weapon," *Eagle Magazine*, May 1945, 9, 19–20; "Sailors, Sailors, and More Sailors," *Writers' War Board Report*, August 1, 1944.

25. Mattie E. Treadwell, *The United States Army in World War II; Special Studies: The Women's Army Corps* (Washington, DC: Office of the Chief of Military History, Department of the Army, 1953), 45, 123–27, 184–88; "Col. Hobby's Report to the WWB on the Recruiting Campaign for the WAACS," WR28.

26. Jeanne Holm, *Women in the Military: An Unfinished Revolution*, rev. ed. (Novato, CA: Presidio, 1992), 24–25, 34–35.

27. Treadwell, *Women's Army Corps*, 186.

28. "WAC Committee Activities," WR27; "Itinerary of Trip for WWB," WR27; "WAC Companies Requested Abroad," *Pittsburgh Courier*, April 24, 1943.

29. "WAC Committee Activities"; obituary of Alice Hughes, *New York Times*, June 21, 1977.

30. "WAC Committee Activities"; Lynn Stone to Clifton Fadiman, May 20, 1943; Fadiman to Hughes, April 21, 1943, both WR28.

31. "WAC Committee Activities"; Fadiman to Lt. Col. E. M. Kirby, June 22, 1943, WR28.

32. "WAC Committee Activities"; Selma G. Hirsh to Fadiman, June 18, 1943, WR28. Irwin Nathanson's unpublished radio script is in WR28.

33. "WAC Committee Activities"; WWB, *Second Annual Report* (New York: WWB, 1944), 8.

34. Treadwell, *Women's Army Corps*, 185, 188; Board Minutes, March 24, 1943, SP47.

35. "Suggestions in re WAACS," WR27.

36. Hildegarde Fillmore, "WAACS, How They Work—Live—Play," *McCall's*, June 1943, 96–97.

37. The July 1943 issue of *Harper's Bazaar* with a cover picture of a striking servicewoman contained numerous references to the WAAC. Sally Kirkland, "The WAACS Take Over," *Vogue*, July 1, 1943, 18–21, 68; "Your Men in Uniform," *Ladies Home Journal*, September 1943, 4–5, 148–49.

38. Mary Hastings Bradley, "The Lieutenant Meets the WAAC," *Cosmopolitan*, July 1943, 28–31, 128–32; Nina Wilcox Putnam, "Arizona Joins the WAACS," *This Week*, July 11, 1943, 10.

39. "WAC Committee Activities."

40. Ibid.; Treadwell, *Women's Army Corps*, 229–30; "Editorial Service," WR57. Two examples of WWB-inspired newspaper coverage are Elsa Maxwell, "Partyline," *New York Post*, June 17, 1943, and H. L. Katzander, "The Truth about WAACS," *Chicago Sun*, June 20, 1943.

41. "WAC Committee Activities"; Clifton Fadiman to Paul Betters, May 18, 1943, WR27.

42. Treadwell, *Women's Army Corps*, 189.

43. "The WAC Recruiting Committee," *Writers' War Board Report*, September 1, 1943.

44. WWB, *Third Annual Report* (New York: WWB, 1945), 9–10; Board Minutes, June 21, 1944, SP47.

45. "WAVES Recruitment Sub-Committee Report," January 10, 1944, WR38; "The WAVES on Active Duty at the Jacksonville Naval Air Station," *Vogue*, December 1, 1943, 74–75; "WAVES—Sky-Workers with Their Feet on the Ground," *Harper's Bazaar*, November 1943, 82–85; "MLLE Wings to See WAVES," *Mademoiselle*, November 1943, 79–81; Pauline Reaves, "Editor Meets the WAVES," *True Confessions*, February 1944, 4, 32–33; Rita Halle Kleeman, "They're Women to Be Proud Of," *Women's Press*, January 1944, 16–17; Kleeman, "Even Chance," *This Week*, January 9, 1944, 14.

46. See, for example, "Mount Holyoke in the Services," *Mount Holyoke Alumnae Quarterly*, February 1944, inside cover.
47. "What's the Matter Girls," *Logan (OH) Daily News*, January 13, 1944.
48. "WAVES Recruitment Sub-Committee Report"; *Second Annual Report*, 9; *Third Annual Report*, 10; "WAVES—And All Women's Services," *Writers' War Board Report*, December 1, 1943; "Editorial Service"; Selma G. Hirsh to Francis McFadden, February 23, 1944, WR37.
49. "WACS and WAVES Make Wonderful Housekeepers," WR37; Board Minutes, June 21, 1944, SP47.
50. Rex Stout, "About Ten Million American Women Are Slackers," *Glamour*, August 1944, 16.
51. "Activities to Date on Behalf of U.S. Cadet Nurse Corps Recruiting," May 5, 1944, WR92; "Wanted: Cadet Nurses," *Parents' Magazine*, June 1944, 40; "From Jitterbug to Angel," WR92; "Tin Pan Alley Turns Out Songs on Production Line," *Milwaukee Journal*, July 19, 1944. At least forty-eight newspapers ran the editorial "From Jitterbug to Angel" including the *Evening Star* (Bradford, PA), March 24, 1944.
52. "The Navy Needs Hospital Corps WAVES," *Writers' War Board Report*, July 1, 1945.
53. Board Minutes, October 20, 1943, SP47; Frederica Barach to WWB, March 29, 1944, WR34.
54. Alan Green to Lt. James M. Hill, January 26, 1945, WR36; *Third Annual Report*, 11–12; "Report on Meeting with Prospective Orientation Speakers at Clifton Fadiman's Home, Tuesday Evening, April 25, [1944]," WR34.
55. Frederica Barach to Marion White, December 12, 1944; John Kenneth Galbraith to Green, January 25, 1945; Arthur Upham Pope to Rex Stout, n.d.; Henry Atkinson to Stout, November 27, 1944, all WR37. This container has several *Army Talk* issues.
56. Green to Katherine L. Bern, June 22, 1944, WR128.
57. Green to Stephen Laird, June 30, 1944; Green to Bennett Cerf, August 15, 1944; Green to Bert L. Shepard, December 4, 1944; Frederica Barach to Green, August 4, 1944, all WR34; *Third Annual Report*, 11–12; Board Minutes, November 29, 1944, SP47.
58. Green to WWB, May 14, 1945, WR34; Board Minutes, May 9, 1945, SP47.
59. *First Annual Report*, 21.
60. "Titles Suggested for *Yarns for Yanks*," WR27; Rex Stout, form letter to writers, May 24, 1943, WR27.
61. "Memorandum of Writers' War Board Projects for the Army," October 13, 1942, WR27.
62. "Committee on Scripts for Soldier and Sailor Shows," WR8; Rex Stout, letter to author, June 15, 1968.
63. "Committee on Scripts for Soldier and Sailor Shows."
64. *First Annual Report*, 23–24; *Second Annual Report*, 6; *Third Annual Report*, 13; "Committee on Scripts for Soldier and Sailor Shows"; "Summary of Writers' War Board Activities—September, 1942"; *Revue Sketches, Vaudeville Comedy Acts, Prepared by the Committee on Scripts for Soldier and Sailor Shows of the Writers' War Board* (Washington, DC: Infantry Journal, 1943); Marvin Young to Dorothy F. Rodgers, January 12, 1945, WR32.

65. Russel Crouse, form letter to Authors' League members, February 28, 1942; Luise Sillcox to Frederica Barach, April 6, 1942, both WR73; *First Annual Report*, 25–26.

66. Eric Brander, "A Different Way of Serving," *On Patrol: The Magazine of the USO*, Fall 2015, 11–15.

67. *Second Annual Report*, 17, 27; *Third Annual Report*, 18; Frederica Barach to Paul Gallico, October 21, 1944; Jean Poletti to R. K. Englander, February 15, 21, 1945, all WR71.

68. Board Minutes, August 8, 1942, SP46.

69. Carter G. Woodson, *The Negro in Our History*, 9th ed. (Washington, DC: Associated Publishers, 1947), 618; John Hope Franklin and Alfred A. Moss Jr., *From Slavery to Freedom: A History of African-Americans*, 8th ed. (New York: Knopf, 2007), 579; Tom Guglielmo, "'Red Cross, Double Cross': Race and America's World War II Era Blood Donor Service," *Journal of American History* 97 (June 2010): 63–90.

70. Howard Lindsay to Rex Stout, August 17, 1942; Stout to Lindsay, August 24, 1942, both WR72.

71. Guglielmo, "'Red Cross, Double Cross,'" 71–79, 90.

72. *First Annual Report*, 13; "Memorandum of Writers' War Board Projects for the Army."

73. Board Minutes, July 8, 1942, SP46.

74. "Memorandum of Writers' War Board Projects for the Army"; "Summary of Writers' War Board Activities—September, 1942"; Don Wharton, "The New MP," *Saturday Evening Post*, September 19, 1942, 20–21, 87; Matt Taylor, "Private McGarry," *This Week*, November 22, 1942, 10.

75. "It's a Big War," *Life*, January 10, 1944, 35.

76. Board Minutes, May 27, 1943, SP47; "It's a Big War."

77. Board Minutes, February 2, 1944, SP47.

78. "Infantry Day Committee Progress Report," August 1, 1944, WR91.

79. George Fielding Eliot, "Wars Are Won in the Mud," *Argosy*, July 1944, 45.

80. "Editorial Service"; "Infantry Day Committee Progress Report"; "Sullivan Salutes the Infantry," *PM* (New York), June 6, 1944.

81. "Infantry Day Committee Progress Report"; *Third Annual Report*, 8–9; "The Infantry," *New York Times*, June 15, 1944.

82. George Fielding Eliot, "The Little Black Line," *Brief Army Camp Items from the Writers' War Board*, May 1944, WR35.

83. Sheldon Stark, "Song of the Infantry," *Look*, May 16, 1944, 28.

84. For two newspapers that published the editorials, see "Hats Off to the Infantry," *Palm Beach (FL) Post*, April 30, 1944, and "How Far Can You Walk?" *Lock Haven (PA) Express*, June 1, 1944.

85. "Infantry Day Committee Progress Report"; Board Minutes, April 19, May 31, 1944, SP47; Oscar Hammerstein II, *The Complete Lyrics of Oscar Hammerstein II*, ed. Amy Asch (New York: Knopf, 2008), 259.

86. *Third Annual Report*, 8–9; "Infantry Day Report as of June 1, 1944," WR91; "City Pays Tribute to Infantry," *New York Times*, June 16, 1944; Julian Street Jr., "High Lights of My Work with Writers and Artists for the Treasury Department: November 1,

1941 to January 31, 1946" (unpublished manuscript), November 22, 1946, 80–84, Peter Odegard Papers, Franklin D. Roosevelt Presidential Library, Hyde Park, NY.

87. "Minutes of the Infantry Committee Meeting, August 7, 1944," WR91; Frederica Barach to WWB, September 6, 1944, WR32; Gen. Lesley J. McNair to Clifton Fadiman, June 21, 1944, WR91.

88. Christopher LaFarge, "For Immediate Release," *American Magazine*, March 1945, 39, 125. For a similar treatment, see also J. C. Furnas, "This Is It," *American Legion Magazine*, April 1944, 9, 30–33.

89. Frederica Barach to WWB, September 6, 1944, WR32; Ernie Pyle, "Forgotten Medics," *New York World Telegram*, September 5, 1944.

90. "Problem #11—Can We Help the Forgotten Medics?" *Bulletin to Cartoonists*, November 1944, WR32.

91. "Army Medics Report," WR32; "The Forgotten Medics," *Writers' War Board Report*, October 1, 1944; "Heroes without Guns," *Writers' War Board Report*, January 1, 1945.

92. Board Minutes, May 5, July 21, 1943, SP47; *Second Annual Report*, 8; "Naval Aviation Committee," *Writers' War Board Report*, July 15, 1943; Fletcher Pratt, *The Navy Has Wings* (New York: Harper and Brothers, 1943); Frederica Barach to Paul Schubert, August 7, 1943, WR37.

93. Adm. Ernest King, quoted in Allan M. Winkler, *The Politics of Propaganda: The Office of War Information, 1942–1945* (New Haven, CT: Yale University Press, 1978), 46.

94. Clifton Fadiman et al. to King, September 4, 1943; King to Fadiman, September 19, 1943; Fadiman to King, September 30, 1943; King to Fadiman, October 14, 1943, all WR39.

95. J. Clarke Maddimore to WWB, January 24, 1944; *Bulletin to Cartoonists*, June 1944; "Naval Air Gunners Interim Report," all WR39.

96. Henry Stimson, quoted in "It's a Tough War," *Life*, January 31, 1944, 17.

97. James T. Sparrow, *Warfare State: World War II Americans and the Age of Big Government* (New York: Oxford University Press, 2011), 215.

98. "Home Front Information for Troops," May 1, 1944, WR44; *Third Annual Report*, 12.

99. "Bonds—Not Bellyaches," *Writers' War Board Report*, May 1, 1944; Christopher LaFarge, "Let Him Know," *Army-Navy Woman*, May 1944, 26–27.

100. Quentin Reynolds, "They Don't Know There's a War On," *Brief Army Camp Items*, August 1944, WR35; *Third Annual Report*, 12.

101. "Labor Committee Minutes," March 1, 1944, WR48; "Private Joe Union," *Brief Army Camp Items*, March 1944, WR35.

102. "Labor Committee Minutes," March 1, 1944, WR48; Alan Green to Jane McGill, March 22, 1944, WR48; Board Minutes, March 22, May 31, 1944, SP47.

103. Board Minutes, March 22, 1944, SP47; Green to McGill, March 22, 1944, WR48.

104. Board Minutes, May 3, 1944, SP47; "Labor Is Fighting Too," *Brief Army Camp*

Items, April 1944, WR35; William H. Davis, "Who Is Labor?" *Brief Army Camp Items*, July 1944, WR35; Sparrow, *Warfare State*, 224–28.

105. William M. Leary Jr., "Books, Soldiers and Censorship during the Second World War," *American Quarterly* 20 (Summer 1968): 237–45.

106. Ibid.; Norman Cousins, "The Taft-Army Meeting," *Saturday Review of Literature*, July 29, 1944, 12, 14; "Censorship of Soldier Vote Committee Report," August 14, 1944, WR7; Council on Books in Wartime, *A History of the Council on Books in Wartime, 1942–1946* (New York: Country Life, 1946), 22–23.

107. "Censorship of Soldier Vote Committee Report"; Alan Green to George Mayberry, August 4, 1944, WR4; Bernard DeVoto, "The Easy Chair," *Harper's Magazine*, September 1944, 330–33; J. L. Qualey, "Sees Taft against Soldiers Voting," *York (PA) Gazette and Daily*, August 7, 1944; Leary, "Books, Soldiers and Censorship."

108. Paul Gallico, "V-E Day—My Hat," *Brief House Organ Items from the Writers' War Board*, December 1944, WR35. See also "Problem #10—V-E Day, What Will It Bring?" *Bulletin to Cartoonists*, November 1944, WR39.

109. Board Minutes, October 11, 1944, SP47.

110. Paul Gallico, "Memorandum from Paul Gallico on the National Service Act," submitted for consideration for January 24, 1945, board meeting, WR11; Board Minutes, January 17, 24, February 7, 1945, SP47.

111. *Third Annual Report*, 12–13; Barbara Bode to Maxwell Aley, December 7, 1944, WR32; materials on project to interview wounded soldiers at Mitchel Field Hospital, WR32.

112. Board Minutes, July 12, 1944, SP47; "Rehabilitation," September 19, 1944, WR31; Alan Green to the Chief of the News Division, (U.S. Army) Bureau of Public Relations, October 13, 1944, WR34; *Third Annual Report*, 12.

113. "14 Point Program on Rehabilitation," WR31; Carl Carmer and Alan Green, "Rehabilitating the Veteran to Civilian Life," WR31; Board Minutes, July 12, 1944, SP47.

114. "Rehabilitation Committee—General Promotion," "Rehabilitation Committee—Newspapers," "Rehabilitation Committee—Radio," "Rehabilitation Committee—Magazines," all WR31; Green to George B. Denny, January 23, 1945, WR91; "We're Getting Somewhere," *Writers' War Board Report*, June 1, 1945. Among the WWB-inspired magazine articles on rehabilitation were Malcolm J. Farrell, "Plain Truths about the N. P.'s ["neuropsychiatrics," a medical term used at the time to refer to those with mental disorders]," *Rotarian*, October 1944, 19, 55–57; Maxine Davis, "Now That He's Home," *Good Housekeeping*, January 1945, 36, 69–70; and Albert Q. Maisel, "Third-Rate Medicine for First-Rate Men," *Cosmopolitan*, March 1945, 35–37, 106–10. For examples of newspaper coverage, see J. A. Heffernan, "The Future of Our Vets," *Brooklyn Daily Eagle*, September 17, 1944, and Thomas L. Stokes, "Aid for Psychiatry," *New York World-Telegram*, January 19, 1945.

115. Maj. Merle Armitage to Frederica Barach, January 20, 1944; Barach to Armitage, February 8, 1944, both WR91; Board Minutes, February 9, 1944, SP47. The unnamed radio program was undoubtedly *Broadway Matinee*, which CBS produced in

cooperation with the OWI. John Dunning, *On the Air: The Encyclopedia of Old-Time Radio* (New York: Oxford University Press, 1998), 121.

Chapter 3: Home Front Propaganda

1. "List of German Economists for the Board of Economic Warfare [for] Sylvia Lowenthal," WR71; Frederica Barach to A. Seymour Houghton; October 20, 1942, Houghton to Barach, December 11, 1942, both WR72; Office of Civilian Defense Newsletter, "How Churches Can Cooperate in Civilian Defense," WR51.
2. "Report on March 15th Income Tax Project," January 8, 1944, WR43; "Bergen Makes with Pay-as-You-Go," *Brief House Organ Items from the Writers' War Board*, December 30, 1943, WR43.
3. "Report on March 15th Income Tax Project"; "How to Keep Your Fellow Citizens out of the Bughouse," *Writers' War Board Report*, December 1, 1943; Sylvia Porter, "The Looming Nightmare of March 15," *Reader's Digest*, January 1944, 1–2.
4. Judson Phillips, "Due—March 15th," *Real Story*, March 19, 1944, 11, 64–65; "Income Tax Again," *Writers' War Board Report*, January 1, 1944.
5. WWB, *First Annual Report* (New York: WWB, 1943), 24.
6. Rex Stout, letter to newspapers, March 12, 1942, WR5; *First Annual Report*, 16–17; winning essays and other materials on the contest, WR5; "Prize Winning Essay in High School Contest," *Boston Herald*, May 22, 1942. A picture of winner Electra Milmazes accompanied the article, and the WWB received credit for the project.
7. *First Annual Report*, 22–23, 25; "Saturday Night *Bond Wagon*," WR40; Board Minutes, November 25, 1942.
8. *First Annual Report*, 23, 25; Julian Street Jr., "High Lights of My Work with Writers and Artists for the Treasury Department: November 1, 1941 to January 31, 1946" (unpublished manuscript), November 22, 1946, 19–20, Peter Odegard Papers, Franklin D. Roosevelt Presidential Library, Hyde Park, NY; Rex Stout to William S. Rainey, October 31, 1942, WR40; Board Minutes, November 25, 1942, SP46.
9. "Report of Work of Poster Committee, August 11, 1942 to December 31, 1942," WR9; *First Annual Report*, 21–22: Street, "High Lights of My Work," 64.
10. "Report of Work of Poster Committee"; *First Annual Report*, 21–22.
11. WWB, *Second Annual Report* (New York: WWB, 1944), 13.
12. Board Minutes, March 1, 1944, SP47; James Kimble, *Mobilizing the Home Front: War Bonds and Domestic Propaganda* (College Station: Texas A&M University Press, 2006), 39; G. H. Gregory, ed., *Posters of World War II* (New York: Gramercy Books, 1993), 10.
13. Street, "High Lights of My Work," 20; Reeves Lewenthal to Frederica Barach, March 7, 1944, WR9.
14. Street, "High Lights of My Work," 20; Julian Brodie to Barach, November 8, 1944; Lewenthal to Rex Stout, April 13, 1944, both WR9; WWB, *Third Annual Report* (New York: WWB, 1945), 14.
15. "Report of Poster Committee," November 10, 1944, WR8; "Fourth War Loan Drive Progress Report," December 7, 1943, WR43.

16. Alan Green to Robert Landry, September 22, 1944, WR15.

17. Street, "High Lights of My Work," 37–38, 42, 44; "Book and Author Bond Rallies," *Writers' War Board Report*, October 1, 1943; Mark Van Doren, "Report on the Book and Author War Bond Committee," November 1943, WR41.

18. Street, "High Lights of My Work," 39–41; Van Doren, "Book and Author War Bond Committee Report," May 1943, WR42; "Treasury Committee Plans Books for Bonds Day," *Publishers Weekly*, January 23, 1943, 351; "Allentown Raises $804,000 in First Books and Authors for Bonds Day," *Publishers Weekly*, March 6, 1943, 1088–93; Dorothy Pratt, "They Sold $188,000,000 Worth of Bonds," *Publishers Weekly*, January 12, 1946, 153–56; *Second Annual Report*, 16; *Third Annual Report*, 14–15; Frederica Barach to Pratt, January 11, 1945, WR41; "Minutes of the Book and Author War Bond Committee, February 26, 1946," WR42.

19. *First Annual Report*, 26–27; Mary Blankenhorn to Selma G. Hirsh, September 5, 1942, WR51; "Now Everyone Can Enlist," September 6, 1942, WR7. One example of magazine coverage is "V-Homes," *Young America*, September 16, 1942, 5.

20. Rex Stout to James M. Landis, September 28, 1942, WR126.

21. Board Minutes, February 9, 16, 1944, SP47; Oscar Schisgall to Stout, February 5, 1944; Frederica Barach to Jack Goodman, October 31, 1944; Richard D. Mathewson to Barach, November 4, 1944, all WR59.

22. Nelson Cruikshank to Barach, July 7, 1942, WR71; Allen Wilson to WWB, February 17, 1943; Frederick W. Wile Jr. to Barach, May 27, 1943, both WR72; "Show Biz to Recruit Labor," *Variety*, February 10, 1943, 1, 30; "War Manpower Commission," *Writers' War Board Report*, April 15, 1943; Dorothy Dana, "We Must Not Fail," *Provo (UT) Daily Herald*, April 27, 1943.

23. Board Minutes, August 9, 1944, SP47; "Crop Corps and Victory Gardens Project—1944," WR47; "Fat Salvage" (speech written for War Production Board), WR71; "When War Workers Go AWOL," *Cumberland (MD) Evening Times*, January 11, 1944; "Junk Goes to War," *Argus-Leader* (Sioux Falls, SD), July 24, 1944; Selma G. Hirsh to Marion White, August 31, 1944, WR71.

24. Board Minutes, June 21, 1944, SP47; "Non-Essential Train Travel Ban Tightened," *New York Herald-Tribune*, June 22, 1944.

25. Berton Braley, "As You Were," *New York Times Magazine*, July 30, 1944, 10; "Civilian Ouster from Trains Near," *New York Times*, June 22, 1944; "Office of Defense Transportation: Progress Report of July 15, 1944," WR93.

26. Clifton Fadiman, "Every Day Is Labor Day—When You Travel Nowadays," *Brief House Organ Items*, July 1944, Harold Moore Collection, MS2007-079, West Virginia State Archives, Charleston, WV.

27. Weare Holbrook, "Why I Sit at Home with a Book—and a Blonde," *Statesville (OH) Daily Record*, August 9, 1944, and many other newspapers; "Office of Defense Transportation: Progress Report of July 15, 1944," WR93.

28. Kenneth D. Rose, *Myth and the Greatest Generation: A Social History of Americans in World War II* (New York: Routledge, 2008), 121–22; Inger L. Stole, *Advertising at War: Business, Consumers, and Government in the 1940s* (Urbana: University of Illinois Press, 2012), 32–33, 45–46, 86–87.

29. "Home Front Pledge Campaign," *Writers' War Board Report*, September 1, 1943; speeches developed by the WWB for the government campaign against the black market, WR51; "Rally Attacks Black Market," *Bridgeport (CT) Herald*, September 5, 1943; Charles Doane, "The White Market," *This Week*, September 5, 1943, 2.

30. Kate Sproehnle, "You Don't Mean Me?" *Woman's Day*, August 1944, 14.

31. Board Minutes, March 8, 1944, SP47.

32. James A. Maxwell and Margaret N. Balcom, "Gasoline Rationing in the U.S.," *Quarterly Journal of Economics* 60 (August 1946): 661–87; 61 (November 1946): 125–55; "'Gas' Racket Held Peril to 'A' Ration," *New York Times*, April 5, 1944; Samuel Dalsimer to Frederica Barach, March 17, 1944, WR52.

33. "Counterfeiters and Black Market Operators May Get It All," *New York World-Telegram*, April 5, 1944. See also "Black Market Perils Gas Supply," *New York Post*, April 5, 1944.

34. Paul Gallico, "The Racketeers Need You," *Army and Navy Woman*, Spring 1944, 14.

35. Pete Martin, "Solid Citizen," *Saturday Evening Post*, May 6, 1944, 34; "Smash the Black Market Menace," *Scholastic*, May 1–6, 1944, 4.

36. For example, see Arthur Bartlett, "Dynamite in Your Gas Tank," *This Week*, April 9, 1944, 2; Betsy Talbot Blackwell, "Memo from the Editor," *Mademoiselle*, June 1944, 10; and "Your Gasoline Coupons—Are They Endorsed?" *New York Motorist*, April 1944, 1.

37. "Report on Black Market Gasoline Campaign," April 28, 1944, WR52; "Supplemental Black Market Campaign," August 4, 1944, WR52.

38. Robert Duffus, "Stop Thief!" *Indiana (PA) Gazette*, June 8, 1944; "Problem #3—Black Market Gasoline—Stolen Gasoline," *Bulletin to Cartoonists*, May 1944, WR56; "Report on Black Market Gasoline Campaign"; "Supplemental Black Market Campaign."

39. Board Minutes, March 21, 1945, SP47.

40. Board Minutes, June 16, 1944, SP47.

41. Ibid.; James Brackett to Rex Stout, June 18, 1943, WR59.

42. "Minutes of the Economic Stabilization Committee Meeting, July 2, 1943," WR59.

43. "The Woman Who Lost Her Head," *Harper's Bazaar*, September 1943, 89.

44. Mildred Russell to Rita Halle Kleeman, October 18, 1943, WR59; "Anti-Inflation Committee, Interim Report, October 20, 1943," WR59; "Anti-Inflation Committee—Additional Progress Report, January 1, 1944," WR59; Rex Stout et al. to Harry Hopkins, October 26, 1943; Voltarine Feingold to Edward Silver, March 13, 1944, both WR59.

45. "Anti-Inflation Committee, Interim Report"; "Anti-Inflation Committee—Additional Progress Report." Newspaper coverage of the topic includes Booth Tarkington, "Are You Choosing to Be Poor?" *New York World-Telegram*, August 3, 1944, and Sylvia Porter, "Your Dollars and the War," *New York Post*, September 18, 1944.

46. "Anti-Inflation Committee—Additional Progress Report"; William Jennings O'Brian, "Dear Joe," *PM* (New York), January 16, 1944; "They're News Because—Luette

Goodbody," *Harper's Bazaar,* February 1944, 20; Goodbody to Carl Carmer, February 1, 1944, WR58; "War Dollars—and Sense," *Look,* March 7, 1944, 8.

47. "Anti-Inflation Committee—Additional Progress Report." See, for example, P. K. Alexander, "Planned Spending—Saving," *Mountain States Banker,* November 1944, 10.

48. "Have You Started Any Spirals Lately?" *Writers' War Board Report,* August 1, 1944.

49. "Committee Report for Anti-Inflation Committee," WR59.

50. Board Minutes, March 21, 28, 1945, SP47.

51. "Help Wanted, Male and Female," WR57; Board Minutes, March 21, 1945, SP47.

52. "This Is Not a Private Fight," *Writers' War Board Report,* June 1, 1945.

53. George E. Sokolsky, "These Days," *New York Sun,* June 9, 1945; Board Minutes, July 3, 1945, SP47.

54. Joseph Hirsh, "Know Your Enemy," *Brief Army Camp Items from the Writers' War Board,* July 1944, WR35; Board Minutes, February 23, 1944, SP47.

55. Stole, *Advertising at War,* 138–49; Board Minutes, February 23, April 5, 1944, SP47; Clifton Fadiman to Mortimer Adler, April 3, 1944; Rex Stout et al. to Will Hayes, May 4, 1944; Carroll Carroll to Fadiman, October 5, 1944, all WR92.

56. Carl Carmer, "Don't Miss Anything," *This Week,* September 24, 1944, 2; "Back to School Campaign: Progress Report as of August 10, 1944," WR47; Board Minutes, July 5, 1944, SP47; Frank Sinatra, "Ninny," *Jackson (MS) Clarion-Ledger,* August 27, 1944.

57. Simon O. Lesser, quoted in Natalie Davison to Frederica Barach, October 18, 1944, WR47.

58. Thomas Howell, "Kansas City's Crusader: Leon Birkhead and the Fight against Fascism," *Missouri Historical Review* 110 (July 2016): 237–59. Among the many news reports on Stout's involvement in the wartime activities of the Friends of Democracy are these *New York Times* articles: "Program to Combat Propaganda Opened," February 28, 1942; "United Action Urged against All Fascists," November 6, 1942; and "Ridder Accuses Writers of Libel," June 8, 1943.

59. Clifton Fadiman, introduction to Norman Corwin, *More by Corwin* (New York: Holt, 1944), xi. The book also contains Corwin's play *To the Young,* 274–87.

60. Board Minutes, April 12, 1944, SP47.

61. "Progress Report—Security of War Information Campaign," May 30, 1944, WR56; Frederica Barach, memo to log, April 18, 1944, WR56; Selma G. Hirsh to Catherine Lanham, April 18, 1944, WR56; "You Can Button Lots of Lips with Your Pen and Typewriter," *Writers' War Board Report,* May 1, 1944.

62. "Pre-Invasion Gossip," *New York Times Magazine,* April 23, 1944, 2.

63. Paul Gallico, "Who Killed My Buddy," *Cosmopolitan,* August 1944, 22–25, 52–59, 165; September 1944, 60–61, 115–22; October 1944, 64–66, 109–12, 115–17.

64. John H. Gardner, "Now Will You Stop Loose Talk?" *Brief House Organ Items,* September 1944, WR35; Frederica Barach, memo to log, April 18, 1944, WR56.

65. Paul Gallico, "Who's Efficient?" *Cosmopolitan,* October 1942, 17, 62.

66. Lee Wright, form letter to writers, May 5, 1942, WR49.

67. *First Annual Report*, 15–16, 24.

68. Ben Brady, "Man Bites Carrot," in U.S. Office of Civilian Defense, Radio Section, *Script Catalog* (Washington, DC: Office of Civilian Defense, 1942), 79; *First Annual Report*, 15–16, 24; "Meeting of the Committee on Civilian Programs, September 1, 1942," WR49; Caroline Simon to Frederica Barach, September 9, 1942, WR49.

69. Barach to Selma G. Hirsh, November 1942; Barach to Knowles Entrikin, May 18, 1943; "Meeting of the Committee on Civilian Programs"; Simon to Barach, September 9, 1942, all WR49; U.S. Office of Civilian Defense, Radio Section, *Script Catalog*.

70. Board Minutes, April 5, 1944, SP47.

71. Edna St. Vincent Millay, *Collected Poems*, ed. Norma Millay (New York: HarperCollins, 2011), 416, 418, 423.

72. James P. Moore Jr., "American Prayers on D-Day and Today," *Washington Post*, June 6, 2004.

73. Louis C. Kesselman, "The Fair Employment Practices Movement in Perspective," *Journal of Negro History* 31 (January 1946): 35–40; John Hope Franklin and Alfred A. Moss Jr., *From Slavery to Freedom: A History of African-Americans*, 8th ed. (New York: Knopf, 2007), 480–81, 496.

74. John Hope Franklin, *From Slavery to Freedom: A History of American Negroes* (New York: Knopf, 1947), 577.

75. Dan J. Puckett, "The Double V Campaign," in *Encyclopedia of African American History*, ed. Leslie M. Alexander and Walter C. Ruckers (Santa Barbara, CA: ABC-CLIO, 2010), 745.

76. Pearl Buck, *American Unity and Asia* (New York: John Day, 1942), 29; "War Scripts of the Month Selections," WR21.

77. Sato Masaharu and Harak Kushner, "Negro Propaganda Operations: Japan's Short-Wave Radio Broadcasts for World War II Black Americans," *Historical Journal of Film, Radio and Television* 19, no. 1 (1999): 5–26.

78. Board Minutes, December 2, 9, 1942, SP46.

79. "War Propaganda among Negroes," WR13; Frederica Barach to Adam Clayton Powell Jr., December 11, 1942, WR13; Powell, "Is This a White Man's War?" *Common Sense*, April 1942, 111.

80. Margaret Leech, "Report to the Writers War Board Re: Negro Newspapers," November 28, 1942, WR13; Board Minutes, December 2, 9, 1942, SP46.

81. Wendy Wall, "'Our Enemies Within': Nazism, National Unity, and America's Wartime Discourse on Tolerance," in *Enemy Images in American History*, ed. Ragnhild Fiebig-von Hase and Ursula Lehmkuhl (Oxford: Berghahn, 1997), 227.

82. Board Minutes, February 9, March 8, 1944, SP47; "How Good an American Are You?" May 22, 1944, WR17; *Third Annual Report*, 28.

83. Board Minutes, March 8, 1944, SP47; Franklin and Moss, *From Slavery to Freedom*, 497.

84. Board Minutes, March 8, 1944, SP47; Violet Edwards, "Note on 'The Races of Mankind,'" in Ruth Benedict, *Race: Science and Politics* (New York: Viking, 1959), 167–68; "Army Drops Race Equality Book; Denies Mag's Stand Was Reason," *New York*

Times, March 6, 1944; "Plans New Edition of Race Pamphlet," *New York Times*, March 8, 1944; Ted Posten to Herbert Little, February 16, 1944, WR16.

85. Board Minutes, March 8, 1944, SP47; form letters signed by Rex Stout and Robert Landry to assorted individuals, their replies, and newspaper clippings, WR16; John T. McManus, "Speaking of Movies," *PM* (New York), July 12, 1944.

86. Stout and Landry, letter to assorted companies and individuals, WR17.

87. Ruth Benedict and Gene Weltfish, *The Races of Mankind* (New York: Public Affairs Committee, 1943), 2–3, 17.

88. "Army Drops Race Equality Book"; "The Races of Mankind," *Commonweal*, March 17, 1944, 532; "Writers Press Fight to Get Book on Races Distributed," *PM* (New York), April 9, 1944; Rex Stout to Chester Barnard, March 14, 1944, WR16.

89. Barnard to Stout, March 15, 1944; Stout to Barnard, March 17, 1944, both WR16.

90. Board Minutes, March 22, 1944, SP47.

91. Rex Stout, form letters to assorted individuals and organizations, April 4, 1944, WR16; Stout, form letters to USO centers, June 21, 1944, and miscellaneous reports from them, WR16; "Ban by USO Criticized," *New York Times*, March 16, 1944; "Writers Press Fight to Get Book on Races Distributed"; "Editorial Service," WR57; "Exploding the Myth," *St. Cloud (MN) Times*, April 19, 1944; Board Minutes, May 24, 1944, SP47.

92. *Third Annual Report*, 17–18; Edwards, "Note on *The Races of Mankind*."

93. Edwards, "Note on *The Races of Mankind*"; Frederick Woltman, "Anti-Reds Backed Pamphlet: *Races of Mankind* Complications," *New York World-Telegram*, April 28, 1944.

94. Board Minutes, April 12, 1944, SP47; Clifton Fadiman to John Tunis, June 22, 1944, WR18.

95. Correspondence with National Urban League, National Conference of Christians and Jews, and Bureau for Intercultural Education, WR18; correspondence with American Council on Race Relations, WR20.

96. Board Minutes, March 22, 1944, SP47.

97. "Memorandum on Mothers' Groups," October 12, 1944, WR18.

98. "Who Will Sit It Out?" *Time*, July 10, 1944, 23.

99. Board Minutes, July 12, 1944, SP47.

100. Board Minutes, May 3, 1944, SP47; Bureau of Intelligence, Office of War Information, Report no. 109, March 15, 1943, quoted in Ronald Takaki, *Double Victory: A Multicultural History of America in World War II* (Boston: Little, Brown, 2000), 51.

101. Board Minutes, August 10, 1944, SP47.

102. *Writers' War Board Script Catalog, November, 1945*, WR21.

103. "Editorial Service"; Frederica Barach to Mary S. Hayes, November 23, 1944, WR48; *Third Annual Report*, 18. For examples of publication, see "Him Today—Me Tomorrow," *Berkshire Eagle* (Pittsfield, MA), June 7, 1944; "Fair Play on the Job," *Bismarck (ND) Tribune*, September 14, 1944; and "Fair Play Now—and Later," *Great Falls (MT) Tribune*, November 14, 1944.

104. Max Perkins to Sylvia Brodow, January 8, 1945, WR48; *Third Annual Report*, 18.

105. Margaret Leech to Julian S. Myrick, February 19, March 5, 1945; Robert Landry to Thomas Dewey, February 27, 1945, all WR20; Frederica Barach to WWB, January

9, 1946; Barach to Janet E. Neuman, February 20, 1946, both WR48; Kesselman, "Fair Employment Practices Movement," 39–46.

106. Barach to WWB, May 27, 1944; Barach to Julian Street Jr., June 1, 1944; WWB to Street, June 6, 1944, all WR44.

107. WWB to Street, June 6, 1944, WR44.

108. Street, quoted in Frederica Barach to WWB, October 25, 1944, WR46.

109. "Report of Japanese-American Campaign," WR82; "Hood River Incident," *Massillon (OH) Evening Independent*, March 19, 1945; "An American Is an American Is an American," *Writers' War Board Report*, April 1, 1945.

110. "Report of Japanese-American Campaign"; "Editorial Service"; "The Blood of Freedom," *Delta Democrat Times* (Greenville, MS), May 16, 1945.

111. Lillian Smith, *Strange Fruit* (New York: Reynal and Hitchcock, 1944); Board Minutes, March 22, 29, April 5, 1944, SP47; "'Strange Fruit' Banned by Boston Booksellers," *Publishers Weekly*, March 25, 1944, 1289–90; "Feverish Fascination," *Time*, March 20, 1944, 99–100; J. Donald Adams, "Speaking of Books," *New York Times*, May 28, 1944.

112. Gwethalyn Graham, *Earth and High Heaven* (Philadelphia: J. B. Lippincott, 1944); Board Minutes, August 2, 1944, SP47; Rita Halle Kleeman, review of *Earth and High Heaven*, WR18; Graham, "Earth and High Heaven," *Collier's*, August 26, 1944, 11–13, 29–31; September 2, 1944, 22–23, 58–60; September 9, 1944, 18, 28–32; September 16, 1944, 24–26, 57–59; Rex Stout to *Colliers's*, July 17, 1944, WR18.

113. Board Minutes, August 2, 1944, SP47; Hawes Publications, "Adult *New York Times* Bestseller Lists for 1945," www.hawes.com.

114. Hortense Powdermaker, *Probing Our Prejudices* (New York: Harper and Brothers, 1944), viii.

115. "Editorial Service"; "Recommended Book," *Writers' War Board Report*, November 1, 1944; Board Minutes, October 18, 1944, SP47; Agnes E. Benedict, review of Hortense Powdermaker, *Probing Our Prejudices*, *Parents' Magazine*, April 1945, 157–58; review of Hortense Powdermaker, *Probing Our Prejudices*, *School and Society*, August 5, 1944, 96.

116. Rita Halle Kleeman to Eleanor Naumburg Sanger, December 7, 1944, WR18; "[Juvenile Committee Report] for the Writers War Board," December 18, 1944, WR18; Kleeman to Frederica Barach, November 2, 1944, WR18.

117. *Second Annual Report*, 15; "War Scripts of the Month Selections"; "Racial Tolerance Series," *Writers' War Board Report*, September 1, 1943; *Writers' War Board Script Catalog, November, 1945*; Fiorello La Guardia to Katharine Seymour, July 22, 1943; Langston Hughes to Seymour, July 29, 1943; Seymour to Barach, August 3, 1943, all WR23; Eve Merriam, *What's Wrong with Me?* WR23; Hughes, *In the Service of My Country*, WR23.

118. Etta Wedge, "Honor Roll in Race Relations, 1944," *Journal of Negro History* 14 (Spring 1945): 267–68.

119. "Books—Authors," *New York Times*, February 29, 1944; *Writers' War Board Script Catalog, November, 1945*.

120. Frederica Barach to Rex Stout, December 30, 1944, WR19; Board Minutes, August 30, 1944, SP47.

121. "Editorial Service"; "Democracy's Way with a Problem," *Provo (UT) Daily Herald*, August 17, 1943.

122. "Editorial Service"; "Later Editorials and Scripts," WR136. For examples of publication, see "Blind Prejudice," *Camden (AR) News*, May 28, 1945; "Bigotry Must Not Win the War," *Greeley (CO) Daily Tribune*, July 11, 1944; and "Open Mouths, Closed Minds," *Pottstown (PA) Mercury*, December 6, 1945.

123. Harry Emerson Fosdick, "Will We Solve Our Negro Problem?" *Brief House Organ Items,* December 30, 1943, WR6; *Third Annual Report*, 5.

124. "Editorial Service"; *Writers' War Board Script Catalog, November, 1945*; *Third Annual Report*, 5; Helen Hayes, "We Have Racial Equity—Do You?" *Brief Army Camp Items*, March 1944, WR35.

125. "German Import," *Writers' War Board Report*, June 1, 1944.

126. Unsigned form letters to editors and publishers, WR17; Rita Halle Kleeman, "Easier Housekeeping Ahead," *Redbook*, June 25, 1944, 28–29; Edward N. Scheiberling, "Tolerance Is Americanism," *American Legion Magazine*, March 1945, 6; Board Minutes, August 16, 1944, SP47.

127. Board Minutes, May 31, 1944, SP47.

128. Jerry McGill, quoted in "Minutes of the Meeting of Radio Writers at Clifton Fadiman's House, June 15, 1944," WR17.

129. "Minutes of the Meeting of Radio Writers, June 15"; Goodman Ace to Fadiman, June 16, 1944, WR17.

130. "Minutes of the Meeting with Radio Writers, June 16, 1944," WR17; Alan Green, form letter to juvenile editors, June 26, 1944; Green to WWB, June 20, 1944, both WR17.

131. Kenneth Gould, *They Got the Blame: The Story of Scapegoats in History* (New York: Association, 1942); Henrietta Wireman, *By Different Boats* (New York: U.S.O. Division, Young Women's Christian Association of the U.S.A. National Board, 1944).

132. Although the board had the best of intentions, *Negroes and the War* (Washington, DC: Office of War Information, Division of Public Inquiries, 1943) was not worth resurrecting even though Congress had opposed it. Leslie Granger of the National Urban League called the pamphlet "a monumental mistake and a disservice to the government and the Negro. I say this . . . because it is like kicking a man who is down and congratulating him because he is not yet dead." Granger, quoted in Franklin and Moss, *From Slavery to Freedom*, 497.

133. Copies of *Negroes and the War*, WR6; Lillian Smith, "There Are Things to Be Done," *South Today* 6 (Winter 1942–43): 35–43; Frederica Barach to Pat S. Klopfer, April 15, 1944, WR16. On the congressional protest against *Negroes and the War*, see "Assails Elmer Davis," *New York Times*, March 9, 1943.

134. Barach to Margaret Seligman Lewisohn, December 26, 1944, WR25. An example of a letter sent at WWB request is Percival E. Jackson to Bristol-Meyers (show sponsor), December 21, 1944, WR25.

135. "The Soap Operas Go Social," *Des Moines Register*, September 28, 1944.

136. [Harvard University, Department of Psychology], *ABC's of Scapegoating* (Chicago: Central YMCA College, [1943?]).

137. Hobe Morrison, form letter to radio writers, March 22, 1945, WR22.

138. "Digest of Comic Magazine Conference, December 7, 1944," WR12.

139. Eric Godal, "The Destroyer," WR17; *Third Annual Report*, 18. Mats of some of the other cartoons in the series are found in WR17.

140. Maxwell C. Gaines, from a story by the East and West Association, "Filipinos Are People"; Henry Kuttner, "A Tale of a City," both *Comic Cavalcade No. 9* (New York: DC Comics, 1945), n.p. A copy of the comic book is located in WR12.

141. Jon L. Blummer, "A Ride in the Sky [The 99th Squadron]," *Comic Calvalcade No. 9*, n.p.; Frederica Barach, memorandum to the WWB, January 22, 1945, WR11. The CIO became part of the AFL-CIO in 1955.

142. Barach to Maxwell C. Gaines, July 21, 1944; Barach, memorandum to WWB, July 12, October 4, 1944; Barach to Walter White, July 11, 1944, all WR11.

143. Alice Marble, "Sojourner Truth," *Wonder Woman Comic No. 13* (New York: All-American Comics, 1945), n.p.; Helen Traeger to WWB, September 21, 1944; Barach to Gaines, September 30, 1944, both WR11. A copy of the comic book is in WR17.

144. Clifton Fadiman to Sheldon Mayer, September 11, 1944, WR11; Gaines, "Filipinos Are People"; Kuttner, "A Tale of a City"; and Blummer, "A Ride in the Sky [The 99th Squadron]," all in *Comic Calvalcade No. 9*, n.p.; Paul Hirsh, "'This Is Our Enemy': The Writers' War Board and Representations of Race in Comic Books, 1942–1945," *Pacific Historical Review* 83 (August 2014): 478–80. Hirsh's article places the efforts of the WWB into the broader context of comic book content on war-related subjects during World War II.

145. Bernard Berelson and Patricia Salter, *Writers' War Board Study* (New York: Bureau of Applied Social Research, Columbia University, 1944); "Gear Show Biz vs. Race Bias," *Variety*, January 10, 1945, 1; Board Minutes, December 27, 1944, SP47; Robert Landry, letter to author, September 28, 1970.

146. Board Minutes, December 27, 1944, SP47.

147. Ibid.; Alan Green, interview by author, August 8, 1968.

148. WWB, *The Myth That Threatens America* (New York: WWB, 1945), 34; "Diverse Intellectuals Use Showmanship to Break Down Prejudice," *Variety*, January 17, 1945, 2; Board Minutes, December 27, 1944, SP47; Noralee Frankel, *Striping Gypsy: The Life of Gypsy Rose Lee* (New York: Oxford University Press, 2010), 151.

149. "Diverse Intellectuals Use Showmanship," 2.

150. Margaret Mead, "Is There an American Type?" 16; Eric Johnston, "Prejudice Is Bad for Business," 9; John Roy Carlson, "It Can Lead to Civil War," 18, all in WWB, *Myth That Threatens America*.

151. Oscar Hammerstein II, *The Complete Lyrics of Oscar Hammerstein II*, ed. Amy Asch (New York: Knopf, 2008), 260; "Diverse Intellectuals Use Showmanship"; Board Minutes, December 27, 1944, SP47. In 1949 Hammerstein tackled the issue of racism in the lyrics of the musical *South Pacific*. Despite criticism that he was being "preachy," he inserted satirical lines like "You've got to be carefully taught before it's too late . . . to hate all the people your relatives hate." Hammerstein, *Complete Lyrics*, 341.

152. Hammerstein, *Complete Lyrics*, 260.

153. "Diverse Intellectuals Use Showmanship," 2.

154. Robert Landry, letter to author, September 28, 1970.

155. WWB, *Myth That Threatens America*, 5; Board Minutes, June 27, 1945, SP47; "Writers' War Board Decides to Continue in Response to Many Requests," *Publishers Weekly*, July 28, 1945, 308; Hugh Fordin, *Getting to Know Him: A Biography of Oscar Hammerstein II* (New York: Da Capo, 1986), 284.

156. Columbia University Bureau of Applied Research, *How Writers Perpetuate Stereotypes: A Digest of Data* (New York: WWB, 1945).

157. Ibid.

158. Board Minutes, June 27, 1945, SP47.

159. Bill V. Mullen, *Popular Fronts: Chicago and African-American Cultural Politics, 1935–46* (Urbana: University of Illinois Press, 1999), 147. For a postwar discussion, see June Blythe, "Can Public Relations Help Reduce Prejudice?" *Public Relations Quarterly* 11 (Autumn 1947): 345–46. The survey was recently cited in Julie Brown, ed., *Ethnicity and the American Short Story* (Milton Park, Abington, UK; Taylor and Francis, 2013), 25.

160. Alberta Altman to WWB, March 30, 1945, WR93; "'I Am an American Day'—May 20, Report on Projects," June 27, 1945, WR93; "Editorial Service"; "I Am an American Day," *The Capital* (Annapolis), May 19, 1945; "How about an Oath for Old Citizens?" *Writers' War Board Report*, May 1, 1945; Ingrid Bergman, "Thank You, Americans," *Brief Army Camp Items*, April 1945, WR35.

161. "'I Am an American Day'—May 20, Report"; "War Scripts of the Month Selections"; *Writers' War Board Script Catalog, November, 1945*.

162. Christopher LaFarge to Rex Stout, November 5, 1944, WR20. See also Luise Sillcox to Rex Stout, n.d., and similar memoranda in WR20.

163. "War Scripts of the Month Selections"; *Writers' War Board Script Catalog, November, 1945*; "Later Editorials and Scripts."

164. "Brief Summary of Business Transacted at the Radio Writers Meeting at Clifton Fadiman's House, June 15, 1944," WR17.

165. Izzy Rowe, "OWI Budget Slash May Kill War Writers Board," *Pittsburgh Courier*, July 7, 1945.

Chapter 4: Propaganda on America's Allies and Enemies

1. "Be Thrifty with Food," *Writers' War Board Report*, January 1, 1945.

2. Alan Green, interview by author, August 8, 1968.

3. WWB to Selma G. Hirsh, May 25, 1942; Rex Stout to Joseph Kastner, June 3, 1942, both WR50; "United Nations Day, June 14, [1942]," WR50; "United Nations in Impressive Flag Day Ceremony at White House," *New York Times*, June 15, 1942.

4. "United Nations Day, June 14, [1943]"; Frederica Barach to Anthony Hyde, April 29, 1943, both WR56.

5. Hyde to Rex Stout, June 25, 1943, WR56; "United Nations Day, June 14, [1943]"; "Writers' War Board Declares Meaning of Old Glory for Flag Day," *Portsmouth (NH) Herald*, June 8, 1943; "War Scripts of the Month Selections," WR21; WWB, *Second Annual Report* (New York: WWB, 1944), 11, 19.

6. Herbert Zim to Clifton Fadiman, October 8, 1943, WR43; "Comics Committee

Progress Report," May 15, 1944, WR11; Board Minutes, February 16, 1944, SP47. Samples of the comic books are located in WR11.

7. Wendell Willkie, *One World* (New York: Simon and Schuster, 1943); Donald B. Johnson, *The Republican Party and Wendell Willkie* (Urbana: University of Illinois Press, 1960), 236–37; *Second Annual Report*, 12, 19, 22.

8. Pearl Buck, *American Unity and Asia* (New York: John Day, 1942); Rex Stout to Arthur J. Goldsmith, July 24, 1942, WR5; Stout, "Memorandum for Arthur Goldsmith," WR5.

9. "Writing Time: 20 Minutes," *Writers' War Board Report*, July 15, 1943; "Chinese Exclusion Activities," WR76; "We Should End the Affront to China," *Saturday Evening Post*, October 23, 1943, 112.

10. Alexander Fadeev later became notorious for describing Stalin as "the greatest humanist the world has ever known." James T. Bennett, *Subsidizing Culture: Taxpayer Enrichment of the Creative Class* (New York: Routledge, 2017), 98.

11. Fadeev to Rex Stout, July 1942; Stout to Fadeev, September 17, 1942, both WR76; Board Minutes, September 16, October 14, 1942, SP46. For an example of WWB use of the Soviet material, see Nikolai Karintsev, "Soviet Drama, Films, Music, Books, Bristle with War Winning Vigor," *Variety*, October 28, 1942, 2, 20.

12. Stout to Foreign Committee, Union of Soviet Writers, June 7, 1943; Frederica Barach to Jack Goodman, July 5, 1943, both WR76.

13. Clifton Fadiman to Marvin McIntyre, September 21, 1942, WR23.

14. Minutes of the Russian Committee, October 13, November 19, 1943, January 5, 25, 1944; Jack Goodman, form letter on War Heroes Tour, January 4, 1944; Richard Condon to Goodman, December 13, 1944, all WR76; Board Minutes, January 5, 1944, SP47.

15. *Second Annual Report*, 17; "Spring Campaign, Russian War Relief," WR75; Booth Tarkington, "Booth Tarkington Writes a Letter to Konstantin Gregorivich Konstantinov" and "Konstantin Tells His Story," *Boys' Life*, September 1943, 13, 30.

16. "War Scripts of the Month Selections"; Joseph E. Davies, "Why We Must Get Along with Russia," *Brief Army Camp Items from the Writers' War Board*, June 1944, WR35.

17. See Warren B. Walsh, "What the American People Think of Russia," *Public Opinion Quarterly* 8 (Winter 1944–45): 513–22.

18. Alan Green, "Not Just Allies—Friends," WR136; *Writers' War Board Script Catalog, November, 1945,* WR21; "Public Opinion Poll Gives Bad News for Mars," *Jackson (MS) Clarion-Ledger*, April 16, 1945. Although the WWB could not have known at the time, *Death and Dr. Burdenko* was an unfortunate choice as a War Script of the Month. Far from being a hero, Burdenko had headed the Russian commission that investigated the Katyn Massacre of Polish officers and erroneously concluded that German troops had carried out the killings. Many years later the Russians admitted that they were to blame. See Anna M. Cienciala, Natalia S. Lebedeva, and Wojciech Materski, eds., *Katyn: A Crime without Punishment* (New Haven, CT: Yale University Press, 2007), 226–29. Duranty also had a problem with accuracy. His incorrect reports about Soviet conditions in the 1930s—particularly his denial of the Ukrainian famine—led to calls for withdrawing his Pulitzer Prize after his death. Karl E. Meyer,

"The Editorial Notebook; Trenchcoats, Then and Now," *New York Times*, June 24, 1990; Sally J. Taylor, *Stalin's Apologist: Walter Duranty, the New York Times's Man in Moscow* (New York: Oxford University Press, 1990).

19. Richard E. Lauterbach, *These Are the Russians* (New York: Harper and Brothers, 1945); Lauterbach, "Russians Are People—and a Lot Like Us," *Brief House Organ Items from the Writers' War Board*, May 1945, WR36; Board Minutes, April 21, 1945, SP47.

20. Robert Bellaire, "Russia in the Pacific," WR57. For one example of publication, see *Burlington (NC) Daily Times-News*, June 2, 1945.

21. George Fielding Eliot, "Confidence Is a Lot of Little Things," *Brief Army Camp Items*, December 1945, WR76.

22. "Canada Bars Dreiser from Making Talks," *New York Times*, September 22, 1942; Joseph Griffin, "Theodore Dreiser Visits Toronto," *Canadian Review of American Studies* 14 (March 1983): 31–48.

23. "WWB News Release," September 24, 1942, WR111; "Writers Assail Dreiser," *New York Times*, September 25, 1942.

24. Theodore Dreiser to WWB, October 31, 1942, WR111. The letter may also be found in Helen Dreiser, *My Life with Dreiser* (New York: World Publishing, 1951), 282–84.

25. Dreiser to WWB, October 31, 1942, WR111.

26. Griffin, "Theodore Dreiser Visits Toronto," 47–48.

27. Paul Gallico, form letters to writers and commentators, January 1943, WR75; "Minutes of the Meeting of the United Nations Committee, December 1, 1942," WR75.

28. Oscar Schisgall, "The Clark and the Clurk," *Collier's,* March 13, 1943, 70–81.

29. "Minutes of the Meeting of the United Nations Committee."

30. Rex Stout to Margaret Leech, December 14, 1942, WR77; Paul Gallico to Stephen Fry, December 19, 1942, WR77.

31. Martha McCleery to Win Nathanson, April 21, 1943, WR5.

32. John Bartlet Brebner and Allan Nevins, *The Making of Modern Britain: A Short History* (New York: Norton, 1943); Board Minutes, June 16, 1943, SP47.

33. John Cornos, "Two Countries—One Heritage," *New York Times,* July 25, 1943.

34. "List of Well Known Writers to Prepare Scripts and Broadcasts in Foreign Languages for Office of War Information Overseas," WR68; Hollister Noble to Frederica Barach, July 19, 1943; Barach to Marion White, September 4, 1943, both WR68; "Progress Report on America and Americans Abroad," WR68.

35. Charles M. Hulton, "How the OWI Operates Its Overseas Propaganda Machine," *Journalism Quarterly* 19 (December 1942): 349–55.

36. Hollister Noble to Frederica Barach, March 20, 1943, WR64; Board Minutes, March 24, 1943, SP47; Barach to Noble, May 11, 1943, WR64; *Second Annual Report*, 20–21.

37. Robert Sherwood to Rex Stout, July 6, 1943, WR64; Board Minutes, June 30, 1943, SP47; *Second Annual Report*, 20–21. Translations of Pearl Buck's article into Egyptian and Icelandic are in WR64, and articles by other prominent authors may be found in WR64–67.

38. Joseph Wood Krutch to WWB, December 2, 1943; Clifton Fadiman to Krutch, December 11, 1943; Frederica Barach to Malcolm Young, February 12, 1945, all WR64.

39. "Projects in 1943 for OWI Overseas," WR68; Board Minutes, June 30, 1943, SP47; Barach to WWB, November 3, 1943, WR68.

40. *The Studio, An Illustrated Magazine of Fine and Applied Art*, June 1944.

41. "Minutes of the Meeting of the United Nations Committee, January 6, 1943," WR75; "*Transatlantic* Magazine," WR124; Geoffrey Crowther, "Transatlantic Commentary," *Transatlantic*, September 1943, 3.

42. John G. Winant to Rex Stout, January 7, 1943; Edward Wood, Lord Halifax, to Stout, January 28, 1943, both WR124.

43. "*Transatlantic* Magazine—Final Memorandum of Working Agreement," February 5, 1943, WR124; "*Transatlantic* Magazine," WR124; *Second Annual Report*, 22, 27; "*Transatlantic*," *Time and Tide*, June 15, 1943, 18–19.

44. Crowther, "Transatlantic Commentary," 3.

45. Ibid.; Crowther, "Transatlantic Commentary," *Transatlantic*, November 1943, 3; Board Minutes, September 8, 1943, SP47.

46. *Transatlantic*, September–December 1943.

47. *Second Annual Report*, 22–23; "Minutes of the Meeting of the *Transatlantic* Committee, May 23, 1944," WR124; "Three Quarters of an Anniversary," *Writers' War Board Report*, June 1, 1944; Alan Green to Margaret Leech, April 20, 1944, WR124; "*Transatlantic*: New Magazine's Mission," *Times* (London), September 6, 1943; WWB, *Third Annual Report* (New York: WWB, 1945), 26–27. Containers WR119–21 have correspondence on the content of *Transatlantic*. One example of a *Transatlantic* article reprinted elsewhere is Stuart Chase, "What the TVA Means," *Reader's Digest*, October 1944, 37–40.

48. Frederica Barach to WWB, October 25, 1943, WR75; Adelaide Sherer to Barach, November 24, 1943, WR74; Franklin D. Roosevelt, "Radio Address on the National War Fund Drive," October 5, 1943, in John T. Woolley and Gerhard Peters, The American Presidency Project, http://www.presidency.ucsb.edu/ws/?pid=16322; "Radio Requests—1943 Campaign, National War Fund," WR75.

49. Benjamin R. Andrews, "Food for Freedom," *Journal of Home Economics* 36 (January 1944): 22–23; "Harold Weston 1894–1972," in "Realism and War," Harold Weston Foundation, 2016, http://www.haroldweston.org/life7.html; George Woodbridge et al., *UNRRA: The History of the United Nations Relief and Rehabilitation Administration* (New York: Columbia University Press, 1950), 1:281–89. After 1945 the new postwar organization (also called the United Nations) took over the operation of the UNRRA.

50. Frederica Barach to WWB, May 20, 1944, WR88; Board Minutes, June 14, 1944, SP47; "Harold Weston 1894–1972."

51. Alan Green to WWB, July 25, 1944, WR88; Woodbridge, *UNRRA*, 1:148–49, 236–37.

52. Green to Luise Sillcox, July 29, 1944, WR88; Board Minutes, July 26, 1944, SP47.

53. "Food and Relief Committee Meeting," September 20, 1944, WR88.

54. Paul Gallico to Rex Stout, [April 1943?], WR82.

55. Board Minutes, September 6, 20, 1944, SP47.

56. E. F. Penrose, *Economic Planning for the Peace* (Princeton, NJ: Princeton University Press, 1953), 140–42, 151–53, 164–66.
57. Ibid.; Alan Green to Rita Weiman, September 12, 1944, WR88.
58. Lizzie Collingham, *The Taste of War: World War II and the Battle for Food* (New York: Penguin, 2012), 477–79.
59. *Third Annual Report*, 26; Woodbridge, *UNRRA*, 1:69; "Mike Steps Up," *Time*, December 25, 1944, 18; Harold Weston to Alan Green, January 20, 1945, WR88.
60. "Be Thrifty with Food," *Writers' War Board Report*, January 1, 1945.
61. "Editorial Service," WR57. An example of nationwide publication is "Food for Friends," *Kokomo (IN) Tribune*, December 29, 1944.
62. Board Minutes, January 17, 1945, SP47.
63. Lawrence Beller to WWB, January 26, 1945, WR90; "United Clothing Collection," January 26, 1945, WR30; "Winter's Coming: United National Clothing Collection," *New Yorker*, July 7, 1945, 15–16. For examples of the publication of statements by prominent individuals, see Sinclair Lewis, "Suggestion: United Clothing Collection," *Rotarian*, April 1945, 18, and Fannie Hurst, "Life-Saving Roundup," *Independent Woman*, April 1945, 107–9.
64. "Editorial Service." One example of nationwide publication is "Their Sunday Best," *Brownsville (TX) Herald*, March 30, 1945.
65. "Special Problem—United National Clothing Collection," *Bulletin to Cartoonists*, April 1945, WR12; "Editorial Service"; "The Capture of 30,000 Cats," *Writers' War Board Report*, March 1, 1945.
66. John W. Dower, *War without Mercy: Race and Power in the Pacific War* (New York: Pantheon, 1986), 53.
67. This National Opinion Research Center poll is cited in Harry H. Field and Louise Van Patten, "If the American People Make the Peace," *Public Opinion Quarterly* 8 (Winter 1944–45): 500–512.
68. Material on the imprisonment of Japanese Americans in the United States during World War II is drawn from Greg Robinson, *By Order of the President: FDR and the Internment of Japanese Americans* (Cambridge, MA: Harvard University Press, 2001).
69. Wallace Irwin, "K.O. for Japanese Shrines," *American Legion Magazine*, April 1944, 19, 34; "Our Enemy—Madame Butterfly," WR128; "A Story from the Pacific," WR128.
70. Board Minutes, January 19, 1944, SP47.
71. Board Minutes, January 31, 1944, SP47.
72. "If He Be Not Fair to Me," *Writers' War Board Report*, October 1, 1944.
73. Alan Green to Rex Stout, February 25, 1944, WR82; Board Minutes, March 1, 1944, SP47.
74. Stout to Julian Brodie, March 9, 1944, WR82.
75. "Editorial Service"; "Hirohito Must Go," *Bend (OR) Bulletin*, May 4, 1944. This newspaper noted WWB authorship, a rare acknowledgment.
76. Board Minutes, August 23, 1944, SP47; "Recommended List of Books on Japan," WR82.
77. Board Minutes, September 6, 1944, SP47.

78. Board Minutes, September 20, 1944, SP47.

79. Rex Stout to George Marshall, October 19, 1944; Henry L. Stimson to Stout, November 15, 1944, both WR82.

80. Stout to James Forrestal, November 21, 1944; Forrestal to Stout, November 23, 1944; Stout to Edward R. Stettinius, November 21, 1944; Stettinius to Stout, November 24, 1944, all WR82.

81. Elmer Davis to Stout, December 1, 1944, WR82.

82. "Japanese Quiz for Writers," *Writers' War Board Report*, November 1, 1944.

83. Clifton Fadiman to J. B. Powell, August 28, 1944, WR82.

84. Powell, "After We Have Occupied Japan," *American Legion Magazine*, November 1944, 16, 48–50; Carl Crow, "The Emperor Must Go," *American Legion Magazine*, January 1945, 19, 34–37.

85. Alan Green to Frederica Barach, April 21, 1944, WR11.

86. Clifton Fadiman to Sheldon Mayer, September 21, 1944, WR11.

87. Christopher LaFarge, "What Is the Writers' War Board?" November 1944, WR93; *Third Annual Report*, 19.

88. "Plant You Now, Hirohito, Dig You Later," *Writers' War Board Report*, June 1, 1945; "Editorial Service"; "Why Coddle Hirohito," *Corsicana (TX) Semi-Weekly Light*, June 22, 1945; Jimmy Young, "The Emperor Eats Octopus for Lunch," *Brief Army Camp Items*, June 1945, WR36; "Shall We Let Japan Off Easy?" *Florence (SC) Morning News*, July 24, 1945.

89. Edgar Salinger, "Statement Concerning the Emperor of Japan," October 1944, WR82.

90. "Letter and Statement to Commentators and Columnists," July 9, 1945, WR89; "Progress Report on Anti-Japanese Campaign," WR82.

91. Rex Stout, "Books and the Tiger," *New York Times Book Review*, March 21, 1943, 11; John W. Dower, "Race, Language, and War in Two Cultures: World War II in Asia," in *The World War Two Reader*, ed. Gordon Martel (New York: Routledge, 2004), 226.

92. "The *Fortune* Survey," *Fortune*, February 1942, 97.

93. "Public Opinion Polls," *Public Opinion Quarterly* 7 (Fall 1943): 478–505. Forty percent said that the German people might not like war but were too easily misled; 27 percent made a similar statement about the Japanese.

94. "Syndicated Messages from Nero Wolfe and Other Famous Fictional Characters," WR6.

95. Thomas Craven, form letter to writers, August 17, 1942, WR9.

96. "Summary of Writers' War Board Activities—September, 1942," WR8; WWB, *First Annual Report* (New York: WWB, 1943), 21–22. See Poster Committee Reports, August–December 1942, November 10, 1943, WR9.

97. "Bibliocaust," *Time*, May 22, 1933, 23; Council on Books in Wartime, *A History of the Council on Books in Wartime, 1942-1946* (New York: Country Life, 1946), 5-7.

98. *First Annual Report*, 20–21; WWB, foreword to Stephen Vincent Benet, *They Burned the Books* (New York: Farrar and Rinehart, 1942), vii.

99. "Report on Activities of the May 10 Book-Burning Committee," WR5;

Council on Books in Wartime, *History of the Council*, 7; *First Annual Report*, 20–21; Leon Feuchtwanger, letter to the editor, *New York Times*, May 11, 1942; Benet, *They Burned the Books*, vii, 3–4.

100. "Report on Activities of the May 10 Book-Burning Committee."

101. WWB, foreword to *They Burned the Books*, vi; "War Scripts of the Month Selections"; Benet, "They Burned the Books," *Saturday Review of Literature*, May 8, 1943, 3–5; Benet, "They Burned the Books," *Scholastic*, September 14, 1942, 25–28; "Report on Activities of the May 10 Book-Burning Committee"; Council on Books in Wartime, *History of the Council*, 7.

102. U.S. Holocaust Memorial Museum, "Fighting the Fires of Hate: America and the Nazi Book Burners," https://www.ushmm.org/exhibition/book-burning/war.php.

103. "Report on Activities of the May 10 Book-Burning Committee."

104. Ibid.; Writers' War Committee to presidents of American colleges and universities, April 24, 1942, WR5; U.S. Holocaust Memorial Museum, "Fighting the Fires of Hate"; Council on Books in Wartime, *History of the Council*, 16–17.

105. U.S. Holocaust Memorial Museum, "Fighting the Fires of Hate"; "Burning of the Books Anniversary Well Publicized," *Publishers Weekly*, May 1, 1943, 1721–23.

106. "Horror in Lidice," *Newsweek*, June 22, 1942, 41–42; Holocaust Education and Research Team, "The Massacre of Lidice," http://www.holocaustresearchproject.org/nazioccupation/ lidice.html.

107. Lidice Committee Minutes, July 15, 1942, WR54.

108. "Report of the Lidice Committee, June 26, 1942," WR54; "Summary of Writers' War Board Activities—September, 1942"; Clifton Fadiman to Elmer Davis, September 11, 1942, WR54.

109. Fadiman, "Committee Report: Lidice Lives Committee," October 1942, WR54; George Bernard Shaw to Fadiman, August 21, 1942, WR53.

110. Fadiman, "Report: Lidice Lives Committee."

111. "Lidice, Illinois," *New York Times*, June 30, 1942; "Summary of Writers' War Board Activities—September, 1942"; "World Awaits Rebirth of Lidice Tomorrow," *Chicago Sun*, July 11, 1942.

112. Clifton Fadiman, "Report: Lidice Lives Committee"; "New Lidice," *Newsweek*, July 20, 1942, 28; Eddie Doherty, "Lidice Reborn as Thousands Honor Martyrs," *Chicago Sun*, July 13, 1942; Wendell Willkie, quoted in "Rebirth of Lidice Hailed by Leaders," *New York Times*, July 13, 1942.

113. "Rebirth of Lidice Hailed by Leaders"; "New Lidice"; Fadiman, "Report: Lidice Lives Committee." WR145 is a scrapbook about the renaming ceremony.

114. "Lidice, in Illinois," *New York Times*, July 14, 1942.

115. Alan Green, interview; "Summary of Writers' War Board Activities—September, 1942"; Clifton Fadiman, "Report: Lidice Lives Committee"; Henry A. Wallace, quoted in "New Lidice in Mexico Hailed by Wallace," *New York Times*, August 31, 1942.

116. Fadiman, "Report: Lidice Lives Committee"; "Summary of Writers' War Board Activities—September, 1942"; "Quebec Town to Change Name," *New York Times*, September 18, 1942; "Not Changing Name to Lidice," *New York Times*, September 22,

1942; "Name Township Here for Martyred Lidice," *Montreal Gazette,* November 17, 1942.

117. "Brazil to Have a Lidice," *New York Times,* June 12, 1943.

118. Clifton Fadiman, "Report: Lidice Lives Committee"; "To Perpetuate the Memory of Lidice," *New York Times,* October 13, 1942; *First Annual Report,* 18.

119. "Summary of Writers' War Board Activities—September, 1942"; "Model of Lidice Monument," *New York Times,* September 19, 1942.

120. "We Refuse to Die," *New York Times,* October 18, 1942; "Station WNEW Shoots the Bankroll in Ballyhoo of Lidice Star-Cast Tie-Up," *Variety,* October 21, 1942, 33; "War Scripts of the Month Selections"; Clifton Fadiman, "Report: Lidice Lives Committee."

121. "Summary of Writers' War Board Activities—September, 1942"; Robert Nathan, "Lidice," *This Week,* September 20, 1942, 2; Nathan, *The Darkening Meadows* (New York: Knopf, 1945), 15–16.

122. Jean Gould, *The Poet and Her Book, A Biography of Edna St. Vincent Millay* (New York: Dodd, Mead, 1969), 264; Edna St. Vincent Millay, quoted in "Miss Millay's 'Lidice,'" *Newsweek,* October 26, 1942, 72.

123. Nancy Milford, *Savage Beauty: The Life of Edna St. Vincent Millay* (New York: Random House, 2001), 470.

124. Clifton Fadiman, "Report: Lidice Lives Committee"; "Miss Millay's 'Lidice,'" 72; "The Radio, the Poet and the News," *Theatre Arts,* December 1942, 733–34; Gould, *The Poet and Her Book,* 264; Erik Barnouw, *The Golden Web* (New York: Oxford University Press, 1968), 168.

125. Edna St. Vincent Millay, *The Murder of Lidice* (New York: Harper and Brothers, 1942), 15, 24–25, 31–32.

126. WWB, quoted in "Miss Millay's 'Lidice,'" 72; Pearl Strachan, review of Edna St. Vincent Millay, *The Murder of Lidice, Christian Science Monitor,* November 14, 1942, 10; "The Radio, the Poet and the News," 735; review of Millay, *The Murder of Lidice, Variety,* October 21, 1942, 34.

127. "The Murder of Lidice," *Life,* October 19, 1942, 90–100; Millay, *The Murder of Lidice*; Millay, *Murder of Lidice Selections,* performed by Basil Rathbone with Blanche Yurka, Columbia Masterworks (11949-D to 11951-D), n.d., 78 rpm, 3 LPs; Clifton Fadiman, "Report: Lidice Lives Committee"; Harry Brown, "The Sanguine Singers," *Common Sense,* December 1942, 425.

128. Paul Fussell, *Wartime: Understanding and Behavior in the Second World War* (New York: Oxford University Press, 1990), 175.

129. Gould, *The Poet and Her Book,* 265; Edna St. Vincent Millay to Cass Canfield, October 1947, in *Letters of Edna St. Vincent Millay,* ed. Allan Roy Macdougall (New York: Harper and Brothers, 1952), 338.

130. Mike Chasar, "In D.C. with Edna St. Vincent Millay, Langston Hughes, and the Writers' War Board," Poetry and Popular Culture (blog), October 3, 2014, mikechasar.blogspot.com/ 2014/10/in-dc-with-edna-st-vincent-millay.html.

131. Clifton Fadiman, "Report: Lidice Lives Committee"; "Summary of Writers' War Board Activities—September, 1942"; Julian Street Jr. to Fadiman, August 7, 1942, WR54.

132. "Lidice Lives Committee Expenses through December 2, 1942," WR54; Fadiman to Joseph Davies, March 31, 1943, WR54.

133. "Germans Raze Villages and Slay Populations in Greece and France," *New York Times*, July 9, 1944; "Anniversary in Greece," *New York Times*, July 13, 1944; Alan Green to WWB, August 4, 1944, WR81; "U.S. Town Urged to Take Name of Distomo Destroyed by the Nazis with 1,100 Residents," *New York Times*, August 31, 1944; "Honor Martyred Heroes of Greece," *New York Times*, September 26, 1944; "Editorial Service." For an example of publication, see "Distomo—Successor to Lidice," *St. Cloud (MN) Times*, October 5, 1944.

134. "Cooperation with Commentators: Memorandum of a Meeting held March 4, 1943," WR8.

135. "Summary of Writers' War Board Activities—September, 1942"; Ben Hecht, "The Extermination of the Jews: 1. 'Remember Us,'" and Eugene Lyons, "The Extermination of the Jews: 2. 'Horror Unlimited,'" *American Mercury* 56 (February 1943): 194–202; Hecht, "Remember Us [abridged]," *Reader's Digest*, February 1943, 107–10.

136. Hecht, "Remember Us [abridged]," 108.

137. *Philadelphia Inquirer*, October 22, 1942. A copy of the newspaper's supplement is located in WR10.

138. Alvin Goldfarb, "The Holocaust on the Air: The Radio Plays of the Writers' War Board," *Journal of American Drama and Theatre* 8 (Spring 1996): 48–58; Morton Wishengrad, "The Battle of the Warsaw Ghetto," in *Radio Drama in Action: Twenty-Five Plays of a Changing World*, ed. Erik Barnouw (New York: Farrar and Rhinehart, 1945), 34–45; "War Scripts of the Month Selections."

139. Board Minutes, December 2, 1942, SP46; Clifton Fadiman to Dorothy Thompson, April 4, 1944, WR106.

140. Goldfarb, "Holocaust on the Air," 58.

141. "Nazi Killings Laid Bare in Camp," *New York Times*, August 30, 1944; *Third Annual Report*, 21; W. H. Lawrence, "Lest We Forget," *Reader's Digest*, November 1944, 32.

142. Board Minutes, July 22, 1942, SP46.

Chapter 5: The Controversial Hate Campaign

1. Thomas J. Fleming, *The Illusion of Victory: America in World War I* (New York: Basic Books, 2003), 135–36; "Sauerkraut May Be Liberty Cabbage," *New York Times*, April 25, 1918.

2. "Gallup and *Fortune* Polls," *Public Opinion Quarterly* 7 (Spring 1943): 161–78. Another 12 percent blamed both the German government and the German people while 3 percent had no opinion.

3. Louis Nizer, "What about the Good Germans?" *Brief Army Camp Items from the Writers' War Board*, April 1944, WR35; Sigrid Undset, "True Justice for the Germans," *Brief Army Camp Items*, November 1944, WR35.

4. "Editorial Service," WR57; Alan Green, "Maybe It's Just Some Guys Named Schmidt," *Traverse City (MI) Eagle*, December 23, 1944.

5. "Report of Committee on Creating a Stronger Feeling against the Enemy," October 24, 1942, WR13.

6. Board Minutes, September 20, 1942, SP46; "Committee Report of Committee on Creating a Stronger Feeling against the Enemy for Inclusion in the *First Annual Report*," WR13. Despite its title, the material does not appear in the *First Annual Report*.

7. WWB, *First Annual Report* (New York: WWB, 1943), 28; "Committee Report for *First Annual Report*"; Clifton Fadiman to WWB, April 1, 1943; Frederica Barach to Robert Landry, October 23, 1943, both WR23.

8. Steven Casey, "The Campaign to Sell a Harsh Peace for Germany to the American Public, 1944–1948," *History* 90 (January 2005): 62–92.

9. "How to Hate Germans Stirs Writers Group," *New York Times*, October 29, 1942.

10. "National Opinion Research Center Survey Results of November 22, 1942," WR10.

11. Board Minutes, November 11, 1942, SP46.

12. Casey, "Campaign to Sell a Harsh Peace," 67, 75.

13. Rick Atkinson, *An Army at Dawn: The War in North Africa, 1942–1943* (New York: Henry Holt, 2002), 461.

14. Paul Gallico, "Slant on Hate," WR8.

15. Carl Carmer, letter to author, April 10, 1969.

16. Rex Stout, "We Shall Hate or We Shall Fail," *New York Times Magazine*, January 17, 1943, 6, 29.

17. Letters to the editor, *New York Times*, January 21, 1943, with the comments of Lambert Fairchild, "Not Built That Way" and George L. Woolley, "Scriptural Injunction."

18. "Mr. Stout Notes Exceptions; He Finds Arguments of Critics of His Article Untenable," *New York Times*, January 23, 1943.

19. Walter R. Bowle, "Hate Is Moral Poison," *New York Times Magazine*, January 31, 1943, 15, 31.

20. Rex Stout, "Mr. Stout Replies," *New York Times*, February 4, 1943.

21. Zelia M. Walters, "Chesterton Quoted," *New York Times*, February 4, 1943.

22. J. Francis Murphy, "Good Hatred Needed," *New York Times*, February 4, 1943.

23. Board Minutes, February 3, 10, 1943, SP46.

24. "Cooperation with Commentators: Memorandum of a Meeting Held March 4, 1943," WR8; bullets added.

25. Ibid.

26. Clifton Fadiman to Walter Winchell, November 21, 1944, WR106; "Walter Winchell on Broadway," *Indianapolis Star*, December 1, 1944.

27. WWB, *Third Annual Report* (New York: WWB, 1945), 20–21; "Around the Cracker Barrel," *Writers' War Board Report*, June 1, 1944.

28. "Take Your Pick," *Brief House Organ Items*, May 1944, WR35.

29. Cecil Brown, "How to Tell a Fascist," *Brief Army Camp Items*, March 1944, WR35; *Bulletin to Cartoonists*, January 1945, WR81; *Third Annual Report*, 21.

30. Alex Somalman to Selma G. Hirsh, August 15, 1944; Sylvia Brodow to Sigrid Schultz, January 12, 1945, both WR81; Sigrid Schultz, "Fritz, the Story of a German

Boy," *Real Life Comics No. 22* (New York: Nedor, 1945), n.p.; Lorraine Beim, "A Loaf of Bread," *Real Life Comics No. 23* (New York: Nedor, 1945), n.p.

31. "War Scripts of the Month Selections," WR21; George Creel, *War Criminals and Punishment* (New York: R. M. McBride, 1944).

32. "Report to Date on Activities of the Committee on Speeches and Speakers," November 5, 1943, WR13; *War Speeches*, WR136.

33. "Report to Date on Activities of the Committee on Speeches"; "Activities of Assignments Committee," WR13; WWB, *Second Annual Report* (New York: WWB, 1944), 4.

34. Heinz Pol, *The Hidden Enemy: The German Threat to Post-War Peace* (New York: Julian Messner, 1943), 248, 256, 9–12, 17–19.

35. John Roy Carlson, *Under Cover: My Four Years in the Nazi Underworld of America—The Amazing Revelation of How Axis Agents and Our Enemies Within Are Now Plotting to Destroy the United States* (New York: Dutton, 1943).

36. Richard M. Brickner, *Is Germany Incurable?* (Philadelphia: Lippincott, 1943).

37. Henry Reed Hoke, *Black Mail* (New York: Readers Book Service, 1944), inside front cover, entitled "About the Author of Black Mail." Although domestic fascist movements did not prove to be a viable threat, they concerned many at the time. See, for example, F. Stuart Chapin, "Some Psychological Cross-Currents That May Affect Peace Plans," *American Sociology Review* 9 (February 1944): 21–27.

38. Sigrid Schultz, *Germany Will Try It Again* (New York: Reynal and Hitchcock, 1944); "Promotion Ideas for the Sigrid Schultz book *They'll* [sic] *Try It Again*," January 20, 1944, WR80.

39. Paul Winkler, *The Thousand Year Conspiracy: Secret Germany behind the Mask* (New York: Charles Scribner's Sons, 1943).

40. Board Minutes, October 6, 1943, SP47; Rosie Goldschmidt Waldeck, *Meet Mr. Blank, the Leader of Tomorrow's Germans* (New York: Putnam, 1943). For an example of a hostile review arranged by the WWB, see Leopold Schwarzschild, "The Countess [Waldeck] Draws a Blank," *The Nation*, November 6, 1943, 531.

41. Clifton Fadiman to W. W. Norton, September 2, 1944, WR81; George W. Schuster and Arnold Bergsträsser, *Germany: A Short History* (New York: Norton, 1944).

42. Rex Stout, "Books and the Tiger," *New York Times Book Review*, March 21, 1943, 11; "Panel Discussion on *Is Germany Incurable?*" *Saturday Review of Literature*, May 29, 1943, 6–10.

43. Lawrence Kubie et al., letter to the editor, *Saturday Review of Literature*, July 31, 1943, 17.

44. Clifton Fadiman to Maxwell C. Gaines, June 30, 1944, WR11.

45. For example, Rex Stout to Vince Fago, June 18, 1943, WR11.

46. Frederica Barach to Sheldon Mayer, November 13, 1944, WR11.

47. "Comic [Book] on Germany," November 17, 1944, WR11.

48. Gardner Fox, "This Is Our Enemy," *All-Star Comics No. 24* (New York: All-Star Comics, 1945), n.p.; Paul Gallico to WWB Advisory Council, February 13, 1945; Oscar Schisgall to Frederica Barach, December 7, 1944, both WR11.

49. Clifton Fadiman to Leo Rosten, March 6, 1943, WR52.

50. "Appraisal of Movies for WWB Ratings," WR12.

51. "Hangmen Also Die Promotion," WR78; Clifton Fadiman to William Fadiman, April 24, 1944, WR12.

52. *What to Do with Germany?* (March of Time)," *Writers' War Board Report*, November 1, 1944.

53. "Progress Report on *What to Do with Germany?*" WR81; "*What to Do with Germany?*" *Writers' War Board Report*, December 1, 1944; Gabriel Heatter, "Sanity—German Style," *Brief Army Camp Items*, January 1945, WR35.

54. Katherine E. R. Smith, *God Bless America: Tin Pan Alley Goes to War* (Lexington: University of Kentucky Press, 2003), 173–78.

55. Noel Coward, "Don't Let's Be Beastly to the Germans," in *The Complete Lyrics of Noel Coward*, ed. Barry Day (London: Methuen Drama, 1998), 207.

56. "How Should the United States Deal with Conquered Germany?" *Newsweek*, November 8, 1943, 106–10; Coward, "Don't Let's Be Beastly"; "Noel Coward Firm on Anti-Nazi Song," *New York Times*, October 25, 1943.

57. Clifton Fadiman to Frank Sullivan, November 8, 1943, WR79.

58. "Coward with Bludgeon," *Newsweek*, December 6, 1943, 94.

59. "Don't Let's Be Beastly to the Germans," *Writers' War Board Report*, January 1, 1944; *Second Annual Report*, 15.

60. "Editorial Service"; "Recipe for Civil War," *Gallup (NM) Independent*, September 14, 1944; "The German General Staff Goes on Forever," *McComb (MS) Daily Journal*, November 14, 1944; "Don't Say We Weren't Warned," *Star-Democrat* (Easton, MD), November 3, 1944. In a very favorable postwar account of Hitler's General Staff, one German historian essentially confirmed the WWB viewpoint. Walter Goerlitz, *History of the German General Staff, 1657–1945* (New York: Praeger, 1953).

61. Letters signed by Jackson Pollock, Booth Tarkington, and Dale Carnegie, WR79. See also Rex Stout to Somerset Maugham, December 27, 1943, WR79.

62. Franklin P. Adams, letter to the editor, *Indianapolis Star*, November 12, 1943.

63. Franklin Adams, "The Germans Hate the U.S.A.," *Brief Army Camp Items*, June 1944, WR35.

64. Clifton Fadiman to Jack Goodman, July 12, 1944, WR79; John Kieran, "Never Again," *American Legion Magazine*, June 1944, 9, 41; Paul Gallico, "Fathers and Sons," *American Legion Magazine*, July 1944, 22, 48; Sumner Welles, "What to Do with the Germans?" *American Legion Magazine*, October 1944, 6, 48; J. B. Powell, "After We've Occupied Japan," *American Legion Magazine*, November 1944, 16, 48–50.

65. William Shirer, "Soft Peace = World War III," *American Legion Magazine*, August 1944, 15, 37; Allan Nevins, "White-Washing the Nazis," *American Legion Magazine*, September 1944, 15, 29.

66. *Third Annual Report*, 21; Board Minutes, September 6, 1944, SP47.

67. Milton Mayer, "The Case against the Jew," *Saturday Evening Post*, March 28, 1942, 18.

68. Mayer, "The War Guilt of Fadiman Kip," *Common Sense*, January 1944, 34.

69. Board Minutes, January 12, 1944, SP47; Mayer, "War Guilt of Fadiman Kip." See also Mayer, "How to Win the War," *Politics* 1 (March 1944): 45–46.

70. Mayer, "War Guilt of Fadiman Kip."
71. Clifton Fadiman to Mayer, January 5, 1944, WR116.
72. Board Minutes, January 19, 1944, SP47.
73. Milton Mayer, "Are Japs Human?" *Common Sense*, April 1944, 140–41.
74. "Too Poor to Tote It," *Common Sense*, August 1944, 287–88.
75. Carl J. Friedrich, quoted in John McAleer, *Rex Stout: A Biography* (Boston: Little, Brown, 1977), 294.
76. Friedrich, "The Role and the Position of the Common Man," *American Journal of Sociology* 49 (March 1944): 421–29, 424, 427 (quotations).
77. Rex Stout, letter to the editor, *American Journal of Sociology* 50 (September 1944): 142.
78. Carl J. Friedrich, letter to the editor, *American Journal of Sociology* 50 (September 1944): 144; Friedrich, "Issues of Informational Strategy," *Public Opinion Quarterly* 7 (Spring 1943): 87.
79. Society for the Prevention of World War III, "It is Time to Call a Spade a Spade" (advertisement), *New York Times*, April 22, 1944.
80. Paul Tillich, quoted in "Council for a Democratic Germany Formed by Religious Leaders Here," *New York Times*, May 3, 1944.
81. "The Shame of American Writers," *Common Sense*, May 1944, 187.
82. Ibid.
83. Elmer Davis, quoted in "American Writers on Germany," *Common Sense*, June 1944, 206.
84. All quoted in ibid., 208, 206–7, 210.
85. All quoted in ibid., 207, 211, 212, 208.
86. WWB, letter to the editor, *Common Sense*, June 1944, 206.
87. Sidney Hertzberg, "The Points at Issue," *Common Sense*, June 1944, 206.
88. Hertzberg, "Review of the Year," *Common Sense*, February 1945, 2.
89. George E. Sokolsky, "These Days," *New York Sun*, January 16, 1945.
90. Board Minutes, May 17, 1944, SP47; Christopher LaFarge, "Postscript to 'Meet the Bruckners' by Max Lerner," WR22.
91. Board Minutes, May 24, 1944, January 12, 19, 1944, SP47. The board made no attempt to publish the three principles because it feared they might foster the idea that the war had already been won.
92. Board Minutes, May 24, 1944, SP47; Alan Green, "Questionnaire on 'What to Do with Germany?'" WR79; Green, interview by author, August 8, 1968.
93. Board Minutes, May 31, 1944, SP47.
94. Board Minutes, June 7, 14, 1944, SP47.
95. "The Position of the Writers' War Board on the German Problem," June 7, 1944, WR8.
96. Ibid.
97. Ibid.
98. Board Minutes, June 28, 1944, SP47; Lewis Gannett to Rex Stout, June 19, 1944, WR80.

99. Board Minutes, June 28, 1944, SP47.

100. Marion K. Sanders, *Dorothy Thompson: A Legend in Her Time* (Boston: Houghton Mifflin, 1973), 197–98, 276–77, 314–15.

101. See, for example, Dorothy Thompson, "The Nazi Retreat and Offensive," *San Francisco Chronicle*, September 20, 1943, and Thompson, "Europe Must Be Free for Peace," *San Francisco Chronicle*, October 7, 1943.

102. Thompson to the WWB, June 21, 1944, WR129.

103. Thompson to the WWB Advisory Council, June 21, 1944, WR80.

104. Board Minutes, July 5, 12, 1944, SP47; Rex Stout to Clifton Fadiman, July 10, 1944, WR80; "Reply of the WWB to the Analysis by Dorothy Thompson of the Board's Position on the German Problem," WR80.

105. "Forum in Turmoil over Reich's Guilt," *New York Times*, June 13, 1944.

106. Leonard Lyons, "The Lyons Den," *New York Post*, June 26, 1944.

107. Clifton Fadiman to Lyons, June 30, 1944; Frederick L. Schuman to Fadiman, July 2, 1944, both WR80; Board Minutes, June 28, 1944, SP47.

108. Schuman to WWB, July 1, 1944; Edward Earle to Fadiman, July 10, 1944; Bernadotte E. Schmitt to Fadiman, July 11, 1944; Fadiman to Schmitt, July 6, 1944, all WR80; Rex Stout, interview by author, August 14, 1968. Stout, who disagreed with these scholars, eventually felt vindicated when a German historian argued that Germany's goals were essentially the same in both world wars. Fritz Fischer, *Germany's Aims in the First World War* (New York: Norton, 1967).

109. Board Minutes, July 12, 1944, SP47; Stout to Fadiman, July 10, 1944; Gordon Cray to Fadiman, July 14 1944; Fadiman to Stout, July 20, 1944, all WR80.

110. "The Position of the Writers' War Board on the German Problem," July 19, 1944, WR80. The document is also included in *Third Annual Report*, 32–36.

111. "Report on 'The Position of the Writers' War Board on the German Problem,'" WR80; John P. Marquand to Alan Green, August 8, 1944, WR128.

112. "Report on 'The Position of the WWB'"; Katherine Brush to Clifton Fadiman, August 10, 1944; George S. Kaufman to Fadiman, August 12, 1944, both WR128.

113. Dorothy Thompson, "On the Record," *Pittsburgh Post Gazette*, August 9, 1944; Joseph Henry Jackson, "Bookman's Notebook," *San Francisco Chronicle*, August 10, 1944.

114. "The Germans," *Writers' War Board Report*, August 1, 1944.

115. "How to Keep Peace with Germany," *Look*, November 14, 1944, 21–25.

116. Harry Hansen, "The First Reader," *New York World-Telegram*, November 9, 1944; Rex Stout to Hansen, November 13, 1944, WR80. For an example of reprinting, see *Carrollton (KY) News*, February 8, 1945.

117. Board Minutes, May 24, June 21, 1944, SP47.

118. Clifton Fadiman to Lester Markel, June 21, 1944, WR80. Fadiman referred to the article "When Germany Cracks: What Will Happen?" *New York Times Magazine*, June 18, 1944, 11, 38.

119. Dorothy Dunbar Bromley, "Many Reich Women Seen Favoring U.S.," *New York Herald-Tribune*, June 27, 1944; Fadiman to Helen Rogers Reid, June 30, 1944, WR80.

120. Fadiman to the Fellowship of Reconciliation, August 17, 1944, WR80; Arno Herzberg to Leland Stowe, August 20, 1944, WR81; Alan Green to Kenneth Leslie, July 31, 1944, WR81.

121. CBS, *Fairness of the Air*, WR25; Board Minutes, August 23, 1944, SP47; Fadiman to WWB, August 24, 1944, WR25; "Time for Decision," *Variety*, August 30, 1944, 25.

122. "Teach Them a Lesson," *Common Sense*, October 1944, 358.

123. Dorothy Thompson, "U.S. Must Be Hard-Headed Too," *San Francisco Chronicle*, October 4, 1944.

124. "The Stout Ire," *Newsweek*, October 30, 1944, 48–49; "Rex Stout Quits Freedom House," *New York Times*, October 21, 1944; "Dorothy Thompson Quits over Stout," *New York Times*, October 23, 1944; "Board Won't Let Two Quit," *New York Times*, October 25, 1944; McAleer, *Rex Stout*, 331.

125. Reinhold Niebuhr to Margaret Widdemar, November 3, 1944, WR88.

126. Paul Gallico to Niebuhr, November 17, 1944; Hiram Motherwell to Gallico, November 29, 1944, both WR88.

127. Robert L. Duffus to Frederica Barach, October 29, 1944, WR57.

128. Rex Stout to Duffus, October 31, 1944, WR58.

129. "Editorial Service"; "War Scripts of the Month Selections"; "Seeing Is Believing," *Writers' War Board Report*, January 1, 1945.

130. Christopher LaFarge, "The Shock Is Late," WR82, and many newspapers including the *Canonsburg (PA) Daily Notes*, June 15, 1945.

131. Board Minutes, June 20, 1945, SP47; "Method to Indict a Whole People," *Arizona Republic* (Phoenix), July 22, 1945.

132. "Editorial Service"; "The Neatest Trick of the Month," *Bradford (PA) Era*, July 18, 1945.

133. Arnold Hartley, *Loving Cups for Murderers*, WR21.

134. Board Minutes, January 17, February 7, 1945, SP47; "Minutes of the First Meeting of the Writers' War Board Committee on POWs," WR81.

135. Board Minutes, March 7, 1945, SP47; "Legion of Despair," *Time*, March 19, 1945, 20–21.

136. "For What I Am," *Time*, June 18, 1945, 26; "Editorial Service."

137. "The German Hitler Feared," *Time*, May 21, 1945, 72; "For What I Am"; G. Bromley Oxnam, "Niemöller Today," *Christian Century*, June 13, 1945, 705–6.

138. Alan Green, "The Pastor Couldn't Fool the GI," WR57, and newspapers such as the *Waukesha (WI) Daily Freeman*, July 27, 1945.

139. Ibid.

140. Eleanor Roosevelt, quoted in G. Bromley Oxnam, "The Attack on Niemöller," *Christian Century*, August 29, 1945, 977–78.

141. "Why Attack Niemöller?" *Christian Century*, September 12, 1945, 1031–32.

142. See, for example, George Rosen, letter to the editor, *Christian Century*, September 29, 1945, 1097–98. The isolationist *Chicago Tribune* used the *Christian Century* article to claim that the WWB was trying to smear Niemöller and wrongly attacked Stout as a "former part owner [of the] . . . *New Masses*, official Communist

newspaper." John Evans, "Trace Attack on Niemöller to WWB 'Smear,'" *Chicago Tribune*, September 9, 1945.

143. Rex Stout, letter to the editor, *Christian Century*, November 21, 1945, 1290. The two pieces to which Stout referred were Ewart Edmund Turner, "The Prisoner of Sachsenhausen," *Christian Century*, June 28, 1939, 818–19, and Paul Hutchinson, "The Strange Case of Pastor Niemöller," *Atlantic Monthly*, October 1937, 514–20.

144. Hutchinson, editorial comment (on Stout's letter to the editor), *Christian Century*, November 21, 1945, 1290.

145. See "The German Hitler Feared"; "For What I Am," 26, 28; "Always a German," *Newsweek*, June 18, 1945, 52, 54; "Niemöller Explains," *Newsweek*, December 16, 1946, 88; and "Down to Size," *Time*, February 3, 1947, 29–30.

146. Lewis Mumford, "German Apologists and the German Record," *Saturday Review of Literature*, August 11, 1945, 5–6, 28, 30; Rex Stout to Mumford, May 19, 1945, WR82.

147. Mumford, "German Apologists," 5–6, 28.

148. "Writers' War Board Themes," WR20. For an example of a work that supports the board's positions, see Daniel Jonah Goldhagen, *Hitler's Willing Executioners: Ordinary Germans and the Holocaust* (New York: Knopf, 1996).

149. Alan Green, interview; Rex Stout, interview; Clifton Fadiman, letter to author, February 17, 1969; Paul Gallico, letter to author, March 17, 1969; Margaret Leech, letter to author, March 12, 1969; Rita Halle Kleeman, letter to author, March 14, 1969; Robert Landry, letter to author, September 28, 1970.

Chapter 6: Shaping the Peace

1. "If the War Ended Today," *Time*, July 20, 1942, 74.

2. Michaela Hönicke, "'Know Your Enemy': American Wartime Images of Germany, 1942–1943," in *Enemy Images in American History*, ed. Ragnhild Fiebig-von Hase and Ursula Lehmkuhl (Oxford: Berghahn, 1997), 234–37, 246–48.

3. "Humanity vs. Germany," *Newsweek*, November 1, 1943, 94.

4. "A Book You Must Read," *Writers' War Board Report*, November 1, 1943.

5. Robert Gilbert Vansittart, *Lessons of My Life* (New York: Knopf, 1943).

6. Emil Ludwig, *How to Treat the Germans* (New York: Willard, 1943), 75–82.

7. Sumner Welles, *The Time for Decision* (New York: Harper and Brothers, 1944); Board Minutes, July 12, 1944, SP47; Welles, "How to Stop the Third World War Now," *Brief Army Camp Items*, October 1944, WR35; Welles, "What to Do with the Germans," *American Legion Magazine*, October 1944, 6, 48; Townsend Hoopes and Douglas Brinkley, *FDR and the Creation of the U.N.* (New Haven, CT: Yale University Press, 2000), 129.

8. Louis Nizer, *What to Do with Germany* (Chicago: Ziff-Davis, 1944). For an example of the WWB promotion of this and other books, see the advertisement for *What to Do with Germany* in the *Chicago Tribune*, January 30, 1944.

9. James K. Pollock, review of Heinz Pol, *The Hidden Enemy: The German Threat to Post-War Peace*, *American Political Science Review* 38 (April 1944): 383.

10. Pol, *The Hidden Enemy: The German Threat to Post-War Peace* (New York: Julian Messner, 1943), 252–53, 260–62.

11. Steven Casey, "The Campaign to Sell a Harsh Peace for Germany to the American Public, 1944–1948," *History* 90 (January 2005): 62–92; "Urges Execution of 1,500,000 Germans," *New York Times*, May 23, 1945.

12. John McAleer, *Rex Stout: A Biography* (Boston: Little, Brown, 1977), 306.

13. John Morton Blum, *From the Morgenthau Diaries*, vol. 3, *Years of War, 1941–1945* (Boston: Houghton Mifflin, 1967), 343–59; Warren F. Kimball, *Swords or Ploughshares? The Morgenthau Plan for Defeated Nazi Germany, 1943–1946* (New York: Lippincott, 1976), 25–31.

14. Blum, *From the Morgenthau Diaries*, 3:359–76; Steven Casey, *Cautious Crusade: Franklin D. Roosevelt, Public Opinion, and the War against Nazi Germany* (New York: Oxford University Press, 2001), 183–85.

15. Blum, *From the Morgenthau Diaries*, 3:377.

16. Casey, *Cautious Crusade*, 185–89.

17. Rex Stout to Franklin D. Roosevelt, September 29, 1944, WR81; "Reparations and Security Campaign," December 6, 1944, WR81; Board Minutes, October 4, 1944, SP47.

18. "Reparations and Security Campaign"; Board Minutes, October 4, 1944, SP47; Frederica Barach to WWB, "Re: Meeting with Robert Sherwood," October 3, 1944, WR81. Sherwood apparently changed his opinion of the plan, referring to its "dangerous implications" three years later. Robert Sherwood, *Roosevelt and Hopkins: An Intimate History* (New York: Harper and Brothers, 1948), 832.

19. Board Minutes, October 4, 1944, SP47.

20. Henry Morgenthau Jr. to Rex Stout, October 6, 1944, WR81; "Reparations and Security Campaign."

21. Casey, "Campaign to Sell a Harsh Peace," 78–79.

22. "Notes on Current Thinking on Post-War Germany," WR81; Board Minutes, November 15, 1944, SP47. See also Shephard B. Clough, "What about Reparations This Time?" *Political Science Quarterly* 59 (June 1944): 220–26.

23. "Notes on Current Thinking on Post-War Germany."

24. Ibid.

25. "Reparations and Security Campaign"; Board Minutes, November 15, 1944, SP47.

26. "Reparations and Security Campaign."

27. "If He Yells for Reparations, He's Giving a Hand to World War III," *Writers' War Board Report*, November 1, 1944; "Reparations and Security Campaign."

28. Rex Stout, "You Have to Give to Get," *Brief Army Camp Items*, January 1945, WR35; "Editorial Service," WR57; "What Do We Want?" WR58. For examples of publication, see "Reparations Booby Trap," *Fort Lauderdale (FL) News*, November 9, 1944, and "What Do We Want?" *Opelousas (LA) Daily World*, January 31, 1945.

29. Board Minutes, December 6, 1944, SP47.

30. Paul Gallico, quoted in "Memoranda on Post-War Germany," WR81.

31. Samuel Grafton, Robert Colwell, and Alan Green, quoted in ibid.

32. "Tabulation of Results on What to Do with Germany," WR81.

33. Robert Colwell, quoted in "Memoranda on Post-War Germany." See also Christopher LaFarge's statement on reeducation in ibid.

34. "Tabulation of Results on What to Do with Germany."

35. WWB, *Third Annual Report* (New York: WWB, 1945), 36–37.

36. "What to Do with Germany after the War," WR81, and *See*, January 1945, 31.

37. "Reparations and Security Campaign"; Board Minutes, February 14, 1945, SP47.

38. Rex Stout to WWB, November 18, 1942, WR1.

39. Stout, quoted in "Sharp Responses Made to Lindbergh," *New York Times*, April 25, 1941.

40. "Comics Committee Progress Report," May 15, 1944, WR11.

41. Anthony Hyde to WWB, April 27, 1943, WR57; "United Nations Day, June 14, [1945]," WR56; *War Speeches*, WR136; "War Scripts of the Month Selections," WR21; Howard Fast, "Tomorrow Will Be Ours," *Scholastic*, May 8, 1944, 13–14.

42. WWB, *Second Annual Report* (New York: WWB, 1944), 19; "One World Pledge Urged by Willkie," *New York Times*, July 5, 1943.

43. Board Minutes, November 18, 1942, SP46.

44. WWB to Joseph Ball, March 19, 1943; Carl Hatch to Rex Stout, March 24, 1943, both WR82; "Eden Asks Caution in Peace Planning," *New York Times*, March 19, 1943; Philip J. Briggs, *Making American Foreign Policy from the Second World War to the Post-Cold War Era*, 2nd ed. (Lanham, MD: Rowan and Littlefield, 1994), 24–28.

45. Kenneth W. Colegrove, *The American Senate and World Peace* (New York: Vanguard, 1944).

46. Rex Stout, "The Post-War World," *Brief House Organ Items*, July 1943, WR35; *Third Annual Report*, 22; Fredric March, "The Price of Freedom," *Brief Army Camp Items*, May 1944, WR35; H. V. Kaltenborn, "United We Stand," *Brief Army Camp Items*, August 1944, WR35.

47. Frederica Barach to Theodore Granik, July 17, 1943; Barach to WWB, August 10, 1943, both WR21; *Second Annual Report*, 19; Christopher LaFarge, "The Simple Idea," WR75.

48. *War Speeches*.

49. *Writers' War Board Script Catalog, November, 1945*, WR21; Norman Corwin, *Untitled and Other Radio Dramas* (New York: Henry Holt, 1947), 45–76.

50. Board Minutes, November 8, 1944, SP47.

51. Clifton Fadiman to Elmer Davis, December 13, 1944, WR23; *Second Annual Report*, 19; "Guest Speakers on Opera Victory Rallies, Season 1943–44," WR23. For a general description of the Victory Rallies, see Paul Jackson, *Saturday Afternoons at the Old Met: The Metropolitan Opera Broadcasts, 1931–1950* (Portland, OR: Amadeus, 1992), 328.

52. Board Minutes, November 24, 1943, SP47.

53. "Post-War Pitch Goes to Plush Audiences, Too; Met Opera Sponsors Forum," *Billboard*, December 4, 1943, 10; "End of Nazi Party Urged by Masaryk," *New York Times*, December 5, 1943.

54. Wendell Willkie, quoted in "Willkie Criticizes Railroad Seizure," *New York Times*, January 9, 1944.

55. Henry Wallace, quoted in "Wallace Demands Peace with Power," *New York Times*, April 2, 1944. "Guest Speakers on Opera Victory Rallies" lists others who gave addresses for the WWB including Elmer Davis, Jan Masaryk, Archibald MacLeish, Senator Harley M. Kilgore, Rex Stout, and Dr. Thomas Parran. The day after they spoke, the *New York Times* regularly printed their speeches in whole or in part. WR23 and WR24 contain several of the full texts.

56. Board Minutes, October 27, 1943, November 8, 1944, SP47.

57. John W. Davis, quoted in "J. W. Davis Backs Oaks Peace Plans," *New York Times*, December 10, 1944; "Metropolitan Victory Rallies: The Fight for Peace," WR23. Some of the speakers that the WWB put on the air in 1944–45 were Sinclair Lewis, Elmer Davis, Henry J. Kaiser, Robert Bellaire, Joseph C. Grew, Herbert Lehman, Raymond Gram Swing, and Christopher LaFarge.

58. *Third Annual Report*, 22–23; "Car Card News Release," September 11, 1944, WR88; Rex Stout to John H. Delaney, September 14, 1944, WR88; "Only Subways Refuse Car-Card for World Cooperation," WR88; "Admits Barring Poster," *New York Times*, September 12, 1944; Walter Winchell, "On Broadway," *Lincoln (NE) Evening Journal*, September 23, 1944.

59. Alan Green, interview by author, August 8, 1968; Stout to R. Rothschild, June 25, 1943, WR87; *Second Annual Report*, 18.

60. Stout to R. Rothschild, June 25, 1943, WR87; Stout to Booth Tarkington, June 15, 1943, WR87; Board Minutes, June 16, 1943, SP47; Clifton Fadiman to Stout, August 24, 1943, WR87.

61. *Second Annual Report*, 27.

62. "Pledge for Peace Is Supported by Justice Roberts," *Baltimore Sun*, November 12, 1943; Carl Carmer, letter to author, March 25, 1969.

63. *Second Annual Report*, 18.

64. "Pledge against War Pushed by Authors," *New York Times*, November 12, 1943; "Debut of a Pledge," *Writers' War Board Report*, December 1, 1943.

65. "Editorial Service"; "Debut of a Pledge"; "A Pledge to Win the Peace," *Brief House Organ Items*, November 25, 1943, WR35. For examples of publication, see "Prescription for Peace," *Argus-Leader* (Sioux Falls, SD), October 6, 1945; "A Four-Square Peace," *Huron (SD) Daily Plainsman*, November 18, 1943; and "The Bugaboo of Sovereignty," *Wisconsin Rapids Daily Tribune*, January 17, 1944.

66. "Report on the Pledge for Peace Campaign," July 1944, WR82. For an example of the publication of the Pledge for Peace, see *Parents' Magazine*, September 1944, 155.

67. "Report on the Pledge for Peace Campaign"; *Second Annual Report*, 18; *Third Annual Report*, 24–25; Board Minutes, March 29, July 12, August 2, 1944, SP47.

68. "Report on the Pledge for Peace Campaign"; *Third Annual Report*, 24–25; Board Minutes, May 10, July 5, 1944, SP47.

69. "Why 'Pledge for Peace' Plays Isolationist Game," *Philadelphia (PA) Record*, May 22, 1944. The *Record*'s typically supportive attitude is illustrated by a second editorial printed alongside it, "Nazis Keep on Fighting in Hopes of a Soft Peace."

70. Board Minutes, May 24, 1944, SP47.
71. Philip Wylie, "Off My Chest," *Nebraska State Journal* (Lincoln), August 27, 1944.
72. "Is This When You Stand?" *Writers' War Board Report*, August 1, 1944.
73. Mark Allen, "The Saga of Bretton Woods," review of Ed Conway, *The Summit: The Biggest Battle of the Second World War—Fought Behind Closed Doors, Finance and Development*, September 2014, www.imf.org/external/pubs/ft/fandd/2014/09/book1.htm.
74. A poll conducted by the National Opinion Research Center in February 1944 showed that 71 percent of Americans thought it would be a good idea to join a union of nations and only 13 percent opposed it. When the Dumbarton Oaks proposals appeared in September 1944 and gave form to the idea, 64 percent favored joining and 26 percent were opposed. Harry H. Field and Louise Van Patten, "If the American People Make the Peace," *Public Opinion Quarterly* 8 (Winter 1944–45): 500–512; "Agreements on Security League Points Way to Better Peace," *Newsweek*, October 9, 1944, 40–41.
75. WWB, form letter on Dumbarton Oaks proposals, September 27, 1944, WR88.
76. Ibid.; Frederica Barach to WWB, September 27, 1944, WR88.
77. Board Minutes, October 11, 1944, SP47.
78. Lewis Mumford to Rex Stout, October 16, 1944, WR88.
79. Stout to Mumford, October 19, 1944, WR88.
80. Board Minutes, October 18, 1944, SP47.
81. Rex Stout, "Questions and Answers about Dumbarton Oaks," WR88 and *Brief Army Camp Items*, December 1944, WR35; Stout, "The Primer of Dumbarton Oaks," mentioned in "Report on Dumbarton Oaks Campaign," WR89, and *Third Annual Report*, 24; "Test for Dumbarton Oaks," in *Third Annual Report*, 24–25.
82. "Report on 'Test for Dumbarton Oaks,'" February 20, 1945, WR88; Board Minutes, February 21, 1945, SP47.
83. J. William Fulbright to WWB, February 21, 1945, WR88.
84. See, for example, M. Black to Douglas Southall Freeman, February 13, 1945, WR88.
85. "Report on Dumbarton Oaks Campaign."
86. Edgar Ansel Mowrer to Edward R. Stettinius Jr., December 18, 1944, quoted in untitled Pledge for Peace paper, WR88.
87. Stettinius to Mowrer, December 21, 1944, quoted in ibid.
88. "Report on Dumbarton Oaks Campaign."
89. Alan Green to WWB, March 7, 1945, WR89; Board Minutes, March 7, 1945, SP47.
90. Board Minutes, March 14, 1945, SP47; Kenneth S. Davis, *A Prophet in His Own Country: The Triumphs and Defeats of Adlai E. Stevenson* (Garden City, NY: Doubleday, 1957), 255–58.
91. Board Minutes, March 14, 1945, SP47.
92. Ibid.; Frederica Barach to Adlai E. Stevenson, March 15, 1945, WR89.
93. Alan Green to WWB, March 7, 1945, WR89; Blum, *From the Morgenthau Diaries*, 3:257–78, 427–34; Board Minutes, March 7, 1945, SP47.
94. "Bretton Woods—A First Step to Lasting Peace," WR88.
95. "Bretton Woods Dinner Meeting, March 19, 1945, at the River Club," March

20, 1945, WR89; Samuel Grafton, "I'd Rather Be Right," *New York Post*, March 20, 1945; "Business and Bretton Woods," *New York Post*, March 21, 1945; "Light on Bretton Woods," *New York Herald-Tribune*, March 22, 1945.

96. Ralph Hendershot, "Pressure Group: Writers' War Board Goes All-Out and More for Bretton Woods Legislation," *New York World-Telegram*, March 15, 1945.

97. "Summary of WWB Activity on Bretton Woods Agreements," WR89.

98. Ibid.; "Road to Peace—Men Working," *Writers' War Board Report*, April 1, 1945; Dean Acheson, "Road to Peace—Under Construction," *Brief Army Camp Items*, March 1945, WR89; Board Minutes, April 18, 1945, SP47.

99. N. S. Byrd to Rex Stout, April 3, 1945, WR89.

100. "Report on International Cooperation," WR90; *Script Catalog*; "Summary of WWB Activity on Bretton Woods."

101. See Jim Cox, *Frank and Anne Hummert's Radio Factory: The Programs and Personalities of Broadcasting's Most Prolific Producers* (London: McFarland, 2003).

102. "Report on International Cooperation."

103. "Keep Special Issues Away from San Francisco," *Writers' War Board Report*, May 1, 1945.

104. "Report on International Cooperation."

105. Rex Stout to Leslie Biffle, May 24, 1945; Biffle to Stout, May 28, 1945, both WR8.

106. "Report on International Cooperation"; Stout, "The United Smiths," *Brief Army Camp Items*, April 1945, WR88.

107. "San Francisco and the Senate," *Writers' War Board Report*, June 1, 1945; "It's Up to You from Here on In," *Writers' War Board Report*, July 1, 1945; Board Minutes, June 27, 1945, SP47.

108. Florence Eldridge March, "Let's Buy It," *Brief House Organ Items*, May 1945, WR36; "Report on International Cooperation"; "Editorial Service"; *Bulletin to Cartoonists*, July 1945, WR36. For an example of nationwide publication, see "The Course of True Love," *Uniontown (PA) Morning Herald*, June 7, 1945.

109. "Cornerstone of Steel," *Time*, January 21, 1946, 26; "Cost of Defeat," *Time*, April 8, 1946, 31.

110. Tony Judt, *Postwar: A History of Europe since 1945* (New York: Penguin, 2005), 54, 55–58.

111. See Gregori Galofré-Vilà et al., "The Economic Consequences of the 1953 London Debt Agreement," working paper no. 22557, National Bureau of Economic Research, October 9, 2016, Centre for Economic Policy Research, http://voxeu.org/article/economic-consequences-1953-london-debt-agreement.

112. David R. Henderson, "German Economic Miracle," in *The Concise Encyclopedia of Economics*, ed. David R. Henderson (Indianapolis, IN: Liberty Fund, 2008), 216–19.

Chapter 7: Reflections on the Writers' War Board

1. "Presidium, Union of Soviet Writers—Cables," December 31, 1943, WR76.

2. Julian Street Jr., "High Lights of My Work with Writers and Artists for the Treasury Department: November 1, 1941 to January 31, 1946" (unpublished manuscript),

November 22, 1946, 16, 19, Peter Odegard Papers, Franklin D. Roosevelt Presidential Library, Hyde Park, NY. Alan Green later recalled his exhilaration and feeling of comradeship during his WWB service. Green, interview by author, August 8, 1968.

3. Street, "High Lights of My Work," 16–17.

4. Russel Crouse to Jimmy Stewart, September 18, 1945; Stewart to Crouse, September 22, 1945, both WR35.

5. "Writers' Board Joins Friends of Democracy," *Variety*, July 18, 1945, 40.

6. "War Writers' Board [sic] to Continue Work," *New York Times*, August 4, 1945.

7. Rex Stout, letter to author, June 15, 1968. The *Writers' War Board Report* continued through July 1, 1945. Publication under the name *Writers' Board Report* extended from November 1945 through March 1, 1946.

8. Rex Stout, interview by author, August 14, 1968; form letters signed by Stout and Pat Klopfer, WR79; Board Minutes, December 5, 1945, SP47.

9. "A Conscience for Christmas," WR88; Board Minutes, December 5, 1945, SP47; "Food for the Hungry," *Newsweek*, December 31, 1944, 27–28; Eleanor Roosevelt, "My Day," syndicated column in numerous newspapers, December 18, 1945, http://www.gwu.edu/~erpapers/myday/displaydoc.cfm?_y=1945&_f=md000211. For an example of publication, see "A Conscience for Christmas," *Pottstown (PA) Mercury*, December 22, 1945.

10. Frederica Barach to Rex Stout, December 17, 1945, WR88.

11. "Truman Aid Asked on World Regime," *New York Times*, February 11, 1946.

12. Frederica Barach to Sol B. Abrams, February 21, 1946, WR126.

13. Rex Stout, interview; Stout, letter to author, June 15, 1968; "Seventeen Writers Form a World Law Plan," *New York Times*, July 4, 1949; Alan Green, interview.

14. John Patric to Representative Fred Bradley, January 17, 1945, WR127.

15. "WWB Economic Stabilization Committee Minutes, July 2, 1943," WR59.

16. Robert Landry, letter to author, September 28, 1970.

17. See, for example, Clifton Fadiman, "Writers' War Board: Second Annual Report," *Authors' League Bulletin*, March 1944, 3; "Additional Memoranda, May 5–May 9, 1945," SP47.

18. Board Minutes, May 3, 10, 1944, SP47; Frederica Barach to Genevieve F. Herrick, April 2, 1944, WR127; Arthur L. Zagat to Rex Stout, June 24, 1942, WR8.

19. Board Minutes, September 30, 1942, SP46; Stout to Elmer Davis, October 7, 1942, WR21; Oscar Schisgall to Stout, February 25, 1944, WR52.

20. See, for example, Joe B. McMillan to WWB, June 3, 1944, WR18.

21. Board Minutes, July 21, 1943, SP47.

22. See, for example, "Omigosh! What an Idea," *Lubbock (TX) Morning Avalanche*, October 17, 1944; Samuel Grafton, "Hey, You Have a Date in November," *Woman's Day*, September 1944, 18; Board Minutes, July 26, 1944, SP47; Frederica Barach to Rex Stout, September 6, 1944, WR93.

23. Steve Neal, *Dark Horse: A Biography of Wendell Willkie* (Garden City, NY: Doubleday, 1984), 227.

24. John Baker to Selma G. Hirsh, April 26, 1944, WR93; Board Minutes, May 3, 1944, SP47.

25. Rex Stout, interview.
26. Paul Gallico, *Confessions of a Story Writer* (New York: Knopf, 1946), 343; Stout, interview; Alan Green, interview.
27. Hannah Arendt, "Approaches to the 'German Problem,'" *Partisan Review* 12 (Winter 1945): 93–106.
28. Steven Casey, "The Campaign to Sell a Harsh Peace for Germany to the American Public, 1944–1948," *History* 90 (January 2005): 62–92.
29. Harold D. Lasswell, *Propaganda Technique in the World War* (London: Kegan Paul, Trench, Trübner, 1927), 9–10.
30. Street, "High Lights of My Work," 17.
31. Walter Johnson, *The Battle against Isolation* (Chicago: University of Chicago Press, 1944), 63–64; Mark Lincoln Chadwin, *The Hawks of World War II* (Chapel Hill: University of North Carolina Press, 1968).
32. WWB, *First Annual Report* (New York: WWB, 1943), 27; WWB, *Second Annual Report* (New York: WWB, 1944), 13; "Playbills," *Writers' War Board Report*, May 15, 1943.
33. Thomas J. Fleming, *The Illusion of Victory: America in World War I* (New York: Basic Books, 2003), 116–19, 148–49; Stewart Halsey Ross, *Propaganda for War: How the United States Was Conditioned to Fight the Great War of 1914–1918*, 2nd ed. (Joshua Tree, CA: Progressive, 2009), 226–37.
34. George Creel, *War Criminals and Punishment* (New York: R. M. McBride, 1944); WWB, *Third Annual Report* (New York: WWB, 1945), 1; Creel, "Let's Not Be Fooled Again," *Pic*, December 5, 1944, 14–16; Richard McDonough, *War Criminals and Punishment* [script based on Creel's book of the same name], 1944; William K. Clarke, *Promise vs. the Deed*, 1944, both listed in "War Scripts of the Month Selections," WR21.
35. Leila J. Rupp, *Mobilizing Women for War: German and American Propaganda* (Princeton, NJ: Princeton University Press, 1978), 91.
36. Robert Landry, letter to author, September 28, 1970.
37. Kenneth D. Rose, *Myth and the Greatest Generation: A Social History of Americans in World War II* (New York: Routledge, 2008), 183.
38. Wendy L. Wall, *Inventing the American Way: The Politics of Consensus from the New Deal to the Civil Rights Movement* (Oxford: Oxford University Press, 2008), 106. Wall characterizes the collective drive for unity as an "infrastructure of consensus."
39. Gallico, *Confessions of a Story Writer*, 345.
40. WWB, foreword to Edna St. Vincent Millay, *The Murder of Lidice* (New York: Harper and Brothers, 1942), v; Rex Stout, interview.
41. Frederica Barach to WWB, November 11, 1944, WR125. In January 1944 the board claimed that it had already furnished the government with "two tons of manuscripts for two percent of the market price." *Second Annual Report*, 1.
42. Frank W. Fox, *Madison Avenue Goes to War: The Strange Military Career of American Advertising, 1941–45* (Provo, UT: Brigham Young University Press, 1975), 66.

INDEX

ABC's of Scapegoating (pamphlet), 121
Ace, Goodman, 120
Adamic, Louis (Advisory Council), 195
Adams, Franklin Pierce "F.P.A." (board member), 25, 47, 57, 60, 92, 186, 233
Advisory Council (WWB), 30, 166, 169, 172, 191, 194, 195, 196, 197, 198, 214, 216, 223, 227, 230, 232, 244, 246–47
African Americans: blood supply segregation (Red Cross), 71–72; Detroit race riot (1943), 107; discrimination against, 107–12; "Double V," 107–8; FEPC, 107, 114–15; job discrimination, 114; *Negroes and the War*, 120–21, 281n132; *The Negro Soldier*, 110; newspapers, 108–10; Posten, 109–11; Powell, A. C., 108–9; *The Races of Mankind*, 110–12; segregation in the armed forces, 71, 108; targeted in Japanese propaganda, 108; Tuskegee Airmen, 122–23, 124; "Will We Solve Our Negro Problem?," 118. *See also* racial tolerance campaign
"After We Have Occupied Japan," 151
Agar, Herbert, 141, 142
"Aggressor Nations, The" (speech), 221
Air Ace, 133
Air Transport Service, 55
Allen, Fredcrick L. (Advisory Council), 143, 191
Allied Control Council, 237–38
All-Star Comics, 181–82
America First Committee (AFC), 3
American Forum of the Air, The (radio program), 219–20
American Journal of Sociology, 188

American Legion Magazine, 119, 148, 151, 186, 210
American Legion Women's Auxiliary, 132
American Magazine, 57, 59, 63, 76–77
American Mercury (periodical), 166
American Red Cross, 4, 70–72, 77
American Senate and World Peace, The (Colegrove), 219
Americans United for World Organization (AUWO), 222, 235
American Theater Wing, 23, 48, 67, 71
American Unity and Asia (Buck), 108, 134
Anderson, Maxwell, 132, 165
anti-inflation campaign, 34, 99–101
anti-racist campaign. *See* racial tolerance campaign
anti-Semitism: Christian Front and Charles Coughlin, 3; *Earth and High Heaven*, 116–17; Holocaust atrocities, 165–68, 201–4; subject of WWB scripts, 36
"Anti-V-E Day" campaign, 82
Ardrey, Robert, 135
Arendt, Hannah, 247
Argosy (periodical), 74
Army Air Forces, 55–59, 85–86, 150
Army Committee (WWB), 72–73
Army Ground Forces, morale campaign, 74–75
Army Medical Corps, 77
Army-Navy Woman (periodical), 79–80
Army Service Forces (ASF) campaign, 73–74
Army Talk (fact sheets), 68
"Around the Cracker Barrel" (column), 177
Assignments Committee (WWB), 28–29, 54

Associated Leagues for an Immediate Declaration of War, 20
Associated Press, 2, 35
Association for Education by Radio, 36
"As You Were" (poem), 96
Author Meets Critic (radio program), 181
Authors' League of America: association with Authors' Guild of America, 21; Dreiser, letter to, 139; formation of WWB, 16–18; Sillcox as secretary-treasurer, 26; WWB weekly meeting venue, 41
"Axis Crimes—Don't Let Them Happen Here," 167
Ayling, Keith, 57, 78

"Back the Attack" (slogan), 91
"Back-to-School" (campaign), 103–4
"Bad News for Mars," 136
Baker, Gretta, 128
Baldwin, Faith (Advisory Council), 44, 54, 57
Ball, Joseph, 218
Barach, Alvan L., 49–50
Barach, Frederica L. "Freddy," 8, 22, 35, 43, 49–50, 181
Barnard, Chester, 111–12
Barnouw, Erik, 35, 132
Battle of the Warsaw Ghetto, The (script), 167
Beck, C. C., 43
Beim, Lorraine, 177
Bellaire, Robert (board member), 25, 137, 152
Benedict, Ruth, 110–11
Beneš, Edvard, 159
Benet, Stephen Vincent (Advisory Council), 30, 36, 155–56, 164
Benny, Jack, 70, 100
Bergen, Edgar, 88
Bergman, Ingrid, 128
Bergsträsser, Arnold, 180
Berlin Diary (Shirer), 45
Bernays, Edward, 7, 236
Biffle, Leslie, 236
Black Mail (Hoke), 180, 185, 293n37
black market campaign, 96–99
"Blind Prejudice," 118
Blondie (radio program), 62
"Blood of Freedom, The," 116

blood supply controversy (Red Cross), 71–72
Boaz, Franz, 110
Bogart, Humphrey, 38, 147
bombardier publicity, 55–58
bond drives, slogans, and posters, 87, 89–90, 92–94, 115
Book and Author War Bond Committee, 92–93
Book of Knowledge Annual 1943, 133
Book of the Month Club, 1, 22, 210
book promotion methods (WWB), 38–39
Books for Bonds rallies, 92–93
Bourke-White, Margaret, 74
Bourne, Nina, 30, 36, 236
Bowle, Walter R., 175
Bowles, Chester, 145–46
Boy from Nebraska (script), 116, 129
Boys' Life, 136
Brady, Ben, 106
Braley, Berton, 96
Brandus, Janet, 178
Brebner, John Bartlet, 140
Bretton Woods Conference proposals, 226, 231–34
Brickner, Richard M., 179–80, 181
Brief Army Camp Items (periodical), 32, 80, 86, 118, 128, 136, 137–38, 152, 170, 177, 183, 210, 215, 219, 234
Brief House Organ Items (periodical), 31–32, 82, 88, 96, 103, 118, 128, 132, 136, 147, 177, 219, 224, 236
Brief Items Committee (WWB), 31, 164
British-American relations, 138–40, 141–42
Britt, George (board member), 25
Broadway Matinee (radio program), 67
Brodie, Julian, 31, 47, 84
Bromfield, Louis (Advisory Council), 93, 191
Bromley, Dorothy Dunbar, 199
Brothers (script), 108
Brown, Cecil, 96, 176, 177, 233
Brown, Harry, 164
Brown, John Mason, 125, 126
Browne, Porter Emerson, 4
Brush, Katharine (Advisory Council), 56, 61, 64
Buchman, Sidney (board member), 25
Buck, Pearl S. (board member), 18, 24–25, 93, 108, 134, 140, 141, 235

"Bugaboo of Sovereignty, The," 224
Bulletin to Cartoonists (periodical), 33, 60, 77, 79, 98, 147, 177, 230, 237
Burdenko, Nikolay, 136, 284n18
Burt, Struthers, 191
Burton, Harold, 218
"Buy Only Necessities for the Duration" (BOND clubs), 100–101
By Different Boats (pamphlet), 120
Byrd, N. S., 234

Calmer, Ned, 235
Canadian Writers' War Committee, 27
Canby, Henry Seidel (Advisory Council), 172, 191, 195, 197, 242
Caniff, Milton, 59
Capra, Frank, 110
Carlson, John Roy, 125, 179
Carlton, Henry Fisk (board member), 25
Carmer, Carl (board member): anti-German campaign, 38, 171, 181; "Back-to-School" campaign, 103; career, 46; Pledge for Peace Committee, 223, 224; racial tolerance campaign, 112, 117; radio debate, 219; "Slant on Hate" assessment, 173–74; submarine publicity for U.S. Navy, 46, 78; Syndicate Committee, 35; *The War against God*, 38; WWB core group, 25
Carroll, Madeleine, 160
Carse, Robert, 59, 60
Cartels (pamphlet), 67
cartoons. *See* comics
"Case against the Jew, The," 187
Catholic Legion of Decency, 103
Cenedella, Robert, 230, 233
censorship: book burnings in Germany, 155; books for American soldiers, 80–82; books WWB opposed, 39; films 39–40
Century Group, 20
Cerf, Bennett, 125, 155
Chamberlin, William Henry, 191
"Change of Heart" (serial), 57
Charlie McCarthy (puppet), 32, 70, 88
Chicago Sun, 158
Chicago Tribune, 3, 21, 25
Chinese Exclusion Act of 1882, 134
Christian, Caye, 129
Christian Century (periodical), 205
Christian Front, 3

Christian Science Monitor, 163
Churchill, Winston, 138–39, 142, 212, 216, 237
civilian morale, 105–7
Civilian Programs Committee (WWB), 106
"Clark and the Clurk, The" (article), 139
Clarke, William K., 178
clothing for war victims, 147
Cole, Charles, 197
Colegrove, Kenneth W., 219
Collier's, 57, 117, 139, 214
Columbia University, 124
Colwell, Robert T. "Bob" (board member), 25, 39, 46, 47, 66, 132, 215, 216
comics: air cadet recruitment, 59; anti-German propaganda, 181–82; anti-Japanese propaganda, 151–52; *Bulletin to Cartoonists*, 33, 60, 77, 79, 98, 147, 177, 230, 237; Comics Committee (WWB), 43, 122–24, 133; gasoline black market campaign, 98; Infantry Day, 75; *Joe Palooka*, 32, 75, 128, 139; racial tolerance campaign, 122–24
Command Performance (radio program), 69
Committee on Cooperation with the Churches (WWB), 44
Committee on Public Information (CPI), 3, 4, 5–6, 247, 248, 249
Committee on Speeches and Speakers/Speech Writers Committee (WWB), 178–79, 230
Committee to Combat Race Hatred (WWB), 109, 124–25
Committee to Defend America by Aiding the Allies, 3, 20, 248
Common Sense, 164, 187, 188, 189–90, 192
Concerning the Red Army (script), 136
Connally, Tom, 218
"Conscience for Christmas, A," 241–42
Corwin, Norman (Advisory Council), 104, 220
Cosmopolitan, 46, 54, 63, 105, 187
Coughlin, Charles, 3, 188
Council for a Democratic Germany (CDG), 189–90, 194–95, 196, 197, 200–201, 204
Council for Democracy, 20, 134, 188
Council on Books in Wartime, 48, 81–82, 134, 155–57
"Course of True Love, The," 237

Country Gentleman (periodical), 56, 71
Cousins, Norman, 235, 236, 242
Coward, Noel, 184–85
Cowles, Gardner, 9–10
Craven, Thomas, 90, 141
Creel, George (Advisory Council), 5–6, 178, 211, 249
Crouse, Russel "Buck" (board member): anti-German campaign, 193; Army Air Forces recruitment, 55; Bretton Woods proposals, 233; career, 24; international cooperation, 218; pro-American propaganda for OWI, 141; racial tolerance campaign, 112; *Salute to the WAACS*, 61; soldier morale materials, 70; United Nations Day, 132; urged Wilkie to run for president (1944), 246; Writers' Board for World Government, 242; WWB founding, 17, 18, 24
Crow, Carl, 151
Crowther, Geoffrey, 142

Dan McGarry (serial character), 73
David, Mack, 57
David Harum (radio program), 98
Davidson, Jo, 160
Davies, Joseph E., 158
Davis, Elmer (board member), 9–10, 25, 150, 157, 190
Davis, John W., 221–22
D-Day Prayer (poem), 106–7
Dead Are Not Liars, The (script), 201
Deane, Martha, 117, 233
"Dear Friend" (song), 23–24
Death and Dr. Burdenko (script), 136, 284n18
"Declaration of Interdependence, The," 143
Declaration of Interdependence, The (radio program), 218
Delaney, John H., 222
DeMille, Cecil, 40
"Democracy's Way with a Problem," 118
Denlinger, Sutherland, 33
Der Führer (and the Great Lie He Borrowed) (play), 178
Derounian, Avedis, 179
Des Moines Register, 121
DeVoto, Bernard (Advisory Council), 81–82, 143
Distomo Committee, 165
Dogs for Defense, 54

domestic culture in wartime America, 12–13
"Don't Let's Be Beastly to the Germans" (song), 183–85
Don't Listen to Him (cartoons), 122
"Don't talk!" (campaign), 104–5
"Double V" (campaign), 107–8
Douglas, Melvyn, 8–9, 28
Dreiser, Theodore, 138–39
Dr. Hopkins' Atomic Bomb (script), 129
Ducas, Dorothy, 9
Duffus, Robert L., 34, 98, 114, 118, 201
Dumbarton Oaks Conference proposals, 226–31, 302n74
Duranty, Walter, 136, 220, 284n18

Each to the Other (LaFarge), 46
Earle, Edward, 197
Earth and High Heaven (Graham), 116–17
East by Southwest (LaFarge), 46
Easy Aces (radio program), 120
Economic Stabilization campaign, 99–102
editorial service (WWB), 33–35
Edmonds, Walter (Advisory Council), 195
Ehrlich, Max, 178
Eldridge, Florence, 230, 234, 236
Eliot, George Fielding, 72–75, 138, 176, 218
"Emperor Must Go, The," 151
ethnic stereotypes, 13–14, 124–30
Eubanks, Sam B. (board member), 25
Eunson, Robert, 150
"Exploding the Myth," 112
"Extermination of the Jews, The," 166

Fadeev, Alexander, 134, 284n10
Fadiman, Clifton (board member): Air Forces recruitment, 55; anti-German campaign, 157, 167, 171–72, 177–78, 181–83, 185, 188, 193–99, 246–47; anti-Japanese campaign, 148, 151, 152; black market campaign, 96; bond drive ideas, 248; Book of the Month Club, 1, 22, 210; book promotions (WWB), 39, 210; "Books for Bonds," 93; Bretton Woods proposals, 233; career, 22–23; Corwin, comment on, 104; Dumbarton Oaks proposals, 227–28; Food and Relief Committee, 144–45; "Hood River Incident," 115; Infantry Day, 74; *Information Please*, 47; Lidice campaign, 157–58, 159–60, 164–65; Mayer, M., attacked by, 187–88; movie promotions

(WWB), 39; peace terms for Germany, 212, 213; "Pledge for Peace" campaign, 222–23, 224, 225; racial tolerance campaign, 120, 129; unnecessary travel campaign, 96; urged Wilkie to run for president (1944), 246; "Victory Gardens," 95; WAAC campaign, 62, 64; Writers' Board for World Government, 242; WWB founding, 18; WWB relationship to government, 11
Fadiman, William, 39
Fair Employment Practice Committee (FEPC), 107, 114–15
fascism, campaigns against American fascists, 104, 177
Fast, Howard, 217
Faulkner, William, 92
Fawcett Magazines, 217
Federal Council of Churches, 175
Feingold, Voltarine, 50
Ferber, Edna (Advisory Council), 59, 198
Ferro, Theodore, 132
Fibber McGee and Molly, 32, 70
Field, Marshall, 52
Fight for Freedom Committee, 3, 20, 248
Filipinos, portrayal of (WWB racial tolerance campaign), 122, 124
Fillmore, Hildegarde, 63
Firepower (periodical), 73
Fischer, Louis, 196
Fish, Hamilton, III, 20–21, 245
Fisher, Dorothy Canfield (Advisory Council), 195, 242
Fisher, Ham, 32, 139
Flag Day, 132
Flanner, Janet, 67
Foerster, Friedrich Wilhelm, 211
Food and Relief Committee (WWB), 144–47
Food for Freedom, 144, 146
"Food for Friends," 147
Foreigners Settled America (script), 128
Foreign Writers' Committee (WWB), 27
Forrestal, James, 150
Fortune, 154
For Whom the Bell Tolls (film), 39–40
Fosdick, Harry Emerson, 118
"Four Musketeers" (comic story), 133
"Four-Square Peace, A," 224
Franco, Francisco, 176
Frankel, Mortimer, 201

Franklin, John Hope, 107
"Free and Equal Blues" (song), 125
Freedom House, 20, 21, 52, 179, 200, 220, 235
Friedrich, Carl J., 188–89
Friend, Ruth Hays, 223, 225
Friends of Democracy (FOD), 20, 48, 104, 179, 277n58
Frissell, Toni, 61, 63
"From Jitterbug to Angel," 67
Fromm, Erich, 181
From Slavery to Freedom (Franklin), 107
fuel oil rationing, editorial on, 34
Fulbright, J. William, 229–30
Furnas, J. C., 134
Fussell, Paul, 164

Gaines, M. C., 123, 152, 181
Gallico, Paul (board member): anti-German campaign, 179, 181, 186, 201, 202–3, 207, 246–47; "Anti-V-E Day," 82; Army Air Forces recruitment, 58; Battle of the Bulge concerns, 82–83; "Bombardier," 56–57; career, 46; civilian morale, 105; "Don't talk!" campaign, 105; gasoline black market campaign, 98; Infantry Day, 74; Newspaper Enterprise Association article, 35; peace plan (WWB), 215–17; postwar regret, 247; pro-American propaganda for OWI, 141; "Slant on Hate," 173–74; *Transatlantic*, 143; United Nations Committee, 139, 251; War Bond Pledge campaign, 92; war correspondent for *Cosmopolitan*, 46; WWB core group, 25
Gang Busters (radio program), 98
Gannett, Lewis (Advisory Council), 2, 89, 195, 196, 197
Gannett News Service, 35
gardens, "Victory Gardens" campaign, 95
Gardner, John H., 104–5
Garland, Hamlin, 4
gasoline, black market campaign, 97–98
German Atrocities Unexpurgated (film), 202
Germany: anti-German books and publications, 179–83; anti-German campaign, 1–2, 13, 36, 154–55, 169–79, 193–99, 206–7, 296n108; anti-German comic book stories, 177–78; anti-German letter-writing campaign, 185–87; anti-German radio broadcasts, 176–77;

Germany (*continued*)
anti-German scripts, 178; anti-German speeches, 178–79; blame for war on all citizens, 13, 170, 172, 177, 179, 182, 184, 190, 246; blame for war on Nazis alone, 13, 170; book burnings, 155–57; criticism of WWB's anti-German campaign, 171–72, 187–201; criticism of WWB's harsh peace terms, 200; "Don't Let's Be Beastly to the Germans," 183–85; "good" Germans, 13, 170; Holocaust atrocities, 165–68, 201–4, 221; Lidice campaign, 157–65; Niemöller, denunciation of, 204–6, 297n142; pan-Germanism, 169, 179, 193–95, 210; "Slant on Hate," 173–74; systematic killing of non-Aryans, 183; "We Shall Hate, or We Shall Fail," 174–76
Germany (Schuster & Bergsträsser), 180
Germany Will Try It Again (Schultz), 180, 185
"Get Tough"/"Goddam Truth"/"Truth and Hate" Committee (WWB), 171
Gianella, Lawrence H., 59
Gilbert, Robert, 200, 209
Glamour, 66
Goebbels, Joseph, 6, 53
Goldfarb, Alvin, 167–68
Goldwyn, Samuel, 158
Golenpaul, Dan, 119–20
Goodbody, Luette, 100–101
Good Housekeeping, 71
Goodman, Jack (board member): anti-German campaign, 155, 171, 175–76, 193–94; anti-Japanese campaign, 149; bond drives, 92; Bretton Woods proposals, 233; career, 47; Dumbarton Oaks proposals, 230; *How Writers Perpetuate Stereotypes*, 127; Labor Committee, 79–80; *Salute to the WAACS*, 61; Union of Soviet Writers, 134–35; United Nations Committee, 139; U.S. Navy publicity chairman, 77–78; "V-Mail" campaign, 94; WWB core group, 25
Gordon, Ruth, 132
Gould, Kenneth, 120, 129
G. P. Putnam, 180
Gracious Lady (Kleeman), 27
Grafton, Samuel (board member), 25, 47–48, 132, 194, 197, 215, 232, 233, 246
Graham, Gwethalyn, 116–17

Graham, Irving, 67
Grant, Jane, 29–30
Grayson, Mitchell, 118
Green, Alan Baer (board member): anti-German campaign, 178, 181, 185, 193, 203, 246–47; anti-Japanese campaign, 149, 152; bond drives, 92; Bretton Woods proposals, 232, 233; career, 46–47; Dumbarton Oaks proposals, 227–28, 230–31; *Earth and High Heaven* promotion, 117; Food and Relief Committee, 144–45, 147; international cooperation, 132, 136; Lidice campaign, 157; Niemöller, denunciation of, 204–5; Orientation Committee (WWB), 67–68; peace terms for Germany, 215–16; racial tolerance campaign, 109, 112, 120, 125, 128; Speech Writers Committee, 36–37; United Nations Day, 132, 136; Writers' Board for World Government, 242; WWB core group, 25; WWB colleagues, praise of, 52; WWB project criteria, 41–42; WWB volume of work, 252
Green Lantern (comic book character), 122
Green Valley, U.S.A (radio program), 62
Greenwood, Michael, 132
Gropper, William, 160
"Gunner's the Man, The," 57
Gunther, John (Advisory Council), 36–37, 71, 176

Hackett, Francis, 67
Hagedorn, Hermann, 4
Halman, Denis, 106
Hammerstein, Oscar, II (board member): career, 23; "Dear Friend," 23–24; "Don't talk!" campaign, 105; Music War Committees (WWB and American Theater Wing), 23; racial tolerance, 112–13, 125–27, 282n151; *South Pacific*, anti-racist lyrics, 282n151; United Nations Day, 132; "We're on Our Way," 75–76; Writers' Board for World Government, 242; WWB core group, 1, 18, 25
Hangmen Also Die! (film), 183
Harbach, Otto, 132
Harper's Bazaar, 62, 63, 65, 100
Harper's Magazine, 81
Hart, Lorenz, 57
Hart, Moss, 125
Hartley, Arnold, 129, 203

INDEX 313

Hatch, Carl, 218
Hate, Incorporated (script), 129
"Hate Is Moral Poison," 175
"Hats Off to the Infantry," 75
Hawley, Adelaide, 74, 224
Hayes, Arthur G., 172
Hayes, Helen, 119
Heatter, Gabriel, 183
Hecht, Ben, 166
"Help Wanted, Male and Female," 102
Hersey, John, 26
Hertzberg, Sidney, 190–93
Heydrich, Reinhard, 157, 161, 164, 183
Hicks, Granville, 192
Hidden Enemy, The (Pol), 179, 210
Hill, Edwin C., 199
Hill, Lister, 218
Hirohito (Emperor of Japan), 148–49, 151, 152–53
"Hirohito Must Go," 151
Hirsch, Joseph, 91
Hirsh, Joseph, 103
Hirsh, Selma G., 11, 49, 51, 144–45
Hitler, Adolf: depiction in anti-German films, 182; *Mein Kampf*, 177. *See also* Germany
Hitler Had a Vision (pageant), 132
Hitler's Madman (film), 164
Hobby, Oveta Culp, 64
Hoke, Henry, 180
Holbrook, Weare, 96
Holiday, Billie, 116
Hollywood Writers' Mobilization (HWM), 28, 233
Holm, Celeste, 185
Holocaust atrocities, 165–68, 201–4, 221
home front propaganda: African American soldiers, 107–12; anti-inflation (Economic Stabilization campaign), 99–102; anti-racism, 107–12, 115; "Back-to-School" campaign, 103–4; black market campaign, 96–99; bond drives, slogans, and posters, 87, 89–94; civilian morale, 105–7; "Don't talk!" campaign, 104–5; fascist organizations in U.S., denunciation of, 104; income tax issues (1943), 88; industrial workers and their contribution to the war, 79–80; Japanese American soldiers, 115; reporting rationing violators 101–2; unnecessary travel, curtailment of, 34,

95–96; venereal disease campaign, 102–3; "Victory" promotions, 93–95. *See also* racial tolerance campaign
"Hood River Incident," 115
Hoover, Herbert, 245
Hoover, J. Edgar, 32
Hope, Bob, 71
Hop Harrigan (comic book character), 122–23, 124
"Horror Unlimited," 166
Hoskins, Louella, 35
Hough, Emerson, 4
Houston, Bryan, 97
How Every Boy Can Prepare for Aviation Service (Ayling), 57
"How Far Can You Walk?," 75
"How to Tell a Fascist," 177
How to Treat the Germans (Ludwig), 209
How Writers Perpetuate Stereotypes (pamphlet), 127
Hughes, Alice, 61, 64
Hughes, Langston (Advisory Council), 30, 108, 117, 119
Hull, Cordell, 211
Hummert Radio Agency, 235
Huntley, Chet, 114, 128
Hurban, Vladimir S., 159
Hurst, Fannie (Advisory Council), 93, 147
Hutchinson, Paul, 205

"I Am an American Day" campaign, 13, 128
"If You Can't Go Across . . . Come Across" (slogan), 92
Illustrious Dunderheads, The (Stout), 20–21
income tax issues (1943), 88
Independent Woman (periodical), 100
Indian Reorganization Act (1934), 113
industrial worker strikes, 79–80
Infantry Day campaign, 13, 74–77
inflation, preventative measures (Economic Stabilization campaign), 99–102
Information Please (radio program), 22, 47, 119, 125
Institute for American Democracy, 121
Internal Revenue Service, 88
internationalism, 13, 217–22, 251, 253
International Monetary Fund (IMF), 232
International News Service, 35
interventionism in the pre-war years, 3, 248
In the Days of McKinley (Leech), 47
In the Service of My Country (script), 117–18

"Invest in Invasion" (slogan), 92
"Iron Curtain" (speech), 237
Irwin, Wallace, 148
Is Fair Play Controversial? (script), 114
Is Germany Incurable? (Brickner), 179–80, 181
isolationism, 208–9, 231, 245–46
"Is This a White Man's War?," 108–9
Ives-Quinn Bill (New York), 115
"I Wanna Marry a Bombardier" (song), 57–58

Jackson, Joseph, 185
Jameson, John Franklin, 4
Japan: anti-Japanese propaganda, 122, 124, 131, 148–53, 154–55; Japanese propaganda targeting African Americans, 108; "Russia in the Pacific," 137. *See also* Hirohito
Japanese Americans, 115–16, 148
job discrimination, 114
Joe Palooka (cartoon), 32, 75, 128, 139
Johnston, Eric, 125
Jordan, Ruth, 132
Judgment (script), 178
Juvenile Writers Committee (WWB), 94, 117

Kagan, Ben, 129
Kaltenborn, H. V., 219
Kate Smith Hour, The (radio program), 105, 116
Kaufman, George S. (Advisory Council), 30, 70, 198
Kazin, Alfred, 191
"Keep Special Issues away from San Francisco," 235
Kerr, Chester, 9, 155
Kieran, John (Advisory Council), 186
King, Ernest, 78–79
Kleeman, Rita Halle (board member): anti-German campaign, 207; career, 27; Committee to Combat Race Hatred, 109; *Earth and High Heaven* review, 116; Economic Stabilization Committee, 99; foreign writers, enlistment on WWB projects, 26–27; Lidice campaign, 157; Merchant Marine recruitment, 59, 60; racial tolerance campaign, 109, 117, 119; WAVES Committee, 65–66; WWB core group, 25
Klopfer, Pat Selwyn, 109
Know Your Enemy (pamphlet), 67

"Know Your Enemy (Blonde, Brunette, or Redhead)," 103
Komroff, Manuel (Advisory Council), 27
Konstantinov, Konstantin, 135
Krutch, Joseph Wood (Advisory Council), 140
Kubie, Lawrence, 84, 85, 181
Kubie, Nora, 84
Kuhn, Ferdinand, 18, 142

Labor Committee (WWB), 79–80
Ladies Home Journal, 63, 199
LaFarge, Christopher (board member): anti-German campaign, 187, 193, 202, 207; anti-Japanese campaign, 148, 149; "The Blood of Freedom," 116; Bretton Woods proposals, 233; career, 46; Dumbarton Oaks proposals, 227–28; Infantry Day campaign, 76–77; racial tolerance campaign, 125, 128–29; soldier morale, 79–80; war correspondent for *Harper's Magazine*, 46; world federation, 219; Writers' Board for World Government, 242; WWB core group, 25
La Guardia, Fiorello, 76, 95, 117
Landis, James, 94
Landry, Robert J. (board member): anti-German campaign, 171; career, 45; Committee to Combat Race Hatred, 109; international cooperation, 218; *The Myth That Threatens America* assessment, 126; racial tolerance campaign, 127–28; Radio Committee, 44–45; script service, 35; "Star-Spangled Banner," fourth stanza, 42; Union of Soviet Writers, 134–35; United Nations, importance of, 236; United Nations Day, 132; WWB core group, 25; WWB work with Roosevelt administration, 244
Laney, Al, 60
Lasswell, Harold D., 247–48
Lauterbach, Richard, 136–37
Lawrence, W. H., 168
Lee, Gypsy Rose, 31, 125
Leech, Margaret (board member): anti-German campaign, 171, 197, 207; career, 47; international cooperation, 218; Merchant Marine recruitment, 59–60; racial tolerance campaign, 109; Roosevelt's fourth-term campaign, 246; "Star-Spangled Banner," fourth stanza,

42; *Transatlantic* Committee, 47, 142; Writers' Board for World Government, 242; WWB core group, 25
Lehman, Herbert, 145
Lessons of My Life (Gilbert), 209
Lest We Forget (sculpture), 160
"Let's Talk about Inflation" (study guide), 100
Leventhal, Albert Rice, 47
Lewenthal, Reeves, 90, 91
Lewis, Sinclair, 147
liberal democracy, 13–14
Liberty Magazine, 58
"Lidice" (poem), 160–61
Lidice campaign and committee, 157–65
Life, 74, 164, 199
"Lifeboat" (story), 59
Lincoln, Abraham, 177
Lindbergh, Charles, 20
Lindsay, Howard (Advisory Council), 16, 17, 24, 66, 72, 143
Lippmann, Walter, 143
Lipschultz, Isidore, 52
Listen, Hans (Thompson), 196
"Loaf of Bread, A" (story), 177
Lodge, Henry Cabot, 228
Look, 5, 56, 57, 199, 214
Loving Cups for Murderers (script), 203
Ludwig, Emil, 209, 211
Lyons, Eugene, 166
Lyons, Leonard, 196–97

MacLeish, Archibald, 231
Mademoiselle, 65
Magazine War Guide, 29
Majdanek concentration camp, 168
"Making Democracy Permanent," 114
Making of Modern Britain, The (Brebner & Nevins), 140
"Man Bites Carrot" (sketch), 106
March, Fredric, 32, 147, 218, 219
Marcoux, George E., 43
Marquand, John P. (board member), 18, 24, 55, 191, 198
Marshall, George, 150
Marshall, James, 219
Marshall, Lee, 145
Martin, Ernest, 128
Masaryk, Jan, 220–21
Mason, Frank, 72–73
Masses, The, 19

Master Detective (pulp magazine), 59
Maxwell, Elsa, 147
May, Andrew J., 111
"Maybe It's Just Some Guys Named Schmidt," 170
Mayer, Milton, 187–88, 191, 200
Mayer, Sheldon, 152, 181–82
McBride, Mary Margaret, 85, 224, 233, 235
McCall's, 63, 64, 71
McCarthy, Joseph, 57
McCleery, Martha, 28–29
McCormick, Robert, 3, 225
McDonough, Richard, 178
McGill, Jerry, 120
McNair, Lesley James, 74, 76, 172–73
Mead, Margaret, 125
Meade, I. J., 7–8
Mechanix Illustrated (periodical), 59, 224
medics (Army Medical Corps), 77
Meet Mr. Blank, the Leader of Tomorrow's Germans (Waldeck), 180
Meet Your Relatives (script), 112
Men for Merchant Marine (film), 60
Merchant Marine recruitment, 59–60
Merriam, Eve, 117
Michael, Sandra, 135
military concerns: air cadet recruitment, 58–59; Air Force Redistribution Center, 85–86; censorship of solders' reading material, 80–81; Dogs for Defense, 54; flight crews, 55–58; glider pilots, 56; ground crews, 55–58; jobs in the services, 72–79; orientation, 67–69; recruitment, 54–67; soldier rehabilitation, 83–85; USO, 70–71; women in the military, 60–67
military police (MPs), 73
Millay, Edna St. Vincent (Advisory Council), 106–7, 161–64
minorities: anti-Semitism in North America, 3, 116, 166–68, 187–88; Chinese Exclusion Act (1882), 134; German Americans, discrimination against (WWI), 169–70; "I Am an American Day," 13, 128; internment of Japanese Americans, 148; Japanese American soldiers, prejudicial treatment, 115–16; lack of inclusion in films, 40–41; *The Myth That Threatens America*, 125–27; Native Americans, 113. *See also* African Americans; racial tolerance campaign
"Miss Subways" (poster), 62–63

Molly Pitcher Day, 62
morale: civilian, 105–7; D-Day prayer, 106–7; soldier, 69–72, 89–90
Morgenthau, Henry, Jr.: Morgenthau Plan, 211–13; Security Plan, 212–17; Treasury Department Defense Savings Program, 15–16
Morgunbladid (newspaper), 141
Morley, Christopher, 105
Morrison, Hobe (board member), 25, 44–45, 105, 109, 115, 121–22
Mothers of Sons Forum, 113
movie promotions, 39–41
Mowrer, Edgar Ansel, 74–75, 230
Mr. District Attorney (radio program), 121
Mr. Keen, Tracer of Lost Persons (radio program), 98
Mumford, Lewis, 206, 228
Muni, Paul, 161
Murder of Lidice, The (poem), 161–64
Murrow, Edward R. (Advisory Council), 30
Music War Committee (WWB), 23
"Must They Die in World War III?" (poster), 222
My Brother Lives in Stalingrad (script), 135
Mystery Theater (radio program), 115
Myth That Threatens America, The (event), 125–27

Nathan, Robert (Advisory Council), 160, 164
Nathanson, Irwin, 62
national anthem, 42
National Blue Star Mothers of America, 113
National Board for Historical Service (NBHS), 3, 4–5
National League of Mothers of America, 3
national service, 82–83
National War Fund (NWF), 144
Nature of the Enemy, The (script), 156
Nature of the Enemy campaign, 154–55, 169, 171, 172, 175–76, 177, 178, 179, 181–82, 183, 185, 187–92, 193, 201, 202–3, 207. *See also* Germany: anti-German campaign
Nazi, The (script), 178
Nazis, 1–2, 170, 175, 179, 194–95, 210, 221, 238
"Neatest Trick of the Month, The," 202–3
Negroes and the War (pamphlet), 120–21, 281n132

Negro Soldier, The (film), 110
Nelson, William, 136, 236
Nevins, Allan (Advisory Council), 5, 140, 143, 187
Newsweek, 163
New World a-Comin' (radio program), 118
New Yorker, 30, 56
New York Herald-Tribune, 60, 89, 191–92, 199, 233
New York Post, 103, 233
New York Times, 2, 75, 140, 158, 159, 189, 222, 244
New York Times Magazine, 105, 174, 175, 181, 199
New York World-Telegram, 97–98, 199, 233
Niebuhr, Reinhold, 200–201
Niemöller, Martin, 204–6, 297n142
Nightmare at Noon (Benet), 155
Nizer, Louis, 170, 183, 210
Norman, Dorothy, 114
"Not Just Allies—Friends" (speech), 136
Not Quite Dead Enough (Stout), 57
Now It Can Be Told (radio program), 102

O'Dea, Mark, 59, 60
Odegard, Peter, 16, 17
Odets, Clifford (Advisory Council), 70, 147
Office of Civilian Defense (OCD): civilian morale campaign, 105–7; collaboration with WWB, 28; "Don't talk!" campaign, 104–5; Douglas, 8–9, 28; V-Homes, 93–94; WWB funding, 7–9, 49
Office of Defense Transportation (ODT), 95–96
Office of Emergency Management (OEM), 7–8
Office of Facts and Figures (OFF), 8
Office of Price Administration (OPA), 96–99, 101–2
Office of War Information (OWI): anti-German campaign, 172; ASF campaign, 73–74; congressional control of, 6, 9–11; Domestic News Bureau, 33–35; Economic Stabilization campaign, 99–102; establishment of, 6, 132; gasoline black market campaign, 97; income tax issues (1943), 88; Japanese atrocities downplayed, 150; Lidice campaign, 157–58; *Magazine War Guide*, 29; *Negroes and the War*, 120–21; Negro Press section, 109–10; overseas propaganda,

140–43, 156; United Nations Day, 132–33; venereal disease campaign, 102–3; V-Mail, 94–95; War Advertising Council, influence on, 49; WWB, relationship with, 4–5, 9–11, 50–53, 240–41, 243–45, 249–50
"Ol' Man Author" (song), 125–27
O'Neill, Eugene (Advisory Council), 30, 92
One World (Wilkie), 133–34
"On the Record" (column), 56
"Open Mouths, Closed Minds," 118
Opera Victory Rallies, 220, 221–22
organizations (non-governmental) that worked with the WWB, 48–50
"Our Chances of Avoiding World War III" (speech), 236
"Our Enemy—Madame Butterfly" (speech), 148
Our Secret Weapon (radio program), 21, 168, 211
overseas pro-American propaganda for the OWI, 140–43

Painton, Frederick C., 43–44
pan-Germanism, 169, 179, 193–95, 210
Parade, 141
Parents' Magazine, 67, 117, 224
Patric, John, 243
peace preparations: Bretton Woods proposals, 226, 231–34; Dumbarton Oaks proposals, 226–31, 302n74; harsh peace terms for Germany, 1, 199–200, 208–11; Morgenthau Plan, 211–13; peace plan (WWB), 215–17; "Pledge for Peace" campaign, 222–26, 229; San Francisco Conference, 226, 234–38; Security Plan, 212–17; UN proposals, 217–22
Pearson, Drew, 17, 85
Pearson, Lester "Mike," 146–47
People's Voice (periodical), 108–9
Pershing, John J., 220
Philadelphia Inquirer, 167
Philadelphia Record, 255
"Pipe Down" (poem), 105
Pittsburgh Courier, 107–8, 129
Pledge for Peace campaign and committee (WWB), 222–26, 230, 232
"Poem and Prayer for an Invading Army" (poem), 106–7
"Points at Issue, The," 192
Pol, Heinz, 179, 210

Poletti, Charles, 25
Poletti, Jean (board member), 25, 109, 118, 128, 234, 235, 246
Polier, Shad, 97
Pons, Lily, 100
Pope, Arthur Upham, 68, 220
Popular Comics, 98
Porter, Sylvia, 88
Posten, Ted, 109–10
Poster Committee (WWB), 90–91, 94–95, 141, 154–55
"Post-War World, The," 219
Powdermaker, Hortense, 117
Powell, Adam Clayton, Jr., 108–9
Powell, J. B., 151, 186
Practical Radio Writing (Seymour & Martin), 45
Pratt, Fletcher (Advisory Council), 78
"Prescription for Peace," 224
Price, Millard, 153
"Price of Freedom, The," 219
"Primer of Dumbarton Oaks, The," 229
Pringle, Henry (board member), 8, 25, 143, 144, 145, 183
Probing Our Prejudices (Powdermaker), 117, 121
Promise vs. the Deed (script), 178
propaganda: pro-American propaganda overseas, 140–43; promotion of U.S. allies, 131–40; war relief efforts, 143–47; World War II, prior to, 3–7. *See also* Germany; home front propaganda; Japan; military concerns
Publishers Weekly, 244
pulp magazines, 43–44
Pulp Writers' Committee, 43–44
Putnam, James, 74
Pyle, Ernie, 74

"Questions and Answers about Dumbarton Oaks" (pamphlet), 229

Races of Mankind, The (pamphlet), 110–12, 118, 120–21
racial tolerance campaign (WWB): attack on Mothers' Groups, 113; comic book storylines, 122–24; Fair Employment Practice Committee, 107, 114–15; "I Am an American Day," 127–28; Ives-Quinn Bill, 115; job discrimination, 114; liberal democracy initiative (WWB), 13–14;

racial tolerance campaign (*continued*)
The Myth That Threatens America, 125–27; overview of campaign, 112–16; *The Races of Mankind*, 110–12, 118; radio programs, books, and other materials against racism, 14, 108, 114–22; stereotypes of minorities and foreign-born citizens, 122–30; WWB criticized as racist, 246–47; WWB meetings with radio writers, 119–22. *See also* African Americans; minorities
Radar (comic book character), 217
Radio Committee, writers, and broadcasters, 36, 44–46, 89–90, 117–22, 176–77
Rains, Claude, 128
Ranch Romances (pulp magazine), 59
Rasher, Howard, 85
rationing: food, 145–46; fuel oil (editorial), 34; gasoline, 97–99; illegal black market, 96–99
Rauschning, Hermann, 199
Reader's Digest, 88, 100, 166, 168
Real Life Comics, 177–78
Real Story (pulp magazine), 88
"Recipe for Civil War," 185
recruitment: industrial workers, 95; soldiers, 54–67; women in the military, 60–67
Redbook, 119
"Release a Man for Combat" (slogan), 61
"Remember Us," 166
Reminder to the Free (script), 132
Reparations and Security Campaign, 213, 217
"Reparations Booby Trap, The," 215
Report to the Nation (radio program), 233
Reuther, Walter, 80
Reveille in Washington, 1860–1865 (Leech), 47
Reynolds, Quentin (Advisory Council), 80, 143, 179
Rice, Elmer (Advisory Council), 132
Ripley, Robert, 100
Rise and Fall of the Third Reich, The (Shirer), 45
"Road to Peace—Under Construction" (speech), 233–34
Roberts, Owen J., 223, 224
Rockefeller, John D., Jr., 52
Rodgers, Dorothy, 70

Rodgers, Richard, 23, 57, 70, 75
Romulo, Carlos P., 93
Roos, S. Edward, 59
Roosevelt, Eleanor, 74, 205
Roosevelt, Franklin D.: criticism of Lindbergh, 20; FEPC, 107; fireside chats, 41, 100; internment of Japanese Americans, 148; Lidice campaign, 159; Morgenthau Plan, 212–13; NWF, 144; OWI establishment, 6, 132; Republican opposition, 6, 48, 81, 105, 212, 249; Southern Democrats, 6, 249; Treasury Department Defense Savings Program, 15; War Advertising Council, 48–49; WWB support for policies of, 1–2, 244, 245–46, 253; Yalta Conference, 216–17
Roosevelt, Theodore, 4, 8
Ross, Malcolm, 114
Rossen, Robert, 28
Rosten, Leo, 9–11, 172
Rosten, Norman, 136, 234
Rotarian, 59
Russell, Bertrand, 181
"Russia in the Pacific," 137
Russian Committee (WWB), 135, 136
"Russians Are People—and a Lot Like Us," 136
Russian War Relief, 135, 143

Salinger, Edgar, 153
Salute to the WAACS (radio program), 61
Sandburg, Carl, 65
San Francisco Examiner, 3
San Francisco Conference, 226, 234–38
Saturday Evening Post, 56–57, 58, 59, 60, 73, 98, 134, 187
Saturday Review of Literature, 156, 181, 206, 235
Scapegoats in History (script), 129
Schisgall, Oscar, 9–11, 51
Schmitt, Bernadotte E., 197
Scholastic, 98, 117, 156
School and Society (periodical), 117
Schreiber, George, 91
Schubert, Paul, 78
Schultz, Sigrid, 178, 180, 185
Schuman, Frederick L., 197
Schuster, George W., 180
scriptwriting: catalog of available plays for the public, 36; Scripts for Soldiers and

Sailors Committee, 79; War Script of the Month, 108, 114, 116, 118, 128, 129, 132, 135, 136, 156, 160, 178, 201, 203, 217–18, 235
Sea Power in Conflict (Schubert), 78
Security Plan, 212–15
See (periodical), 177, 216
segregation in the armed forces, 71, 108
Selznick, David O., 40
Series E savings bonds, 15
Seymour, Katharine (board member), 25, 44–46
"Shall We Let Japan Off Easy?," 153
Shaw, George Bernard, 158
Sherwood, Robert, 9, 212, 235, 242–43, 299n18
Shimkin, Leon, 99, 100
Shirer, William (board member), 1, 25, 44–45, 186–87, 196, 197, 203, 233, 246
"Shock Is Late, The," 202
Sillcox, Luise (board member), 16–18, 25–26, 28–29, 197
Simon and Schuster, 22, 30, 47, 99
"Simple Idea, The" (speech), 219
Sinatra, Frank, 100, 103
Since You Went Away (film), 40
Skinner, Cornelia Otis, 147
"Slant on Hate" (document), 173–74
Smith, Gerald L. K., 120
Smith, Kate, 42, 171
Smith, Lillian, 116, 118, 121
Snow Goose, The (Gallico), 46
Society for the Prevention of World War III (SPWW3), 21, 48, 52, 189–90, 193, 205, 210–11, 214
"Soft Peace = World War III," 186–87
Sokolsky, George E., 102, 192
soldiers: military jobs, publicity about, 72–79; morale, 69–72, 79–80; orientation, 67–69; reading materials for, 80–82; recruitment, 54–67; rehabilitation, 83–85; resentment of striking industrial workers, 79–80; soldier and sailor shows, 70; women in the military, 60–67; writing contests, 69–70. *See also* military concerns
Sound of Music, The, 23, 24
Sour, Bob, 67
South Pacific, anti-racist lyrics, 282n151
Souvaine, Henry, 220

Soviet Union, 134–38, 214, 219–20, 237
Speaking of Liberty (radio program), 20
Special Assignments Committee of the WWB (for OWI-Overseas projects), 140
speeches: bond drives, 92; catalog of available addresses, 37; soldier orientation, 68–69; Speech Writers Committee, 36–37, 42, 148
Sprague, Carter, 64
Stack, Robert, 203
Stalin, Joseph, 134, 135, 216, 284n10
Standard Magazines (pulp magazines), 78
Stark, Sheldon, 75
Starr, Martin, 40
Stars Fell on Alabama (Carmer), 46
"State of the States" (column), 143
Stearns, Martin, 230
Steinbeck, John (Advisory Council), 30, 244
stereotypes in the media, 124–27
Stern, David, 225
Stettinius, Edward R., Jr., 150, 230
Stevenson, Adlai, 231
Stevenson, George, 83, 84
Stewart, Jimmy, 241
Stickney, Dorothy, 66
Stimson, Henry L., 79, 150, 202, 211–12
St. John, Robert (Advisory Council), 96, 179
"Stop Thief!," 98
"Story from the Pacific, A" (speech), 148
Story of Dr. Wassell, The (film), 40
"Story of Fritz, The" (documented story), 178
Stout, J. Robert "Bob," 19
Stout, Pola, 51
Stout, Rex (board member): advocacy of international organization with policing powers, 217; anti-German campaign, 154, 157, 168, 172, 181, 185, 187–89, 207, 246–47, 296n108; anti-Japanese campaign, 148, 149–50; attack on American woman "slackers," 66; Baldwin, encouragement to write for pulp magazines, 44; Barnard and the controversy over *The Races of Mankind*, 111–12; blood supply segregation (Red Cross), concern over, 72; Bretton Woods proposals, 233; career, 18–22; *Collier's*, appreciation to, 117; Committee

Stout, Rex (*continued*)
on Scripts for Soldier and Sailor Shows, praise for, 70, 117; controversy over WWB position on the German question, 193–99; Dumbarton Oaks proposals, 227–31; early promoter of American intervention in World War II, 19–21; Fadiman, C., view of, 22; Freedom House, 20–21, 176, 200, 220; Friedrich, animosity toward, 188–89; Friends of Democracy, 104, 277n58; Hertzberg, attack on, 189–92; Morgenthau Plan supporter, 212–13; Nero Wolfe detective novels, 19, 21, 57, 154; *Our Secret Weapon*, 21; OWI relationship with WWB, 10–11, 52; Pledge for Peace, 224, 225–26, 229; racial tolerance campaign, 121, 125, 128–29; reaction to Goebbels's criticism of WWB, 53; Roosevelt's fourth-term campaign, 246; *Speaking of Liberty*, 20; SPWW3, 21, 189–90, 205; Thompson, argument with, 195–97; United Nations Charter, 236; United Nations Day, 132; urged early American intervention in World War II, 19–21; V-Homes complaint, 94; war talks (WWB), discussion of, 37–38; "We Shall Hate, or We Shall Fail," 174–76; Writers' Board for World Government, 242; WWB chair, 1, 21–22; WWB founding, 16–18; WWB funding and finances, 7–8, 49, 51, 52; WWB volume of work, 2, 252
Strange Fruit (book and song), 116
Street, Julian, Sr., 16
Street, Julian Jr., 4, 15–18, 91, 92–93, 239–40, 248
strikes by industrial workers, 79–80
Studio, The (periodical), 141
Sullivan, Frank (Advisory Council), 74, 185
Superman (comic book and character), 75, 100, 181
Swing, Raymond Gram, 37, 156
Syndicate Committee, 35, 43

"Taffy at War," 54
Taft, Robert A., 81, 245
"Take Your Pick" (column), 177
"Take Your Place at the Peace Table" (speech), 236
Tannenbaum, Ellen, 50
Tarbell, Ida M., 4

Tarkington, Booth, 4, 100, 135, 147, 186
tax filing, problems with 1943 income tax, 88
Taylor, Matt, 73
Terry and the Pirates (comic strip), 181
"Test for Dumbarton Oaks," 229, 231
Tetens, T. H., 211
"Thank You, Americans," 128
Theatre Arts Monthly (periodical), 46, 163
"Their Sunday Best," 147
There Are Things to Be Done (script), 118, 121, 129
There Go the Ships (Carse), 59
These Are Americans (script), 128
These Are the Russians (Lauterbach), 136
They Burned the Books (radio script), 36, 155–56
They Got the Blame (pamphlet), 120
They Got the Blame (script), 129
They Shall Be Heard (script), 234–35
"This Is Our Enemy" (comic story), 181–82
This Life Is Mine (radio program), 61–62
This Month (periodical), 143
This Week (Sunday newspaper supplement), 59, 63–64, 65, 73, 103, 143
Thomas, Lowell, 96
Thompson, Dorothy (Advisory Council), 56, 167, 195–97, 198–99, 200
Thousand Year Conspiracy, The (Winkler), 180
Thrilling Love (pulp magazine), 64, 100
Thursday Club (radio program), 117
Tillich, Paul, 189
"Till We Meet Again, Buy War Bonds" (poster), 91
Time, 113
Time for Decision, The (Welles), 209–10
Tojo, Hideki, 149
Tomorrow Will Be Ours (script), 217–18
"Too Hot to Handle," 118
To the Young (script), 104
Tovrov, Orin, 156
Towne, Charles Hanson, 4
Town Meeting of the Air (radio program), 213
Tracy, Spencer, 62
Traeger, Helen, 123
Transatlantic (periodical), 141–43
Transatlantic Committee, 142
travel, unnecessary, 34, 95–96
Treadwell, Mattie E., 64

Treasury Bond Wagon (radio program), 89–90
Treasury Department: anti-inflation campaign, 34, 99–101; bond drives, 87, 89–94; Defense Savings Program publicity, 15–18; income tax issues (1943), 88; radio programs, 89–90; WWB relationship with, 89–90, 239–40
Treasury Star Parade (radio program), 89
True Confessions (pulp magazine), 65, 224
True Detective (pulp magazine), 59
"True Justice for the Germans," 170
Truman, Harry, 242
Truth, Sojourner, 123, 124
Turner, Ewart Edmund, 205
Tuskegee Airmen, 122–23, 124

Under Cover (Carlson), 179
Undset, Sigrid, 170
Union of Soviet Writers, 134–35, 239
United National Clothing Collection, 147
United Nations: charter, 234, 235; international peacekeeping organization, discussions about, 217–22; restructuring recommendations, 242–43; San Francisco Conference, 234–38; United [Allied] Nations Committee of the WWB, 139–40
United [Allied] Nations Day, 132–33
United Nations Relief and Rehabilitation Administration (UNRRA), 144–46, 241
"United We Stand," 219
Unity at Home—Victory Abroad (radio program), 117
Untitled (script), 220
U.S. Army Signal Corps, 110
U.S. Cadet Nurse Corps, 66–67
U.S. Coast Guard, 85
U.S. Holocaust Memorial Museum, 157
U.S. Navy publicity campaign, 77–79
USO (United Service Organizations), 70–71, 111–12, 144
U.S. Senate, 218–19, 241–42
U.S. State Department, 150–51, 172, 231

Vandercook, J. W., 233
Vanderlip, Frank A., 16
Van Doren, Carl (Advisory Council), 125, 143, 235
Van Doren, Mark (Advisory Council), 92, 93, 140, 191, 196, 242

Vanguard Press, 19
Van Loon, Hendrick (Advisory Council), 67
Variety, 45, 125, 126, 163, 200, 244
venereal disease campaign, 102–3
Venuta, Benay, 125
veterans, disabled, 83–85
V-Homes, 93–94
Victory Clothing Drive, 147
"Victory" promotions, 93–95
Vigilantes, 3–4, 16
V-Mail, 94–95
Vogue, 63, 65

Waldeck, Rosie Goldschmidt, 180
Wallace, Henry A., 159, 221
Wallister, Ruth, 28
War Activities Committee (film industry), 110
War Advertising Council, 48–49, 91, 96, 99, 103
War against God, The (Carmer, ed.), 38
War Criminals and Punishment (script), 178, 249
"War Guilt of Fadiman Kip, The," 187
War Heroes Tour (Russian), 163
War Manpower Commission, 95
War Production Board, 95
war relief in various countries, 143–47, 241–42
War Script of the Month, 108, 114, 116, 118, 128, 129, 132, 135, 136, 156, 160, 178, 201, 203, 217–18, 235
War Script of the Month Committee, 37–38, 42
"Washington Letter" (column), 143
"Washington Newsletter" (*McCall's*), 64
Washington Post, 107
Watch on the Rhine (film), 40
WAVES (Women Accepted for Volunteer Emergency Service), 65–67
We Are All Brothers—What Do You Know about Race? (filmstrip), 112
"We Discovered America," 118
"We Fought Through to Murmansk" (serial), 59
"We Have Racial Equity—Do You?," 118–19
Welles, Orson, 220, 233
Welles, Sumner, 186, 209–10
Weltfish, Gene, 110–11
We Refuse to Die (film), 160

"We're on Our Way" (song), 75–76
"We Shall Hate, or We Shall Fail," 174–76
Weston, Harold, 144, 147
"We the Tools" (sketch), 106
"What about the Good Germans?," 170
"What America Means to Me," 140, 141
"What Do We Want?," 215
"What's the Matter Girls?," 65–66
What's Wrong with Me? (script), 117
What to Do with Germany? (film), 183
What to Do with Germany (Nizer), 183, 210
When a Girl Marries (radio program), 67
Whitcup, Leonard, 57
White, W. L. (Advisory Council), 56
"White-Washing the Nazis," 187
"Who Is Our Enemy?" (speech), 178
"Why Coddle Hirohito?," 152
"Why the U.S. and Russia Must Be Friends" (speech), 136, 236
"Why We Need the San Francisco Charter" (speech), 236
Widdemer, Margaret (Advisory Council), 147
Wilder, Thornton (Advisory Council), 30
Williams, Norman, 178
Willkie, Wendell, 133–34, 143, 159, 171, 218, 221, 246
"Will We Solve Our Negro Problem?," 118
Wilson, Woodrow, 5, 228
Winant, John G., 142
Winchell, Walter, 85, 117, 177, 222, 233
Winkler, Paul, 180
Wireman, Henrietta, 120
Wishengrad, Morton, 167
"Woman's Place, A" (song), 67
Woman's Views, A (radio program), 61
women: Economic Stabilization campaign, 99–101; industrial workers, 95; Mothers' Groups, 113, 122; recruitment for military service, 56, 60–67
Women's Army Auxiliary Corps (WAAC)/ Women's Army Corps (WAC), 60–67, 83
Wonder Woman Comics, 123
Wood, Edward, 142
Woollcott, Alexander, 161, 171
World Bank, 232

writers, enlistment of authors to contribute to WWB, 25–30
Writers' Board for World Government, 242–43
Writers' Board of the Friends of Democracy, 241
Writers' War Board (WWB): *Across the Board* (proposed radio program), 45–46; board members, original six, 18–25; collaboration with private organizations, 48–50; demise of, 240–43; enlistment of writers for, 25–30; estimate of volume of work produced at its behest, 2, 252; funding and financial operations, 2, 7–9, 50–52, 240–41, 266n135; goals, 1–2, 14; influence on domestic culture of wartime America, 12–13; liberal democracy initiatives, 13–14; OWI, relationship with, 9–11; quasi-governmental status of, 11–12, 247–50; significance of, 11–14, 250–53; Street's assessment of, 239–40
Writers' War Board Report, 29–30, 39–40, 54, 58, 60, 77, 79–80, 88, 102, 114, 119, 131, 134, 147, 149, 151, 152, 177, 224, 235, 236, 241
writing contests for soldiers, 69–70
WWB (Writers' War Board). *See* Writers' War Board
WWB publications, audience and purpose: *Brief Army Camp Items*, 32; *Brief House Organ Items*, 31–32; *Bulletin to Cartoonists*, 33; editorials, 33; *First Annual Report*, *Second Annual Report*, and *Third Annual Report*, 244, 255; War Script of the Month, 35–36; War Speeches, 36, 256; *Writers' War Board Report*, 29–30
Wylie, Philip, 225–26

Yalta Conference, 216–17
Yarns for Yanks (radio program), 69
Young, Jimmy, 152–53
Young, Marvin, 70
Your Job in Germany (film), 202

Zim, Herbert, 133

THOMAS HOWELL, a Texas native, grew up in Louisiana, where he earned a doctorate at Louisiana State University. He later received a Mellon fellowship and did further study in Berlin and Belfast. In 1987 he taught at the University of Iceland as a Fulbright professor. A frequent public speaker who has presented programs for the Louisiana Endowment for the Humanities, Dr. Howell recently retired from William Jewell College in Liberty, Missouri, after fifty-two years in college teaching. He continues to chair the National Eligibility Committee of the National Association of Intercollegiate Athletics, a position he has held for more than twenty years. His articles have appeared in *The Historian*, the *Missouri Historical Review*, and *Louisiana History*.

www.ingramcontent.com/pod-product-compliance
Lightning Source LLC
Chambersburg PA
CBHW031435230426
43668CB00007B/538